ASTRONOMICAL OBJECTS FOR
SOUTHERN TELESCOPES

TO MY WIFE

ASTRONOMICAL OBJECTS

FOR SOUTHERN TELESCOPES

WITH AN ADDENDUM FOR NORTHERN OBSERVATORIES

A handbook for amateur observers

BY

E.J.HARTUNG

Emeritus Professor of Chemistry in the
University of Melbourne

CAMBRIDGE
AT THE UNIVERSITY PRESS
1968

Published by the Syndics of the Cambridge University Press
Bentley House, 200 Euston Road, London, N.W. 1
American Branch: 32 East 57th Street, New York, N.Y. 10022

© Cambridge University Press 1968

Standard Book Number: 521 05224 6

Printed in Great Britain
at the University Printing House, Cambridge
(Brooke Crutchley, University Printer)

CONTENTS

PLATES

PREFACE

This book is based on many years of telescopic observation of the sky between 50° N declination and the south pole, and it is designed mainly for amateur observers of the southern sky, who are not well served by existing publications. An observing list of some 4,000 objects was drawn up from standard double star, nebular and other catalogues, and all of these have been observed individually, many of them several times. From the accumulated material, about 1,000 of the more interesting and attractive objects have been selected for tabulation and description. For the use of observers in more northerly stations than my own, and for northern observers generally, the remaining 12 per cent of the sky has been covered in an addendum, with descriptions drawn from various sources.

The arrangement of the material has been carefully considered. Simple sequence in right ascension as adopted by Admiral Smyth in his *Cycle of Celestial Objects* has much to commend it, but the Rev. T. W. Webb's grouping in constellations has endeared itself to amateurs and often enables relationships to be brought out which tend otherwise to be hidden. I have tried to adopt the best of both systems.

All objects are listed in sequence in R.A. with positions for the epoch 1950 and decennial variations, together with very brief descriptions. Each object is denoted by a serial number and the constellation in which it lies. The constellations are then treated in alphabetical order and each object may be found more fully described here, where it is located by its constellation and serial number. The five northern constellations hidden from my observatory are included here, but the eighty objects selected from them are given only in the addendum on the same plan as in the main table, but with fuller descriptions in the table itself. It is hoped that this general arrangement will enable observing lists to be drawn up quickly without the encumbrance of descriptive matter which when needed may be found in its own place.

My observations have been made with a 30 cm Newtonian reflector located in clean country air well removed from city glare and haze. The use of instruments of this aperture is now quite common amongst amateurs, but in each case I have indicated what may be expected from smaller telescopes. Five introductory chapters give some information about the various types of objects available for study. As the book is primarily an aid to observing, this introduction is necessarily concise but it may be useful in promoting interest in what is seen. It should be emphasized however that these chapters are not meant to take the place of a good text-book on astronomy, of which many are available. I have added a few remarks on equipment and observing which long experience has shown me to be useful. Star charts have been avoided. Norton's star atlas is recommended for every private observatory; in addition to eighteen very clear star maps and lists of objects, it contains much condensed information of great value to the astronomer. For more detailed delineation of fainter stars and objects, the sixteen excellent sheets of the Skalnate Pleso atlas of A. Becvar are recommended.

Many books and scientific papers have been consulted, and a list of these is given at the end of the book. In addition I wish to acknowledge with sincere thanks the kindly help and encouragement which I have received from the Mount Stromlo Observatory, Canberra, and especially from the late Dr A. R. Hogg who read the manuscript and offered useful comment, from Professor S. C. B. Gascoigne and M. J. Miller. The fine photographic plates have also come from this observatory. Nor can I conclude without paying a tribute to the maker of the mirror used in my observations, F. J. Hargreaves, Kingswood, Surrey, England. This mirror is a superb example of optical craftsmanship, and in many years of observing on every favourable occasion I have never had steady enough atmospheric conditions to test the limits of its performance.

Lavender Farm,   E.J.H.
Woodend,
Victoria,
Australia

1

RADIATION

Meteorites are the only extra-terrestrial bodies which are yet available for direct examination. Material from the moon and even some of the planets may soon be obtained but nearly all astronomical objects are likely to be known solely by the radiation received from them by the earth. This radiation is of two general kinds, one involving the transmission of energy only and the other being associated with the transference of electrically charged material particles known as ions. Such particles in the form of cosmic rays from interstellar regions, or as streams from the sun especially following solar flares, have important influences on the electrical condition of the atmosphere and the magnetic field of the earth. Auroral displays and some of the phenomena of the tails of comets depend on them. However such particulate radiation lies outside the scope of this book.

It is easy to show that a radiating body is losing energy and that an absorbing body is gaining it. It is thus usual to speak of radiation as a form of energy which passes from the radiator to the absorber. It is able to pass in the absence of any material medium of transmission but the passage is not instantaneous. Careful experiment has shown that there is always a time delay between emission and absorption which in a vacuum depends only on the distance between the emitter and the absorber, and not on the type of radiation. This is expressed by saying that radiation travels with constant speed c, and experiment shows that the actual value of c is 299,793 kilometres per second.

Radiation from different sources may differ in quality and also in intensity. Differences in quality are referable to three factors—frequency, coherence and polarization, and each of these will be discussed briefly.

Frequency

Each specific type of radiation is associated with a definite time interval or period, the reciprocal of which is known as the oscillation or vibration frequency and is expressible as number of oscillations per second. In comparison with the vibrations of material bodies, such as a harp-string or a suspension bridge, radiation frequencies are extremely high. Nevertheless they are finite and may be measured with such precision as to be used for identification of the radiation. They range from the very high frequency gamma-rays associated with atomic nuclear changes in descending order through X-rays, ultra-violet and visible radiation, infra-red and heat radiation, microwaves and finally the comparatively low frequency radiation used in television and broadcasting. The radiation spectrum is thus continuous from the highest to the lowest frequencies physically measurable.

Radiation may also be characterized by its wavelength; this depends on the frequency because the product of both equals the speed of radiation or
$$c = \text{frequency} \times \text{wavelength}.$$

However, though for a specific type of radiation the frequency is a fixed quantity, the wavelength is not. When radiation traverses material bodies, as for example light through glass, its speed becomes less and so does the wavelength, while the frequency remains unchanged.

The wave theory of radiation was at one time thought sufficient to account for all optical phenomena, for refraction, reflection, dispersion and interference found a ready explanation by its means. Now however a vast array of experimental facts can only be interpreted on the assumption that radiation is discontinuous, being emitted and absorbed in units or quanta which have received the name of photons. These photons for all types of radiation are equal in magnitude when this is expressed in terms of a concept known as action, represented by the symbol h. Where photons of different types of radiation differ is in the associated time interval or period, and so also in energy content, for these two are related so that always

$$\text{energy} \times \text{period} = h.$$

As the frequency of oscillation is the reciprocal of the period, it is clear that
$$\text{energy} = h \times \text{frequency}.$$

The value of the quantum of action h, known also as Planck's constant, is in conventional units $6 \cdot 625 \times 10^{-27}$ erg second and it no doubt represents a very fundamental entity in the structure of the universe, for it is only in units of action of this magnitude that radiation is able to pass from one material body to another.

Emission and absorption of radiation are essentially atomic processes. Ions, atoms and molecules are able to exist in various stages of internal energy characteristic for each entity, and the emission or absorption of a photon of radiation involves passage from one energy level to another, the difference in energy being precisely the same as the energy quantum carried by the photon which is emitted or absorbed during the change. As these atomic energy levels are sharply defined and specific for the radiating or absorbing entity, their recognition in the energy quanta carried by the photons serves for identification of the entities themselves. This is the basis of spectrum analysis, and the spectrometer is simply a device for separating out the various photons in the radiation and identifying them through their associated frequencies or energies.

The greatest differences in atomic energy levels are found in nuclear changes and the photons of the associated gamma-radiation deliver very high energy quanta on absorption. X-radiation of lower energy quanta comes from changes in the inner electron levels near the atomic nucleus, while changes in energy level of the outer electrons give ultra-violet and visible radiation. The energy levels associated with molecules are still lower, though usually very complex, and changes between them furnish infra-red radiation. In all these cases the radiating atom or molecule must first be stimulated to pass from a lower to a higher energy state; reversal of this process then produces the photon of radiation. Stimulation or excitation may be effected by thermal or electrical means, or by the absorption of radiation itself.

Radio-frequency radiation familiar in television and broadcasting is associated with energy quanta too low to be produced by individual atomic or molecular changes. Such radiation arises when large numbers of electrons are made to oscillate in specially designed electric circuits which are tuned to the required frequency. The reception of this radiation does not involve the absorption of photons by single atoms or molecules; it excites oscillatory movement of large numbers of electrons in appropriately designed and tuned electric circuits. The small electric currents so produced are amplified and recorded. This type of reception applies also to the two known cases of radio-frequency emission by individual particles, the so-called 21 cm radiation of neutral hydrogen and the 18 cm radiation of the hydroxyl molecule.

There are many reasons why a radiating body is not likely to emit radiation restricted to one particular frequency. The number of possible energy levels in most individual atoms is large and in addition very many atoms will be radiating at the same time. The characteristic spectrum of a single chemical element is therefore complex and on analysis shows a series of narrow lines, each corresponding to a particular frequency. The relative intensity of these lines is a measure of the relative probability of excitation of the atoms between the different energy levels concerned.

Sharp narrow spectrum lines imply sharply defined frequencies in the radiation, and these can come only from tenuous gases where the radiating atoms are free from mutual interference. If the pressure of the gas be increased, the atoms begin to exert mutual influence by attraction and collision; this results in modification of the internal energy levels which shows itself in a broadening of the spectrum lines. In highly compressed gases, and in incandescent liquids and solids, the broadening has proceeded so far that the lines have merged with one another and the spectrum is continuous. Even in tenuous gases under excitation, some broadening of the spectrum lines takes place because of thermal or turbulent motion of the radiating entities. Photons from those moving towards the receiver will register slightly higher than normal frequency, and photons from those moving away, slightly lower. The range of received frequencies is thus increased and the lines become broadened; this is the well-known Doppler effect. In addition the presence of electric and magnetic fields in the region of the radiating entities modifies the emitted frequencies. These are complicating influences but at the same time they offer valuable means for studying the conditions under which radiation is emitted from extra-terrestrial bodies.

The atmosphere of the earth absorbs a great deal of extra-terrestrial radiation which is thus prevented from reaching the surface and can only be investigated by instruments carried above the atmosphere in rockets or orbiting satellites. This applies to all radiation of higher frequency than the near ultra-violet, and generally to radiation of lower frequency than the near infra-red. The optical telescope uses therefore a kind of window in the atmospheric blanket which admits the visible spectrum from violet to red with some extension at either end. There is fortunately another window in the radio-frequency part of the spectrum, between wavelengths of about 1 cm to 2,000 cm through which the radio-telescope operates. This window permits the transmission of the 21 cm radiation of neutral hydrogen, from the study of which remarkable results have followed.

Coherence

When radio-frequency radiation is generated by oscillating electrons in electric circuits, the oscillations of the radiation itself are all in step, or in other words the photons are emitted in phase. Such radiation is known as coherent. This however is not the case for radiation consisting of photons generated by individual ions, atoms or molecules, as for example in usual light sources. Emission of photons is here a random process, and photons even of the same frequency are not all in phase with one another. Such radiation is known as incoherent; the wave-trains of the individual photons are inevitably superimposed on one another in the total radiation and, not being all in phase, the combination results in a small spread in frequency. A spectrum line, instead of being ideally sharp corresponding to a single frequency, shows a certain natural width corresponding to a small group of frequencies. It is true that radio-frequency radiation generated electrically is also not ideally sharp in frequency, but this is not due to lack of coherence. It results from the nature of electric circuits and in particular from the necessity of using components such as resistors and capacitors which themselves vary slightly in properties with surrounding conditions. This relative instability broadens the tuning and prevents the oscillation frequency from being peaked with ideal sharpness.

Recently it has been found possible, by the stimulated emission of photons from individual atoms in appropriate conditions, to generate coherent radiation in which the photons are all in phase. This radiation can be made very intense; it differs from ordinary light in that its frequency is defined with very great precision, and that a parallel beam diverges very little even over long distances. These properties offer great advantages which are now being developed rapidly and in which astronomy will surely share. Devices for generating coherent radiation in the visible spectrum are known as lasers and their discovery is a most far-reaching achievement.

Polarization

Polarized radiation differs from ordinary radiation in showing a certain structure. The simplest way to visualize this is to imagine the wavetrains of the photons of the radiation as oscillating in planes perpendicular to the direction of propagation. A mechanical analogy is the movement of ocean water particles up and down while the waves themselves move onwards. If these particles move only up and down, and not sideways nor in any other direction as well, the ocean waves may be described as plane polarized.

Unpolarized radiation may therefore be imagined as propagated by oscillations which take place at random in a plane perpendicular to the direction of propagation. If however these oscillations are linearly restricted to one direction in this plane, or are elliptical or circular in this plane, the radiation is plane or elliptically or circularly polarized. This may be brought about in unpolarized radiation by reflection from suitable surfaces, by refraction through a medium with its own regular structure such as a crystal, or by scattering from tiny particles. It may also be generated by the action of a magnetic field on the source of radiation itself. Polarization is detected and measured by devices known as analysers which will only accept the polarized radiation if they are properly orientated with regard to it. Extra-terrestrial radiation is often partly polarized and valuable information may thus be obtained about conditions existing in other parts of the universe.

Intensity

The intensity of radiation is determined by the number of photons received per unit area in unit time. Various devices are used for measuring intensity, as for example the photographic plate or film for visible and ultra-violet radiation. By this means the radiation may be integrated, for, provided that the incoming photons deliver individually quanta of energy sufficiently large to alter the photo-sensitive units in the film upon which they fall, the radiation however feeble will be recorded and added up. In this way are produced the remarkable photographs of extra-terrestrial objects which even the largest telescope cannot show directly to the eye, lacking as this organ does any capacity for integration. Electronic devices for recording radiation and multiplying its effects are now in wide use, while for the reception and measurement of radio-frequency radiation, carefully designed electric circuits are employed.

2

STARS

Stars are self-luminous bodies generating within themselves the energy which they radiate continuously in all directions into their surroundings. The individual character of a star depends on its composition and is largely influenced by its size, its mass and its luminosity. These three quantities are so great in comparison with terrestrial standards that it is usual to record them in terms of the corresponding quantities for the sun as units. Star luminosities may differ in extremes more than a million-fold; the same applies to star diameters but in mass the range is only about 300-fold, with the sun near the centre of the sequence. The astronomer has therefore ample material for study, both in numbers and in variety.

The apparent brightness of stars is recorded in magnitudes on an arbitrary scale in which 5 magnitudes represent 100-fold alteration in brightness, which diminishes steadily as the number expressing the magnitude increases. However these magnitudes depend on the way in which the brightness is measured. For example, the brightness may be estimated visually by eye, or by the diameter of the star image on a standardized photographic film or by photo-electric devices, or by measuring the total radiation with a bolometer, or in other ways. Qualifying symbols expressing visual, photographic, bolometric and so on must therefore be added to the apparent magnitude m to denote the method of measurement.

In order to free the apparent brightness from the effect of distance, absolute magnitudes M are used to denote the apparent brightness at a distance of 10 parsecs. The difference between these two quantities $m - M$ is known as the distance modulus which, after correction for the influence of interstellar absorption, depends only on the distance R of the star in terms of the simple equation

$$m - M = 5 \log R - 5$$

so that the distance modulus is zero at this distance of 10 parsecs.

The absolute magnitude of a star may therefore be used as a measure of its total luminosity, which depends largely on its size and surface temperature. With the exception of certain classes of stars known as

7

variables, the total luminosity of most stars changes only very slowly over immense periods of time. This means that the star is in radiative equilibrium in the sense that the rate of production of energy in its interior by nuclear processes is the same as its rate of escape as radiation from the surface, and it is clear that such a steady state can only be maintained by a balance of opposing tendencies. These are the enormous inward pull of gravitation tending to make the star smaller and the equally enormous outward thrust of the thermal motion of the atoms composing the star, combined with the pressure of the radiation trying to escape. For the photon of radiation has mass in virtue of its energy, and therefore has momentum which it delivers when it is absorbed; this gives the effect of an outward pressure in the interior of the star. The thermonuclear processes which generate the energy of the star are sensitive to temperature and to pressure, both of which steadily increase from the surface of the star inwards until they become high enough for nuclear fusion to begin. Should these actions proceed too rapidly, the increasing temperature gradient causes the star to expand. This not only tends to reduce the temperature and pressure but also gives a larger surface from which energy is lost as radiation. In this way the star is able to preserve an equilibrium.

It is also clear that the more rapidly energy is generated inside the star, the more massive must the star be in order to hold itself together by its gravitation against the outward pressures of the thermal motion of its atoms and its own radiation. In general, therefore, high mass in a star is associated with high internal temperature and high luminosity. There is however an upper limit to the massiveness of a star, for at very high temperatures the radiation pressure may become so great as to blow the star apart. The great problem facing the terrestrial generation of energy by thermonuclear fusion is how to hold together material heated to many million degrees against the expansive pressure of the thermal motion of its atoms; the star manages this by its enormous gravitation.

The surface temperature of a star is difficult to define for several reasons, one being the indefinite character of the surface itself. In general the temperature determines the amount of radiation which passes outwards through unit area of the surface in unit time, and also the energy distribution in the spectrum in relation to frequency. The radiation coming from the interior of the star gives a continuous spectrum, but the maximum of the energy distribution in this spectrum steadily shifts towards higher frequencies as the temperature rises.

8

Stars with relatively cool surfaces are therefore judged to be red, and as surface temperatures rise, the colours progress through orange and yellow to white and finally bluish or greenish for the hottest stars. These are the only colours which stars inherently show to normal vision but they may be modified by contrast, by atmospheric dispersion and by lack of perfect achromatism in telescope lenses. The only sure way to describe the radiation from a star is in terms of its spectrum.

The usual spectral classification of stars is based in general on a descending sequence in surface temperature, which is not however a sequence in stellar evolution. The main spectral classes are denoted by the letters

O   B   A   F   G   K   M

and each class is divided into 9 groups. The O stars at one end of the sequence are bluish or greenish white and the M stars at the other end are orange red. There are however other classes. Thus the O class stars are sometimes subdivided into the very hot greenish white W stars, and the M class stars are subdivided into the relatively rare deep red stars of classes N, R and S.

Practical determination of the class and group rests on careful analysis of the lines denoting characteristic frequencies distributed on a background of continuous radiation in the spectrum. The lines originate in the cooler tenuous gaseous layers of the outer regions of the star through which the continuous radiation must pass outwards. Those atoms and ions in the tenuous outer regions which are able to absorb photons from the continuous radiation will do so, the frequency of the photon absorbed being determined in each case by the available energy levels of the absorbing entity. The absorbed photons are quickly radiated again as the excited atoms or ions drop back to their former energy levels, and the process is repeated indefinitely. However as the regenerated photons are radiated in all directions, relatively few will travel in the same direction as the incident radiation, and a distant observer notices therefore a dark line in the continuous spectrum of the star for each frequency which has been absorbed. The intensity of this dark line is a measure of the number of absorbing atoms or ions in the line of sight.

While therefore recognition of the lines characteristic of a particular chemical element in the spectrum of a star indubitably shows the presence of this element in the star's atmosphere, absence of these lines does not prove that it is not there, for suitable conditions for the excitation of the element may not exist. These conditions are largely determined by the surface temperature of the star. In general, the higher the temperature the simpler is the absorption spectrum, because at high temperatures the more easily removable electrons are stripped from the atoms, and the resulting positive ions are no longer capable of absorbing, and therefore of emitting, radiation in the spectral regions available for observation. The hottest stars with surface temperatures approaching 25,000° K show little else on an intense continuous background but the spectrum lines of ionized helium (He II), doubly ionized carbon, oxygen and nitrogen (C III, O III and N III) and trebly ionized silicon (Si IV). Sirian stars of spectral type A 0 and surface temperature about 11,000° K show strong absorption lines of hydrogen but no helium lines as the temperature is not high enough for their excitation. Solar stars, including the sun itself, of spectral type G 0 and surface temperature about 6,000° K show innumerable absorption lines of a majority of the chemical elements, while the spectra of comparatively cool red stars are loaded with heavy absorption bands which indicate that some chemical molecules are able to form and suffer excitation in their atmospheres.

It may be mentioned that if the tenuous atmosphere of a star is very extensive, projecting far beyond the more concentrated region from which the continuous spectrum comes, this continuous spectrum may show superposed bright lines from the extended atmosphere. A notable example for southern observers is the bright star Gamma Velorum, in the spectrum of which even a small telescope will show splendid bright broad lines of helium.

The broadening of spectral lines has already been mentioned when discussing radiation; in addition the lines may be modified by electric and magnetic fields and also show partial polarization, while the relative intensities of the lines of an element may give useful information about the conditions of their excitation. Further if the star is moving towards or away from the earth the spectrum lines show displacement towards higher or lower frequency. Careful measurement of these displacements enables the speed of the star in the line of sight towards or away from the earth to be estimated. Moreover if some of the lines in the star's spectrum do not show this movement, or show it to a different extent, it is clear indication that these lines do not represent absorption in the atmosphere of the star but in the interstellar space between the star and the earth, or in the earth's atmosphere itself. Stars with simple spectra themselves render the detection of such lines easier, and most interstellar lines have been discovered in the spectra of very hot stars.

It is evident therefore that a great deal of information may be obtained from the close examination of the spectra of extra-terrestrial bodies, and one of the main functions of large telescopes—optical as well as radio—is to collect sufficient radiation to enable the spectrum to be dispersed as widely as possible, so that its details may be revealed and measured accurately. In the case of very faint stars, even recognition of spectral type gives valuable information, for the absolute magnitude may often be inferred from this with fair security, and so the distance of the star.

Binary stars

Many stars on examination with the telescope are seen to consist of two and sometimes more components apparently close together. If the stars are moderately bright and the apparent separation is small, the chances are very greatly in favour of their physical connection, the stars revolving in elliptical orbits round a common centre of inertia.

This is made apparent by a simple calculation. There are some 96,000 stars in the Milky Way system brighter than, and including, apparent magnitude 9. If these stars were uniformly distributed over the 41,253 square degrees of the whole sky, each star would have available to itself about 1,500 square minutes of arc, and the mean apparent separation of adjacent stars would be about 38'. The chances of two stars of magnitude 9 or brighter being fortuitously within a few seconds of arc of one another are thus quite small.

Physical connection between two stars is disclosed when careful measurements of angular separation and position angle over a sufficient period prove beyond doubt that the stars are describing elliptical orbits round a common centre. What is actually measured is the apparent orbit of one star with respect to the other; this too will be an ellipse but the reference star will only be at one focus if the orbit plane is perpendicular to the line of sight. Usually this plane is more or less inclined to the line of sight, which not only alters the shape or eccentricity of the ellipse but also displaces the reference star from the focus. Careful analysis of the measurements is therefore necessary to determine the elements of a binary orbit, and these measurements must be very accurate for trustworthy results. Binary star work is hence exacting.

If the distance of a binary star is known, as for example from parallax measures, the actual dimensions of the orbit may be calculated from the apparent size; knowing this and the period of revolution, the combined masses of the stars may be obtained from Kepler's third law. If in addition the position of the centre of inertia between the stars can be found by close analysis of their proper motions, the individual stellar masses can be determined. This is the fundamental method and all others for inferring the masses of stars are based upon it, so that the importance of binary star study is evident.

Many pairs are so close that even large telescopes are unable to separate their components. However two superimposed spectra in the combined spectrum may be detected, and measurements of the Doppler displacements of the two sets of lines give not only the period of revolution but also the variable motions of the stars in the line of sight. These are the spectroscopic binaries. Conditions are still more favourable if the stars happen to eclipse one another more or less completely at regular intervals; the pair then forms an eclipsing variable star and both individual masses and diameters may be determined.

Often the orbit of a binary star is so large and the period so long that very little change in separation and position angle of the components can be detected over many years. Physical connection is inferred in these cases by this very fixity, for it implies a common proper motion of both stars, which would be most unlikely for two unrelated stars fortuitously appearing nearly in the same line of sight. If however the proper motions are both extremely small, physical connection may be less certain.

Many ternary star systems are known, in which three stars describe orbits under the influence of their mutual gravitation, but little progress has been made in their investigation because of observational difficulties. Quaternary and higher multiple stars also occur and they pass with increasing complexity into star clusters, where the individual motions of the components are so intricate that they admit of only generalized mathematical treatment. It is likely that these star associations are able to maintain their identity for very long periods and that the stars in them have had a common origin. This seems to be the case with binary stars also. The fortuitous meeting of two stars is most unlikely and they could not form a permanent system without the intervention of a third body, which is still more unlikely. The frequent differences in size and spectral type of the components offer difficult but not insoluble problems.

Variable stars

Most stars shine very steadily without noticeable change in brightness over long periods. This has been discovered by systematic comparison, one star with another, making due allowance for changing meteorological conditions. Some stars however show variability of brightness when observed over a sufficient period, and this variability is usually accompanied by changes in the spectrum of the star.

Leaving out of consideration what may be regarded as mechanical examples of variability, such as eclipsing binaries, ellipsoidal rotating stars, and stars passing behind obscuring matter, variation in real brightness implies a state of periodical instability in the star. The actual physical causes of variability may be due to change in surface temperature, in surface area, in atomic and molecular absorption in the stellar atmosphere, or finally in general obscuration by more or less opaque clouds, particularly in relatively cool S type stars.

The causes of instability must lie in a lack of balance of opposing tendencies which regulate the equilibrium of a star. It has already been mentioned that the very high temperatures in the interior of a star are maintained by the emission of energy in the process of nuclear fusion leading to the production of complex atomic types from simpler ones. The rates at which these processes take place are very sensitive to temperature and, as the radiation generated during fusion reactions tends finally to be degraded into heat, some form of compensation must operate to keep the energy production under control. The most obvious is increase in volume under the rising pressure; this results in internal cooling and increase in radiation from the enlarged surface of the star. In most cases compensation seems to be effective enough to result in a steady state, in which the energy produced in the interior of the star is so exactly balanced by that leaving the surface as radiation that only very slow changes in luminosity take place during immense periods of time.

In some cases however, and possibly at some stage in the evolution of most stars, exact compensation becomes difficult. One reason for this lies in the steadily growing complexity of atomic composition as the star ages. Initially the star consists largely of hydrogen and nuclear fusion is a relatively simple process, but it becomes increasingly intricate as new atomic types are produced and enter themselves into fusion processes, each with its own characteristics and rate of energy production. The later synthesis of more complex chemical elements actually requires absorption of energy, and as more than one hundred atomic types are known, the difficulty of handling the theoretical problem of the maintenance of stability may be imagined.

As evolution proceeds with steadily changing composition, there may come a period in the history of the star when the surface layers become unstable and begin gradually to oscillate in a regular manner. As the emitted radiation changes in step with this oscillation, the brightness of the star varies regularly also with a definite time interval. Sometimes these oscillations become so violent and turbulent that temporary relief is obtained through a surface explosion at intervals, giving rise to an irregular variable star. If the instability develops to such an extent as to cause a very violent explosion, the blaze of radiation accompanying it is recorded as a nova. In these upheavals, which may be repeated at intervals in the same star, relatively little of the material of the star appears to be lost, most of it falling back again under the influence of gravitation. Should however the internal stability of the star fail, much of its substance may be lost in a colossal outburst, resulting in the much rarer supernova.

Two types of short period regular variables are of special value in estimating stellar distances; these are the Cepheid variables named from Delta Cephei which was the first one discovered, and the RR Lyrae stars.

Cepheid variables are giant stars of high luminosity with diameters from 10 to 100 times that of the sun, and absolute magnitudes from zero to about −4·5. The range of variation is usually less than one magnitude, characterized by a rather steep rise and slower fall, and very regular periods ranging from less than one day to about 50 days. The spectral type varies between F and G, and all these characters serve for recognition. It has been found that the period is related to the absolute magnitude and if the former can be determined, the absolute magnitude and therefore the distance of the star may be inferred.

RR Lyrae variables are sometimes called cluster-type variables as they are by far the most plentiful type found in globular clusters. They are but little larger than the sun but far more luminous, with absolute magnitudes about zero. They vary very regularly with periods shorter than one day and their spectra cannot easily be classed. Their recognition gives again a means of inferring their distances from their absolute magnitudes.

Long period variables are giant orange or red stars of high luminosity with periods ranging from 90 to 600 days. They usually vary over several magnitudes and belong to late spectral types from K to M onwards, so that if bright enough for the equipment of the observer they exhibit fine absorption spectra.

Amongst irregularly variable stars may be mentioned those of:

R Coronae Borealis type which remain steady for long intervals before decreasing several magnitudes and then returning to normal.

U Geminorum type which remain at a minimum brightness for long intervals before rising suddenly several magnitudes to a series of long and short maxima and then returning to normal.

RV Tauri type with a series of variable maxima and variation about two magnitudes.

The observation of variable stars has always formed a prominent part of the work of amateur astronomers whose interests in this respect are fostered by several organizations. Two of these are the Variable Star Section of the British Astronomical Association in England, and the American Association of Variable Star Observers in the United States of America.

3

STAR CLUSTERS

Star clusters fall into two general groups, known respectively as galactic and globular clusters. The former are almost entirely restricted to the central plane of the Milky Way, while the latter are more isolated and scattered in a vast system round the centre of the galaxy.

Galactic clusters

Galactic clusters are groups of associated stars which may be distinguished visually from the starry background by their greater concentration. They range in apparent diameter from several degrees across to not more than about 2′, and vary in the number of component stars. According to the usual convention, poor clusters contain less than fifty stars and rich ones more than one hundred, although the total number is often much greater. They vary also in the degree of concentration of the component stars; some clusters are broadly scattered while others show marked gathering towards the centre, although this is never so pronounced as in typical globular clusters.

Well over seven hundred of these galactic or open clusters, as they are also called, have been recorded in the Milky Way system and these clearly represent but a small part of the total number, for the situation of the sun in the central plane towards one edge precludes any view of the more distant regions of the Milky Way, or even of its centre. Obscuring clouds of interstellar gas and dust limit examination by optical means to a few thousand parsecs round the sun in the central plane of the galaxy and all the known open clusters lie within this distance. The actual diameters range from about 1·5 to occasionally 20 parsecs; those with pronounced central condensation are usually smaller in actual diameter than those with more open scattering of their stars.

The criterion for membership of an open cluster is common proper motion. Were this not so, the cluster would be merely a fortuitous gathering of stars of relatively short persistence as a group, and this is most unlikely to be the case. On the contrary, theory indicates that the gravitational pull of the rest of the stellar system combined with the individual motions of the cluster stars will gradually disperse them,

16

although even in the most favourable circumstances this is a very slow process requiring hundreds of millions of years. It seems clear that each galactic cluster has developed as a group of stars of common origin.

This view is supported by the frequent association of both luminous and dark diffuse nebulae with such clusters, which makes it highly likely that the cluster stars are the result of gradual coalescence from this scattered material under the influence of gravitation. The common proper motion of the cluster stars is thus a reflection of the motion of the generating nebula which itself may have disappeared long ago. Further evidence of this is found in the pronounced patterns which are so often shown by the stars in relation to one another, and which may be the relics of the internal motion and the structure of the original nebula. In some diffuse nebulae small dark nodules have been detected which may represent incipient star formation.

From a determination of the spectral types of cluster stars the absolute magnitudes may be assessed and by comparing these with the apparent magnitudes, the distance of the cluster may be obtained. This method when applied to a cluster is more secure than when applied to individual stars, for the members of a cluster will be all at about the same distance from the earth, and this imposes a check. However as galactic clusters lie mainly near the central plane of the Milky Way where gas and dust clouds also lie, allowance must be made for light absorption which, by lessening the apparent brightness of the cluster stars, makes the inferred distance too great. Estimation of the extent of this absorption is often difficult and uncertain but fortunately it varies with radiation frequency, becoming progressively greater as this increases. Red light penetrates haze more easily than violet, and the relatively low frequency radio-radiation passes readily through obscuring interstellar clouds which are quite impenetrable to light. We find as expected therefore that stars of distant galactic clusters are definitely more red than those of similar spectral type in nearer ones, and this gives a means of estimating the extent of interstellar absorption.

Another way of assessing the distances of galactic clusters is by measurement of their apparent diameters. The actual dimensions of known clusters differ so greatly that little reliance can be placed on such a method without some attempt at classification. However, by dividing clusters into classes depending on the central condensation and the distribution of their stars, some estimate of the probable dimensions of each class can be made. By comparing these estimated diameters with the apparent diameters obtained from observation, the probable distance of the cluster is obtained. This method has greatest value for very distant faint clusters and is less subject to interference by interstellar absorption.

Many of the galactic clusters make attractive telescopic objects, especially with moderate magnification and a sufficiently large field. The interest and beauty of some of them are enhanced by association with bright diffuse nebulae, to which they stand in obvious relationship. Others however merge so imperceptibly into rich star fields that they look like mere local increases in star density, while numbers of those described by John Herschel in the southern sky contain relatively few loosely scattered and often inconspicuous stars and are likely to pass unnoticed by the casual observer.

Globular clusters

Globular clusters are comparatively isolated aggregations of stars forming part of the Milky Way system. They are much larger and more symmetrical than galactic clusters, and far richer in individual stars. They show also in general much greater central condensation which gives most of them a very characteristic appearance in the telescope. They have usually high velocities relative to the sun and comparatively few of them are found very near to the central plane of the Milky Way, to which galactic clusters are so largely restricted. This may be due partly to obscuration by interstellar material, for globular clusters are in general very remote objects, but a contributing factor may be their highly eccentric orbits round the centre of the galactic system with steep inclination to its central plane. They appear to be very ancient systems and may have been formed before the Milky Way acquired its present spiral character. They also seem to be observationally free from nebulosity which is so often associated with galactic clusters. With adequate optical means all of them may be resolved completely into stars, and their spectra show no trace of gaseous type.

The number of globular clusters now recognized in the Milky Way system is 119 and these are scattered irregularly round the galactic centre, usually at vast distances from it. Owing to the position of the sun far out towards the edge of the galaxy, most of the globular clusters appear in the sky in the general direction of its centre, and the constellations of Ophiuchus, Scorpius and Sagittarius contain nearly half of them. They are therefore admirably placed for southern observers.

Very few are nearer to the sun than 3,000 parsecs and the most distant appear to be almost extra-galactic.

Although showing a considerable range in size, globular clusters are in the main very large systems, the average diameter being about 70 parsecs. The apparent angular diameters range from about 30′ downwards but are often difficult to estimate if the clusters show widely scattered outliers, as many of them do. The same applies to integrated photographic magnitudes which range from 5·3 to 12·7 for clusters which can be seen telescopically, a few recently discovered by photography with large instruments being much fainter. Integrated magnitudes are however only a general guide to visibility in the telescope because this is greatly influenced by the angular diameter and the degree of central condensation. For example, one of the most difficult to see in a small telescope is NGC 7492 in Aquarius where an integrated magnitude of 12·3 is combined with an apparent diameter of 3·3′ and little central concentration, whereas NGC 6517 in Ophiuchus with integrated magnitude 12·7 and apparent diameter 1·5′ and considerable central concentration is relatively easy.

Globular clusters are mostly spherical or ellipsoidal with usually well marked symmetry. Resolution in the telescope depends on the apparent magnitudes of at least the brighter stars being within the capacity of the instrument. If all the stars are below this limit, the cluster looks not unlike an extra-galactic nebula of spherical type and like it will show a continuous spectrum band if examined through a direct-vision prism. Most of the clusters are very rich in stars, some of the larger ones showing at least 100,000 and therefore containing probably a much greater number, for only the brighter stars can be seen and photographed. The clusters show a great range in central condensation which H. Shapley in 1933 expressed by dividing them into twelve classes, designated in the order of diminishing condensation by the Roman numerals I to XII. A somewhat similar classification was adopted by A. C. Mowbray in 1946 with fourteen classes numbered in half units from one to seven, in very general agreement with those of Shapley.

The distances of globular clusters are obtained primarily from a study of their variable stars; of these the RR Lyrae type with mean absolute magnitude zero have proved the most useful. Other types are much rarer. The problem is complicated, particularly near the galactic plane, by interstellar absorption just as in the case of galactic clusters, but of course for such distant objects this may be very difficult to assess. It is therefore not surprising that considerable uncertainty appears for this reason in the distance estimates of different astronomers. Other methods of inferring the distance depend on assessing the absolute magnitudes of the brightest stars in the cluster from their spectral types, on measures of diameters as recorded on blue- and red-sensitive plates, and on estimating the absolute integrated magnitude of the whole cluster from the degree of central condensation. Much of this information leads to results of a largely statistical nature, but nothing else is available for faint and remote clusters.

It was from an analysis of the brighter stars of M 13 and other globular clusters that W. Baade in 1944 proposed a distinction between two star populations: (i) which included stars in the outer regions of the central plane of the galaxy and therefore typical of galactic clusters and (ii) which included stars typical of globular clusters and the vast cloud of scattered stars which forms a kind of halo round the centre of the galaxy. The distinction between these two star populations depended on differences in colour-magnitude relations and later investigations have shown it to be of limited value. The colour-magnitude diagram of a cluster represents the magnitudes of its stars in relation to their spectral types, the latter being expressed quantitatively as colour-index. The position of a star in this diagram depends largely on its stage of evolution, during which its original store of hydrogen is being steadily depleted with formation of more complex atoms. There is thus a progressive change in the chemical composition of a star as evolution proceeds, but stars do not follow this evolutionary course at the same rate. Stars of high mass evolve faster than stars of low mass, so that even in an assemblage of very old stars such as a globular cluster, there are still many which are in the early stages of evolution. On the other hand, most, though not all, of the galactic clusters are comparatively young; this is particularly the case when they are associated with diffuse nebulae, for the formative stages are still active. The stars of such clusters are likely to be therefore in the earlier part of their life.

A globular cluster furnishes thus an isolated star system in which the individuals are all at about the same distance from the sun and presumably of much the same age, but are at different stages of evolution because of their originally different masses. The intrinsic value of the study of such a system is plain but the evidence from all sources is still too fragmentary to give a clear picture of stellar evolution. It seems likely however that even old stars such as the sun which still have large stores of hydrogen in their outer regions are slowly becoming hotter in the interior, where helium is accumulating. The resulting induction of new nuclear processes leading to the formation of more complex atoms causes expansion and steadily increasing luminosity until a giant stage is reached, when the gravitational forces at the surface are unable to prevent the escape of large amounts of the material of the star. Long before this happens to the sun all life on the earth will have been extinguished by the rising temperature. The ultimate stage of evolution appears to be a very slowly cooling burnt out dwarf star.

Most globular clusters are very interesting telescopic objects, the larger and brighter ones being most beautiful in instruments capable of resolving them and showing clearly their myriads of clustering stars. Practically all are visible to the southern observer, the most northerly being the bright NGC 6229 in Hercules.

4

GALACTIC NEBULAE

Galactic nebulae are more or less luminous clouds of gaseous or solid particulate material, often of enormous extent, which form part of the system of the Milky Way. As telescopic objects they fall into two distinct types—planetary nebulae which are comparatively small and circumscribed, each associated with a particular star, and diffuse nebulae bright or dark, which are much larger and irregular in form. These diffuse nebulae are local condensations of interstellar material, rendered luminous by the presence of sufficiently hot stars in the vicinity. Otherwise they show as dark absorption regions if the starry background is rich enough to render them visible by projection against it. In addition vast tracts of very tenuous interstellar material exist, the presence of which is shown by the general absorption of radiation from distant stars, by absorption lines in the spectra of stars lying behind them, and by faint luminescence and the emission of radio-frequency radiation.

Planetary nebulae

Planetary nebulae were so named by William Herschel because of the planet-like appearance which many of them show in the telescope. They appear usually as small round or somewhat elliptical bodies, often quite bright white or pale blue, with fairly well defined edges. Some of them look annular with fainter central region which may be due simply to the effect of projection on a plane of a luminous but very tenuous gaseous sphere. Although visually they seem to shine with fairly even light, yet photographs with large instruments often reveal much irregular and sometimes filamentous structure which suggests turbulence. They range in apparent diameter from almost stellar points to objects 100″ or more across, by far the largest being the faint annulus NGC 7293 in Aquarius which is 15′ in diameter.

All planetary nebulae show gaseous bright line spectra in which so-called forbidden frequencies of elements such as oxygen, nitrogen and neon are prominent, together with lines denoting hydrogen and helium. Forbidden frequencies are associated with transitions between energy states in atoms which are extremely unlikely to occur, and in any

22

experimentally manageable quantity of tenuous gas in the laboratory, such radiation on excitation is so feeble as to be practically undetectable. It is the vast size of the nebula which gives sufficient forbidden radiation for recognition. The luminosity owes its origin to fluorescence excited in the very tenuous gas by ultra-violet radiation from a small but very hot star in the centre. Some of the atoms or ions energized by absorption of photons of ultra-violet frequency lose this energy in stages, emitting photons of lower frequency in the visible region of the spectrum. Many planetary nebulae show such a central star to visual observation, but in most of them it is either hidden by the greater luminosity of the gaseous envelope or else most of the radiation of the star is so far in the ultra-violet that it can be detected only by photography.

Planetary nebulae may be well studied by means of the slitless spectrograph which, instead of isolating a portion of the image of the nebula by a narrow slit, admits the whole of the image. With sufficient dispersion this is separated by the instrument into a succession of images, each corresponding to a particular frequency present in the nebular radiation. A study of these images, which often show great differences, indicates the distribution of various chemical elements in the nebula and also the conditions of local excitation. The spectrum of the central star is marked by a narrow continuous band on which the nebular images appear to be strung; it extends far into the ultra-violet and often shows bright emission lines due to the very high temperature. These central stars have in general the highest known surface temperatures, which may exceed $30,000°$ K, but owing to their small size the absolute magnitudes appear to be about zero, although those of the nebulae themselves may be as high as -3 or -4.

There seems to be no doubt that a planetary nebula is the result of surface explosions from the hot central star. In some of them there is plain evidence of several successive outbursts at intervals, and it is clear that stellar instability has been responsible. In many of them spectroscopic evidence indicates much turbulence. Some novae have subsequently developed luminous gaseous envelopes which however do not exhibit the relative permanence which is a marked feature of planetary nebulae, although the spectra may show considerable similarity. The relation between novae and planetaries is still by no means clear.

Planetary nebulae differ too much in actual size and luminosity for measurements of apparent size and brightness to afford useful estimates of their distances. One method of attacking this problem is to estimate the parallax but, instead of using the diameter of the earth's orbit as a baseline which is so useful for the nearer stars, the motion of the sun in its orbit round the galaxy is used to obtain the secular parallax. This has the advantage of increasing steadily year after year, but the proper motion of the nebula itself contributes to the observed displacement, and the problem admits of no easy solution. Most of these nebulae appear to be fairly remote objects, the nearest to the sun being about 180 parsecs distant.

Planetary nebulae may occur in any galactic latitude but most of them show a marked concentration towards the centre of the galaxy, and the constellation of Sagittarius is particularly rich in them. Most of these however are so far away as to appear very small and, as they occur usually in rich star fields, they are difficult to pick out in the telescope, even if bright enough to be seen. However a small direct-vision prism held between the eye and the ocular of the instrument will show them at once, for while the stars are spread by the prism into narrow faint streaks because of their continuous spectra, the planetary nebula remains as a point of light since most of its visible radiation is concentrated into two very close frequencies due to doubly ionized oxygen. For nebulae of appreciable size, the single prism images of about the same dimensions demonstrate at once their gaseous nature. Many of these nebulae are attractive telescopic objects, and their actual diameters in astronomical units are obtained by multiplying the distance in parsecs by the apparent diameter in seconds of arc.

Diffuse luminous nebulae

These nebulae are limited almost entirely to the vicinity of the central plane of the Milky Way and they represent largely the denser regions of the interstellar medium which have stars sufficiently near, and hot enough, to excite this medium to luminosity. The spectra are typically gaseous as shown by bright lines, which however denote a lower degree of excitation than most planetary nebulae because the exciting stars are not so hot. For example the radiation from doubly ionized oxygen which is so prominent in most planetaries is relatively feeble in diffuse nebulae, being replaced by radiation from the singly ionized element. Many, and probably all, diffuse nebulae contain solid particles or dust as well as gas, which shine by reflection and therefore contribute some continuous stellar spectrum to that of the fluorescent gases. Some are almost entirely dust nebulae, as for example the nebula in which the stars of the Pleiades are entangled; in this case the gas spectrum is lacking but the nebulosity is more blue than the light of the exciting stars. This indicates some fluoresence which may come from the solid particles themselves.

A typical diffuse nebula consists of tenuous gases, mostly hydrogen but also helium, oxygen and other permanent gases as well as solid particles which are thought to be graphite, ice, methane, carbon dioxide and other simple compounds. If the surface temperature of a nearby star is high enough, this rich source of ultra-violet radiation will cause the gases to fluoresce. In the case of hydrogen the limiting surface temperature of the exciting star is about 20,000° K corresponding to spectral type B 1, for below this temperature there is not enough of the requisite radiation to ionize the hydrogen atoms.

Diffuse nebulae assume many forms; they are usually very irregular with faint hazy edges and extensions where the material thins out or the exciting radiation becomes feeble. Some of them are so large that they are hardly telescopic objects in the accepted sense. For example in the constellations of Scorpius and Ophiuchus wide regions of the sky are luminous and faint stars are blotted out. Diffuse nebulae are often associated visibly with stars and star clusters from which the exciting radiation emanates. Many of these stars have very high surface temperatures corresponding to spectral type O, and their luminosity is so great that their stores of hydrogen are being used up rapidly. They must therefore be young stars and their astronomical lives will be relatively short unless they are able to replenish their supply of hydrogen from the surrounding nebula by accretion.

If these nebulae are observed in the telescope through the direct-vision prism, the continuous spectra of the stars are seen as streaks but the nebula itself remains fairly well gathered together in a single image, though usually not so clearly as a planetary nebula. This is because the diffuse nebulae have much less distinct outlines, are larger and often show some continuous spectrum from solid particles. Frequently they have dark lanes or rifts or bays, due to opaque clouds projected against them. If bright enough to exhibit colour, this is usually pale greenish or bluish white.

The only method of estimating the distance of a diffuse nebula is by the stars responsible for its luminescence, which are either in the vicinity or immersed in it. If the absolute magnitudes of some of these stars can be found, the distance of the nebula may be inferred and so also the actual dimensions of its luminous regions.

Dark diffuse nebulae

These nebulae vary in apparent size from the small dark and often well-defined objects outlined against rich star fields to the huge elongated clouds which obscure parts of the Milky Way and diversify its appearance. They were first brought into prominence in 1889 by the wonderful photographs of the Milky Way taken by E. E. Barnard with a lens giving a very wide and sharply defined field. They consist of interstellar material which is not only sufficiently opaque to absorb some of the light of stars lying in and behind it, but also has no neighbouring stars hot enough to excite it to luminosity. Barnard was the first to show that some dark nebulae are indeed feebly luminous. One of the nearest and best known of the dark nebulae is the Coal Sack immediately following Alpha Crucis, and specially conspicuous because it is completely surrounded by the Milky Way which is very bright in this region; it contains however many faint and mostly red stars. Some diffuse nebulae show dark rifts and patches, good examples being the trifid nebula NGC 6514 in Sagittarius and the great nebula round Eta Carinae, NGC 3372; these represent clouds of opaque material projected on the bright background luminosity.

Dark nebulae seem to be similar in composition to luminous ones and consist of clouds of gas and dust. It may be that they represent an early stage in the condensation of tenuous interstellar material into stars, which grow by steady accretion and ultimately become hot enough for nuclear processes to begin the production of energy. When this happens, the increasing radiation from the new stars finally becomes able to excite the still uncondensed material, and the nebula becomes luminous. Photographs of some diffuse nebulae, such as that encircling the cluster NGC 2244 in Monoceros, show small well-defined dark globules on the luminous field which may be the initial condensations of future stars.

The distance and the extent in depth of a dark nebula may be estimated by application of the observational result that there is a progressive increase in the number of stars of each succeding magnitude per unit area of sky in regions for which there is no evidence of obscuring matter. Such star counts were first made by William Herschel who drew attention to the appearance of ever-increasing numbers of stars for each succeeding degree of faintness. A dark nebula interrupts this magnitude-number sequence at a point depending on its distance and for an interval depending on its thickness or depth. By making magnitude-number star counts over the nebula and in the surrounding regions, it is possible to estimate both distance and depth. The method is subject to much uncertainty and requires great care and experience in its application, so that the results must be interpreted with caution. However it seems to be reasonably well established that all the dark nebulae so far investigated lie within a distance of about 1,000 parsecs from the sun.

5

EXTRA-GALACTIC SYSTEMS

One of the most striking results of the introduction of photographic methods into astronomy towards the end of last century has been the discovery of immense numbers of small nebulous objects which do not belong to the Milky Way system at all, their apparent smallness and faintness being brought about by their great distance. Many hundreds of these objects had been discovered by William and John Herschel, who referred to them simply as nebulae, and their number continually increased by new discoveries during the nineteenth century. However it required systematic photographic surveys with large reflectors to reveal that these small faint objects exceeded the stars in number, and that they were in reality very large systems which lay far beyond the confines of the Milky Way. For such extra-galactic bodies the term galaxy has come to stay. This term has the merit of brevity but it is not well chosen because time-honoured usage has long applied it to the Milky Way itself and most extra-galactic systems are different from the galaxy in size, shape and structure.

These objects may be distinguished from galactic nebulae by their spectra, which are essentially continuous, by their apparent forms which are mostly round, elliptical or spindle-shaped and by their distribution in the sky. They are probably fairly evenly scattered over the celestial sphere, with a tendency to clustering in some regions, but are shut out from observation in and near the central plane of the galaxy by obscuring clouds of gas and dust. That this occlusion is real is shown by the occasional presence of gaps in the interfering screen through which these distant objects may be seen.

Although anomalies and irregularities in structure are frequent, yet extra-galactic systems may be divided very generally into two broad groups—the spiral and the non-spiral types. Depending on their inclination to the line of sight, the former appear round, elliptical or spindle-shaped and sometimes very elongated, and either show definite evidence of spiral structure or are inferred from their shape to possess it. When visible this structure takes the form of two or more spiral arms which emerge from a bright central mass, or sometimes from the ends of a diametrical bar. The nearest and brightest of the spirals have been resolved by means of the largest telescopes, and they show a structure and composition akin to that of the Milky Way system which is evidently one of the same type. They are composed of a vast more or less spherical aggregation of old stars round the nucleus, with bright comparatively young stars scattered along the flattened extended spiral arms, where also star clusters, diffuse gaseous nebulae and dark obscuring clouds are located. In some of them, numbers of globular clusters have been detected which are distributed round the centre much as in the galaxy itself.

Some of the nearest and brightest of the non-spiral types have also been resolved. These spherical or ellipsoidal bodies appear to consist of myriads of ancient stars with no evidence of gas or dust clouds. They are in fact gigantic globular clusters which they resemble also in appearance by a steady increase in concentration from the outer regions to the centre, and by a notable absence of any detailed structure. In general no extra-galactic system is resolvable by small telescopes but for the brighter ones the use of the direct-vision prism between ocular and eye will demonstrate at once their starry nature by spreading the image into a band because of the essentially continuous spectrum. The two Magellan Clouds form exceptions; these are near enough for small telescopes to show globular and other star clusters, gaseous nebulae and myriads of faint stars in them.

The distances of the nearer extra-galactic systems are estimated by recognizing in them objects such as stars, globular clusters and gaseous nebulae, of which the absolute magnitudes or dimensions may be inferred from their spectra and character. Cepheid variables, novae often in considerable numbers, and occasional supernovae have all been used as distance indicators. The results of such primary methods of distance measurement are in general agreement but some doubt remains owing to the difficulty of estimating the extent of interstellar absorption over these great distances. For more remote systems which cannot be resolved into recognizable objects, secondary methods such as estimations of apparent integrated magnitude and of apparent size are employed. These methods are open to grave errors, for extra-galactic systems differ greatly from one another in actual luminosity and dimensions but by classifying them from their appearance, and by comparison with nearer systems to which primary methods may be applied, it is possible to make a general estimate of what the absolute magnitudes and sizes of the different types are likely to be. In these ways, distance moduli may be inferred.

In 1912 it was discovered by V. M. Slipher of the Lowell Observatory that certain recognizable dark absorption lines in the spectra of some extra-galactic systems, notably the H and K lines of ionized calcium in the near ultra-violet, showed a displacement towards the red end of the spectrum, and by 1925 he had extended his results to some fifty of the brighter systems. These red shifts were interpreted as Doppler displacements which indicated recession from the sun, and the fact that a few of the brightest systems, notably M 31 in Andromeda, showed not recession but approach was explained by the rotation of the galaxy itself masking the recession for regions near the sun. As these results were gradually extended to objects of increasing remoteness, as indicated by diminishing brightness and size, the red shifts were found to increase progressively, until for extremely faint objects the shift was so great as to displace the two absorption lines right through the visible spectrum.

Now whatever be the interpretation of the red shift, the fact that it increases roughly with the faintness and diminishing size of the objects showing it in their radiation has led to the plausible assumption that it may be used as a measure of distance, and indeed it is so used now almost as a matter of course. However if the red shift is interpreted as an actual Doppler displacement, extremely high speeds of recession from the sun and so from the galaxy are indicated, in some cases exceeding 100,000 kilometres per second. It is not surprising therefore that doubts have been raised as to the validity of this interpretation. It may be that photons in transit over immense distances lose energy which will show itself as a shift in frequency towards the red end of the spectrum. There is no way of testing such an assumption and it raises the further problem of what becomes of the lost energy. It seems also to undermine the foundations of the quantum theory which is so firmly entrenched in modern science.

If the recession velocities are real, they involve the consequence that the radiation as received by the terrestrial observer has been weakened in intensity as well as altered in character. The observed brightness of a distant object must therefore be corrected for the effect of the speed of recession in order to estimate the distance. Moreover this brightness refers to the object at a remote era in time and, if the brightness of such a system changes with its gradual evolution, the distance estimate is no longer reliable. There is the further question of why extra-galactic objects should be moving apart at speeds increasing with the distance. This leads to difficult and disputed problems in modern cosmology, where it is quite usual to pile unverified assumptions on top of one another in order to see what may emerge. Great hopes are entertained from the help which the newer science of radio-astronomy is now giving so abundantly, and it is most unfortunate that man-made radio interference is becoming such a serious factor in limiting its potentiality.

One of the results of distance estimates has been to show that extragalactic systems have a clustering tendency, well-known groups occurring in Virgo, Ursa Major, Coma Berenices, Fornax and other constellations. The Milky Way system itself belongs to such a group which contains about sixteen members, of which the two Magellan Clouds are the nearest and M 31 in Andromeda with M 33 in Triangulum compare with the galaxy in dominance. Five of them are so faint that they are not included in the NGC and it is possible that more of these may be discovered. As only four of the local group are spirals, it may be that this type is not the most frequent in general occurrence but only appears to be so because of superior brightness and size, the small and faint systems being undetected unless they are relatively near to the galaxy. There is already evidence that, in the Virgo group, dwarf systems comparable to the smallest in the local group may be as abundant as the largest types. Possibly these dwarf systems form a generally distributed field in which only the large systems form groups. If this be so, the local group would contain only seven members—M 31, M 32 and NGC 205 in Andromeda, M 33 in Triangulum, the two Magellan Clouds and the Milky Way system itself, one of the largest and situated on the edge of the group which is about 600,000 parsecs across. The dimensions of the Milky Way system are usually given as about 30,000 parsecs in diameter; the sun lies far out near the central plane at a distance of about 10,000 parsecs from the centre, the direction of which is in R.A. 17^h 42^m and Dec. $-29°$. This is in the constellation of Ophiuchus, close to its borders with Scorpius and Sagittarius.

6

AMATEUR OBSERVING

This is a personal chapter which expresses simply my own preferences and procedure. Its only justification is that of being based on nearly twenty years of observing on every available occasion. One is bound to learn something during that time.

The instrument

As the telescope is a constant companion for use in darkness, it should be simple, robust and efficient. Elaborate fittings and devices, however pleasant to look at and indeed necessary for the exacting work of the professional astronomer, are not needed. They waste precious time, get in the way in the dark and are subject to damage. In regard to type, I choose unhesitatingly the simple Newtonian reflector of focal length seven to eight times the aperture, which should be as large as possible, remembering that 30 cm is near the limit for convenient amateur use. Such a telescope is relatively easy to make and to keep in adjustment; it is also pleasant to use and reasonably fast for photography. In comparison the Cassegrain reflector has too many disadvantages to compensate for the merit of compactness. It is more difficult to make and to keep in adjustment, and usually much slower for photography. Also to avoid the great inconvenience, shared in common with the refractor, of direct vision for objects at high elevation, a star diagonal must be employed. This loses about 10 per cent of the available light and must be accurately made to avoid decentration of the field on rotation. Further the warm breath of the observer near the mirror requires that this be completely enclosed in the bottom of the telescope tube, which is undesirable for good definition.

The refractor is expensive and inconvenient except in small apertures in spite of its admirable qualities for precision measurements. The focal length is rarely less than fifteen times the clear aperture, which makes larger instruments unwieldy, and it needs a star diagonal with its accompanying disadvantages. It is also slow and requires a filter for photographic work, owing to secondary spectrum. Indeed this lack of complete achromatism makes the recognition of fine nuances of colour quite impossible with a refractor.

32

There is much satisfaction in making one's own mirror but, if this be undertaken, it should be done really well, for there is little pleasure in observing with defective optical parts. My own mirror was made in England by F. J. Hargreaves of Kingswood, Surrey; it is 30·8 cm in diameter and 213 cm in focal length, and has been greatly admired by those who know for its brilliant polish and perfection of figure. These qualities are important in attaining the black field free from scattered light which is so valuable for detecting faint objects. Orthoscopic microscope oculars are recommended; they give fine wide fields and are much easier in use than the screwed type. There is a certain relationship between magnification and aperture which gives the best viewing conditions for faint objects; these become too dispersed if magnification is high, and sky brightness obtrudes itself if it is low. My experience leads me to recommend a magnification about five times the aperture of the mirror expressed in cm. I have used both flat and prism in the telescope and much prefer the former. The prism is in some respects easier to adjust but it is heavy, not quite achromatic, subject to ghosts of bright objects, and expensive as it must be made of first-class optical glass and has three polished surfaces instead of one.

The frame of my telescope is made of selected wood known as aeroplane spruce, accurately dressed to square or rectangular cross-section as required. This is very easily cut and assembled into a square section open lattice girder, firmly screwed together and provided with stiff perforated 3-ply partitions. All the parts were covered with shellac varnish before assembly and the whole frame was treated subsequently in the same way. This girder has held its shape remarkably through years of use in a mountain climate of very variable humidity. The mirror is supported by an open wooden triangle on three rounded brass studs which make contact with it symmetrically at points two-thirds of the radius from the centre. Four small adjustable curved brass pads lined with cork touch it lightly at the sides and permit of centration. The wooden triangle is loosely pivoted at one corner and the other corners may be raised or lowered by rotating two long brass rods which are accessible from the ocular tube—a simple device which permits very easy and accurate collimation. This method of mounting the mirror at the lower end of an open girder allows ready circulation of air all round the glass without detectable flexure or distortion of any kind, and experience has shown that the mirror settles down in about 10 minutes after uncovering and then holds its figure remarkably well for the night's observing. There are of course no tube currents to interfere with definition.

The mount of the flat is held by four thin strips of hard rolled blackened aluminium which terminate in pairs at opposite edges of the mount and not at its centre; this arrangement ensures that they are easily kept firm and tight. Experience has shown that if the flat is protected when not in use by tying a clean handkerchief loosely round it instead of putting on a hard cap, the telescope maintains its optical adjustment well over long periods. The ocular tube is fixed to a panel on the side of the girder away from the declination axis. This is very convenient for observing objects in or near the meridian and indeed also with considerable hour angle, except for those which pass within about 5° on either side of the zenith; in these cases there is some awkwardness between about 1 and 2 hours east or west. I have found this restriction only a trifling inconvenience. It would of course be obviated if the telescope or its upper part could be rotated, but the accuracy in construction needed for this if centration and setting are to remain unimpaired is beyond most amateurs.

The equatorial mount

A sturdy and reasonably accurate equatorial mount is essential for any serious work. The main thing to ensure is that all parts of the instrument are balanced so that the driving clock has the same load in all positions and there are no overturning forces which tend to pull the polar axis out of position. The telescope should balance about the declination axis, the declination axis with its loads should balance about the polar axis, and the polar axis, short, wide and massive, should sit firmly on top of the supporting column under full load without any tendency to overturn, even if not bolted down. The number of ways in which the polar axis may be constructed and supported is of course legion, but these simple precepts are recommended. If the pillar itself is stable, the polar axis will remain accurately in position year after year without attention, and finding will be easy and precise.

In my instrument (Plate 1), the support for the polar axis is a solid cast-iron block in one piece, flanged and planed off below. At an angle to the bottom of the flange corresponding approximately to the co-latitude of the observatory—in my case 52° 38′—is machined a flat circular plane about 24 cm in diameter, from the centre of which projects the short heavy steel polar axis. Near the periphery of this plane, a circular groove of semi-circular section is machined out, into which about 100 steel balls are packed in grease. Over this fits a thick disk of cast-iron, perforated to take the polar axis and grooved correspondingly to make a large ball race with the steel balls. Round the lower outside edge of the disk are cut 360 teeth for a suitable worm drive, and just above is the 22 cm diameter movable hour circle divided accurately in 5-minute intervals, which can be fixed in any required position by suitable grub screws. Above this again, on the top and outside edges of the disk are the carefully machined surfaces which act as a wide bearing for the inside rim of a heavy cast-iron cap carrying the declination axis. This cap may be clamped to the clock-driven disk below it, and the polar axis just passes through it and is secured by a small plate.

This equatorial head is sturdy, stable and reliable and has given long service without any trouble. It is supported on the heavy wide flange of a 6-inch steel pipe filled with concrete, the lower flange of which is bolted to a heavy steel plate 3 ft in diameter. This itself has three large levelling screws and is mounted on a massive concrete block in the earth below the observatory floor. The polar axis is adjusted in the meridian by slight horizontal movement between the supporting flanges, and in latitude by slight adjustment of the levelling screws of the base, before tightening the holding bolts down. The supporting pillar is free from the floor of the observatory and the clock drive on this floor communicates with a reduction gear box on the pillar by a thin rubber belt, thus avoiding all possibility of vibration.

The declination circle 22 cm in diameter is one of the counter weights, divided accurately in degrees round the periphery. It is a mistake to divide circles more finely than this, for close lines are confusing and cannot be seen well in the dim light available. By dividing the degrees into tenths by eye with the help of a small fixed lens, and the 5-minute intervals on the hour circle into half minutes, ample accuracy is obtained for finding. It is rare for this operation to require more than 15 or 20 seconds and I should not tolerate arrangements which took much longer. It should be mentioned also that with the telescope described, slow motions in R.A. and Dec. are not needed unless photography is attempted; in fact their use wastes time. All that is necessary is to clamp the telescope very lightly. When the object is in the field, gentle hand pressure on the telescope brings it to the centre in a moment or two, and the surrounding regions may also be quickly examined. This method of using the instrument has another advantage in protecting the worm drive from strain due to accidental contacts in the dark.

3-2

The observatory

A small observatory is a great convenience and comfort; it saves much time and enables a permanently mounted instrument to be protected. My own is 12 ft by 10 ft with timber frame sheeted with thin hard rolled aluminium, and the roof 14 ft by 11 ft runs off on roller bearings to the south (Plate 1). I believe that this type of roof is preferable to the dome; it is much easier to construct and affords a view of the whole sky all the time, which has advantages and saves a good deal of time. It is true that it offers no more protection from cold and wind than the walls of the observatory are able to afford, but the serious observer will not mind exposure, especially when he knows that the protection of a dome inevitably means warm air currents passing out through the observing slot with interference to definition. Free exposure ensures rapid temperature stabilization and, if the floor of the observatory is made of wood a foot or two above the ground and ventilated beneath, dewing is not likely to occur. On some observing nights here, the dew has been so heavy that it has trickled down the metal stand of the telescope, but I have never experienced the slightest trouble from clouding of either mirror or flat. On very cold nights the front lenses of oculars may cloud from the moist warm surface of the eye, but this is easily avoided by keeping the oculars when not in use in a box containing a hot-water bag suitably wrapped up.

The observatory faces north and has a pair of wide doors which open outwards and may be hooked back. The horizontal bar above the doors acting as a transom can then be unbolted and lifted away, thus affording a clear view right down to the northern horizon. As the south pole is clear above the roof when it is run off, there is no restriction to viewing except low down to the east and west due to the 6 ft walls of the observatory. I have found that this type of structure meets all requirements, and a short sturdy pair of double-sided steps with flat top will suffice for all the climbing about that may be necessary.

Lighting

The eyes are very easily desensitized and as little light as possible should be used for reading scales and recording observations. My observatory is situated in clean country air at an altitude of 2,200 ft and well removed from interfering lights and luminous city haze. Nevertheless, although the sky is often very dark, there is usually enough general auroral glow to see the location of objects in the observatory when the roof is run off, and no lighting is needed. The telescope scales are illuminated feebly by under-run pea lamps of low voltage from a transformer to avoid accidents in the dark from possible frayed or damp leads. For recording notes, a small white plastic torch is useful, again under-run by using a higher voltage bulb in place of the usual one. The feeble glimmer illuminates a circle an inch or so wide on the paper, which is sufficient for all purposes. It is interesting to note that even a short viewing of the television screen will cause stars to appear reddish for a considerable time. This is caused by lack of red in the fluorescent screen light, so that the eyes are not desensitized at this end of the spectrum. In any case, the viewing of television is a very poor preparation for observing with the telescope.

Clothing

It is unfortunate that some of the best nights for observing are the coldest, and that many of the most interesting regions of the southern sky culminate in winter. All astronomers know the value of adequate protection from cold and even the most devoted look somewhat ruefully at the ice crystals growing steadily on the metal parts of their instruments or on the observatory floor.

I have always found that it is most important to protect the head and neck, where circulation is rapid and heat losses are high. One can do this pretty well with a thick scarf, a lined balaclava and a beret. As for the rest, fleece-lined flying boots are a great comfort and so are mittens with the finger tips free. I always wear outside of everything else a pair of unlaundered overalls known locally as a boiler-suit, the smooth surface of which does not flap about and shed fluff, some of which would sooner or later find its way to the surface of the mirror. And it has ample pockets.

Special equipment

Direct-vision prism. One of the most useful appliances is a small direct-vision prism;* these are usually about 3 × 1 cm and may be mounted in a small cardboard or plastic tube. By applying the mount directly to the ocular of the telescope, a little practice enables one to look through and

* This prism is composed of three small right-angled isosceles prisms cemented together in line. Deviation between hydrogen C and F is 4·6°, with undeviated wavelength approximately 5,130 A.

see the spectra of objects near the centre of the field. The prism is most effective in picking out small planetary nebulae from fields of stars, and generally in distinguishing objects with gaseous spectra from unresolved clusters and extra-galactic nebulae which have continuous spectra. For seeing stellar spectra, the narrow line of light must be broadened slightly by change of focus which will bring any well-marked spectrum lines into view if the air is fairly steady. Long period variables if bright enough well repay examination.

Position micrometer. The elaborate micrometers used in binary star measurements of precision are not needed by the amateur observer unless he wishes to undertake this exacting work seriously. However a simple form of instrument will give him much information about changing pairs by enabling him to estimate separations and position angles reasonably well. All that is needed is a small cleavage rhomb of clear calcite about 2 mm thick and 1 cm wide, and providers of chemical reagents or perhaps a geological museum may be able to furnish a few pieces for trial. The rhomb is simply cemented between two micro-slide covers with a drop of any clear colourless varnish and then mounted in a tube—mine is turned from a piece of vulcanite—in which it can be viewed with a small positive ocular giving a magnification of 250 or so on the telescope. This makes in effect a polarizing ocular and it is held in a mount which turns in the ocular tube of the telescope and is provided with an outside flange graduated at intervals of 5°. These graduations may be read against a fixed index on the ocular tube of the telescope.

Now if a double star be observed, four images will be seen because of the double refraction of the calcite. Adjustment must be made on a known pair, and Gamma Arietis is useful here, because both stars are bright and practically fixed at 8·0″ and 360°. On rotating the micro-meter, the two pairs of images will move round in the field, and the calcite rhomb must be rotated in its own mount until the four images are exactly in line when the index reads 360°. The adjustment requires care and patience, but need be done only once and may be helped by rotating the ocular tube of the telescope in its own mounting if this can be done, not neglecting to mark its final position so that it can always be found again in case of displacement. The separation of the two images of each star should now be estimated by eye and noted, remembering that the separation between the two stars of the pair is 8·0″. In my instrument this separation is very close to 15″. To measure approxi-mately an unknown pair, the micrometer is rotated until the four images are accurately in line when the angle may be read on the index, always remembering that double-image micrometers will give two readings of angle exactly 180° apart. Knowledge of the four quadrants of the field will enable the correct one to be chosen, position angles being always measured from the north counter-clockwise. A guess at the separation of the stars may also be made by comparing it with the known separation of the two images of either star.

Siderial clock. A siderial clock is not really necessary as the hour circle of the telescope can be set quickly at the commencement of work by reference to a known star near culmination. Nevertheless it is a great convenience, and useful for checking the running of the driving clock. I found that a well-known type of electric wall clock for 240 volt 50 cycle supply had three gear ratios in train, making a total reduction of 150 : 1 between the synchronous motor and the hands. These were 8 : 40, 9 : 45, and 9 : 54. By altering these to 8 : 30, 7 : 47, 17 : 101, the clock will keep siderial time with a rate of only +0·06 second per day, which is amply sufficient for finding with an equatorial. A firm of precision engineers in Melbourne made the alterations neatly for me and changed the hour hand rate to one revolution in 24 hours. This cost more than the value of the original clock but the whole was much less expensive than an observatory siderial clock and it has been running faultlessly for nearly twenty years.

Aids to observing

A set of circular limiting diaphragms of blackened ply-wood is useful; these fit into the top of the telescope girder, those of 10 cm diameter and less being in my case extra-axial to avoid interference from the flat. On nights of relatively poor definition it is surprising how useful these diaphragms can be. A neutral grey optical glass filter absorbing about three stellar magnitudes is also occasionally useful; it will often show the companion to Sirius or to Beta Centauri when otherwise the glare of the primary is too great. Another convenience is a small wooden rack attached to the telescope frame near the ocular, and protected by a plastic sheet. This holds spare oculars, the position micrometer and the direct-vision prism ready for use.

Spectacles are inconvenient for observing and are not necessary unless astigmatism is present. Those whose eyes are astigmatic, as in my case, can help themselves by selecting oculars with a plane surface on the front lens. On this surface is cemented by a drop of cedar-wood oil a small cylindrical lens of the appropriate correction, cut by means of a diamond from the larger spectacle lens which any optician will supply. For observing, the ocular is rotated until the extra-focal image of a star in the centre of the field is quite round, and remains so on focusing. There is in fact a certain advantage in having astigmatic eyes when observing stellar spectra by the direct-vision prism, for the star may be focused to a short bright line before using this. The width of the spectrum so produced makes details in it easier to see.

In endeavouring to see faint diffuse nebulae, it should be remembered that on most nights which seem otherwise clear, bright stars show more or less pronounced diffuse haloes round them, which are partly instrumental and partly atmospheric. Even such experienced observers as the Herschels were sometimes deceived in this way. For this reason I am never quite sure that I really see the dust nebula involving some of the Pleiades. However fainter stars usually show dark areas round them, where the field appears to be blacker, and this is due to contrast. If a few such stars are scattered in an otherwise almost empty field, it is easy to imagine that between them an ill-defined faintly luminous hazy object exists, due simply to the greater apparent brightness of the field in comparison with that close to the stars. This has often led observers into error. Moonless nights are of course necessary for an observation like this, because moonlight blots out faint objects and is detrimental to the appearance of star clusters and nebulae. However some of the brighter double stars look very beautiful in a moonlit field, or in twilight.

In conclusion it may be said that observation should be made with both eyes open, completely relaxed and looking into the far distance. Some people screw their eyes up to see something close at hand, which soon leads to eye strain. Black velvet on the ocular panel of the telescope will prevent disturbing images in the unused eye.

GENERAL LIST OF
TELESCOPIC OBJECTS FOR
SOUTHERN OBSERVERS

The following list has been selected from nearly 4,000 objects which have been observed individually in a programme extending over many years. The included objects have been chosen as likely to interest the observer, and cover the sky south of the limit of about 50° N declination. The excluded portion of the sky amounting to less than 12 per cent of the total area is inaccessible from my observatory, but about eighty objects from it are listed in the addendum.

It is necessary to emphasize that the selection is a personal one, based largely on my own estimate of the interest and beauty of the various objects. Some endeavour has been made to space the chosen objects round the R.A. circle so that diversity is available at all times of the year, but the overwhelming richness of some regions of the southern sky has inevitably made parts of the circle very crowded. In regard to double stars of which tens of thousands are known, preference has been given to the closer and brighter pairs as being more interesting and attractive. About 1,000 planetary nebulae are known, most of which are very difficult objects discovered only by photography; the list includes about seventy of the brighter ones, which should provide sufficient examples of these interesting bodies. All the brighter diffuse nebulae are given, and a limited selection from the vast array of extra-galactic nebulae. Of the many open galactic clusters, only those have been included which make good telescopic objects or have some special claim. However, because of their diversity, intrinsic interest and often wonderful beauty, all the globular clusters within the range of amateur telescopes find places. Variable stars have been largely omitted, not because of lack of interest but because their character is disclosed only after repeated observation, often over prolonged periods. A few long-period variables are however scattered through the list for their fine spectra.

The objects in the list are arranged in R.A. sequence and are numbered. Then follow the name, and the R.A. and Dec. for the epoch 1950, with decennial variations in minutes of time and minutes of arc respectively. Variations in R.A. are all positive unless otherwise shown; variations in Dec. are positive or negative as indicated. Then come a very brief

41

description and the constellation in which the object occurs, in the usual 3-letter contraction. For stars, visual magnitude and spectral type are given, and for pairs the separation and position angle as well; these refer to 1960 unless otherwise stated.* These values are approximate only, for double stars are subject to change and star magnitudes often show discrepancy when taken from different sources. It should be remembered that position angles are measured from north counter-clockwise, and that diurnal star movement through the telescope field proceeds from 90° to 270° (from f. to p.) with north on the left hand. In regard to naming, the NGC and IC numbers have preference for clusters and nebulae. A few of the planetary nebulae are not found in the NGC; these are denoted by their numbers in the Vorontzov–Veljaminov list and prefaced by the letters VV. For stars, the letters of the Greek alphabet are used, and then the numbers in Flamsteed's British Catalogue of 1725. Pairs not covered by these are numbered with the appropriate symbol from the discoverer's lists.

Fuller description and information about each object may be found under the constellation in which it occurs, where it is located by list number and name. The constellations are given in alphabetical order, and in each case after a short introduction the selected objects follow. These descriptions indicate what 30 cm aperture may be expected to show on a clear dark night of fair definition, but the performance of smaller apertures is also given. Magnifications are not stated, for seeing conditions are important and the observer soon learns to select the best ocular for the occasion. A few difficult objects are useful, partly as tests for instrument and conditions, and partly as exercises in finding. Estimates of distances are approximate as they tend to be modified as the result of observational and theoretical advances; they are given in parsecs and may be converted to light years by multiplying with 3·26. Amongst the constellations, Nubecula Major and Minor will be found for convenience, with the contractions NMa and NMi respectively. The date of culmination of each constellation refers to its central meridian at midnight; this takes place 28 minutes earlier for each succeeding week.

The following abbreviations are used:

NGC	New General Catalogue 1887.	Var.	Decennial variation.
IC	Index Catalogues 1894 1907.	N	North.
R.A.	Right Ascension.	S	South.
Dec.	Declination.	p.	preceding.

* Conventionally the angle is given before the separation. The order is here reversed so that the two factors upon which resolution mainly depends—magnitude of the fainter star and separation—may be seen at a glance.

f.	following.		eg.	extra-galactic.
pa.	position angle.		m.	apparent visual magnitude.
pc	parsec.		R	distance (in parsecs).

No.	Name	R.A.	Var.	Dec.	Var.	Description	Con.
		h m	m	° ′	′		
1	κ Scl	0 6·8	+0·51	−28 16	+3·3	6·2 6·3 1·5″ 84° F2. F2. Fine pair	Scl
2	35 Psc	0 12·4	0·51	+ 8 33	3·3	5·9 8·1 12″ 148° gA9. dA9. Binary	Psc
3	NGC 55	0 12·5	0·50	−39 30	3·3	Long bright edgewise eg. spiral	Scl
4	38 Psc	0 14·8	0·51	+ 8 36	3·3	7·0 8·0 4·5″ 236° dG1. dA9. Elegant	Psc
5	AC 1	0 18·3	0·52	+32 42	3·3	7·5 8·0 1·5″ 288° dF4. Close binary	And
6	NGC 104	0 21·9	0·44	−72 21	3·3	47 Tuc. Superb globular cluster	Tuc
7	NGC 134	0 27·9	0·49	−33 32	3·3	Large fairly bright eg. spindle	Scl
8	β Tuc	0 29·3	0·46	−63 14	3·3	4·5 4·5 27″ 169° B9. A2. Brilliant	Tuc
9	β 395	0 34·7	0·52	−25 2	3·3	6·4 6·5 0·2″–0·8″ dG7. Short period	Cet
10	55 Psc	0 37·3	0·52	+21 10	3·3	5·6 8·5 6·5″ 194° gG7. Fine pair	Psc
11	NGC 205	0 37·6	0·54	+41 25	3·3	Fairly bright elliptical eg. nebula	And
12	NGC 221	0 40·0	0·54	+40 36	3·3	M 32. Small companion to M 31	And
13	NGC 224	0 40·0	0·54	+41 0	3·3	M 31. Very large bright eg. spiral	And
14	NGC 246	0 44·6	0·50	−12 9	3·3	Faint large annular nebula	Cet
15	NGC 247	0 44·6	0·50	−21 1	3·3	Large diffuse elliptical eg. nebula	Cet
16	NGC 253	0 45·1	0·49	−25 34	3·3	Very fine large edgewise spiral	Scl
17	65 Psc	0 47·2	0·53	+27 26	3·3	6·3 6·3 4·5″ 296° gF0. gF0. Fine pair	Psc
18	NGC 288	0 50·2	0·49	−26 51	3·3	Open type globular cluster	Scl
19	NGC 300	0 52·6	0·47	−37 58	3·2	Large diffuse elliptical eg. nebula	Scl
20	NGC 330	0 54·5	0·34	−72 44	3·2	Small compact star cluster	NMi
21	NGC 346	0 57·4	0·34	−72 27	3·2	Bright irregular gaseous nebula	NMi
22	IC 1613	1 0·6	0·51	+ 1 41	3·2	Large faint local eg. system	Cet
23	NGC 362	1 1·6	0·35	−71 7	3·2	Bright well-resolved globular cluster	Tuc
24	NGC 371	1 1·9	0·33	−72 20	3·2	Large irregular star cloud	NMi
25	NGC 376	1 2·3	0·32	−73 5	3·2	Bright small compact cluster	NMi
26	β Phe	1 3·9	0·45	−46 59	3·2	4·1 4·1 1·4″ 344° G4. Close binary	Phe
27	ζ Phe	1 6·3	0·42	−55 31	3·2	4·1–4·5 8·2 6·2″ 243° B8. Fine pair	Phe
28	NGC 404	1 6·6	0·56	+35 27	3·2	Fairly bright round eg. nebula	And
29	NGC 419	1 6·8	0·30	−73 9	3·2	Remote round globular cluster	NMi
30	β 303	1 7·0	0·54	+23 32	3·2	7·1 7·3 0·7″ 289° F0. Test pair	Psc
31	IC 1644	1 7·7	0·29	−73 28	3·2	Small bright planetary nebula	NMi
32	φ Psc	1 11·0	0·54	+24 19	3·2	4·6 10·1 7·5″ 223° gG7. Fine pair	Psc
33	ζ Psc	1 11·1	0·52	+ 7 19	3·2	5·6 6·5 23″ 63° A5. dF6. Wide pair	Psc
34	NGC 456	1 12·4	0·28	−73 34	3·2	Chain of remote star clusters	NMi
35	κ Tuc	1 14·1	0·32	−69 8	3·2	5·1 7·3 5·2″ 334° F2. Fine pair	Tuc
36	h. 2036	1 17·5	0·49	−16 4	3·2	6·8 7·3 1·8″ 350° G0. Elegant pair	Cet
37	NGC 524	1 22·1	0·52	+ 9 16	3·2	Conspicuous round eg. nebula	Psc
38	NGC 602	1 28·4	0·22	−73 49	3·1	Interesting gaseous nebula	Hyi
39	η Psc	1 28·8	0·53	+15 5	3·1	3·7 11·0 1·0″ 20° gG3. Difficult pair	Psc
40	NGC 598	1 31·1	0·56	+30 24	3·1	M 33. Very large eg. spiral system	Tri

No.	Name	R.A.	Var.	Dec.	Var.	Description	Con.
		h m	m	° ′	′		
41	NGC 613	1 32·0	+0·46	−29 40	+3·1	Barred spiral eg. nebula	Scl
42	NGC 625	1 32·9	0·44	−41 41	3·1	Fairly bright edgewise eg. spiral	Phe
43	Σ 138	1 33·4	0·52	+ 7 23	3·1	7·6 7·6 1·6″ 53° F8. Dainty pair	Psc
44	τ Scl	1 33·8	0·46	−30 10	3·1	6·0 7·1 1·2″ 112° Fo. Fo. Changing	Scl
45	NGC 628	1 34·0	0·54	+15 32	3·1	M 74. Round symmetrical eg. spiral	Psc
46	p. Eri	1 37·9	0·38	−56 27	3·0	6·0 6·1 11″ 201° dK2. dK5. Fine pair	Eri
47	NGC 650–1	1 39·1	0·62	+51 19	3·0	M 76. Large planetary nebula	Per
48	ε Scl	1 43·3	0·47	−25 18	3·0	5·4 8·8 4·5″ 40° dF1. Fine pair	Scl
49	1 Ari	1 47·4	0·55	+22 2	3·0	6·2 7·4 2·8″ 167° gG9. A2. Fine pair	Ari
50	γ Ari	1 50·8	0·56	+19 3	2·9	4·8 4·8 8·0″ 0° Ao. Ao. Beautiful pair	Ari
51	Σ 186	1 53·3	0·51	+ 1 36	3·0	6·9 6·9 1·5″ 49° dGo. Fine binary	Cet
52	h. 3475	1 53·7	0·32	−60 33	2·9	7·2 7·3 2·5″ 68° Fo. Elegant pair	Hyi
53	χ Eri	1 54·0	0·39	−51 51	3·0	3·7 11·0 4·6″ 202° gG4. Difficult pair	Eri
54	NGC 752	1 54·8	0·59	+37 26	2·9	Large open star cluster	And
55	NGC 772	1 56·6	0·55	+18 46	2·9	Fairly bright eg. nebula	Ari
56	α Psc	1 59·5	0·52	+ 2 31	2·9	4·3 5·2 2·0″ 294° A2. A3. Fine binary	Psc
57	γ And	2 0·8	0·61	+42 5	2·9	2·3 5·1 9·9″ 63° gK3. Ao. Beautiful	And
58	6 Tri	2 9·5	0·58	+30 4	2·8	5·4 7·0 3·8″ 72° gG4. dF4. Fine pair	Tri
59	NGC 869	2 15·5	0·69	+56 55	2·8	Very fine open star cluster	Per
60	o Cet	2 16·8	0·50	− 3 12	2·7	2·0–10·1 10 0·9″ 130° M6–M9. Mira	Cet
61	NGC 884	2 18·9	0·70	+56 53	2·7	Very fine twin cluster to NGC 869	Per
62	NGC 891	2 19·3	0·62	+42 7	2·7	Long eg. edgewise spiral nebula	And
63	NGC 908	2 20·8	0·46	−21 27	2·7	Fairly bright elliptical eg. nebula	Cet
64	NGC 936	2 25·1	0·51	− 1 22	2·7	Bright round eg. nebula	Cet
65	ω For	2 31·7	0·44	−28 27	2·6	5·0 7·8 11″ 244° B9. Fine white pair	For
66	ν Cet	2 33·2	0·52	+ 5 23	2·6	5·0 9·6 8·0″ 83° gG5. Fine pair	Cet
67	NGC 1023	2 37·2	0·62	+38 52	2·6	Fairly bright elliptical eg. nebula	Per
68	NGC 1049	2 37·7	0·42	−34 29	2·6	Remote eg. globular cluster	For
69	84 Cet	2 38·6	0·51	− 0 54	2·6	5·7 9·2 4·0″ 313° dF6. Elegant pair	Cet
70	NGC 1039	2 38·8	0·64	+42 34	2·6	M34. Bright large scattered cluster	Per
71	NGC 1068	2 40·1	0·51	− 0 14	2·5	M77. Bright elliptical eg. nebula	Cet
72	γ Cet	2 40·7	0·52	+ 3 2	2·5	3·7 6·2 3·0″ 294° A2. dF3. Very fine	Cet
73	NGC 1097	2 44·3	0·43	−30 29	2·5	Conspicuous elliptical eg. nebula	For
74	π Ari	2 46·5	0·56	+17 15	2·5	5·3 8·4 3·1″ 119°; 10·5 25″ 110° B8	Ari
75	θ Eri	2 56·4	0·38	−40 30	2·4	3·4 4·4 8·2″ 88° A2. A2. Very fine	Eri
76	ε Ari	2 56·4	0·57	+21 8	2·4	5·2 5·5 1·5″ 206° A4. A4. Fine binary	Ari
77	Σ 336	2 58·4	0·61	+32 13	2·4	6·7 8·0 8·5″ 7° G5. A5. Elegant pair	Per
78	β 11	3 0·2	0·49	− 7 53	2·4	5·5 9·6 2·8″ 84° gG5. Little change	Eri
79	β Per	3 4·9	+0·65	+40 46	2·3	2·2–3·5 B8. Eclipsing variable	Per
80	h. 3568	3 9·2	−0·34	−79 11	2·3	5·7 7·8 15″ 226° Fo. Fine pair	Hyi
81	α For	3 9·9	+0·42	−29 11	2·4	4·0 7·0 1·6″ 298° dF5. Fine binary	For
82	Jc 8	3 10·7	0·35	−44 36	2·3	6·4 7·0 0·45″–1·0″; 9·5 3·2″ 206° F2	Eri
83	NGC 1261	3 10·9	0·26	−55 24	2·2	Bright compact globular cluster	Hor
84	NGC 1291	3 15·5	0·37	−41 17	2·2	Bright round eg. nebula	Eri
85	Jc 1	3 17·3	0·44	−21 55	2·2	4·0 10·5 6·0″ 288° gM3. Fine pair	Eri

LIST OF TELESCOPIC OBJECTS

No.	Name	R.A.	Var.	Dec.	Var.	Description	Con.
		h m	m	° ′	′		
86	NGC 1313	3 17·6	+0·12	−66 40	+2·2	Fairly bright bar-spiral eg. nebula	Ret
87	NGC 1316	3 20·8	0·38	−37 24	2·1	Two eg. nebulae in same field	For
88	NGC 1325	3 22·3	0·45	−21 43	2·1	Remarkable comet-like nebula	Eri
89	NGC 1350	3 29·1	0·39	−33 48	2·0	Conspicuous elliptical eg. nebula	For
90	NGC 1360	3 31·4	0·43	−26 0	2·0	Large diffuse planetary nebula	For
91	NGC 1365	3 31·8	0·38	−36 18	2·0	Fine bar-spiral eg. nebula	For
92	NGC 1379	3 34·2	0·39	−35 37	2·0	Three eg. nebulae in same field	For
93	Σ 422	3 34·2	0·51	+ 0 26	2·0	6·1 8·9 6·5″ 261° dG9. dK6. Elegant	Tau
94	NGC 1380	3 34·6	0·39	−35 9	2·0	Conspicuous elliptical eg. nebula	For
95	NGC 1399	3 36·6	0·38	−35 37	1·9	Two bright eg. nebulae in fine field	For
96	Σ 425	3 37·0	0·63	+33 57	1·9	7·6 7·6 2·0″ 79° F5. Elegant pair	Per
97	NGC 1433	3 40·4	0·31	−47 24	1·9	Large elliptical e.g. nebula	Hor
98	NGC 1448	3 42·1	0·33	−44 48	1·9	Long eg. edgewise spiral nebula	Hor
99	IC 351	3 44·3	0·64	+34 54	1·9	Very small planetary nebula	Per
100	30 Tau	3 45·5	0·55	+10 59	1·9	5·0 9·6 9·0″ 59° B3. Fine unequal pair	Tau
101	Δ 16	3 46·8	0·37	−37 46	1·8	4·9 5·4 7·9″ 212° B8. B9. Very fine	Eri
102	OΣ 65	3 47·3	0·60	+25 26	1·8	6·0 6·3 0″–0·7″ A3. Changing binary	Tau
103	ζ Per	3 51·0	0·63	+31 44	1·8	2·9 9·3 13″208°B1.Wide unequal pair	Per
104	32 Eri	3 51·8	0·50	− 3 6	1·8	4·9 6·3 7·0″ 348° gG4. A1. Beautiful	Eri
105	ε Per	3 54·5	0·67	+39 52	1·7	3·0 8·3 9·0″ 9° B1. Little change	Per
106	NGC 1511	3 59·3	0·04	−67 46	1·7	Small eg. edgewise spiral nebula	Hyi
107	Σ 495	4 4·9	0·56	+15 2	1·6	6·0 8·7 3·8″ 222° dF2. dG8. Elegant	Tau
108	NGC 1531	4 10·1	0·38	−32 59	1·6	Two fine eg. nebulae in same field	Eri
109	47 Tau	4 11·2	0·54	+ 9 8	1·6	5·0 8·0 1·1″ 351° gG5. Close pair	Tau
110	NGC 1535	4 11·9	0·47	−12 52	1·5	Fine bright planetary nebula	Eri
111	39 Eri	4 12·0	0·48	−10 23	1·5	5·1 9·0 6·4″ 146° gK2. Fine pair	Eri
112	40 Eri	4 13·0	0·46	− 7 44	1·0	4·5 9·6 82″ 105°; BC 9·6 11 4″ 340°	Eri
113	NGC 1549	4 14·9	0·22	−55 48	1·5	Fine field with two bright nebulae	Dor
114	NGC 1559	4 17·0	0·12	−62 55	1·5	Bright elliptical eg. nebula	Ret
115	θ Ret	4 17·1	0·11	−63 23	1·5	6·2 8·0 4·5″ 2° B9. Elegant pair	Ret
116	NGC 1566	4 18·9	0·22	−55 4	1·5	Bright eg. spiral nebula	Dor
117	β 744	4 19·4	0·41	−25 51	1·4	6·6 6·6 0·7″ 280° dF2. Changing pair	Eri
118	β 87	4 19·4	0·59	+20 42	1·4	6·1 8·8 2·0″ 171° gMo. Ao. Orange	Tau
119	NGC 1574	4 21·0	0·20	−57 5	1·4	Bright round eg. nebula	Ret
120	56 Per	4 21·4	0·65	+33 51	1·4	5·8 8·8 4·0″ 30° dF5. Bright yellow	Per
121	ADS 3201	4 22·4	0·59	+22 8	1·4	9·5 9·8 6″ 330°. Brilliant field	Tau
122	h. 3650	4 25·0	0·34	−40 38	1·4	7·0 8·8 3·0″ 184° Ao. Delicate pair	Cae
123	Σ 559	4 30·6	0·58	+17 55	1·3	7·0 7·0 3·1″ 277° B8. Little change	Tau
124	α Tau	4 33·0	0·57	+16 25	1·2	1·1 gK5. Brilliant orange; spectrum	Tau
125	Σ 572	4 35·4	0·62	+26 51	1·2	7·2 7·2 4·0″ 195° dF3. dF2. Elegant	Tau
126	R Dor	4 36·2	0·12	−62 11	1·2	4·8–6·8 gM7. Remarkable spectrum	Dor
127	α Cae	4 38·9	0·32	−41 57	1·2	4·5 13 6″ 120° F1. Difficult test	Cae
128	h. 3683	4 39·5	0·16	−59 2	1·2	7·1 7·3 2·3″ 91° (1946) Go. Interesting	Dor
129	55 Eri	4 41·2	0·48	− 8 53	1·1	6·7 6·8 9·3″ 317° gG6. dF3. Fine pair	Eri
130	NGC 1647	4 43·2	0·58	+18 59	1·1	Large open galactic cluster	Tau

No.	Name	R.A.	Var.	Dec.	Var.	Description	Con.
		h m	m	° ′	′		
131	NGC 1672	4 44·9	+0·16	−59 20	+1·1	Fairly bright eg. nebula	Dor
132	NGC 1679	4 48·1	0·38	−32 4	1·0	Curious round diffuse nebula	Cae
133	ι Pic	4 49·8	+0·22	−53 33	1·0	5·6 6·4 12″ 58° Fo. Fo. Fine pair	Pic
134	NGC 1711	4 51·0	−0·07	−70 4	1·0	Small bright compact star cluster	NMa
135	NGC 1714	4 52·0	+0·02	−67 0	1·0	Small bright gaseous nebula	NMa
136	NGC 1722	4 52·2	−0·06	−69 28	1·0	Gaseous nebula and star clouds	NMa
137	NGC 1841	4 52·5	−1·61	−84 5	1·0	Rather faint globular cluster	Men
138	NGC 1743	4 54·5	−0·06	−69 17	0·9	Fine field with several nebulae	NMa
139	ω Aur	4 55·9	+0·68	+37 49	0·9	5·0 8·0 5·3″ 359° Ao. dF9. Fine pair	Aur
140	NGC 1763	4 57·1	0·02	−66 30	0·9	Lovely field with nebulae and cluster	NMa
141	R Lep	4 57·3	0·45	−14 53	0·9	6·0–10·4 N6. Remarkable spectrum	Lep
142	γ Cae	5 2·6	0·36	−35 33	0·8	4·6 8·5 3·0″ 308° K5. Orange pair	Cae
143	NGC 1792	5 3·5	0·34	−38 4	0·8	Bright elliptical eg. nebula	Col
144	NGC 1818	5 4·2	0·01	−66 30	0·8	Small bright condensed cluster	NMa
145	14 Ori	5 5·2	0·54	+ 8 26	0·8	5·9 6·7 0·8″ 72° gF2. A2. Close pair	Ori
146	NGC 1808	5 5·9	+0·35	−37 34	0·8	Fine elliptical eg. nebula	Col
147	NGC 1837	5 6·2	−0·11	−70 40	0·7	Beautiful star cloud	NMa
148	Σ 644	5 6·9	+0·68	+37 14	0·7	6·8 7·1 1·7″ 221° K. B2. Fine colour	Aur
149	Σ 652	5 9·2	+0·52	+ 0 59	0·7	6·3 7·8 1·8″ 185° F5. Close pair	Ori
150	NGC 1850	5 9·4	−0·05	−68 52	0·7	Three clusters in fine field	NMa
151	ι Lep	5 10·0	+0·47	−11 56	0·7	4·5 10 12″ 335° B8. Fine white pair	Lep
152	ρ Ori	5 10·7	0·52	+ 2 48	0·7	4·7 8·5 6·5″ 62° gK3. Orange	Ori
153	κ Lep	5 10·9	0·46	−13 0	0·7	4·5 7·5 2·3″ 357° B8. Fine pair	Lep
154	β Ori	5 12·1	0·48	− 8 15	0·7	0·3 6·7 9·5″ 203° B8. B5. Brilliant	Ori
155	14 Aur	5 12·1	0·65	+32 38	0·7	5·0 11 11″ 352°; 7·2 14″ 225° gA7	Aur
156	NGC 1851	5 12·4	0·33	−40 6	0·7	Fine condensed globular cluster	Col
157	τ Ori	5 15·2	+0·49	− 6 54	0·6	3·7 11·5 35″ 250° B8. Test pair	Ori
158	NGC 1903	5 18·3	−0·05	−69 22	0·6	Two bright nebulae and star cloud	NMa
159	38 Lep	5 18·3	+0·43	−21 17	0·6	4·8 9·5 4·0″ 282° B9. Fine pair	Lep
160	41 Lep	5 19·7	0·41	−24 49	0·6	5·5 6·7 3·2″ 97° gG2. A3. Bright pair	Lep
161	η Ori	5 22·0	+0·50	− 2 26	0·6	3·8 4·8 1·5″ 80° Bo. Brilliant pair	Ori
162	NGC 1935	5 22·1	−0·03	−68 0	0·5	Lovely field of nebulae and star cloud	NMa
163	NGC 1904	5 22·1	+0·41	−24 34	0·5	M 79. Fine globular cluster	Lep
164	θ Pic	5 23·6	0·23	−52 22	0·5	6·3 6·8 38″ 286° Ao. Ao. Wide pair	Pic
165	IC 418	5 25·2	0·46	−12 44	0·5	Small bright planetary nebula	Lep
166	NGC 1912	5 25·3	0·67	+35 48	0·5	M 38. Large rich open cluster	Aur
167	β Lep	5 26·1	0·43	−20 48	0·5	3·0 11·0 2·4″ 330° gG1. Very unequal	Lep
168	Σ 716	5 26·2	+0·61	+25 7	0·5	5·9 6·6 4·8″ 206° B9. Fine pair	Tau
169	NGC 1983	5 28·1	−0·07	−69 2	0·5	Beautiful irregular star clusters	NMa
170	NGC 1931	5 28·1	+0·66	+34 12	0·5	Curious diffuse galactic nebula	Aur
171	33 Ori	5 28·6	0·52	+ 3 15	0·5	5·5 7·3 2·0″ 26° B3. Fine close pair	Ori
172	δ Ori	5 29·5	+0·51	− 0 20	0·4	2·5 6·9 53″ 0° Bo. B3. Beautiful	Ori
173	NGC 2004	5 30·8	−0·02	−67 19	0·4	Bright compact cluster in rich field	NMa
174	NGC 1964	5 31·2	+0·42	−21 59	0·4	Fairly bright elliptical eg. nebula	Lep
175	NGC 1952	5 31·5	0·60	+21 59	0·4	M 1. Bright gaseous nebula	Tau

No.	Name	R.A.	Var.	Dec.	Var.	Description	Con.
		h m	m	° ′	′		
176	λ Ori	5 32·4	+0·55	+ 9 54	+0·4	3·7 5·6 4·5″ 42° O8. B2. Very fine	Ori
177	NGC 1976	5 32·8	0·49	− 5 25	0·4	M 42. Great diffuse nebula	Ori
178	42 Ori	5 32·9	0·49	− 4 52	0·4	4·6 8·6 1·6″ 210° B2. Fine field	Ori
179	ι Ori	5 33·0	0·49	− 5 56	0·4	2·9 7·3 11·5″ 140° O8. Brilliant field	Ori
180	NGC 1960	5 33·0	+0·66	+34 7	0·4	M 36. Fine open galactic cluster	Aur
181	NGC 2029	5 35·3	−0·03	−67 36	0·4	Three gaseous nebulae; fine field	NMa
182	NGC 2027	5 35·5	0·01	−66 59	0·4	Compact cluster and star cloud	NMa
183	I 277	5 35·9	−0·14	−71 10	0·4	7·7 11·1 3·9″ 190° K2. Dainty pair	Men
184	σ Ori	5 36·2	+0·50	− 2 38	0·4	Multiple star in beautiful field	Ori
185	NGC 2017	5 37·1	+0·44	−17 53	0·3	Interesting group of 8 stars	Lep
186	NGC 2057	5 37·7	−0·11	−70 15	0·3	Complex field with many nebulae	NMa
187	NGC 2055	5 37·7	−0·08	−69 27	0·3	Fine star cloud and nebula	NMa
188	ζ Ori	5 38·2	+0·50	− 1 58	0·3	2·0 4·2 2·5″ 160° Bo. Fine pair	Ori
189	NGC 2070	5 39·0	−0·07	−69 8	0·3	Wonderful looped nebula round 30Dor	NMa
190	NGC 2022	5 39·3	+0·55	+ 9 4	0·3	Small planetary nebula; starry field	Ori
191	NGC 2024	5 39·3	+0·50	− 1 53	0·3	Dark nebula in luminous field	Ori
192	NGC 2080	5 40·1	−0·09	−69 42	0·3	Several gaseous nebulae in fine field	NMa
193	γ Lep	5 42·4	+0·42	−22 27	0·3	3·8 6·4 96″ 350° dF6. dK5. Fine pair	Lep
194	NGC 2100	5 42·5	−0·08	−69 14	0·3	Bright cluster in beautiful field	NMa
195	NGC 2068	5 44·2	+0·51	+ 0 2	0·2	M 78. Diffuse gaseous nebula	Ori
196	52 Ori	5 45·3	0·54	+ 6 26	0·2	6·0 6·1 1·4″ 210° dA5. Elegant pair	Ori
197	β 94	5 47·3	0·45	−14 30	0·2	5·6 9·4 2·5″ 172° gG6. Bright yellow	Lep
198	NGC 2099	5 49·0	0·65	+32 33	0·2	M 37. Very fine large open cluster	Aur
199	α Ori	5 52·5	+0·54	+ 7 24	0·1	0·1–1·2 M2. Var. Brilliant spectrum	Ori
200	NGC 2134	5 52·7	−0·14	−71 7	0·1	Bright irresolvable compact cluster	NMa
201	IC 2149	5 52·6	+0·74	+46 7	0·1	Small fairly bright planetary nebula	Aur
202	θ Aur	5 56·3	+0·68	+37 13	0·1	2·7 7·2 3·0″ 320° A1. G. Fine pair	Aur
203	NGC 2156	5 58·6	−0·05	−68 31	0·0	Triangle of 3 star clusters	NMa
204	3 Mon	5 59·5	+0·47	−10 36	+0·0	5·0 9·0 1·8″ 351° B8. Close, unequal	Mon
205	h. 3834	6 3·2	0·29	−45 5	−0·1	5·9 9·9 0·4·7″ 221° F5. Fine field	Pup
206	NGC 2158	6 4·3	0·62	+24 6	0·1	Globular cluster in fine field	Gem
207	NGC 2168	6 5·7	0·61	+24 21	0·1	M 35. Very fine bright open cluster	Gem
208	NGC 2169	6 5·7	0·57	+13 59	0·1	Remarkable triangular cluster	Ori
209	41 Aur	6 7·8	0·77	+48 43	0·1	6·1 6·8 7·8″ 356° Ao. Ao. Pale yellow	Aur
210	η Gem	6 11·9	0·60	+22 31	0·2	3·2–4·2 8·8 1·3″ 260° gM3. Spectrum	Gem
211	NGC 2207	6 14·3	0·43	−21 21	0·2	Fairly bright elliptical eg. nebula	CMa
212	Σ 3116	6 19·1	0·47	−11 45	0·3	5·5 10·4 4·2″ 22° B2. Elegant pair	CMa
213	IC 2165	6 19·5	0·49	−12 57	0·3	Bright bluish planetary nebula	CMa
214	ε Mon	6 21·1	0·53	+ 4 37	0·3	4·5 6·5 13″ 28° A6. dF4. Beautiful	Mon
215	h. 3857	6 22·3	0·35	−36 41	0·3	5·7 9·3 13″ 255° G5. Fine wide pair	Col
216	β Mon	6 26·4	0·48	− 7 0	0·4	4·7 5·2 7·2″ 131°; 5·6 2·8″ 107° All B3	Mon
217	β 753	6 26·8	0·37	−32 20	0·4	6·0 7·6 1·3″ 42° B3. Pale yellow	CMa
218	Δ 30	6 28·6	0·25	−50 12	0·4	5·3 9·0 12″ 312° F2. Each a close pair	Pup
219	NGC 2244	6 29·7	0·53	+ 4 54	0·4	Fine cluster in large nebulous ring	Mon
220	NGC 2245	6 29·9	0·55	+10 12	0·4	Curious fan nebula with apex star	Mon

LIST OF TELESCOPIC OBJECTS

No.	Name	R.A.	Var.	Dec.	Var.	Description	Con.
		h m	m	° ′	′		
221	μ Pic	6 31·2	+0·15	−58 43	−0·5	5·8 9·3 2·3″ 233° B9. White pair	Pic
222	β 755	6 33·7	0·35	−36 44	0·5	6·1 6·8 1·3″ 258° B9. Fine field	Col
223	ν CMa	6 34·2	0·44	−18 37	0·5	5·8 7·9 17″ 263° gG3. dA8. Beautiful	CMa
224	NGC 2261	6 36·4	0·55	+ 8 47	0·5	Bright fan nebula with apex star	Mon
225	Δ 31	6 37·3	0·27	−48 10	0·5	5·0 7·3 13″ 320° G7. Ao. Very fine	Pup
226	NGC 2264	6 38·2	0·55	+ 9 57	0·6	Bright star group in nebulosity	Mon
227	S 534	6 40·7	0·42	−22 24	0·6	6·3 9·0 18″ 143° Fo. Fine field	CMa
228	α CMa	6 42·9	0·45	−16 39	0·6	−1·6 8·4 3·7″–11·4″ A2. F. Binary	CMa
229	OΣ 156	6 44·5	0·58	+18 15	0·7	6·7 7·2 0·6″ 260° Ao. Fine field	Gem
230	NGC 2287	6 44·9	0·43	−20 41	0·7	M 41. Very fine scattered cluster	CMa
231	AC 4	6 46·7	0·45	−15 5	0·7	5·4 8·0 1·0″ 315° B7. Pale yellow	CMa
232	NGC 2298	6 47·2	0·35	−35 57	0·7	Globular cluster in starry field	Pup
233	β 324	6 47·7	0·41	−24 1	0·7	6·6 7·6 1·6″ 205° Ao. Fine field	CMa
234	NGC 2301	6 49·2	0·51	+ 0 31	0·7	Beautiful open star cluster	Mon
235	38 Gem	6 51·8	0·56	+13 15	0·8	4·7 7·4 6·9″ 150° dA8. dG4. Very fine	Gem
236	μ CMa	6 53·8	0·46	−13 59	0·8	5·2 8·0 2·6″ 340° Mo. Beautiful	CMa
237	B 122	6 55·5	0·41	−24 34	0·8	5·7 7·2 1·1″ 270° dFo. Fine field	CMa
238	ε CMa	6 56·7	0·39	−28 54	0·8	1·6 8·0 7·5″ 161° B1. Brilliant pair	CMa
239	NGC 2323	7 0·6	0·48	− 8 16	0·9	M 50. Beautiful open star cluster	Mon
240	Δ 39	7 2·5	0·15	−59 6	0·9	6·1 6·9 1·8″ 82° B9. Close binary	Car
241	h. 3928	7 3·7	0·36	−34 42	0·9	6·7 7·8 3·1″ 149° Fo. Bright yellow	Pup
242	β 328	7 4·3	0·47	−11 13	0·9	5·6 6·8 0·6″ 114°; 9 17″ 353° B2. Fine	CMa
243	Σ 1027	7 5·9	+0·58	+16 59	0·9	8·1 8·2 7·0″ 355° gK5. gK5. Orange	Gem
244	γ Vol	7 9·2	−0·08	−70 25	1·0	3·9 5·8 14″ 299° Ko. Go. Beautiful	Vol
245	Σ 1037	7 9·7	+0·62	+27 19	1·0	7·1 7·2 0·2″–1·3″ dF6. Close binary	Gem
246	β 757	7 10·7	0·36	−36 28	1·0	6·1 8·8 2·5″ 66° B5. Elegant pair	Pup
247	L² Pup	7 12·0	0·30	−44 33	1·0	3·1–6·3 M5. Var. Fine spectrum	Pup
248	NGC 2353	7 12·2	0·48	−10 13	1·0	Fine open star cluster	Mon
249	h. 3945	7 14·5	0·42	−23 14	1·1	4·8 6·8 26″ 55° gMo. dFo. Beautiful	CMa
250	NGC 2359	7 15·2	0·46	−13 7	1·1	Curious gaseous nebula in fine field	CMa
251	λ Gem	7 15·2	0·57	+16 38	1·1	3·6 10·3 10″ 34° A2. Long period	Gem
252	NGC 2360	7 15·5	0·45	−15 33	1·1	Large rich star cluster	CMa
253	NGC 2362	7 16·6	0·41	−24 52	1·1	Beautiful cluster round 30 CMa	CMa
254	δ Gem	7 17·1	0·60	+22 5	1·1	3·5 8·2 6·5″ 217° dA8. dK6. Fine pair	Gem
255	Rmk 6	7 19·2	0·24	−52 13	1·1	6·4 7·0 9·5″ 23° F2. Deep yellow	Car
256	See 78	7 20·9	0·41	−25 40	1·2	7·5 gM4. Orange red nebulous star	CMa
257	NGC 2380	7 21·8	0·40	−27 26	1·2	Small nebula in fine field	CMa
258	NGC 2371	7 22·5	0·63	+29 35	1·2	Curious bi-nuclear planetary nebula	Gem
259	NGC 2384	7 22·9	0·43	−20 56	1·2	Two small clusters in fine field	CMa
260	η CMi	7 25·4	0·54	+ 7 3	1·2	5·3 11·3 4·0″ 26° gFo. Elegant pair	CMi
261	β 332	7 25·5	0·47	−11 27	1·2	5·9 8·2 1·0″ 170° F8. Two stars near	CMa
262	NGC 2392	7 26·2	0·59	+21 1	1·2	Bright planetary nebula; central star	Gem
263	Δ 49	7 26·9	0·38	−31 45	1·2	6·5 7·2 9·0″ 53° B3. B3. Beautiful	Pup
264	Σ 1104	7 27·1	0·46	−14 53	1·3	6·2 7·8 1·9″ 1° dF4. Fine field	Pup
265	σ Pup	7 27·6	0·32	−43 12	1·2	3·3 9·4 22″ 74° Mo. G5. Beautiful	Pup

48

No.	Name	R.A.	Var.	Dec.	Var.	Description	Con.
		h m	m	° ′	′		
266	α Gem	7 31·4	+0·64	+32 0	−1·3	2·0 2·8 2·2″ 168° A2. Ao. Brilliant	Gem
267	HN 19	7 32·2	0·42	−23 22	1·3	5·9 6·0 9·4″ 113° dF4. dF5. Fine pair	Pup
268	NGC 2422	7 34·3	0·46	−14 22	1·3	Bright open cluster with 2 fine pairs	Pup
269	NGC 2419	7 34·8	+0·67	+39 0	1·3	Remote faint globular cluster	Lyn
270	h. 3997	7 36·4	−0·20	−74 10	1·4	7·2 7·3 2·0″ 120° B9. Elegant pair	Vol
271	NGC 2442	7 36·5	−0·02	−69·25	1·4	Large faint eg. nebula	Vol
272	H III 27	7 36·8	+0·41	−26 41	1·4	4·5 4·6 9·9″ 138° B8. B5. Very fine	Pup
273	Σ 1126	7 37·5	0·53	+ 5 21	1·4	6·4 6·7 1·2″ 157° Ao. Slow change	CMi
274	NGC 2437	7 39·5	0·46	−14 42	1·4	M 46. Rich star cluster and nebula	Pup
275	NGC 2440	7 39·7	0·45	−18 5	1·4	Bright bluish planetary nebula	Pup
276	κ Gem	7 41·4	+0·60	+24 31	1·4	3·7 8·5 7·0″ 238° gG7. Fine pair	Gem
277	ζ Vol	7 42·4	−0·12	−72 29	1·4	3·9 9·0 17″ 117° Ko. Orange & white	Vol
278	NGC 2447	7 42·5	+0·42	−23 45	1·4	M 93. Very fine open cluster	Pup
279	NGC 2452	7 45·5	0·41	−27 13	1·5	Faint planetary nebula in fine field	Pup
280	5 Pup	7 45·6	0·47	−12 4	1·5	5·5 8·2 2·2″ 5° dF5. dG3. Yellow	Pup
281	NGC 2467	7 50·4	0·42	−26 16	1·6	Gaseous nebula in rich field	Pup
282	NGC 2477	7 50·5	0·35	−38 25	1·6	Fine open cluster of small stars	Pup
283	I 26	7 55·9	0·30	−47 45	1·6	6·5 7·4 0·6″ 50° B5. Fine field	Pup
284	NGC 2516	7 57·5	0·17	−60 44	1·6	Very fine bright galactic cluster	Car
285	β 202	7 59·9	0·41	−27 4	1·7	6·6 9·2 7·5″ 160° B9. Very fine field	Pup
286	h. 4038	8 1·0	0·34	−41 10	1·7	5·6 8·5 27″ 346° B9. Beautiful pair	Pup
287	Σ 1177	8 2·6	0·61	+27 40	1·7	6·5 7·4 3·5″ 350° B9. Elegant	Cnc
288	h. 4046	8 3·8	0·39	−33 26	1·7	6·0 8·2 21″ 87°; 9·5 28″ 58° G5. Fine	Pup
289	ε Vol	8 7·8	0·03	−68 28	1·8	4·5 8·0 6·1″ 22° B8. Fine pair	Vol
290	γ Vel	8 8·0	0·31	−47 11	1·8	2·2 4·8 42″ 219° OW9. B3. Spectrum	Vel
291	Δ 63	8 8·1	0·34	−42 30	1·8	6·7 7·9 5·5″ 81° Ao. Beautiful field	Pup
292	NGC 2547	8 9·2	0·30	−49 7	1·8	Large bright open cluster	Vel
293	h. 4051	8 9·2	0·37	−37 9	1·8	6·3 13 18″ 265°; 13 17″ 206° A3. Fine	Pup
294	ζ Cnc	8 9·3	0·57	+17 48	1·8	5·66·30·7″−1·2″;6·06·0″84°dF7. dG2	Cnc
295	NGC 2548	8 11·3	0·49	− 5 39	1·8	Large bright scattered cluster	Hya
296	β 454	8 13·9	0·40	−30 46	1·8	6·6 7·8 1·9″ 7° G5. Beautiful field	Pup
297	Rmk 8	8 14·5	0·15	−62 46	1·9	5·3 8·5 4·0″ 66° A2. Fine bright pair	Car
298	I 67	8 21·0	0·31	−48 20	1·9	5·2 6·6 0·8″ 139° B2. Close pair	Vel
299	φ² Cnc	8 23·8	0·61	+27 6	2·0	6·3 6·3 5·1″ 216° A2. A2. Elegant	Cnc
300	h. 4093	8 24·5	0·37	−38 54	2·0	6·7 7·3 8·1″ 124° Ao. Fine field	Pup
301	h. 4104	8 27·5	0·32	−47 46	2·0	5·7 7·9 3·4″ 245° B5. Striking field	Vel
302	Δ 70	8 27·8	0·34	−44 33	2·0	5·2 6·7 4·5″ 350° B5. Fine pair	Vel
303	I 489	8 29·3	0·45	−19 24	2·0	5·9 6·5 0·5″ 60° Ao. Difficult pair	Pyx
304	Slr 8	8 30·7	0·28	−53 2	2·0	6·1 7·3 0·8″ 291° G5. Ao. Close pair	Vel
305	β 205	8 30·9	0·43	−24 26	2·0	6·9 7·1 0·5″ 128° dA7. Difficult pair	Pyx
306	NGC 2610	8 31·1	0·46	−15 58	2·1	Pale planetary nebula in fine field	Hya
307	NGC 2613	8 31·1	0·44	−22 48	2·1	Elongated edgewise eg. spiral	Pyx
308	Σ 1245	8 33·2	0·53	+ 6 48	2·1	6·3 7·2 10″ 25° dF6. dG5. Yellow	Cnc
309	β 208	8 37·0	0·44	−22 30	2·1	5·4 6·9 2·0″ 212° dG6. Fine pair	Pyx
310	NGC 2632	8 37·2	0·58	+20 9	2·1	M 44. Very large brilliant cluster	Cnc

LIST OF TELESCOPIC OBJECTS

No.	Name	R.A.	Var.	Dec.	Var.	Description	Con.
		h m	m	° ′	′		
311	h. 4128	8 38·2	+0·21	−60 9	−2·1	6·9 7·6 1·5″ 211° Ao. Fine field	Car
312	~~IC 2391~~	~~8 38·9~~	~~0·29~~	~~−52 45~~	~~2·1~~	~~Brilliant field including o Vel~~	~~Vel~~
313	h. 4130	8 39·5	0·25	−57 22	2·1	6·5 8·8 3·8″ 239° A2. Fine field	Car
314	NGC 2660	8 40·9	0·33	−47 0	2·2	Distant galactic cluster in fine field	Vel
315	IC 2395	8 41·6	0·33	−48 0	2·2	Bright open star cluster	Vel
316	δ Vel	8 43·3	0·28	−54 31	2·2	2·0 6·6 2·5″ 152° Ao. Brilliant pair	Vel
317	ι Cnc	8 43·7	0·61	+28 57	2·2	4·2 6·6 30″ 308° gG6. A5. Beautiful	Cnc
318	Rmk 9	8 43·9	0·24	−58 32	2·2	7·0 7·1 4·0″ 292° B8. Elegant pair	Car
319	ε Hya	8 44·1	0·53	+ 6 36	2·2	3·5 6·9 3·0″ 271° dF8. dF7. Fine pair	Hya
320	Σ 1282	8 47·6	0·63	+35 15	2·2	7·5 7·5 3·6″ 279° F8. Dainty pair	Lyn
321	NGC 2682	8 48·5	0·55	+12 0	2·2	M 67. Fine open cluster of small stars	Cnc
322	Hd 205	8 48·9	0·34	−46 20	2·2	4·9 10 3·5″ 82° Bo. Beautiful field	Vel
323	15 Hya	8 49·1	0·49	− 6 59	2·2	5·6 9·0 0·9″ 125° dFo. Close pair	Hya
324	NGC 2683	8 49·6	0·63	+33 38	2·3	Large fairly bright eg. spindle	Lyn
325	57 Cnc	8 51·2	0·61	+30 46	2·3	6·1 6·6 1·5″ 318° gG7. Ko. Orange	Cnc
326	R 87	8 54·8	0·30	−52 32	2·3	4·9 7·7 2·5″ 336° B5. Fine field	Vel
327	NGC 2736	8 58·7	0·35	−45 42	2·3	Faint long streak in rich field	Vel
328	h. 4165	9 0·2	0·31	−51 59	2·4	5·6 7·1 0·9″ 117° B9. Fine pair	Vel
329	h. 4166	9 1·2	0·41	−33 24	2·4	6·7 7·4 14″ 153° Ao. Beautful field	Pyx
330	Σ 1316	9 5·4	0·49	− 6 56	2·4	8·4 11·5 7·1″ 138°; 10·5 2·8″ 208° dF9	Hya
331	IC 2448	9 6·6	0·10	−69 44	2·4	Bright bluish planetary nebula	Car
332	RS Cnc	9 7·6	0·61	+31 10	2·4	5·3–6·8 M6. Var. Fine spectrum	Cnc
333	NGC 2775	9 7·7	0·53	+ 7 15	2·4	Small fairly bright eg. nebula	Cnc
334	NGC 2784	9 10·1	0·45	−23 58	2·5	Fairly large eg. edgewise spiral	Hya
335	NGC 2792	9 10·6	0·38	−42 14	2·5	Moderately bright planetary nebula	Vel
336	h. 4188	9 10·7	0·37	−43 24	2·5	6·1 6·9 2·7″ 283° B8. Fine pair	Vel
337	NGC 2808	9 10·9	0·20	−64 39	2·5	Very bright condensed globular cluster	Car
338	I 11	9 13·4	0·36	−45 21	2·5	6·7 7·8 0·8″ 280° Ao. Fine field	Vel
339	NGC 2818	9 14·0	0·40	−36 24	2·5	Planetary nebula in large cluster	Pyx
340	Σ 1333	9 15·4	0·62	+35 35	2·5	6·4 6·7 1·8″ 45° A4. A5. Yellowish	Lyn
341	38 Lyn	9 15·8	0·62	+37 1	2·5	4·0 5·9 2·8″ 229° B9. Fine pair	Lyn
342	Σ 1338	9 17·9	0·63	+38 24	2·5	6·5 6·7 1·2″ 225° dF3. dF2. Yellow	Lyn
343	NGC 2867	9 20·0	0·28	−58 6	2·6	Bright planetary nebula in fine field	Car
344	NGC 2899	9 25·5	0·31	−55 54	2·6	Gaseous nebula in beautiful field	Vel
345	ω Leo	9 25·8	0·54	+ 9 17	2·6	5·9 6·7 0·4″–1·1″ dF8. Close binary	Leo
346	ζ¹ Ant	9 28·6	0·43	−31 40	2·6	6·4 7·2 8·0″ 212° Ao. Ao. Fine pair	Ant
347	ψ Vel	9 28·8	0·40	−40 15	2·6	3·9 5·1 0·3″–1·1″ dF7. Short period	Vel
348	NGC 2903	9 29·3	0·57	+21 44	2·6	Conspicuous elliptical eg. nebula	Leo
349	R. Car	9 31·0	0·25	−62 34	2·7	3·9–9·6 gM4–M7. Fine spectrum	Car
350	h. 4220	9 31·9	0·36	−48 47	2·7	5·8 6·4 2·0″ 214° B3. Fine pair	Vel
351	IC 2501	9 37·3	0·29	−59 52	2·7	Small planetary nebula in fine field	Car
352	Σ 1374	9 38·3	0·62	+39 11	2·7	7·0 8·3 3·0″ 300° dG2. Test pair	LMi
353	NGC 2997	9 43·5	0·44	−30 58	2·8	Large faint nucleated eg. nebula	Ant
354	h. 4245	9 44·2	0·38	−45 41	2·8	7·0 9·5 9·0″ 213° G5. Beautiful	Vel
355	R Leo	9 44·9	0·54	+11 40	2·8	5·0–10·5 gM8. Fine spectrum	Leo

No.	Name	R.A.	Var.	Dec.	Var.	Description	Con.
		h m	m	° ′	′		
356	υ Car	9 45·9	+0·25	−64 50	−2·8	3·2 6·0 5·0″ 128° Fo. Brilliant pair	Car
357	γ Sex	9 50·0	0·50	− 7 52	2·8	5·8 6·0 0·3″–0·65″ Ao. Difficult pair	Sex
358	Δ 81	9 52·3	0·39	−45 3	2·8	5·9 8·0 5·0″ 240° B5. Beautiful	Vel
359	NGC 3114	10 1·1	0·32	−59 53	2·9	Very fine large scattered cluster	Car
360	Hrg 47	10 2·0	0·31	−61 38	2·9	6·4 8·0 1·2″ 351° B8. Beautiful field	Car
361	NGC 3115	10 2·8	0·50	− 7 28	2·9	Bright eg. spindle with faint halo	Sex
362	NGC 3132	10 4·9	0·42	−40 11	2·9	Planetary nebula with central star	Vel
363	α Leo	10 5·7	0·54	+12 13	2·9	1·3 7·6 176° 307° B6. dK1. Brilliant	Leo
364	IC 2553	10 7·8	0·31	−62 22	2·9	Bright planetary nebula in fine field	Car
365	S Car	10 7·8	+0·32	−61 18	2·9	5·5–8·8 K7–M4. Fine spectrum	Car
366	NGC 3195	10 10·1	−0·09	−80 37	3·0	Fairly bright bluish planetary nebula	Cha
367	NGC 3166	10 11·4	+0·52	+ 3 41	3·0	Two conspicuous eg. nebulae	Sex
368	λ 118	10 13·3	0·37	−55 18	3·0	6·7 12·0 14″ 145° Ko. Very fine field	Vel
369	OΣ 215	10 13·6	0·55	+17 59	3·0	7·0 7·2 1·1″ 185° dF2. Yellow pair	Leo
370	Hld 101	10 14·4	0·48	−20 25	3·0	6·5 9·8 1·3″ 110° F5. Close, closing	Hya
371	NGC 3199	10 15·0	0·36	−57 43	3·0	Large crescent nebula in fine field	Car
372	NGC 3190	10 15·4	0·55	+22 5	3·0	Two eg. nebulae in fine field	Leo
373	NGC 3201	10 15·5	0·41	−46 9	3·0	Resolved globular cluster of faint stars	Vel
374	NGC 3211	10 16·2	0·33	−62 24	3·0	Small planetary nebula in fine field	Car
375	γ Leo	10 17·2	0·55	+20 6	3·0	2·6 3·8 4·3″ 122° gK1. gG5. Brilliant	Leo
376	h. 4306	10 17·5	0·31	−64 25	3·0	7·0 7·0 2·2″ 134° Ao. Pale yellow	Car
377	Rmk 13	10 19·0	0·37	−55 47	3·0	4·6 8·7 7·0″ 102°; 9·8 37″ 190° B5	Vel
378	β 219	10 19·2	0·47	−22 17	3·0	6·7 8·4 2·2″ 187° Ao. Pale yellow	Hya
379	NGC 3228	10 19·7	0·39	−51 28	3·0	Bright straggling star group	Vel
380	NGC 3242	10 22·4	0·48	−18 23	3·0	Bright bluish planetary nebula	Hya
381	NGC 3245	10 24·5	0·57	+28 46	3·1	Fairly bright elliptical eg. nebula	LMi
382	IC 2581	10 25·5	0·37	−57 23	3·1	Cluster round bright star	Car
383	NGC 3256	10 25·7	0·43	−43 38	3·1	Elliptical eg. nebula in starry field	Vel
384	δ Ant	10 27·3	0·46	−30 21	3·1	5·6 9·3 11″ 225° Ao. Unequal pair	Ant
385	NGC 3271	10 27·8	0·45	−35 6	3·1	Brightest of 5 small eg. nebulae	Ant
386	49 Leo	10 32·4	0·53	+ 8 55	3·1	5·7 8·7 2·5″ 158° Ao. Fine pair	Leo
387	NGC 3293	10 33·9	0·38	−57 58	3·1	Beautiful open cluster	Car
388	NGC 3309	10 34·3	0·47	−27 16	3·1	Field with 4 small eg. nebulae	Hya
389	U Hya	10 35·1	0·49	−13 7	3·1	4·8–5·9 N. Fine spectrum	Hya
390	NGC 3324	10 35·5	0·38	−58 22	3·1	Large diffuse nebula in fine field	Car
391	Δ 94	10 36·8	0·38	−58 55	3·1	4·7 8·3 14·5″ 20° M1. A. Fine field	Car
392	Gls 152	10 37·1	0·38	−58 34	3·1	6·1 9·1 21″ 77° M2. Beautiful field	Car
393	NGC 3347	10 40·5	0·46	−36 6	3·1	One of 3 small eg. nebulae	Ant
394	35 Sex	10 40·8	0·52	+ 5 1	3·1	6·3 7·4 6·8″ 340° gK4. gG7. Orange	Sex
395	NGC 3351	10 41·3	0·53	+11 58	3·1	M 95. Round symmetrical eg. nebula	Leo
396	NGC 3372	10 43·1	0·39	−59 25	3·2	Great diffuse nebula round η Car	Car
397	NGC 3368	10 44·2	0·53	+12 5	3·2	M 96. Bright elliptical eg. nebula	Leo
398	μ Vel	10 44·6	0·43	−49 9	3·2	2·9 6·8 0·7″ 90° (1942) G5. Difficult	Vel
399	δ Cha	10 44·8	0·10	−80 12	3·2	6·1 6·4 0·6″ 78° K1. Close pair	Cha
400	NGC 3384	10 45·7	0·53	+12 54	3·2	Interesting field with 3 eg. nebulae	Leo

No.	Name	R.A.	Var.	Dec.	Var.	Description	Con.
		h m	m	° ′	′		
401	40 Sex	10 46·8	+0·51	− 3 46	−3·2	6·9 7·7 2·4″ 9° A2. Yellow pair	Sex
402	h. 4383	10 52·1	0·33	−70 27	3·2	6·6 7·2 1·7″ 284° B8. B8. Binary	Car
403	54 Leo	10 52·9	0·54	+25 1	3·2	4·5 6·3 6·5″ 109° B9. A1. Very fine	Leo
404	R 164	10 57·2	0·40	−61 3	3·2	6·4 10·2 3·5″ 78° B9. Fine field	Car
405	IC 2621	10 58·4	0·38	−64 58	3·2	Minute planetary nebula among stars	Car
406	NGC 3532	11 4·4	0·42	−58 24	3·3	Remarkable large bright cluster	Car
407	65 Leo	11 4·4	0·51	+ 2 14	3·3	5·7 11·5 2·4″ 102° gG7. Deep yellow	Leo
408	NGC 3582	11 10·0	0·42	−61 1	3·3	Gaseous nebulae in rich field	Car
409	NGC 3603	11 13·0	0·43	−60 59	3·3	Hazy galactic cluster of small stars	Car
410	h. 4423	11 14·1	0·47	−45 36	3·3	7·1 7·4 2·3″ 276° F2. Elegant pair	Cen
411	ξ UMa	11 15·5	0·54	+31 49	3·4	4·4 4·9 1·0″–3·1″ dGo. dGo. Binary	UMa
412	NGC 3621	11 15·9	0·48	−32 32	3·3	Bright elliptical eg. nebula	Hya
413	υ UMa	11 15·8	0·54	+33 22	3·3	3·7 10·1 7·2″ 148° gK3. Orange	UMa
414	NGC 3623	11 16·3	0·52	+13 23	3·3	M 65. Long elliptical eg. nebula	Leo
415	Σ 1527	11 16·4	0·52	+14 33	3·3	6·9 8·1 2·8″ 25° dF7. Elegant pair	Leo
416	NGC 3627	11 17·6	0·52	+13 17	3·3	M 66. Conspicuous eg. nebula	Leo
417	NGC 3628	11 17·7	0·52	+13 53	3·3	Very long not bright eg. spindle	Leo
418	h. 4432	11 21·2	0·43	−64 41	3·3	5·7 6·8 2·3″ 304° B7. Fine pair	Mus
419	ι Leo	11 21·3	0·52	+10 48	3·3	4·1 6·8 1″ 225° dF4. Close binary	Leo
420	γ Crt	11 22·4	0·50	−17 25	3·3	4·1 9·5 5·2″ 96° A5. Fine bright pair	Crt
421	NGC 3699	11 25·6	0·45	−59 41	3·3	Bright round nebula in beautiful field	Cen
422	VV 60	11 26·3	0·46	−52 40	3·3	Small planetary nebula in fine field	Cen
423	57 UMa	11 26·4	0·54	+39 37	3·3	5·3 8·4 5·5″ 358° A2. dG5. Fine pair	UMa
424	Jc 16	11 27·2	0·50	−24 11	3·3	5·8 8·9 7·7″ 80° Ao. Elegant pair	Crt
425	H III 96	11 29·8	0·50	−28 59	3·3	5·8 5·9 9·2″ 209° dF6. dF7. Very fine	Hya
426	I 78	11 31·2	0·49	−40 19	3·3	6·3 6·3 1·0″ 96° A2. Pale yellow	Cen
427	90 Leo	11 32·1	0·52	+17 4	3·3	5·8 7·3 3·4″ 208° B3. B6. Fine pair	Leo
428	NGC 3766	11 33·8	0·46	−61 19	3·3	Beautiful open galactic cluster	Cen
429	h. 4455	11 34·1	0·49	−33 18	3·3	6·0 8·2 3·5″ 243° Ko. Orange	Hya
430	NGC 3918	11 47·8	0·49	−56 54	3·3	Very bright bluish planetary nebula	Cen
431	Cor 130	11 49·4	0·49	−64 56	3·3	5·2 7·8 1·6″ 157° B7. Fine pair	Mus
432	β Hya	11 50·4	0·50	−33 38	3·3	5·0 5·4 1·0″ 6° B9. Fine pair	Hya
433	ε Cha	11 57·1	0·49	−77 57	3·3	5·4 6·2 1·1″ 188° B9. Pale yellow	Cha
434	NGC 4038	11 59·3	0·51	−18 35	3·3	Two elliptical eg. nebulae in contact	Crv
435	NGC 4062	12 1·5	0·51	+32 10	3·3	Faint elongated eg. nebula	UMa
436	2 Com	12 1·7	0·51	+21 44	3·3	6·0 7·5 3·8″ 238° dA8. dF2. Fine pair	Com
437	h. 4498	12 3·8	0·52	−65 26	3·3	6·2 7·9 8·7″ 60° F5. A3. Fine pair	Mus
438	NGC 4103	12 4·1	0·51	−60 58	3·3	Open star cluster in rich region	Cru
439	NGC 4105	12 4·1	0·51	−29 31	3·3	Two conspicuous eg. nebulae	Hya
440	NGC 4147	12 7·6	0·51	+18 49	3·3	Bright resolved globular cluster	Com
441	NGC 4192	12 11·3	0·51	+15 11	3·3	M 98. Long fairly bright eg. spindle	Com
442	Rmk 14	12 11·4	0·52	−45 27	3·3	5·5 6·5 2·6″ 243° Mo. Fine pair	Cen
443	β 920	12 13·2	0·52	−23 4	3·3	6·5 7·0 1·4″ 295° F5. Changing pair	Crv
444	NGC 4216	12 13·4	0·51	+13 25	3·3	Long narrow edgewise eg. spiral	Vir
445	2 CVn	12 13·6	0·50	+40 56	3·3	5·8 8·0 11″ 260° gMo. dF6. Fine pair	CVn

No.	Name	R.A.	Var.	Dec.	Var.	Description	Con.
		h m	m	° ′	′		
446	NGC 4244	12 15·0	+0·50	+38 5	−3·3	Faint very long eg. nebula	CVn
447	Σ 1627	12 15·6	0·51	− 3 40	3·3	6·6 7·0 20″ 196° dF4. dF5. Fine pair	Vir
448	NGC 4254	12 16·3	0·51	+14 42	3·3	M 99. Conspicuous round eg. nebula	Com
449	NGC 4258	12 16·5	0·50	+47 35	3·3	Large elongated eg. nebula	CVn
450	β 605	12 17·6	0·52	−21 54	3·3	6·2 8·3 0·4″ 187° dG2. Difficult pair	Crv
451	NGC 4281	12 17·8	0·51	+ 5 40	3·3	Five small eg. nebulae in 12′ field	Vir
452	Σ 1633	12 18·2	0·50	+27 20	3·3	7·0 7·1 9·0″ 245° dF2. dF2. Elegant	Com
453	NGC 4303	12 19·4	0·51	+ 4 45	3·3	M 61. Large round eg. nebula	Vir
454	17 Vir	12 20·0	0·51	+ 5 35	3·3	6·5 9·0 20″ 337° dF7. dK5. Fine pair	Vir
455	NGC 4321	12 20·4	0·51	+16 6	3·3	M 100. Large diffuse eg. nebula	Com
456	NGC 4349	12 21·7	0·54	−61 37	3·3	Fine open cluster of small stars	Cru
457	Σ 1639	12 21·9	0·50	+25 52	3·3	6·6 7·8 1·0″ 320° dA6. Close binary	Com
458	NGC 4361	12 21·9	0·52	−18 30	3·3	Planetary nebula with central star	Crv
459	NGC 4374	12 22·6	0·51	+13 10	3·3	M 84. Round bright eg. nebula	Vir
460	NGC 4382	12 22·9	0·51	+18 28	3·3	M 85. Conspicuous eg. nebula	Com
461	NGC 4372	12 23·0	0·57	−72 23	3·3	Large faint globular cluster	Mus
462	α Cru	12 23·8	0·55	−62 49	3·3	1·6 2·1 4·4″ 116°; 5·1 91″ 205°. B1. B3	Cru
463	NGC 4406	12 23·7	0·51	+13 13	3·3	M 86. Bright elliptical eg. nebula	Vir
464	δ Crv	12 27·3	0·52	−16 14	3·3	3·1 9·2 24″ 218° Ao dK2. Fine pair	Crv
465	NGC 4472	12 27·3	0·51	+ 8 16	3·3	M 49. Round conspicuous eg. nebula	Vir
466	β 28	12 27·5	0·52	−13 7	3·3	6·4 10·2 1·6″ 310° dF8. Changing pair	Crv
467	NGC 4486	12 28·3	0·51	+12 40	3·3	M 87. Conspicuous round eg. nebula	Vir
468	γ Cru	12 28·4	0·55	−56 50	3·3	1·6 M 4. Brilliant; fine spectrum	Cru
469	NGC 4517	12 29·0	0·51	+ 0 21	3·3	Long rather faint eg. spindle	Vir
470	NGC 4501	12 29·5	0·51	+14 42	3·3	M 88. Conspicuous eg. ellipse	Com
471	NGC 4526	12 31·6	0·51	+ 7 58	3·3	Bright elliptical eg. nebula	Vir
472	24 Com.	12 32·6	0·52	+18 39	3·3	5·2 6·7 20″ 271° gG9. A9. Beautiful	Com
473	NGC 4552	12 33·1	0·51	+12 50	3·3	M 89. Small bright round eg. nebula	Vir
474	NGC 4559	12 33·5	0·50	+28 14	3·3	Large elliptical eg. nebula	Com
475	NGC 4565	12 33·9	0·50	+26 16	3·3	Large extended eg. nebula; dark bar	Com
476	NGC 4567	12 34·0	0·51	+11 32	3·3	Two rather faint eg. nebulae in contact	Vir
477	NGC 4569	12 34·3	0·51	+13 26	3·3	M 90. Large elliptical eg. nebula	Vir
478	NGC 4579	12 35·1	0·51	+12 5	3·3	M 58. Fairly bright eg. ellipse	Vir
479	NGC 4590	12 36·8	0·53	−26 29	3·3	M 68. Fine large globular cluster	Hya
480	NGC 4594	12 37·4	0·52	−11 21	3·3	Bright eg. spindle with dark lane	Vir
481	Σ 1669	12 38·7	0·52	−12 44	3·3	6·0 6·1 5·5″ 308° dF6. dF1. Yellow	Crv
482	γ Cen	12 38·7	0·55	−48 41	3·3	3·1 3·1 1·6″ 5° Ao. Bright binary	Cen
483	γ Vir	12 39·1	0·50	− 1 11	3·3	3·7 3·7 5·1″ 308° Fo. Fo. Very fine	Vir
484	31 Vir	12 39·4	0·51	+ 7 5	3·3	5·5 11·6 4·0″ 36° B9. Pale yellow	Vir
485	NGC 4621	12 39·5	0·51	+11 55	3·3	M 59. Bright elliptical eg. nebula	Vir
486	NGC 4631	12 39·8	0·49	+32 49	3·3	Very long fairly bright eg. spindle	CVn
487	NGC 4649	12 41·1	0·51	+11 49	3·3	M 60. Bright round eg. nebula	Vir
488	NGC 4656	12 41·6	0·49	+32 26	3·3	Irregular rather faint eg. nebula	CVn
489	NGC 4666	12 42·6	0·51	− 0 12	3·3	Long fairly bright eg. spindle	Vir
490	β Mus	12 43·2	0·61	−67 50	3·3	3·9 4·2 1·5″ 15° B3. Brilliant pair	Mus

No.	Name	R.A.	Var.	Dec.	Var.	Description	Con.
		h m	m	° ′	′		
491	β Cru	12 44·8	+0·58	−59 25	−3·3	1·5 B1. Brilliant white; red star near	Cru
492	NGC 4697	12 46·0	0·52	− 5 32	3·3	Bright elliptical eg. nebula	Vir
493	NGC 4710	12 47·1	0·50	+15 26	3·3	Fairly bright eg. spindle	Com
494	NGC 4725	12 48·1	0·49	+25 46	3·3	Large diffuse elliptical eg. nebula	Com
495	NGC 4736	12 48·6	0·47	+41 23	3·3	M 94. Bright round eg. nebula	CVn
496	NGC 4754	12 50·0	0·50	+11 33	3·3	Fine field with 2 bright eg. nebulae	Vir
497	NGC 4755	12 50·7	0·59	−60 5	3·3	Vivid cluster with delicate colours	Cru
498	35 Com	12 50·8	0·49	+21 31	3·3	5·2 8·0 1·0″ 331°; 9·0 29″ 127° gG8	Com
499	μ Cru	12 51·6	0·58	−56 54	3·3	4·3 5·5 35″ 17° B3. B3. Fine pair	Cru
500	NGC 4782	12 51·9	0·52	−12 18	3·3	Two small eg. nebulae in contact	Crv
501	α CVn	12 53·7	0·47	+38 35	3·2	2·9 5·4 19″ 229° A1. Ao. Beautiful	CVn
502	NGC 4826	12 54·3	0·49	+21 57	3·2	M 64. Fine eg. ellipse with dark spot	Com
503	NGC 4833	12 56·0	0·66	−70 36	3·2	Fine globular cluster in fine field	Mus
504	48 Vir	13 1·3	0·52	− 3 24	3·2	7·2 7·3 0·8″ 206° dA7. Close pair	Vir
505	NGC 4945	13 2·4	0·58	−49 12	3·2	Long bright eg. spindle in fine field	Cen
506	R 213	13 4·3	0·61	−59 36	3·2	6·7 6·9 0·9″ 23° B9. Close pair	Cen
507	θ Mus	13 4·9	0·64	−65 2	3·2	5·7 8·0 5·5″ 188° Bo. Fine field	Mus
508	IC 4191	13 5·5	0·65	−67 22	3·2	Small planetary nebula in fine field	Mus
509	NGC 4976	13 5·9	0·58	−49 14	3·2	Bright eg. nebula in fine field	Cen
510	θ Vir	13 7·4	0·52	− 5 16	3·2	4·4 9·0 7·2″ 341° A2. Beautiful pair	Vir
511	α Com	13 7·6	0·49	+17 48	3·2	5·2 5·2 0·1″–0·6″ dF4. Close binary	Com
512	β 931	13 8·3	0·50	+13 34	3·2	7·3 11·8 4·9″ 205° gK2. Test pair	Vir
513	NGC 5005	13 8·5	0·46	+37 19	3·2	Fairly bright elliptical eg. nebula	CVn
514	I 424	13 9·2	0·62	−59 39	3·2	4·8 8·0 1·9″ 354° B8. Fine field	Cen
515	OΣ 261	13 9·7	0·47	+32 21	3·2	7·2 7·7 2·1″ 342° dF4. Elegant pair	CVn
516	NGC 5024	13 10·5	0·49	+18 26	3·2	M 53. Fine resolved globular cluster	Com
517	54 Vir	13 10·8	0·53	−18 34	3·2	6·3 7·3 5·2″ 33° A1. A2. Elegant pair	Vir
518	NGC 5055	13 13·5	0·45	+42 17	3·2	M 63. Large elliptical eg. nebula	CVn
519	NGC 5053	13 13·9	0·49	+17 57	3·2	Large faint globular cluster	Com
520	β 800	13 14·4	0·49	+17 17	3·2	6·6 10·2 5·0″ 109° dK3. dM2. Orange	Com
521	NGC 5061	13 15·3	0·55	−26 36	3·2	Bright eg. nebula in fine field	Hya
522	Dark neb.	13 22	0·66	−63 20	3·1	Conspicuous dark nebula in rich field	Cen
523	NGC 5128	13 22·4	0·58	−42 45	3·1	Bright round eg. nebula with dark bar	Cen
524	NGC 5139	13 23·8	0·59	−47 3	3·1	ω Cen, finest of globular clusters	Cen
525	R Hya	13 27·0	0·55	−23 1	3·1	4·2–9·8 gM6–M9. Fine spectrum	Hya
526	NGC 5194	13 27·8	0·42	+47 27	3·1	M 51. Well-known spiral nebula	CVn
527	λ 180	13 28·4	0·59	−42 12	3·1	6·7 9·2 3·7″ 231°. Ko. Orange & white	Cen
528	NGC 5189	13 29·9	0·69	−65 43	3·1	Irregular gaseous nebula in fine field	Mus
529	HN 69	13 34·0	0·55	−26 14	3·1	5·5 7·0 10·2″ 191° A2. Fine pair	Hya
530	NGC 5236	13 34·3	0·56	−29 37	3·1	M 83. Large bright eg. nebula	Hya
531	R 223	13 34·8	0·65	−58 9	3·1	6·4 10·7 2·5″ 23° Ko. Fine field	Cen
532	NGC 5248	13 35·1	0·50	+ 9 8	3·1	Fairly bright elliptical eg. nebula	Boo
533	25 CVn	13 35·2	0·44	+36 33	3·1	5·1 7·0 1·7″ 109° A3. Long period	CVn
534	NGC 5247	13 35·3	0·54	−17 38	3·1	Large faint diffuse eg. nebula	Vir
535	VV 66	13 35·9	0·73	−67 7	3·1	Very small planetary nebula, as test	Mus

No.	Name	R.A.	Var.	Dec.	Var.	Description	Con.
		h m	m	° ′	′		
536	1 Boo	13 38·3	+0·48	+20 12	−3·0	5·7 8·5 4·5″ 138° A3. dF8. Fine pair	Boo
537	Δ 141	13 38·5	0·64	−54 18	3·0	5·7 7·1 5·3″ 163° B9. Fine white pair	Cen
538	NGC 5272	13 39·9	0·46	+28 38	3·0	M 3. Beautiful globular cluster	CVn
539	84 Vir	13 40·6	0·51	+ 3 47	3·0	5·6 8·2 3·2″ 228° gK3. dG5. Fine pair	Vir
540	NGC 5281	13 43·1	0·70	−62 39	3·0	Open cluster in beautiful field	Cen
541	NGC 5286	13 43·3	0·63	−51 7	3·0	Bright globular cluster in fine field	Cen
542	86 Vir	13 43·3	0·53	−12 11	3·0	5·8 10·5 1·6″ 298° gG7. Close pair	Vir
543	Cor 157	13 43·7	0·69	−62 20	3·0	6·2 10·4 10″ 318° G5. Very fine	Cen
544	Hwe 24	13 46·0	0·57	−35 27	3·0	6·5 9·3 11″ 355° dF8. Unusual colour	Cen
545	Σ 1785	13 46·8	0·46	+27 14	3·0	7·8 8·2 3·0″ 143° dK6. dK6. Orange	Boo
546	NGC 5307	13 47·8	0·63	−50 58	3·0	Bright bluish planetary nebula	Cen
547	Rmk 18	13 48·8	0·64	−52 34	3·0	5·7 7·7 18″ 290° B8. A3. Wide pair	Cen
548	3 Cen	13 48·9	0·58	−32 45	3·0	4·7 6·2 7·9″ 108° B5. B8. Very fine	Cen
549	β 343	13 49·1	0·57	−31 22	3·0	6·6 7·9 0·8″ 60° F8. Close binary	Cen
550	NGC 5315	13 50·2	0·73	−66 16	3·0	Small bright bluish planetary nebula	Cir
551	4 Cen	13 50·3	0·57	−31 41	3·0	4·8 8·5 15″ 186° B7. Fine wide pair	Cen
552	Σ 1788	13 52·3	0·53	− 7 49	3·0	6·5 7·7 3·4″ 91° dF7. dG1. Elegant	Vir
553	R 227	13 53·0	0·65	−53 53	2·9	6·7 8·0 1·8″ 6° A2. Pale yellow	Cen
554	NGC 5367	13 54·7	0·60	−39 44	2·9	Small double star in nebular haze	Cen
555	h. 4632	13 54·7	0·74	−65 34	2·9	6·2 10·2 6·5″ 12° K0. Fine field	Cir
556	β 1197	14 0·1	0·58	−31 27	2·9	6·6 8·0 2·0″ 213° F5. Elegant pair	Cen
557	β Cen.	14 0·3	0·70	−60 8	2·9	0·9 4·1 1·3″ 251° B3. Difficult pair	Cen
558	NGC 5466	14 3·2	0·45	+28 46	2·9	Large faint globular cluster	Boo
559	Slr 19	14 4·4	0·64	−49 38	2·9	7·2 7·6 1·4″ 296° G0. Changing pair	Cen
560	Cor 167	14 11·4	0·73	−61 28	2·8	6·7 8·7 3·0″ 159° O5. Fine field	Cen
561	R Cen	14 12·9	0·72	−59 41	2·8	6·0–10·7 gM4. Fine spectrum	Cen
562	β 1110	14 16·7	0·60	−36 38	2·8	6·9 11·7 4·0″ 130° Mb. Red & white	Cen
563	h. 4672	14 17·0	0·64	−42 50	2·8	5·8 8·7 3·5″ 303° G5. Elegant pair	Lup
564	Δ 159	14 19·0	0·71	−58 14	2·7	5·1 7·0 9·3″ 160° G3. Fine pair	Cen
565	IC 4406	14 19·3	0·63	−43 55	2·7	Fairly bright planetary nebula	Lup
566	R 244	14 19·4	0·65	−48 6	2·7	6·3 9·4 4·5″ 120° B2. Starry field	Lup
567	Σ 1835	14 20·9	0·49	+ 8 40	2·7	5·1 6·6 6·3″ 192° B9. dF2. Beautiful	Boo
568	Σ 1837	14 22·0	0·54	−11 27	2·7	6·7 8·5 1·4″ 290° dF1. Yellow pair	Lib
569	Sh 179	14 22·7	0·56	−19 45	2·7	6·4 7·3 35″ 295° A0. A0. Ternary	Lib
570	φ Vir	14 25·6	0·52	− 2 0	2·7	5·0 9·7 4·5″ 110° dF8. dK0. Fine pair	Vir
571	NGC 5617	14 26·0	0·74	−60 30	2·7	Open galactic cluster in rich field	Cen
572	NGC 5634	14 27·0	0·53	− 5 45	2·7	Fairly bright globular cluster	Vir
573	Hd 232	14 27·0	0·66	−49 18	2·7	5·5 11·7 23″ 20° A2. Difficult	Lup
574	h. 4690	14 34·0	0·65	−45 55	2·6	5·5 8·9 19″ 26° G7. A. Beautiful	Lup
575	α Cen	14 36·2	0·72	−60 38	2·5	0·3 1·7 1·8″–22″ G0. K5. Brilliant	Cen
576	NGC 5694	14 36·7	0·58	−26 19	2·6	Bright remote globular cluster	Hy
577	π Boo	14 38·4	0·47	+16 38	2·6	4·9 5·8 5·6″ 107° A0. A0. Bright pair	Boo
578	α Cir	14 38·4	0·81	−64 46	2·6	3·4 8·8 16″ 231° F0. Fine wide pair	Cir
579	α Lup	14 38·6	0·66	−47 10	2·6	2·9 13·5 27″ 232° B2. Difficult test	Lup
580	ζ Boo	14 38·8	0·48	+13 57	2·6	4·4 4·8 1·1″ 309° A2. Close binary	Boo

No.	Name	R.A.	Var.	Dec.	Var.	Description	Con.
		h m	m	° ′	′		
581	β 414	14 38·9	+0·60	−30 43	−2·6	6·8 8·0 1·0″ 347° B9. White pair	Cen
582	NGC 5746	14 42·4	0·51	+ 2 10	2·5	Long fairly bright eg. spindle	Vir
583	ε Boo	14 42·8	0·44	+27 17	2·5	2·7 5·1 2·8″ 337° gKo. A3. Beautiful	Boo
584	54 Hya	14 43·1	0·58	−25 14	2·5	5·2 7·1 8·5″ 125° dF1. dF9. Fine pair	Hya
585	5 Lib	14 43·2	0·55	−15 15	2·5	6·6 11·0 3·5″ 240° gK2. Orange	Lib
586	h. 4698	14 43·5	0·70	−52 10	2·5	5·2 13·4 9·0″ 255° G6. (Cf. no. 573)	Lup
587	Σ 1884	14 46·2	0·44	+24 34	2·5	6·3 8·0 2·0″ 55° dF6. Deep yellow	Boo
588	μ Lib	14 46·6	0·55	−13 57	2·5	5·8 6·7 1·8″ 356° A4. A4. Fine pair	Lib
589	I 236	14 48·1	0·99	−73 0	2·5	5·7 8·5 2·0″ 117° G5. In a fine field	Aps
590	ξ Boo	14 49·1	0·46	+19 18	2·5	4·8 6·8 6·8″ 348° dG5. dK5. Very fine	Boo
591	IC 4499	14 52·7	1·58	−82 2	2·4	Remote faint globular cluster	Aps
592	h. 4715	14 53·1	0·68	−47 41	2·4	5·8 7·3 2·2″ 278° B9. Elegant pair	Lup
593	HN 28	14 54·5	0·58	−21 11	2·7	5·8 8·9 22″ 302° dK5. dM2. Very fine	Lib
594	59 Hya	14 55·7	0·59	−27 27	2·4	6·3 6·6 0·8″ 335° A5. Close pair	Hya
595	κ Cen	14 55·9	0·65	−41 54	2·4	3·4 11·5 3·9″ 82° B2. Very unequal	Cen
596	δ Lib	14 58·3	0·53	− 8 19	2·4	4·8−6·2 Ao. Algol-type variable	Lib
597	β 348	14 59·3	0·51	+ 0 3	2·4	6·0 8·3 0·4″ 115° gM2. Difficult pair	Vir
598	NGC 5824	15 0·9	0·61	−32 53	2·4	Small very bright globular cluster	Lup
599	σ Lib	15 1·1	0·58	−25 5	2·4	3·4 gM4. Bright orange; fine spectrum	Lib
600	Cp 15	15 1·3	0·99	−71 59	2·4	6·9 8·7 1·5″ 43° Ao. Fine field	Aps
601	NGC 5822	15 1·6	0·73	−54 9	2·3	Very large open galactic cluster	Lup
602	π Lup	15 1·7	0·68	−46 51	2·3	4·7 4·8 1·5″ 72° B5. Fine pair	Lup
603	Σ 1910	15 5·1	0·49	+ 9 25	2·3	7·3 7·4 4·4″ 211° dG5. dG5. Elegant	Boo
604	κ Lup	15 8·5	0·70	−48 33	2·3	4·1 6·0 27″ 143° B9. Ao. Fine pair	Lup
605	ι Lib	15 9·4	0·57	−19 36	2·3	4·7 9·7 59″ 111° B9. Triplet	Lib
606	NGC 5873	15 9·5	0·64	−37 54	2·3	Very small bright planetary nebula	Lup
607	NGC 5882	15 13·4	0·68	−45 28	2·2	Small bright bluish planetary nebula	Lup
608	NGC 5897	15 14·5	0·57	−20 50	2·2	Fine large globular cluster	Lib
609	μ Lup	15 15·0	0·69	−47 42	2·2	5·1 5·3 1·3″ 140°; 7·2 23″ 130° B8	Lup
610	NGC 5904	15 16·0	0·51	+ 2 16	2·2	M 5. Fine large globular cluster	Ser
611	I 332	15 16·1	0·92	−67 18	2·2	6·5 9·1 1·0″ 110° B5. Starry field	TrA
612	Σ 1932	15 16·2	0·43	+27 1	2·2	7·2 7·5 0·8″ 50° dF8. Close pair	CrB
613	5 Ser	15 16·7	0·52	+ 1 57	2·3	5·2 10·0 11″ 35° dF6. Near M 5	Ser
614	Hwe 76	15 18·3	0·64	−38 2	2·2	6·7 8·8 5·0″ 123° Ao. Elegant pair	Lup
615	VV 72	15 19·4	0·58	−23 27	2·2	Tiny bluish planetary nebula	Lib
616	γ Cir	15 19·4	0·79	−59 9	2·2	5·2 5·3 1·1″ 42° B5. F8. Fine pair	Cir
617	η CrB	15 21·1	0·41	+30 28	2·2	5·6 6·1 0·4″−1·1″ dF9. Binary	CrB
618	μ Boo	15 22·6	0·38	+37 31	2·1	4·5 6·7 108″ 171° dA7. dGo. Ternary	Boo
619	NGC 5927	15 24·4	0·72	−50 30	2·1	Large globular cluster in fine field	Lup
620	γ Lup	15 31·8	0·66	−41 0	2·0	3·6 3·8 0″−0·8″ B3. Changing binary	Lup
621	NGC 5946	15 31·8	0·72	−50 30	2·0	Small globular cluster in fine field	Nor
622	δ Ser	15 32·4	0·48	+10 42	2·0	4·2 5·2 4·0″ 178° dA7. dA9. Very fine	Ser
623	h. 4788	15 32·4	0·69	−44 48	2·0	4·9 7·6 2·5″ 2° B3. Fine close pair	Lup
624	ζ CrB	15 37·5	0·38	+36 48	1·9	5·1 6·0 6·3″ 305° B8. B5. Fine pair	CrB
625	β 122	15 37·0	0·58	−19 36	1·9	7·6 7·8 1·9″ 216° F2. Elegant pair	Lib

No.	Name	R.A.	Var.	Dec.	Var.	Description	Con.
		h m	m	° ′	′		
626	γ CrB	15 40·6	+0·42	+26 27	−1·9	4·0 7·0 0″−0·7″ 295° Ao. Binary	CrB
627	β 619	15 40·8	0·47	+13 50	1·9	7·0 7·4 0·5″ 358° G3. Difficult test	Ser
628	Hwe 79	15 41·0	0·67	−41 40	1·9	6·6 8·0 3·8″ 343° Ao. Elegant pair	Lup
629	Hld 124	15 41·3	0·73	−50 38	1·9	6·8 8·7 2·5″ 201° A2. Pale yellow	Nor
630	NGC 5986	15 42·8	0·65	−37 37	1·9	Fine resolved globular cluster	Lup
631	Rmk 20	15 43·3	0·90	−65 17	1·9	6·5 6·5 2·0″ 149° A5. A5. In fine field	TrA
632	NGC 5979	15 43·5	0·84	−61 3	1·9	Conspicuous planetary nebula	TrA
633	NGC 5999	15 48·2	0·79	−56 20	1·8	Large open star cluster	Nor
634	2 Sco	15 50·6	0·60	−25 11	1·8	4·8 7·3 2·4″ 273° B3. Bright pair	Sco
635	Slr 11	15 50·6	0·83	−60 36	1·8	6·5 8·2 1·4″ 103° B8. In a starry field	TrA
636	h. 4813	15 51·3	0·83	−60 2	1·8	6·0 9·8 4·0″ 100° A3. Elegant pair	Nor
637	ξ Lup	15 53·7	0·64	−33 49	1·8	5·4 5·7 10·5″ 49° Ao. Ao. Very fine	Lup
638	η Lup	15 56·8	0·66	−38 15	1·7	3·6 7·9 15″ 20° B3. Beautiful pair	Lup
639	NGC 6026	15 58·1	0·64	−34 25	1·7	Planetary nebula with central star	Lup
640	NGC 6025	15 59·4	0·84	−60 22	1·7	Bright open cluster in fine field	TrA
641	ι Nor	15 59·5	0·81	−57 38	1·7	5·5 5·8 0·2″−0·8″; 7·5 11″ 244° A2	Nor
642	ξ Sco	16 1·6	0·55	−11 14	1·6	4·8 5·1 0·2″−1·3″; 7·2 7·5″ 53° dF4. dG7	Sco
643	β Sco	16 2·5	0·58	−19 40	1·6	2·9 5·1 14″ 23° B2. B3. Very fine	Sco
644	Brs 11	16 6·3	0·64	−32 31	1·6	6·7 7·5 7·7″ 84° G5. Fine pair	Sco
645	ν Sco	16 9·1	0·58	−19 20	1·6	4·3 6·5 41″ 336° B3. A. Double pair	Sco
646	12 Sco	16 9·2	0·62	−28 17	1·6	5·8 8·6 4·0″ 74° B9. White & orange	Sco
647	NGC 6067	16 9·3	0·80	−54 5	1·6	Beautiful open cluster in fine field	Nor
648	IC 4593	16 9·3	0·47	+12 12	1·6	Planetary nebula with central star	Her
649	NGC 6072	16 9·6	0·65	−36 7	1·5	Fairly bright planetary nebula	Sco
650	VV 78	16 10·6	0·79	−54 50	1·5	Small planetary nebula in fine field	Nor
651	σ CrB	16 12·8	0·38	+33 59	1·5	5·8 6·7 6·2″ 229° dF8. dGo. Fine pair	CrB
652	NGC 6093	16 14·1	0·60	−22 52	1·5	M 80. Beautiful globular cluster	Sco
653	NGC 6087	16 14·7	0·83	−57 47	1·5	Scattered star cluster in fine field	Nor
654	σ Sco	16 18·1	0·61	−25 28	1·4	3·1 8·7 20″ 273° B1. Fine pair	Sco
655	NGC 6101	16 20·0	1·12	−72 6	1·4	Diffuse globular cluster in fine field	Aps
656	NGC 6121	16 20·6	0·61	−26 24	1·4	M 4. Very fine globular cluster	Sco
657	h. 4850	16 21·5	0·63	−29 35	1·4	5·9 6·6 5·4″ 354° Go. Go. Deep yellow	Sco
658	NGC 6124	16 22·2	0·68	−40 33	1·4	Large open cluster of bright stars	Sco
659	ρ Oph	16 22·6	0·60	−23 20	1·4	5·2 5·9 3·2″ 345° B5. B5. In nebula	Oph
660	ι TrA	16 23·3	0·92	−63 57	1·4	5·3 9·7 13″ 12° F3. Optical pair	TrA
661	ε Nor	16 23·5	0·73	−47 27	1·4	4·8 7·5 22″ 335° B5. A. Fine wide pair	Nor
662	NGC 6134	16 24·0	0·74	−49 2	1·4	Scattered star cluster	Nor
663	NGC 6144	16 24·2	0·61	−25 56	1·4	Faint resolved globular cluster	Sco
664	NGC 6139	16 24·3	0·68	−38 44	1·4	Well-condensed globular cluster	Sco
665	Σ 2048	16 26·1	0·54	− 8 1	1·3	6·6 9·0 5·0″ 298° dF3. dK1. Elegant	Oph
666	α Sco	16 26·3	0·61	−26 19	1·3	1·2 5·4 3·0″ 276° Ma. A3. Brilliant	Sco
667	NGC 6153	16 28·1	0·68	−40 9	1·3	Fairly bright planetary nebula	Sco
668	λ Oph	16 28·4	0·50	+ 2 6	1·3	4·0 6·1 0·6″−1·5″ A1. Changing binary	Oph
669	NGC 6171	16 29·7	0·59	−12 57	1·3	Large resolved globular cluster	Oph
670	NGC 6167	16 30·6	0·75	−49 30	1·3	Scattered cluster in fine field	Nor

No.	Name	R.A.	Var.	Dec.	Var.	Description	Con.
		h m	m	° ′	′		
671	R Ara	16 35·5	+0·83	−56 54	−1·2	6·8–7·9 8·3 3·5″ 123° B9. Fine field	Ara
672	NGC 6188	16 36·0	0·75	−48 55	1·2	Faint irregular gaseous nebula	Ara
673	NGC 6193	16 37·6	0·75	−48 40	1·2	Large fine scattered cluster	Ara
674	ζ Her	16 39·4	0·38	+31 41	1·1	3·0 5·6 0·5″–1·6″ dG0. Changing	Her
675	NGC 6205	16 39·9	0·36	+36 33	1·1	M 13. Beautiful globular cluster	Her
676	β 1116	16 41·2	0·62	−27 22	1·1	6·4 10·4 2·1″ 3° Ao. Pale yellow	Sco
677	NGC 6210	16 42·4	0·42	+23 53	1·1	Bright bluish planetary nebula	Her
678	NGC 6218	16 44·6	0·52	− 1 52	1·1	M 12. Very fine globular cluster	Oph
679	NGC 6229	16 45·6	0·28	+47 37	1·1	Bright condensed globular cluster	Her
680	Cor 201	16 46·8	0·76	−49 58	1·1	7·3 7·3 3·2″ 41° A5. Elegant pair	Ara
681	h. 4889	16 47·6	0·67	−37 26	1·0	6·2 8·1 6·7″ 5° B9. Fine pair	Sco
682	21 Oph	16 48·9	0·51	+ 1 18	1·0	5·6 7·5 0·9″ 128° A2. Close pair	Oph
683	Σ 2107	16 49·8	0·40	+28 45	1·0	6·7 8·0 0·8″ 70° dF5. Close binary	Her
684	NGC 6235	16 50·4	0·60	−22 6	1·0	Small irregular globular cluster	Oph
685	NGC 6231	16 50·6	0·70	−41 43	1·0	Beautiful bright open cluster	Sco
686	I 576	16 51·5	0·70	−41 4	1·0	6·0 12·5 5·5″ 265° O7. Beautiful field	Sco
687	NGC 6242	16 52·2	0·69	−39 26	1·0	Large scattered galactic cluster	Sco
688	24 Oph	16 53·8	0·60	−23 5	0·9	6·3 6·5 0·9″ 293° Ao. Close pair	Oph
689	NGC 6254	16 54·5	0·53	− 4 2	0·9	M 10. Fine large globular cluster	Oph
690	λ 316	16 56·7	0·75	−48 35	0·9	6·4 7·7 1·0″ 175° G5. Orange yellow	Ara
691	NGC 6266	16 58·0	0·64	−30 2	0·9	M 62. Very fine globular cluster	Oph
692	IC 4634	16 58·6	0·60	−21 44	0·9	Small bright planetary nebula	Oph
693	NGC 6273	16 59·5	0·62	−26 12	0·9	M 19. Fine large globular cluster	Oph
694	NGC 6281	17 1·4	0·68	−37 50	0·8	Open star cluster in fine field	Sco
695	NGC 6284	17 1·4	0·61	−24 42	0·8	Small remote globular cluster	Oph
696	IC 4637	17 1·6	0·70	−40 48	0·8	Bright bluish planetary nebula	Sco
697	NGC 6287	17 2·1	0·60	−22 39	0·8	Globular cluster in obscured field	Oph
698	NGC 6293	17 7·1	0·62	−26 31	0·8	Beautiful globular cluster in fine field	Oph
699	η Oph	17 7·5	0·57	−15 40	0·8	3·2 3·7 0·6″ 200° (1946) A2. Binary	Oph
700	Hwe 86	17 10·4	0·68	−38 14	0·7	6·8 9·8 2·8″ 145° F5. Fine field	Sco
701	NGC 6302	17 10·4	0·68	−37 3	0·7	Very bright elliptical gaseous nebula	Sco
702	h. 4926	17 11·0	0·69	−39 43	0·7	6·6 9·9 15″ 335°; 10·5 17″ 210° K5	Sco
703	NGC 6309	17 11·2	0·56	−12 52	0·7	Fairly bright planetary nebula	Oph
704	NGC 6304	17 11·4	0·63	−29 24	0·7	Heavily veiled globular cluster	Oph
705	36 Oph	17 12·3	0·62	−26 32	0·9	5·3 5·3 4·4″ 164° dK2. dK1. Fine pair	Oph
706	α Her	17 12·4	0·46	+14 27	0·7	3·1–3·9 5·4 4·6″ 107° gM5. dF8. Fine	Her
707	δ Her	17 13·0	0·41	+24 54	0·7	3·2 8·3 9·5″ 242° Ao. dG4. Optical pair	Her
708	NGC 6316	17 13·5	0·63	−28 5	0·7	Compact not bright globular cluster	Oph
709	U Oph	17 14·0	0·51	+ 1 16	0·7	5·7–6·4 13 20″ 355° B5. Algol-type	Oph
710	41 Oph	17 14·0	0·51	− 0 23	0·7	4·8 7·6 1·0″ 346° gK4. Orange pair	Oph
711	NGC 6325	17 15·0	0·61	−23 42	0·7	Remote veiled globular cluster	Oph
712	o Oph	17 15·0	0·61	−24 14	0·7	5·4 6·9 10·3″ 354° gK1. dF5. Fine pair	Oph
713	Brs 13	17 15·3	0·74	−46 35	0·7	5·7 8·2 6·1″ 234° dKo. Fine binary	Ara
714	Mlb 4	17 15·5	0·68	−34 56	0·7	6·3 7·1 0·6″–1·9″ dK5. Rapid binary	Sco
715	NGC 6341	17 15·6	0·31	+43 12	0·6	M 92. Very fine globular cluster	Her

No.	Name	R.A.	Var.	Dec.	Var.	Description	Con.
		h m	m	° ′	′		
716	NGC 6333	17 16·3	+0·59	−18 28	−0·6	M 9. Large bright globular cluster	Oph
717	NGC 6326	17 16·7	0·79	−51 42	0·6	Small bluish-grey planetary nebula	Ara
718	β 126	17 17·0	0·58	−17 42	0·6	6·4 7·5 2·0″ 264°; 11·7 11″ 141° Ao	Oph
719	NGC 6342	17 18·2	0·59	−19 32	0·6	Remote veiled globular cluster	Oph
720	NGC 6337	17 18·9	0·69	−38 25	0·6	Delicate pale blue annular nebula	Sco
721	NGC 6356	17 20·7	0·58	−17 46	0·6	Bright globular cluster in fine field	Oph
722	Dark neb.	17 20·7	0·61	−23 30	0·6	Dark S-formed nebula; difficult	Oph
723	IC 4651	17 20·8	0·77	−49 53	0·6	Fine loose cluster of small stars	Ara
724	NGC 6355	17 20·9	0·62	−26 19	0·6	Remote hazy globular cluster	Oph
725	γ Ara	17 21·2	0·84	−56 20	0·6	3·5 10·4 18″ 330° B1. Very unequal	Ara
726	NGC 6352	17 21·6	0·76	−48 26	0·6	Large globular cluster in fine field	Ara
727	ρ Her	17 22·0	0·35	+37 11	0·6	4·5 5·5 4·0″ 317° B9. A6. Bright pair	Her
728	h. 4949	17 23·2	0·74	−45 48	0·5	6·0 6·8 2·2″ 257° B9. In a rich field	Ara
729	NGC 6366	17 25·1	0·53	− 5 2	0·5	Faint large globular cluster	Oph
730	NGC 6369	17 26·3	0·61	−23 43	0·5	Rather faint annular nebula	Oph
731	NGC 6362	17 26·6	1·03	−67 1	0·5	Fine resolved globular cluster	Ara
732	Σ 2173	17 27·8	0·51	− 1 1	0·5	5·9 6·3 0·25″–1·2″ dG6. Rapid binary	Oph
733	I 40	17 28·1	0·74	−46 0	0·5	6·3 10·5 18″ 210° Go. Fine field	Ara
734	NGC 6383	17 31·4	0·65	−32 33	0·4	Bright star in small loose cluster	Sco
735	NGC 6380	17 31·9	0·69	−39 2	0·4	Faint remote globular cluster	Sco
736	NGC 6388	17 32·6	0·73	−44 43	0·4	Beautiful globular cluster; fine field	Sco
737	NGC 6402	17 35·0	0·53	− 3 13	0·4	M 14. Large resolved globular cluster	Oph
738	NGC 6401	17 35·6	0·61	−23 53	0·4	Fairly bright hazy globular cluster	Oph
739	NGC 6397	17 36·6	0·81	−53 39	0·3	Beautiful globular cluster; stars bright	Ara
740	NGC 6405	17 36·8	0·65	−32 11	0·3	M 6. Large bright open cluster	Sco
741	IC 4663	17 41·8	0·73	−44 53	0·3	Small planetary nebula in fine field	Sco
742	61 Oph	17 42·1	0·50	+ 2 36	0·3	6·2 6·6 20″ 94° Ao. Ao. Fine pair	Oph
743	NGC 6426	17 42·4	0·50	+ 3 12	0·3	Faint remote globular cluster	Oph
744	μ Her	17 44·5	0·40	+27 46	0·3	3·5 9·5 33″ 247° dG4. dM4. Triplet	Her
745	NGC 6440	17 45·9	0·60	−20 21	0·2	Heavily veiled globular cluster	Sgr
746	NGC 6445	17 46·3	0·59	−20 0	0·2	Pale grey planetary nebula	Sgr
747	h. 4978	17 46·4	0·81	−53 36	0·2	5·9 9·5 12″ 268° B3. Elegant pair	Ara
748	NGC 6441	17 46·8	0·68	−37 2	0·2	Fine globular cluster and orange star	Sco
749	NGC 6451	17 47·5	0·64	−30 12	0·2	Open star cluster in fine field	Sco
750	NGC 6453	17 48·0	0·67	−34 37	0·2	Remote globular cluster in fine field	Sco
751	NGC 6476	17 50·7	0·64	−29 7	0·1	Luminous star fields of Milky Way	Sgr
752	NGC 6475	17 50·7	0·67	−34 48	0·1	M 7. Brilliant open star cluster	Sco
753	90 Her	17 51·7	0·33	+40 1	0·1	5·1 9·2 1·7″ 123° gK4. Fine pair	Her
754	Dark neb.	17 53·2	0·63	−28 54	0·1	Large dark nebula in rich field	Sgr
755	NGC 6494	17 54·0	0·59	−19 1	0·1	M 23. Large scattered star cluster	Sgr
756	Σ 2245	17 54·2	0·44	+18 20	0·1	7·3 7·3 2·6″ 294° A2. Elegant pair	Her
757	I 1013	17 54·5	0·69	−39 8	0·1	6·6 8·5 0·8″ 150° Ao. In fine field	Sco
758	NGC 6496	17 55·4	0·73	−44 14	0·1	Faint uncondensed globular cluster	CrA
759	h. 5003	17 55·9	0·64	−30 15	0·1	5·3 7·0 5·5″ 105° Mo. In fine field	Sgr
760	VV 133	17 56·8	0·69	−38 49	0·1	Tiny planetary nebula in rich field	CrA

No.	Name	R.A.	Var.	Dec.	Var.	Description	Con.
		h m	m	° ′	′		
761	NGC 6517	17 59·1	+0·55	− 8 57	−0·0	Faint small globular cluster	Oph
762	NGC 6514	17 59·4	0·61	−23 2	0·0	M 20. Remarkable gaseous nebula	Sgr
763	95 Her	17 59·4	0·42	+21 36	−0·0	5·1 5·2 6·3″ 258° A1. gG3. Fine pair	Her
764	NGC 6520	18 0·3	0·63	−27 54	+0·0	Star cluster and dark nebula	Sgr
765	τ Oph	18 0·4	0·54	− 8 11	0·0	5·3 6·0 2·0″ 272° dF3. Very fine	Oph
766	NGC 6522	18 0·4	0·64	−30 3	0·0	Small fairly bright globular cluster	Sgr
767	NGC 6523	18 0·7	0·61	−24 23	0·0	M 8. Very large bright diffuse nebula	Sgr
768	NGC 6535	18 1·3	0·51	− 0 18	0·0	Faint globular cluster; cf. no. 771	Ser
769	NGC 6528	18 1·6	0·64	−30 4	0·0	Small not bright globular cluster	Sgr
770	NGC 6531	18 1·7	0·61	−22 30	0·0	M 21. Fine open galactic cluster	Sgr
771	NGC 6539	18 2·1	0·54	− 7 35	+0·0	Heavily obscured globular cluster	Ser
772	70 Oph	18 2·9	0·50	+ 2 31	−0·1	4·3 6·0 1·7″–6·8″ dK1. dK6. Beautiful	Oph
773	h. 5014	18 3·2	0·72	−43 26	+0·1	5·8 5·8 1·5″ 206° A3. Close binary	CrA
774	Σ 2276	18 3·4	0·46	+12 0	0·1	7·0 7·4 7·1″ 258° Ao. Ao. Elegant	Oph
775	NGC 6544	18 4·3	0·62	−25 1	0·1	Compact globular cluster in fine field	Sgr
776	NGC 6541	18 4·4	0·73	−43 44	0·1	Very fine globular cluster and field	CrA
777	100 Her	18 5·8	0·40	+26 6	0·1	5·9 6·0 14″ 183° A3. A3. Fine pair	Her
778	NGC 6553	18 6·3	0·62	−25 56	0·1	Nearest globular cluster, much veiled	Sgr
779	IC 1275	18 6·7	0·61	−23 50	0·1	Diffuse nebulosity surrounding stars	Sgr
780	β 245	18 6·9	0·64	−30 44	0·1	5·6 8·2 4·0″ 353° Ko. Orange yellow	Sgr
781	73 Oph	18 7·1	0·50	+ 3 59	0·1	5·9 7·4 0·6″ 46° (1947) dFo. Difficult	O h
782	NGC 6558	18 7·1	0·65	−31 46	0·1	Small globular cluster in fine field	Sgr
783	ε Tel	18 7·5	0·74	−45 58	0·1	4·6 13·5 19″ 231° G5. Test pair	Tel
784	Σ 2289	18 7·9	0·45	+16 28	0·1	6·5 7·6 1·2″ 224° dF3. Ao. Close pair	Her
785	NGC 6563	18 8·8	0·66	−33 52	0·1	Delicate planetary nebula	Sgr
786	NGC 6572	18 9·7	0·49	+ 6 51	0·1	Small very bright planetary nebula	Oph
787	NGC 6569	18 10·4	0·65	−31 50	0·2	Bright globular cluster in fine field	Sgr
788	β 131	18 10·7	0·57	−15 37	0·2	7·1 9·2 3·0″ 279°; 11·6 8·0″ 288° F5	Ser
789	NGC 6567	18 10·8	0·59	−19 5	0·2	Small planetary nebula in fine region	Sgr
790	η Sgr	18 14·3	0·68	−36 47	0·2	3·2 9·2 3·6″ 104° gM4. Very fine pair	Sgr
791	NGC 6584	18 14·6	0·80	−52 14	0·2	Conspicuous globular cluster	Tel
792	IC 4699	18 14·8	0·74	−46 1	0·2	Small planetary nebula in starry field	Tel
793	NGC 6603	18 15·5	0·59	−18 27	0·2	M 24. Star cluster in very rich field	Sgr
794	NGC 6611	18 16·0	0·57	−13 48	0·2	M 16. Fine cluster in luminous haze	Ser
795	Σ 2303	18 17·4	0·54	− 8 0	0·3	6·5 9·2 2·0″ 230° dF2. Veiled field	Ser
796	NGC 6618	18 17·9	0·58	−16 12	0·3	M 17. Large bright gaseous nebula	Sgr
797	ξ Pav	18 18·6	0·92	−61 31	0·3	4·2 8·1 3·5″ 155° M1. Very fine	Pav
798	NGC 6624	18 20·5	0·64	−30 23	0·3	Bright globular cluster in fine field	Sgr
799	NGC 6626	18 21·5	0·62	−24 54	0·3	M 28. Fine bright globular cluster	Sgr
800	AC 11	18 22·4	0·52	− 1 36	0·3	6·8 7·0 0·7″ 359° dF2. Close binary	Ser
801	21 Sgr	18 22·4	0·59	−20 34	0·3	5·0 8·3 1·8″ 287° gK1. Ao. Fine pair	Sgr
802	NGC 6629	18 22·7	0·61	−23 13	0·3	Small pale grey planetary nebula	Sgr
803	β 133	18 24·6	0·62	−26 40	0·4	6·9 7·0 1·5″ 252° A5. Elegant pair	Sgr
804	59 Ser	18 24·6	0·51	+ 0 10	0·4	5·3 7·8 4·0″ 318° Go. A2. Bright pair	Ser
805	NGC 6630	18 27·6	0·96	−63 19	0·4	Faint planetary nebula, as test	Pav

No.	Name	R.A.	Var.	Dec.	Var.	Description	Con.
		h m	m	° ′	′		
806	NGC 6638	18 27·9	+0·62	−25 32	+0·4	Small fairly bright globular cluster	Sgr
807	NGC 6637	18 28·1	0·65	−32 23	0·4	M 69. Fine bright globular cluster	Sgr
808	IC 1287	18 28·7	0·56	−10 50	0·4	Large diffuse nebula containing pair	Sct
809	IC 4725	18 28·8	0·59	−19 17	0·4	M 25. Large bright scattered cluster	Sgr
810	NGC 6642	18 28·9	0·61	−23 30	0·4	Compact globular cluster in fine field	Sgr
811	NGC 6644	18 29·5	0·62	−25 10	0·4	Very small bright planetary nebula	Sgr
812	NGC 6645	18 29·8	0·58	−16 56	0·4	Open cluster of rather faint stars	Sgr
813	κ CrA	18 29·9	0·69	−38 46	0·4	6·0 6·6 21″ 359° B8. B9. Fine field	CrA
814	NGC 6652	18 32·5	0·66	−33 2	0·5	Compact globular cluster in fine field	Sgr
815	NGC 6656	18 33·3	0·61	−23 57	0·5	M 22. Fine large globular cluster	Sgr
816	OΣ 358	18 33·7	0·45	+16 56	0·5	6·7 7·1 1·8″ 170° dGo. dF8. Fine	Her
817	α Lyr	18 35·2	0·34	+38 44	0·5	0·14 10·5 64″ 177° Ao. Fine spectrum	Lyr
818	NGC 6681	18 40·0	0·65	−32 21	0·6	M 70. Small bright globular cluster	Sgr
819	NGC 6694	18 42·5	0·55	− 9 27	0·6	M 26. Irregular star cluster	Sct
820	IC 4776	18 42·6	0·66	−33 24	0·6	Small bright planetary nebula	Sgr
821	ε Lyr	18 42·7	0·33	+39 36	0·6	4·7 4·5 208″ 172° A2. A3. Double pair	Lyr
822	Σ 2375	18 43·0	0·49	+ 5 27	0·6	6·2 6·6 2·4″ 118° Ao. Pale yellow	Ser
823	Σ 2373	18 43·1	0·55	−10 33	0·6	7·1 8·1 4·2″ 334° F2. Elegant pair	Sct
824	R 314	18 43·6	1·23	−73 3	0·6	6·3 8·7 1·8″ 270° Ao. Close pair	Pav
825	NGC 6684	18 44·1	0·99	−65 14	0·6	Bright round eg. nebula	Pav
826	β Lyr	18 48·2	0·37	+33 18	0·7	3·4–4·3 7·8 45″ 150° B2. Eclipsing	Lyr
827	Σ 2404	18 48·4	0·47	+10 55	0·7	7·0 8·0 3·6″ 179° K5. Orange pair	Aql
828	NGC 6705	18 48·4	0·54	− 6 20	0·7	M 11. Fine open star cluster	Sct
829	NGC 6709	18 49·1	0·47	+10 17	0·7	Scattered star cluster in fine field	Aql
830	Σ 2411	18 50·0	0·46	+14 28	0·7	6·5 9·8 13″ 96° gKo. In starry field	Her
831	NGC 6712	18 50·3	0·55	− 8 46	0·7	Conspicuous globular cluster	Sct
832	NGC 6720	18 51·7	0·37	+32 58	0·8	M 57. Bright large annular nebula	Lyr
833	NGC 6715	18 51·9	0·64	−30 32	0·8	M 54. Compact globular cluster	Sgr
834	IC 1295	18 52·0	0·55	− 8 51	0·8	Faint planetary nebula in fine field	Sct
835	NGC 6717	18 52·1	0·61	−22 47	0·8	Small faint hazy globular cluster	Sgr
836	θ Ser	18 53·7	0·50	+ 4 8	0·8	4·5 5·4 22″ 104° A5. A5. Bright pair	Ser
837	I 113	18 55·1	0·76	−48 34	0·8	6·5 10·5 3·0″ 229° K5. Elegant pair	Tel
838	β 648	18 55·2	0·37	+32 50	0·8	5·2 8·2 0·4″–1·3″ dGo. Close binary	Lyr
839	NGC 6723	18 56·2	0·68	−36 42	0·8	Attractive globular cluster	Sgr
840	Brs 14	18 57·7	0·67	−37 8	0·8	6·6 6·8 13″ 281° B9. B9. White pair	CrA
841	NGC 6729	18 58·5	0·67	−37 1	0·8	Small diffuse variable nebula	CrA
842	ζ Sgr	18 59·4	0·64	−29 57	0·9	3·4 3·6 0·2″–0·8″ A4. Close binary	Sgr
843	h. 5082	19 0·1	0·59	−19 19	0·9	6·0 9·5 7·5″ 88°; 10·7 20″ 114° gG6	Sgr
844	HN 126	19 1·3	0·60	−21 36	0·9	7·6 7·8 1·1″ 220° Go. Fine field	Sgr
845	ζ Aql	19 3·1	0·47	+13 47	0·9	3·0 12·0 7·0″ 50° B9. Difficult test	Aql
846	γ CrA	19 3·1	0·68	−37 8	0·9	5·0 5·0 2·5″ 31° dF7. Fine binary	CrA
847	NGC 6751	19 3·2	0·54	− 6 4	0·9	Rather faint planetary nebula	Aql
848	R Aql	19 4·0	0·48	+ 8 9	0·9	5·5–11·8 M6. Fine spectrum	Aql
849	NGC 6744	19 5·0	0·96	−63 56	0·9	Large elliptical eg. nebula	Pav
850	NGC 6752	19 6·4	0·89	−60 4	1·0	Very beautiful globular cluster	Pav

No.	Name	R.A.	Var.	Dec.	Var.	Description	Con.
		h m	m	° ′	′		
851	Σ 2470–4	19 7·0	+0·36	+34 36	+1·0	Field with two very similar pairs	Lyr
852	NGC 6760	19 8·6	0·51	+ 0 57	1·0	~~Heavily veiled globular cluster~~	~~Aql~~
853	β 139	19 10·3	0·45	+16 46	1·0	6·7 8·0 0·8″ 139° B9. Close pair	Sge
854	η Lyr	19 12·1	0·34	+39 4	1·0	4·5 8·5 28″ 82° B5. Ao. Wide pair	Lyr
855	IC 1297	19 14·0	0·72	−39 42	1·1	Small bright planetary nebula	CrA
856	Σ 2489	19 14·2	0·46	+14 27	1·1	5·5 8·9 8·3″ 345° Ao. dG2. Fine pair	Aql
857	NGC 6779	19 14·6	0·39	+30 6	1·1	M 56. Conspicuous globular cluster	Lyr
858	2 Vul	19 15·6	0·42	+22 56	1·1	5·4 9·5 2·0″ 128° Bo. Pale yellow	Vul
859	NGC 6778	19 15·7	0·52	− 1 43	1·1	Planetary nebula and dark nebula	Aql
860	NGC 6781	19 16·0	0·49	+ 6 26	1·1	Faint large round planetary nebula	Aql
861	23 Aql	19 16·0	0·51	+ 1 0	1·1	5·3 9·5 3·4″ 7° gK1. Fine pair	Aql
862	β Sgr	19 19·0	0·72	−44 33	1·1	4·2 7·1 28″ 76° B8. A3. Fine pair	Sgr
863	NGC 6790	19 20·4	0·51	+ 1 25	1·1	Small bright planetary nebula	Aql
864	HN 119	19 26·8	0·62	−27 5	1·2	5·6 7·8 7·7″ 143° Ko. Elegant pair	Sgr
865	NGC 6802	19 28·4	0·44	+20 10	1·3	Distant open cluster of faint stars	Vul
866	β Cyg	19 28·7	0·40	+27 51	1·3	3·2 5·3 34″ 55° gK1. B9. Beautiful	Cyg
867	NGC 6803	19 29·0	0·48	+ 9 58	1·3	Minute planetary nebula as test	Aql
868	NGC 6804	19 29·2	0·48	+ 9 7	1·3	Large faint planetary nebula	Aql
869	AQ Sgr	19 31·5	0·57	−16 29	1·3	6·6–7·6 N3. Red; fine spectrum	Sgr
870	Σ 2545	19 36·0	0·55	−10 16	1·4	6·6 8·1 3·7″ 325° A5. Elegant pair	Aql
871	NGC 6809	19 36·9	0·64	−31 4	1·4	M 55. Fine large globular cluster	Sgr
872	NGC 6819	19 39·6	0·34	+40 4	1·4	Rich open cluster of faint stars	Cyg
873	χ Aql	19 40·2	0·47	+11 42	1·4	5·6 6·8 0·5″ 77° dF5. Close pair	Aql
874	NGC 6818	19 41·1	0·57	−14 17	1·4	Bright large planetary nebula	Sgr
875	NGC 6822	19 42·1	0·57	−14 53	1·4	Faint eg. nebula of local group	Sgr
876	δ Cyg	19 43·4	0·31	+45 0	1·5	3·0 6·5 2·0″ 245° A1. Fine pair	Cyg
877	17 Cyg	19 44·5	0·38	+33 37	1·4	5·0 9·2 26″ 69° dF5. K5. Fine field	Cyg
878	π Aql	19 46·3	0·47	+11 41	1·5	6·0 6·8 1·4″ 110° dF2. A2. Close pair	Aql
879	ζ Sge	19 46·8	0·44	+19 1	1·5	5·0 8·7 8·3″ 312° A2. Fine field	Sge
880	χ Cyg	19 48·6	0·38	+32 47	1·5	3·3–14·2 gM7. Mira-type; spectrum	Cyg
881	Δ 227	19 48·7	0·80	−55 6	1·5	6·1 6·8 23″ 148° G5. A2. Fine pair	Tel
882	Σ 2587	19 49·0	0·50	+ 3 58	1·5	6·6 9·2 4·1″ 103° Ko. In fine field	Aql
883	NGC 6838	19 51·5	0·45	+18 39	1·6	M 71. Fine rich globular cluster	Sge
884	Σ 2597	19 52·6	0·53	− 6 52	1·6	6·8 7·8 0·8″ 83° F2. Close pair	Aql
885	NGC 6842	19 52·9	0·40	+29 9	1·6	Large faint planetary nebula, as test	Vul
886	OΣ 390	19 53·1	0·40	+30 4	1·6	6·4 9·2 9·6″ 22°; 11·0 16″ 174° B8	Cyg
887	NGC 6853	19 57·4	0·43	+22 35	1·6	M 27. Beautiful large planetary nebula	Vul
888	13 Sge	19 57·8	0·45	+17 23	1·6	5·6 12·0 28″ 206° gM4. Fine spectrum	Sge
889	16 Vul	19 59·9	0·42	+24 48	1·7	5·9 6·3 1·0″ 115° dFo. Close pair	Vul
890	Σ 2616	20 0·4	0·46	+14 26	1·7	6·7 9·7 3·2″ 265° Ko. Elegant pair	Aql
891	β 57	20 3·1	0·46	+15 21	1·7	6·6 10·6 2·3″ 116° gM2. Fine field	Aql
892	NGC 6864	20 3·2	0·59	−22 4	1·7	M 75. Small bright globular cluster	Sgr
893	NGC 6871	20 4·0	0·38	+35 38	1·7	Large open cluster in rich field	Cyg
894	Σ 2628	20 5·4	0·48	+ 9 15	1·7	6·4 8·2 4·0″ 344° dF2. Deep yellow	Aql
895	NGC 6868	20 6·3	0·73	−48 31	1·7	Bright round eg. nebula	Tel

No.	Name	R.A.	Var.	Dec.	Var.	Description	Con.
		h m	m	° ′	′		
896	θ Sge	20 7·7	+0·44	+20 46	+1·8	6·3 8·4 12″ 326° dF1. dG5. Fine pair	Sge
897	h. 5173	20 7·9	0·65	−36 13	1·5	5·3 12·0 8·3″ 121° dK4. Test pair	Sgr
898	NGC 6879	20 8·2	0·46	+16 47	1·8	Minute planetary nebula, as test	Sge
899	NGC 6882	20 9·8	0·42	+26 22	1·8	Two bright open clusters in contact	Vul
900	Σ 2644	20 10·0	0·51	+ 0 43	1·8	6·8 7·1 3·0″ 207° Ao. Ao. Elegant pair	Aql
901	NGC 6886	20 10·5	0·45	+19 50	1·8	Small planetary nebula as test	Sge
902	Σ 2653	20 11·5	0·43	+24 5	1·8	6·5 10·1 2·6″ 270° Ao. Fine field	Vul
903	NGC 6891	20 12·8	0·47	+12 35	1·8	Small bright planetary nebula	Del
904	NGC 6894	20 14·4	0·40	+30 25	1·9	Faint annular planetary nebula	Cyg
905	α Cap	20 15·1	0·55	−12 41	1·9	4·6 3·8 6·5′ 110° G5. gG8. Very fine	Cap
906	Σ 2666	20 16·3	0·35	+40 35	1·9	6·0 8·2 2·7″ 250° O8. White pair	Cyg
907	h. 5188	20 17·4	0·62	−29 21	1·9	6·4 9·5 4·0″ 50° Ao. Striking field	Sgr
908	IC 4997	20 17·9	0·46	+16 34	1·9	Small bright planetary nebula	Sge
909	β Cap	20 18·2	0·56	−14 56	1·9	3·2 6·2 205″ 267°. Complex system	Cap
910	NGC 6905	20 20·2	0·45	+19 57	1·9	Rather faint planetary nebula	Del
911	β 763	20 20·5	0·68	−42 35	1·9	5·9 7·5 1·0″ 235° A3. Pale yellow	Sgr
912	π Cap	20 24·5	0·57	−18 22	2·0	5·2 8·7 3·2″ 148° B8. Fine pair	Cap
913	ρ Cap	20 26·0	0·57	−17 59	2·0	5·0 10 0·5″ 158° (1958) dF1. Binary	Cap
914	o Cap	20 27·0	0·57	−18 45	2·0	6·1 6·6 22″ 239° A2. A3. Bright pair	Cap
915	1 Del	20 27·9	0·48	+10 44	2·0	6·1 8·0 1·1″ 354° Ao. Pale yellow	Del
916	β 987	20 28·0	0·48	+19 15	2·0	6·6 11·5 2·1″ 132° A2. Fine field	Del
917	NGC 6925	20 31·2	0·63	−32 9	2·0	Fairly bright elliptical eg. nebula	Mic
918	NGC 6934	20 31·7	0·49	+ 7 14	2·0	Bright globular cluster	Del
919	NGC 6940	20 32·5	0·42	+28 8	2·1	Rich open star cluster	Vul
920	β Del	20 35·2	0·47	+14 25	2·1	4·1 5·1 0·2″–0·7″ dF3. Close binary	Del
921	Δ 232	20 35·8	1·18	−75 31	2·1	7·1 7·6 17″ 17° G5. G5. Deep yellow	Oct
922	49 Cyg	20 39·0	0·40	+32 8	2·1	6·0 8·1 3·0″ 43° gG7. A1. Fine pair	Cyg
923	Σ 2723	20 42·5	0·48	+12 8	2·2	6·7 8·2 1·2″ 116° dA7. Pale yellow	Del
924	NGC 6960	20 43·6	0·41	+30 32	2·2	Irregular nebulosity involving 52 Cyg	Cyg
925	γ Del	20 44·3	0·46	+15 57	2·2	4·5 5·5 10″ 268° gK1. dF6. Very fine	Del
926	β 677	20 45·2	0·40	+34 11	2·2	5·2 12·0 10″ 122° gK3. Fine field	Cyg
927	α Mic	20 46·9	0·63	−33 58	2·2	5·0 9·5 21″ 166° G6. Wide pair	Mic
928	IC 5052	20 47·5	0·97	−69 25	2·2	Rather faint elongated eg. spindle	Pav
929	Rmk 26	20 47·5	0·83	−62 37	2·2	7·2 7·5 2·3″ 87° A2. Fine pair	Pav
930	4 Aqr	20 48·8	0·53	− 5 49	2·2	6·3 7·6 1·1″ 3° dF3. Close binary	Aqr
931	NGC 6981	20 50·7	0·55	−12 44	2·3	M 72. Fairly bright globular cluster	Aqr
932	Σ 2735	20 53·2	0·50	+ 4 20	2·3	6·3 7·8 2·1″ 284° gG6. Deep yellow	Del
933	NGC 6992	20 54·3	0·41	+31 30	2·3	Extensive irregular gaseous nebula	Cyg
934	1 Equ	20 56·6	0·50	+ 4 6	2·3	5·7 6·2 1·0″ 286°; 7·1 10″ 69° dFo	Equ
935	NGC 7006	20 59·1	0·47	+16 0	2·4	Very distant globular cluster	Del
936	2 Equ	20 59·7	0·49	+ 6 59	2·4	7·1 7·1 2·7″ 218° dF3. Elegant pair	Equ
937	12 Aqr	21 1·4	0·53	− 6 1	2·4	5·9 7·3 2·7″ 194° gG4. A3. Fine pair	Aqr
938	NGC 7009	21 1·4	0·55	−11 34	2·4	Very bright planetary nebula	Aqr
939	Hd 305	21 4·2	1·05	−73 22	2·4	5·8 14·5 7·9″ 130° gK6. Test pair	Pav
940	61 Cyg	21 4·7	0·43	+38 30	2·9	5·6 6·3 28″ 142° dK6. dMo. Fine pair	Cyg

No.	Name	R.A.	Var.	Dec.	Var.	Description	Con.
		h m	m	° ′	′		
941	NGC 7027	21 5·2	+0·37	+42 2	+2·4	Small bright planetary nebula	Cyg
942	Σ 2762	21 6·5	0·42	+30 0	2·4	5·6–5·8 7·7 3·5″ 309° B8. Bright pair	Cyg
943	γ Equ	21 7·9	0·49	+ 9 56	2·4	4·8 11·0 2·5″ 273° F1. Not easy	Equ
944	τ Cyg	21 12·8	0·40	+37 50	2·6	3·8 8·0 0·5″–1·2″ dF0. Close binary	Cyg
945	NGC 7049	21 15·6	0·69	−48 47	2·5	Small fairly bright eg. nebula	Ind
946	β 163	21 16·2	0·48	+11 22	2·5	7·0 9·0 1·0″ 260° dF8. Close binary	Equ
947	θ Ind	21 16·3	0·71	−53 40	2·5	4·6 7·2 6·0″ 275° A5. Beautiful pair	Ind
948	β 271	21 16·9	0·57	−26 33	2·5	6·5 9·0 3·5″ 257° dG4. dG6. Elegant	Cap
949	Σ 2786	21 17·2	0·49	+ 9 19	2·5	7·3 8·4 2·6″ 186° A2. White pair	Equ
950	OΣ 437	21 18·7	0·42	+32 14	2·6	6·9 7·6 2·1″ 30° G5. Starry field	Cyg
951	β 766	21 21·2	0·64	−41 13	2·6	6·4 7·0 0·8″ 272° A0. Close pair	Mic
952	ζ Cap	21 23·8	0·57	−22 38	2·6	3·9 12·7 21″ 10° G4. Test pair	Cap
953	Mlb 6	21 23·8	0·64	−42 46	2·6	5·7 8·3 2·8″ 148° A3. Fine pair	Mic
954	NGC 7078	21 27·6	0·48	+11 57	2·6	M 15. Very fine globular cluster	Peg
955	NGC 7092	21 30·4	0·36	+48 13	2·7	M 39. Large bright open cluster	Cyg
956	NGC 7089	21 30·9	0·52	− 1 3	2·7	M 2. Beautiful globular cluster	Aqr
957	NGC 7090	21 32·9	0·71	−54 47	2·7	Fairly bright long narrow eg. spindle	Ind
958	NGC 7099	21 37·5	0·57	−23 25	2·7	M 30. Fine irregular globular cluster	Cap
959	μ Cyg	21 41·9	0·44	+28 31	2·7	4·7 6·1 1·5″ 282° dF6. dF3. Yellow	Cyg
960	κ Peg	21 42·4	0·45	+25 25	2·8	4·3 10·8 13″ 295° dF2. Wide pair	Peg
961	λ Oct	21 43·5	1·52	−82 57	2·8	5·5 7·6 3·0″ 69° G5. A3. Bright pair	Oct
962	Σ 2848	21 55·5	0·50	+ 5 42	2·9	7·3 7·6 11″ 56° A2. Elegant pair	Peg
963	IC 5150	21 56·2	0·61	−39 39	2·9	Faint annular planetary nebula	Gru
964	η PsA	21 58·0	0·57	−28 42	2·9	5·8 6·6 1·8″ 115° B8. Fine pair	PsA
965	NGC 7172	21 59·2	0·59	−32 7	2·9	Three small eg. nebulae in field	PsA
966	29 Aqr	21 59·7	0·55	−17 12	2·9	7·2 7·4 3·8″ 245° A2. Elegant pair	Aqr
967	NGC 7209	22 3·3	0·40	+46 15	2·9	Large scattered star cluster	Lac
968	NGC 7205	22 5·1	0·69	−57 40	2·9	Conspicuous elliptical eg. nebula	Tuc
969	NGC 7213	22 6·2	0·63	−47 25	2·9	Bright round eg. nebula	Gru
970	41 Aqr	22 11·5	0·55	−21 19	3·0	5·6 7·4 5·0″ 115° G8. Fine pair	Aqr
971	Σ 2878	22 12·0	0·50	+ 7 44	3·0	6·6 8·0 1·4″ 120° A0. Pale yellow	Peg
972	NGC 7243	22 13·3	0·39	+49 38	3·0	Fairly bright scattered cluster	Lac
973	Σ 2894	22 16·7	0·44	+37 31	3·0	6·1 8·2 16″ 194° dF2. Wide pair	Lac
974	π Gru	22 20·0	0·61	−46 11	3·0	Two bright stars, each a pair	Gru
975	51 Aqr	22 21·5	0·52	− 5 6	3·0	6·6 6·6 0·7″ 330° A0. Close binary	Aqr
976	IC 5217	22 21·9	0·40	+50 43	3·0	Small bright planetary nebula	Lac
977	δ Tuc	22 23·8	0·71	−65 13	3·1	4·8 9·2 7·0″ 282° B9. Fine pair	Tuc
978	53 Aqr	22 23·9	0·54	−17 0	3·1	6·4 6·6 4·1″ 323° G0. Bright yellow	Aqr
979	34 Peg	22 24·1	0·51	+ 4 8	3·1	5·8 12·5 3·2″ 218° dF5. Unequal pair	Peg
980	Σ 2906	22 24·5	0·44	+37 11	3·1	6·4 10·6 4·2″ 3° B2. White pair	Lac
981	ζ Aqr	22 26·2	0·51	− 0 17	3·1	4·4 4·6 1·9″ 261° dF2. dF1. Beautiful	Aqr
982	NGC 7293	22 27·0	0·55	−21 6	3·1	Very large planetary nebula	Aqr
983	37 Peg	22 27·4	0·51	+ 4 11	3·1	5·8 7·2 1·0″ 117° F5. Close binary	Peg
984	β PsA	22 28·7	0·57	−32 36	3·1	4·4 7·8 30″ 172° A0. Fine pair	PsA
985	NGC 7314	22 33·0	0·56	−26 18	3·1	Fairly bright large eg. nebula	PsA

No.	Name	R.A.	Var.	Dec.	Var.	Description	Con.
		h m	m	° ′	′		
986	NGC 7331	22 34·8	+0·46	+34 10	+3·1	Fairly bright elliptical eg. nebula	Peg
987	NGC 7332	22 35·0	0·48	+23 32	3·1	Field with 2 small eg. spindles	Peg
988	h. 5356	22 37·0	0·56	−28 36	3·1	7·2 8·0 3·0″ 67° F5. Elegant pair	PsA
989	Σ 2942	22 41·8	0·45	+39 12	3·1	6·2 8·4 3·0″ 270° gK5. gK1. Orange	Lac
990	ξ Peg	22 44·2	0·50	+11 55	3·1	4·3 12·0 12″ 105° dF3. Unequal pair	Peg
991	γ PsA	22 49·8	0·56	−33 8	3·2	4·5 8·5 4·2″ 262° Ao. Fine pair	PsA
992	NGC 7410	22 52·1	0·57	−39 56	3·2	Large pretty bright eg. spindle	Gru
993	NGC 7408	22 52·8	0·67	−63 58	3·2	Faint fairly large planetary nebula	Tuc
994	δ PsA	22 53·2	0·56	−32 48	3·2	4·3 10·5 5·3″ 240° G3. Yellow pair	PsA
995	52 Peg	22 56·7	0·50	+11 28	3·2	6·0 7·5 0·9″ 259° Fo. Long period	Peg
996	β Peg	23 1·3	0·48	+27 49	3·2	2·6 gM2. Bright orange; fine spectrum	Peg
997	β 773	23 4·1	0·56	−39 10	3·2	5·6 9·1 1·1″ 211° (1948) Ao. Close pair	Gru
998	θ Gru	23 4·1	0·57	−43 47	3·2	4·5 7·0 1·2″ 71° F4. Fine pair	Gru
999	Δ 246	23 4·4	0·58	−50 57	3·2	6·1 6·8 8·6″ 256° F5. Elegant pair	Gru
1000	NGC 7492	23 5·8	0·53	−15 54	3·2	Very faint remote globular cluster	Aqr
1001	I 1467	23 10·4	0·57	−49 53	3·3	6·8 8·3 1·0″ 230° G5. Changing pair	Gru
1002	NGC 7552	23 13·5	0·56	−42 53	3·3	Fairly bright elliptical eg. nebula	Gru
1003	NGC 7582	23 16·2	0·56	−42 34	3·3	Field with 3 eg. nebulae	Gru
1004	NGC 7606	23 16·5	0·52	− 8 46	3·3	Fairly bright elliptical eg. nebula	Aqr
1005	94 Aqr	23 16·5	0·52	−13 44	3·3	5·6 7·6 13″ 350° dG4. dK3. Fine pair	Aqr
1006	NGC 7619	23 18·0	0·51	+ 7 55	3·3	Field with 2 bright eg. nebulae	Peg
1007	Σ 3007	23 20·3	0·50	+20 17	3·3	6·6 9·6 5·8″ 91° dGo. dK6. Elegant	Peg
1008	Σ 3009	23 21·7	0·51	+ 3 26	3·3	6·8 8·8 7·2″ 230° gK2. dF4. Very fine	Psc
1009	NGC 7662	23 23·5	0·48	+42 16	3·3	Very bright bluish planetary nebula	And
1010	Hwe 93	23 34·4	0·53	−32 9	3·3	6·6 9·8 5·3″ 252° Ko. Orange	Scl
1011	θ Phe	23 36·8	0·54	−46 55	3·3	6·8 7·4 3·8″ 275° A3. Fine pair	Phe
1012	R Aqr	23 41·2	0·52	−15 34	3·3	5·8–11·5 M6. Fine spectrum	Aqr
1013	78 Peg	23 41·5	0·50	+29 5	3·3	5·0 8·1 1·0″ 235° gG8. Deep yellow	Peg
1014	107 Aqr	23 43·4	0·52	−18 57	3·3	5·7 7·0 6·5″ 136° A5. Fine pair	Aqr
1015	NGC 7793	23 55·3	0·52	−32 51	3·3	Very large elliptical eg. nebula	Scl
1016	Σ 3050	23 56·9	0·51	+33 27	3·3	6·6 6·6 1·5″ 277° dGo. dGo. Binary	And
1017	85 Peg	23 59·5	0·52	+26 49	3·2	5·8 11·0 0·4″–0·8″ dG1. Rapid binary	Peg

DESCRIPTION OF CONSTELLATIONS
AND OBJECTS

Andromeda (And)

In the mythology of ancient Greece, Andromeda represents the chained maiden, daughter of Cepheus and Cassiopeia, who is rescued from the sea monster Cetus by the hero Perseus. This large northern constellation of area 722 sq. deg. was recognized by Ptolemy who assigned twenty-three stars to it. The unaided eye sees the only conspicuous feature as an irregular line of the four brightest stars extending Nf. from the great square of Pegasus, of which α And—Alpheratz—forms one corner. The northern limit of Andromeda encroaches on the Milky Way; it is rather low in the sky for most southern observers and the centre culminates at midnight about September 30th.

The finest of the many pairs is the beautiful Almak—γ And—which in large instruments is a triplet. Only one of the three open clusters is effective in the telescope, which applies also to the three known planetary nebulae. There is no diffuse galactic nebula nor globular cluster, but many extra-galactic nebulae occur, including the two Messier objects M31 and M32. The former is the well-known spiral nebula which is the largest and brightest of its class in the sky.

1009. NGC 7662. In good conditions this bright planetary nebula shows a vivid pale blue disk about 25″ across, even in light and fairly well defined; no central star is visible but the single elliptical prism image shows evidence of a central streak. Even 7·5 cm shows the prism image easily. R is 550 pc.

1016. Σ 3050. The components of this close deep yellow equal pair have been steadily closing since W. Struve found 3·8″ and 191° in 1832, and the angle is now in the fourth quadrant so that the orbit should soon be determinable. In 1961 the stars were just in contact with 10·5 cm.

5. AC 1. In a field with a few widely scattered fainter stars, this deep yellow star has a bright orange-red gem 4·5′ Sp. 10·5 cm resolves it clearly, and both angle and separation are slowly increasing.

11. NGC 205. One of the companions of M 31, this large ellipsoidal system belongs to the local group containing the galaxy. Photographs with large instruments show an extension of 26′ × 16′ in pa. 165° and resolve it into a vast assemblage of ancient stars with only slight evidence of interstellar dust and gas. It is low for southern observers, but not difficult for small apertures; 30 cm shows a fairly bright diffuse luminous haze $3\cdot5' \times 2'$ with no apparent structure, rising broadly to the centre. The field is sprinkled with stars.

12. NGC 221. This companion of M 31 lies $25'$ S of its centre; in large instruments it is $12' \times 8'$ and resolved into stars, so that like NGC 205 it resembles a gigantic globular cluster far advanced in evolution. I see it as a hazy almost round object about $1\cdot5'$ across with very bright nucleus, which the prism spreads into a strong band. In spite of low altitude it is quite easy to see with $7\cdot5$ cm.

13. NGC 224. Visible to the unaided eye and recorded in the tenth century, this immense system resembles the galaxy in size and general composition. It is a vast spiral, well tilted to the line of sight, and the regions of its central plane contain bright and dark diffuse nebulae, star clusters and many young very hot stars, while round it is a halo of ancient stars and more than 300 globular clusters. In photographs the apparent dimensions are about $3° \times 1\cdot5°$, though visually much less, especially for southern observers where the altitude is low. 30 cm shows me an extended elliptical haze in pa. $40°$, very bright in the central region, with a dark rift near the Np. edge and extending N of the centre. $7\cdot5$ cm shows the bright centre about $5'$ long. R is 570,000 pc.

28. NGC 404. The very bright deep yellow β And is $6\cdot5'$ Sf. and interferes somewhat with the observation of this object. It is a round fairly bright haze about $1'$ across with a continuous spectrum as indicated by the prism band. It can be seen as a small spot with $10\cdot5$ cm if the star is hidden.

54. NGC 752. An interesting cluster of scattered stars, m. 8–9 and fainter, with no central condensation; it is about $45'$ across and needs a large field with low magnification. In it are two strongly curved lines of stars p. R is about 400 pc.

57. γ And. This beautiful and brilliant pair, orange-yellow and pale blue (by contrast) completely dominates the field of a few scattered stars. There has been no change since the measures of W. Struve in 1830, but O. Struve in 1842 resolved B into two stars of m. 5·4 and 6·6. These form a binary of period 55 years and very eccentric orbit. The stars were very close in 1945 and will be widest $0\cdot6''$ in 1971, but owing to low altitude southern observers will need very good conditions to resolve this pair.

62. NGC 891. Photographs reveal this object as a very fine edgewise spiral $12' \times 1'$ in pa. $24°$ with heavy dark absorption along the central axis. From northern stations 30 cm will show something of this as a dark band across the brighter central region, but at low altitude I see only a faint spindle $7' \times 1'$ with no apparent nucleus, in a field well sprinkled with stars.

Antlia (Ant)

Antlia, the air pump, is one of the constellations introduced by Lacaille about 1752; it is a group of inconspicuous stars lying on the edge of the Milky Way between Hydra and Vela with an area of 239 sq. deg. Its centre culminates at midnight about February 22nd.

Apart from a few double stars, and the noted eclipsing binary S Ant ($9^h 30 \cdot 1^m$; $-28° 24'$ $6 \cdot 4$-$6 \cdot 8$) with a period of only $7^h 47^m$, the only objects of interest are extra-galactic nebulae which however show little diversity in small telescopes and none of which is bright. From thirty-three of these examined, NGC 2997 is selected because of its size, and two fields are given containing several of them.

346. ζ^1 Ant. This is an effective pair for small apertures; the pale yellow stars dominate a field well sprinkled with stars. There has been no appreciable change since the measures of John Herschel in 1836, and if the stars are connected the period must be very long.

353. NGC 2997. In a field of scattered stars this interesting object is a large faint ellipse of luminous haze about $5' \times 4'$, of fairly even light except for a well-defined much brighter nucleus less than $10''$ across. A suggestion of concentric structure is probably illusory although the nebula is an extra-galactic spiral. 15 cm shows it only very dimly.

384. δ Ant. These two stars, pale yellow and ashy, have shown no real change since measured by Jacob in 1856, and common proper motion denotes a binary of long period. Two spectra seem to be superposed in that of A, which may itself be composite. $7 \cdot 5$ cm shows the faint star plainly.

385. NGC 3271. This is about the brightest of five small extra-galactic nebulae in a field $12'$ across; all are rather similar, elliptical and fairly bright with a small nucleus. They are all spirals except the second (in R.A.) and give bands in the prism. 15 cm shows four of them with care.

393. NGC 3347. In an interesting field sprinkled with many stars are three extra-galactic nebulae, of which this is the first; all are classed as spirals and the prism extends them into bands. The first and third are elliptical, and the second is small, faint and nearly round. 15 cm shows only the two ellipses, and rather dimly.

Apus (Aps)

The origin of this constellation is usually attributed to Johann Bayer in 1603, but he seems to have adopted it from the accounts of voyagers to the southern hemisphere in the previous century who would be acquainted with the bird of paradise which it is supposed to represent. It is a comparatively small group of area 206 sq. deg. lying S of Circinus and Triangulum Australe, and the centre culminates at midnight about May 21st.

There are only four stars of moderate brightness and all are orange. Of the several mostly wide pairs which have been measured, two of the closer brighter ones are given. There are two globular clusters, but no other galactic objects and the extra-galactic nebulae are all small and faint.

589. I 236. In a field sown profusely with small stars this bright deep yellow star has a less bright companion very close Sf., quite clearly shown by 7·5 cm. Precise measures in 1901 gave 1·7″ and 102°, since when both values have increased. The proper motion of A does not account for this, and the stars probably form a binary system.

591. IC 4499. This globular cluster, missed by John Herschel, was discovered photographically from Arequipa. It is a faint irregularly round haze nearly 3′ across in a field of rather faint stars, and three very faint stars in it are probably superposed. On a clear dark night it is not difficult for 30 cm because of its size, but 20 cm is hardly enough. R is about 18,000 pc.

600. Cp 15. In a field sown with less bright stars this fairly bright pale yellow star has a white companion very close Nf. which, though difficult, can sometimes be made out with 7·5 cm and is quite clear with 10·5 cm. The orange CPD 1718 is 5·5′ p. There has been no real change since Russell's measures in 1880, and little can be said about this pair.

655. NGC 6101. In fine contrast with a field sown profusely with stars is this rather faint but very rich globular cluster; it is irregularly round, rising broadly to the centre, about 3′ across with rays of faint stars emerging. Resolution is apparent with 20 cm while 10·5 cm shows plainly an unresolved haze. R is about 8,400 pc.

Aquarius (Aqr)

Aquarius, the water pourer, is the eleventh constellation of the Zodiac, to which Ptolemy assigned forty-two stars, including Fomalhaut which is now α PsA. Although not conspicuous for brightness or pattern in its stars, the group has an ancient history for even in very early Babylonian times these stars were taken to represent a man pouring water from an urn. It is a large constellation of 980 sq. deg. lying just S of the equator and extending over more than 3 hours in R.A.; the centre culminates at midnight about August 26th. Due to precession the zodiacal sign of Aquarius is now almost entirely in the constellation of Capricornus.

There are many fine pairs, of which nine have been selected. Four globular clusters are known, one of which was discovered photographically at Palomar and is beyond the reach of amateur telescopes. No diffuse galactic nebulae nor open clusters have been found but there are two interesting planetary nebulae. Almost all of the innumerable extragalactic nebulae are small faint objects; from twenty-six examined only one is given, the edgewise spiral NGC 7606.

930. 4 Aqr. This bright deep yellow binary was discovered by W. Struve in 1829, the measures being 0·7″ and 25°. The motion is direct and the separation is now increasing after a minimum of 0·2″ early in this century. 15 cm showed the stars clearly apart in 1960. The period is about 152 years.

931. NGC 6981. Méchain discovered this conspicuous globular cluster in 1780; it is of the open little compressed type, irregularly round, about 1·5′ across and resolved into star points which may be seen scattered in the luminous haze with 20 cm, while 10·5 cm shows an easy nebulous spot. Two wide pairs nearby Sf. and f. add interest to the field. R is about 19,000 pc.

937. 12 Aqr. This bright unequal pair, deep yellow and white, is an effective telescopic object, beautifully divided by 7·5 cm. The angle has increased slightly since W. Struve measured it in 1831 and common proper motion indicates a binary system of long period.

938. NGC 7009. Photographs of this bright bluish planetary nebula show very intricate structure and two short equatorial rays with almost stellar condensations at the ends. 30 cm however indicates little of this; the light seems even and the faint rays can be seen only on very clear nights. The nebula is elliptical, about 20″ × 15″ in pa. 70°, and no nucleus is visible; the single prism image is bright, and easy for 7·5 cm. R is 440 pc.

956. NGC 7089. Discovered by Maraldi in 1746, this very fine object is a mass of innumerable stars concentrated towards the centre and dispersing outwards into irregular wispy rays of outliers about 5′ across. Resolution is just evident with 15 cm, and with 10·5 cm the cluster is conspicuous and granular, with outlier haze. R is about 15,000 pc.

966. 29 Aqr. This beautiful easy pair, yellow and white, shines brightly in a thin field of faint stars. Little change has occurred since the measures of Dembowski in 1866 and the proper motions are very small.

970. 41 Aqr. Excellent for small apertures, this unequal well-separated pair, deep and paler yellow, lies in a field with several fairly bright stars. Change has been slight since the earliest accurate measures, but common proper motion indicates that the stars are connected.

975. 51 Aqr. Dembowski found 0·46″ and 20° for this pair in 1875; since then the separation has increased and the angle steadily diminished, so that in 1961 25 cm separated the stars cleanly. This seems to be a true binary, but little is known of the orbit yet.

978. 53 Aqr. Here is an unusual case of two bright stars forming a close optical pair. Since South found 10″ and 303° for these stars in 1823, separation has diminished and angle increased due to difference in proper motions. Nearest approach will be 2·3″ in 20° about 2030, after which the stars will separate linearly again. This is a fine object for small apertures.

981. ζ Aqr. Dominating a field of widely scattered stars, this very bright yellow pair is well shown by 7·5 cm. It is a binary of long period, with values steadily diminishing since W. Struve's measures of 3·6″ and 360° in 1825, and there is some evidence of a third invisible component.

982. MGC 7293. This remarkable object is the nearest planetary nebula so far known, R being 180 pc. It is a large rather faint annulus about 14′ × 12′ with a dark centre about 6′ across and central star of m. 12. The brightest parts of the ring are Nf. and Sp., and the faintest part is Np. where the luminous haze is broadest and four small stars are involved. The single prism image, just visible with 15 cm, indicates the gaseous nature; the nebula itself may be seen as a faint round haze with 7·5 cm.

1000. NGC 7492. This very distant globular cluster, estimated at about 30,000 pc, is completely isolated and, lying even farther from the central plane of the galaxy than the Magellan Clouds, may possibly be extra-galactic. It is a very large uncondensed cluster since the apparent diameter is 3·5′ and, as the integrated magnitude is only 12·3, it is a very faint telescopic object. However 20 cm will show it and with 30 cm it is a large round patch of faint fairly even haze showing evidence of very faint stars. This is a good test for a clear dark night; as a guide it lies between a faint star and a faint wide pair 7′ f., about half way somewhat S.

1004. NGC 7606. Photographs show this object as a fine edgewise spiral with narrow compact whorls. With 30 cm it is an elongated elliptical haze about 3′ × 1′ in pa. 150°, the central regions much brighter and showing easily a band in the prism; the extensions are faint and there is a small nucleus. 15 cm is needed to show the elongation and the general form is clear at 20 cm.

1005. 94 Aqr. This bright wide pair, yellow and orange, is a good object for small apertures; the angle is increasing very slowly. Similar proper motion indicates a connection but the period must be very long.

1012. R Aqr. Near maximum this variable of period 387 days is a bright orange red star in a rather barren field; the spectrum is fine, with a succession of bright and dark lines plainly evident with 15 cm. Merrill in 1919 discovered nebular lines in the spectrum and a blue companion (not seen yet) must be near to excite them. The surrounding nebulous glow is difficult to see.

1014. 107 Aqr. Since the first measures of this pair in 1823, change has been very slow; the separation has slightly increased and the angle lessened. It is a fine bright object, pale and deeper yellow, shown well by 7·5 cm. The proper motions are very similar and no doubt this is a physical system of long period.

Aquila (Aql)

Aquila, the eagle, is a moderately large constellation of area 652 sq. deg. It is of ancient origin and Ptolemy assigned nine stars to it, but the six southerly stars which he placed in the obsolete Antinous are now included in it. Aquila lies across the celestial equator in the Milky Way and is easily recognized by the bright pale yellow Altair with its two deeper yellow flanking stars β and γ, the former being the less bright. The centre of the constellation culminates at midnight about July 12th.

Apart from a number of fine pairs, Aquila as a Milky Way constellation is rather disappointing to the observer and it contains no Messier object. Of the five known open clusters, only NGC 6709 has any distinction as a telescopic object. There are two globular clusters, one heavily obscured by interstellar dust and the other, discovered at Palomar photographically, much beyond the reach of amateur instruments. The constellation is however rich in planetary nebulae, and several of these make interesting objects. Extra-galactic nebulae in this region are all small and faint.

827. Σ 2404. In a field spangled with stars the components of this unequal orange pair shine like gems, making a fine sight. Very little change has occurred since W. Struve measured them in 1829; he recorded the colours as yellow and blue, repeated by Webb with the note that the colours are remarkable, which shows how unreliable such estimates are when made with refractors.

829. NGC 6709. This group of medium bright stars about $15' \times 12'$ lies in a fine field and has little central condensation; there are three pointed lobes Np. and an orange star f. The cluster is fairly rich, but not effective with small apertures. R is about 700 pc.

845. ζ Aql. This brilliant pale yellow star so dominates the field that it will tax 30 cm to show the faint companion Nf.; it is useless to look for it unless definition is good on a clear night. Burnham discovered the pair in 1878 with the 26-inch refractor at Washington and there has been slow retrograde motion with increase in separation. It is likely that the stars are in orbit.

847. NGC 6751. In a field sprinkled with stars is a greyish rather diffuse disk of luminous haze about 20″ across, with no visible central star. 15 cm will show it but the single prism image needs more aperture. R is about 2,500 pc.

848. R Aql. This red star in a thinly sprinkled field with period from 302 to 329 days varies greatly in brightness. During the brighter range the prism shows a fine spectrum crossed by many strong well-marked dark bands.

852. NGC 6760. The faintness of the Milky Way background shows the very heavy obscuration which exists in the region of this globular cluster; it amounts to m. 5·4. The cluster is only 2,500 pc distant and yet is comparatively faint; it is about 2′ across with little central condensation and some very faint stars can be made out with 30 cm, while 15 cm shows only a dim round haze.

856. Σ 2489. Since W. Struve's measures in 1828 there has been little change in this pair and, as proper motion is small, not much is known about it yet. It is easy for small apertures and the fainter star looks reddish by contrast.

859. NGC 6778. This planetary nebula appears as a fairly bright luminous disk about 15″ across with ill-defined edges and single prism image. About 10′ N is a dark area 10′ × 4′ extending roughly Np.–Sf., outlined by faint field stars. Good aperture and a dark clear night are needed. R is given as 4,000 pc.

860. NGC 6781. In a field sprinkled with stars is a large faint grey object about 2′ across of even illumination and showing a single prism image. 15 cm is needed for it and if the distance of 2,900 pc is reliable, this is a very large planetary nebula about 1·5 pc in diameter.

861. 23 Aql. This bright deep yellow star has a whitish companion close Nf. which 7·5 cm will show with care. No real change has occurred since 1830. In 1905 Burnham found a third star (13·7 12″ 61°) which I have not been able to see.

863. NGC 6790. The tiny pale blue disk of this nebula can be seen amongst the scattered stars of the field, a star m. 11 being 30″ p. The single prism image can just be seen with 7·5 cm and is easy with 10·5 cm. R is 1,750 pc.

867. NGC 6803. The image of this planetary nebula is star like, showing a tiny disk only with high magnification. With two stars it forms an acute triangle 2′ long and the single prism image is just discernible with 10·5 cm. R is 1,750 pc.

868. NGC 6804. In a field of scattered stars is an elliptical luminous haze about 40″ across, pale grey and fairly even except for the diffuse edges. 20 cm shows the single prism image but 15 cm only the nebula itself, and dimly. R is 4,000 pc.

73

870. Σ 2545. This dainty close pair, pale and deep yellow, is converted to a triplet by a faint star Sf. (11·0 27″ 166°) which 7·5 cm will just show. The angle of the pair has slowly increased since 1829 and all 3 stars may be connected.

873. χ Aql. I have not found this bright deep yellow star easy to resolve, but 25 cm will do it in good conditions. It is a long period binary which O. Struve first measured in 1850 as 0·6″ and 75°, and there has been very little change since then.

878. π Aql. Dominating a field sown with medium and faint stars, this bright deep yellow star has a close companion Sf., the two just in contact with 10·5 cm. It is probably a binary system with little change since W. Struve's measures in 1829.

882. Σ 2587. This is a very pretty pair in a field sown with stars, and an easy object for small apertures. Change has been slow since 1828 and little is known about the stars yet.

884. Σ 2597. The stars of this yellow pair are closing with slow decrease in angle and I have found it difficult. In 1961 30 cm showed the fainter star very close f. and 25 cm was fairly certain, but good conditions are needed. This is no doubt a true binary and will repay watching.

890. Σ 2616. A fine pair in a field sown with stars, quite clearly seen with 7·5 cm. There has been no real change since W. Struve's measures in 1829 and the stars have evidently the same proper motion. Little is known of them yet.

891. β 57. This orange star shines like a gem in a field sown with stars and the faint companion close Sf. is visible with care with 7·5 cm. Change has been very slow since Dembowski's measures in 1875 and little is yet known about the pair.

894. Σ 2628. Both separation and angle seem to be decreasing very slowly since W. Struve measured this pair in 1830; both stars are yellow and small apertures show them well. Common proper motion suggests a long period binary.

900. Σ 2644. This white nearly equal pair looks clean and neat in a black field when shown with 7·5 cm. Change is very slow but separation and angle seem to be diminishing and similar proper motion indicates a physical connection.

Ara (Ara)

Ara, the altar, appears amongst the forty-eight constellations of Ptolemy as the censer, to which he assigned seven stars. It is a small group of area 237 sq. deg. lying in the Milky Way immediately S of the tail of Scorpius where a few third and fourth magnitude stars mark its position. The centre culminates at midnight about June 12th.

The Milky Way in this region is rich and bright, and in places obscured by dark nebular clouds sometimes showing faint luminosity; an example of this is NGC 6188. There are nine open clusters in Ara, the most effective being NGC 6193. The three globular clusters are all fine objects, and the brightest of the planetary nebulae is not difficult. The few extra-galactic nebulae outside the visible edge of the Milky Way are all faint.

671. R Ara. In a field sown profusely with stars is a fine combination of an elegant yellow close pair with a red star 4′ N. John Herschel measured the pair in 1836 as 4·0″ and 127° and there has been a slight diminution in both values since. It is likely that this is a ternary system, for A is an eclipsing binary of period 4·42 days.

672. NGC 6188. This region of the Milky Way is obscured by dark diffuse and also faintly luminous nebular material, so that the field is only thinly scattered with rather faint stars. A fairly bright star 20′ Sp. the centre of the bright cluster NGC 6193 is involved in faint nebulosity about 100″ across which extends irregularly towards the cluster and the brightest parts show gaseous character in the prism. A clear dark night and good aperture are needed for this object.

673. NGC 6193. This straggling cluster needs a large field; it shows remarkable long curved chains and lobes of stars with a small group near the centre. The field is beautiful and makes a good demonstration piece which is still effective with small apertures and there is some faint nebulosity involved. The brightest star is a close pair (5·6 8·5 1·5″ 20°) in which change is slow; in 1963 it was clearly resolved with 10·5 cm. R is about 500 pc.

680. Cor 201. In a field with many scattered stars on a rich faint ground is a dainty equal yellow pair, cleanly shown with 7·5 cm. First measured by Pollock in 1889, there has been no real change since. It seems to be a distant binary.

690. λ 316. This close pair was first measured by See in 1897 as 0·6″ and 179°; the angle has since decreased slightly and the separation increased. In 1963 the two star disks were clearly apart with 15 cm. Common proper motion indicates a connection between the stars. The Milky Way field is sown with stars.

713. Brs 13. This beautiful pair, deep yellow and orange, lies in a field sprinkled with faint stars. The components at present are in fairly rapid direct motion and form an easy object for small apertures, but in 1907 the pair was irresolvable while in 1947 Mt Stromlo found 4·9" and 223°. The period is not short.

717. NGC 6326. This small round nebula is quite conspicuous in a star sprinkled field; it is fairly well defined and brighter towards the centre, and two stars are very close N and f. The prism image is single and can just be made out with 10·5 cm. The nebula is 25" across and R is about 2,500 pc.

723. IC 4651. An irregular gathering of numerous stars fairly uniform in brightness, about 15' across with stragglers to 20'. The stars are in lines, curves and chains enclosing dark spaces so that the pattern is open without much condensation. 15 cm is needed to show the cluster well. R is about 1,200 pc.

725. γ Ara. 10·5 cm will just show the companion of this brilliant white star which dominates a well-sprinkled field. There has been no change in separation since John Herschel's measures in 1835 and only a small increase in angle. Little is known about these stars.

726. NGC 6352. In this fine field sown profusely with stars is one of the less-condensed type of globular cluster, irregularly round, about 2·5' across and resolved into very faint stars, some of which can be seen with 15 cm scattered through the haze and the outlying region. Absorption is here assessed as m. 2·4 and R is about 4,300 pc. It is surprising that John Herschel's thorough sweeping missed this conspicuous object.

728. h. 4949. This is a really fine pair in beautiful contrast with the surrounding starry field; the stars are pale yellow and clearly shown with 7·5 cm. John Herschel in 1835 found 3·2" and 268° and both values have slowly diminished since then. It is no doubt a binary system of long period.

731. NGC 6362. This globular cluster in a fine field extends with outliers about 4' across; it rises broadly to the centre and is beautifully resolved into faint stars on a hazy ground. This resolution is quite clear with 15 cm but 10·5 cm shows only granularity. The edges are very irregular with arcs and rays of faint stars. Absorption is assessed as m. 1·1 and R is about 6,300 pc.

733. I 40. In this fine field sown with stars on a profuse faint ground is a bright yellow star with a less bright orange star 4' Sf.; the yellow star has a companion wide Sp. which 10·5 cm will show with care. There has been little change since Innes measured the stars in 1900 and not much is known about them.

739. NGC 6397. On a clear dark night this cluster makes a wonderful sight, with bright scattered outliers over an area 20' wide round the well-condensed centre 3' across; there are orange stars in it and some of the outliers are in arcs and sprays. This is one of the best globular clusters for small telescopes, 7·5 cm resolving it well. It was discovered by Lacaille in 1752 who described it as a 'small star enveloped in a nebula', which is a comment on the quality of his telescope. Absorption is here about m. 1·5 and the cluster is relatively near with R about 2,000 pc (Plate 8).

747. h. 4978. This well-separated pair, pale yellow and ashy bluish, has shown no change since John Herschel measured it in 1835 and common proper motion suggests a binary with very long period. There is evidence of two spectra for A which may be a spectroscopic binary. 7·5 cm shows the companion with care.

Aries (Ari)

Aries, the first constellation of the zodiac, is a very ancient star group, and although known by a variety of names in the historical records of early peoples, seems usually to have represented a sheep or a ram. The modern name is due to the Romans for whom and the early Greeks it was associated with the legend of the golden fleece. Ptolemy recorded thirteen stars in Aries in A.D. 150, and five additional stars to the N. The area is 441 sq. deg., most of which lies N of the ecliptic and the constellation is easily recognized by the narrow triangle of the brightest stars. In the southern hemisphere the evening rising of this triangle, balanced on its narrow apex, marks the coming of summer. It is interesting to note that owing to the somewhat similar proper motions of α, β and γ Ari, the appearance of the triangle has altered little in the last precessional cycle of 26,000 years. It is very slowly extending in length and tilting away from the meridian due to the greater motion of α Ari to the east. The triangle culminates at midnight about October 20th.

There are some attractive pairs in Aries but otherwise no objects of telescopic interest except extra-galactic nebulae. None of these is really bright, the best being the spiral system NGC 772.

49. 1 Ari. Fine colour contrast, deep yellow and white, is shown by this elegant pair in conformity with spectral type; it is an easy object and little real change has occurred since W. Struve's measures in 1830.

50. γ Ari. This beautiful pair is one of the best known in the sky, and one of the first to be discovered; the pale yellow stars dominate a field well sprinkled with scattered stars. There has been no change since at least 1830 and common proper motion indicates a physical system of very long period.

55. NGC 772. Photographs show this object as a well-marked spiral system 11′ × 7′ in pa. 125° but all I see with 30 cm is a fairly bright round haze nearly 2′ across, rising much to the centre but with no real nucleus. It is a small faint hazy spot with 10·5 cm.

74. π Ari. Three stars almost in line have shown no change since the measures of W. Struve in 1832 and it is likely that they form a physical system. A is also a spectroscopic binary and Young in 1917 found a period of 3·85 days.

76. ε Ari. There has been a slow increase in both separation and angle of this pair since W. Struve measured it in 1830, but the period must be very long. The bright pale yellow stars should be separated cleanly with 7·5 cm.

Auriga (Aur)

Auriga, the wagoner, is a large constellation of ancient origin to which Ptolemy assigned fourteen stars. Its area is 657 sq. deg. and with a northern limit of 56° N, it is low in the sky and even partly hidden to many southern observers. The Milky Way passes across the Sp. corner and is here not conspicuous as it lies opposite in direction to the galactic centre in Ophiuchus, which gives it much less depth. The leader is the brilliant Capella (5^h $13\cdot0^m$; $+45°$ $57'$) with solar-type spectrum which gives a remarkable display of coruscating colour in the telescope when low on the northern horizon. This star is a spectroscopic binary of period 104 days and it culminates at midnight about December 9th.

Auriga contains nine open clusters, of which the three brightest are fine objects in the Messier list. There are two planetary nebulae, one of which is relatively easy, and a single globular cluster discovered photographically at Palomar which is beyond the reach of any but large instruments. Many fine pairs occur but no diffuse nebulae, and the few extra-galactic nebulae are small and faint.

139. ω Aur. This bright unequal pair, pale and deep yellow, is changing only very slowly with lessening separation and increasing angle. Common proper motion indicates a very long period binary.

148. Σ 644. In good conditions 10·5 cm will separate this close orange and white pair; if merely elongated the appearance of the ellipse is striking with one end orange and the other white. W. Struve measured the stars in 1828 as 1·6″ and 219° and subsequent change has been small; if binary the period must be long.

155. 14 Aur. This pale yellow star is a spectroscopic binary of period 3·79 days; many scattered stars are in the field and it has two well-separated companions. The brighter has similar proper motion and may be connected with A but the fainter lying N seems to be a field star, for the proper motion of A accounts for small changes which have occurred since W. Struve's measures in 1830.

166. NGC 1912. Discovered by Messier in 1764 this fine scattered cluster is 20′ across with a rather empty centre, and showing roughly the form of an oblique cross. The stars are numerous and elegantly dotted in arcs and small groups, the structure plain with 10·5 cm. R is about 900 pc.

170. NGC 1931. This curious object discovered by W. Herschel in 1793 appears as a bright round nebulous haze about 1′ across with indefinite edges; near the centre is a close triplet, the Np. star much the faintest, which 15 cm will show. This nebula is classed as galactic but it is apparently not gaseous for the prism extends it into a band. Perhaps it is a dust nebula, like that in the Pleiades; it is in a field sown with stars. R is estimated as 2,500 pc.

180. NGC 1960. This fine cluster, discovered by Messier in 1764, has a central region about 10′ across from which emerge several irregularly curved arms to give a roughly spiral pattern; the stars are numerous with a small pair near the centre. 10·5 cm shows the cluster well. R is about 1,300 pc.

198. NGC 2099. Small apertures give this beautiful rich cluster a nebulous appearance as remarked by Messier in 1764; it consists however only of stars extending with outliers about 25′ across. An orange star is near the centre which is considerably concentrated, with a lobed pattern and radiating arms, the whole effect very fine. R is about 800 pc.

201. IC 2149. This bluish planetary nebula is markedly elliptical, about 12″ × 8″ in 75°; the hydrogen spectrum is strong and a second prism image near the fused images of ionized oxygen can be made out. The planetary character is evident with 10·5 cm with a faint prism image. R is about 870 pc.

202. θ Aur. Since the measures of O. Struve in 1871 there has been slow increase in separation and steady diminution in angle for this long period binary system. 7·5 cm shows the companion close to the brilliant pale yellow primary even when low altitude or poor definition renders large apertures ineffective.

209. 41 Aur. The scattered star field is dominated by this bright pale yellow pair which is very easy with 7·5 cm. There has been little change since W. Struve's measures in 1830 and similar proper motions indicate a binary system.

Bootes (Boo)

Bootes, the ploughman, was used as the title of this large northern constellation by the ancient Greeks nearly 3,000 years ago. Ptolemy assigned twenty-three stars to it and the modern area is 907 sq. deg. The leader is the brilliant orange-yellow Arcturus (14ʰ 13·4ᵐ; + 19° 27′), a star with about 100 times the luminosity of the sun and at a distance of 12·5 pc showing the large proper motion of 2·3" annually. The centre of the constellation culminates at midnight about April 30th.

Bootes is far removed from the Milky Way and no open clusters nor planetary nebulae occur in it. The single globular cluster though large is faint, and of the many extra-galactic nebulae scattered through it, only one is sufficiently bright to make a good telescopic object. There are however many fine pairs.

532. NGC 5248. Photographs disclose a fine bright spiral nebula 8′ × 6′ in pa. 140° with many condensations but 30 cm shows only a conspicuous diffuse haze about 2·5′ × 1·5′ in a field with a few scattered stars. This rises broadly and then rapidly to a small nucleus somewhat Sp. the centre. 15 cm shows a large dim formless haze which is perceptible with 10·5 cm.

536. I Boo. This bright pale yellow star, with another less bright 3·5′ N, has a companion close Sf. which looks reddish; 7·5 cm will show it with care. Both angle and separation have very slowly diminished since W. Struve's measures in 1831, and shared proper motion indicates a long period binary.

545. Σ 1785. The period of this direct motion orange pair seems to be about 155 years; the stars were closest in 1922 at 1·1″ and 21° while the discoverer W. Struve found 3·5″ and 164° in 1830. At present it is very easy with 7·5 cm; the spectroscopic parallax gives a distance of only 12 pc.

558. NGC 5466. This globular cluster is of the uncondensed scattered type similar to NGC 7492 in Aquarius but not nearly so remote; it is a large irregularly round cloud of numerous very faint stars about 5′ across, and 25 cm will show some resolution while 20 cm will only reach the object itself in good conditions. R is about 15,000 pc.

567. Σ 1835. Dominating a field of scattered stars, this beautiful bright pair, white and deep yellow, has shown only slight increases in angle and separation since W. Struve's measures in 1832. The system is ternary since B was found by Burnham in 1889 to be a very close pair of period 40·5 years; with maximum separation of only 0·3″, few amateurs could resolve it.

577. π Boo. The angle of this very fine pale yellow pair is slowly increasing with little change in separation since W. Struve measured it in 1830. It is probably a long period binary and makes an excellent object for small apertures.

580. ζ Boo. This bright pale yellow binary system was measured by W. Struve in 1830 as 1·2″ and 309°; the angle diminished slowly and the separation steadily until in 1897–8 the stars could not be resolved. When they separated again in 1899 the angle was 341° so that B had passed through three quadrants in less than 4 years, indicating a very eccentric orbit. The period seems to be about 126 years and the stars are now closing with slow diminution of angle. In 1961 15 cm just resolved them.

583. ε Boo. A well-known demonstration object for small apertures, this beautiful pair, deep yellow and white (or bluish by contrast) was measured by W. Struve in 1829 as 2·6″ and 321°. The angle is slowly increasing and the stars form a binary system with common proper motion.

587. Σ 1884. This close unequal pair is not difficult to resolve with 7·5 cm. The separation has slowly increased since W. Struve found 1·2″ and 52° in 1829 but there is little angular change. Common proper motion indicates a long period binary.

590. ξ Boo. The colours of this beautiful binary are striking, being yellow and deep orange. The period is about 150 years; the stars were closest at 2·1″ in 1914 and will be widest at 7·2″ in 1982. The motion is retrograde and the distance from the sun only 6·8 pc, so that this is one of the best-known pairs.

603. Σ 1910. These two dwarf yellow stars form no doubt a binary of long period. It is an attractive object with slowly increasing separation but no real change in angle since the measures of W. Struve in 1832.

618. μ Boo. This interesting ternary system is formed of a bright wide pair, pale and deep yellow, which has not changed appreciably since 1834. The less bright star is a close pair which closed to 0·4″ in 1860 and is now widening with diminishing angle; the period seems to be about 260 years. In 1961 at 2·0″ and 24° B was clearly resolved with 7·5 cm.

Caelum (Cae)

This constellation is one of the southern groups designated by Lacaille in 1752; it represents the engraving tool or burin used by craftsmen in metal and ivory, and consists of about a score of inconspicuous stars in an area of 125 sq. deg. between Eridanus and Columba. The centre culminates at midnight about November 30th.

The two brightest stars are α and γ Cae, both of which are pairs; there are no clusters and the only nebula of interest is NGC 1679 about which little is known.

122. h. 3650. This elegant unequal pair lies in a field well sprinkled with stars; it is an easy object for 7·5 cm and there has been little change since the measures of John Herschel in 1836.

127. α Cae. The faint companion of this bright yellow star is difficult and needs 30 cm on a clear dark night of good definition to show it. Both separation and angle seem to be increasing slowly. It was discovered at Harvard in 1898 and I find that the companions of many of these Harvard pairs are fainter than the designated magnitudes. Little is known about this pair.

132. NGC 1679. This curious object is a round diffuse fairly bright nebulous haze about 2′ across in which three faint stars are immersed with what appears to be a nucleus in the f. part. It is evidently not gaseous as the prism extends it into a band and, as it has not been classed as extra-galactic, may be a dust nebula in the Milky Way system. Discovered by John Herschel in 1835, it is faintly visible with 15 cm.

142. γ Cae. Missed by John Herschel and first measured by Jacob in 1852, this fine unequal pair, orange and white, has shown little change. Common proper motion indicates a long period binary; 7·5 cm shows the fainter star clearly.

Camelopardus (Cam)

The long faint constellation of the giraffe was formed in 1614 by Bartschius. It stretches almost from the north pole to Lynx and Auriga, and there is little to distinguish it in the sky. The area is 757 sq. deg. and the centre culminates at midnight about December 23rd.

There are many double stars scattered over this wide area, and interest centres mainly in them and in the brighter extra-galactic nebulae. In the corner of the constellation encroaching on the Milky Way near Perseus, seven galactic clusters are recognized but only NGC 1502 makes a good telescopic object. No globular clusters occur, but two of the planetary nebulae are given in the addendum with other objects of interest.

Cancer (Cnc)

Cancer, the crab, is the fourth constellation of the ancient zodiac to which Ptolemy assigned thirteen stars, one of which he noted as a nebulous collection. This was in fact the open cluster Praesepe which is one of the distinguishing marks to the unaided eye of this inconspicuous constellation. The modern area is 506 sq. deg. and none of the stars is brighter than magnitude 4. The centre culminates at midnight about January 30th.

Apart from a number of pairs and the interesting ternary system ζ Cnc, telescopic interest is limited to the two fine clusters M 44 and M 67. Neither diffuse nor planetary nebulae are known and no globular clusters, while only one of the many small and faint extra-galactic nebulae is bright enough for mention; this is NGC 2775.

287. Σ 1177. W. Struve measured this long period binary in 1828 as 3·5″ and 355°, since when the angle has slowly diminished. 7·5 cm shows it well as two small white points in a black field.

294. ζ Cnc. This fine ternary system makes an interesting telescopic object. The period of the close pair is about 60 years; in 1961 I found 1·2″ and 357°, and 15 cm resolved it well. The motion is retrograde as is that of the third star, although in this case so slow that the period must be several hundred years. From irregularities in the motion of C however, the presence of a dark companion in circular orbit of about 18 years has been inferred. The stars are deep yellow and the distance from the sun about 24 pc.

299. ϕ^2 Cnc. In a sparsely sprinkled field, this attractive pale yellow pair was measured by W. Struve in 1829 as 4·6″ and 212°, since when both values have increased very slowly. It is no doubt a binary system of long period.

308. Σ 1245. A good object for small apertures, this deep yellow unequal pair lies in a field sprinkled with stars. There has been no real motion since W. Struve's measures in 1832 and common proper motion indicates a long period binary. A is also a spectroscopic pair of period 14·296 days.

310. NGC 2632. Praesepe is rather too large for the telescope and requires a wide field. It is a very open and scattered cluster with three bright triangles, one of which has a fine orange star with less bright wide reddish companion Nf. in beautiful contrast with the other stars. Messier noted the cluster in 1769 but it was known to Hipparchus. R is about 150 pc.

317. ι Cnc. Fine colour contrast, orange yellow and pale blue, is shown by this bright wide pair, although the spectrum of B indicates that it is actually pale yellow. There has been no change since 1828 and the stars probably form a binary of long period.

321. NGC 2682. Noted by Messier in 1780, this really fine group of medium bright stars about 15′ across is well differentiated from the field; it contains an orange star Nf. and a red star f., both clear with 10·5 cm. There is evidence of curvilinear pattern and R is about 700 pc.

325. 57 Cnc. This long period binary shows no certain change in separation but slow lessening in angle since the measures of W. Struve in 1830. Both stars are orange, with the disks just in contact with 10·5 cm.

332. RS Cnc. The period of this fairly bright pale reddish variable star has been given from 120 to 239 days, so that it is apparently not regular. The spectrum is crossed by heavy absorption bands which give it almost a sectioned appearance. This can be seen with care with 10·5 cm.

333. NGC 2775. Photographs show this object as a slightly elliptical spiral 2′ long with bright stellar nucleus, and 30 cm discloses a conspicuous round haze about 1·5′ across, rising much to a bright nucleus spread into a band by the prism, but with no sign of structure. 10·5 cm shows the nebula clearly though faintly.

Canes Venatici (CVn)

Most of the stars of Canes Venatici, the hunting dogs, were once included in the ancient constellation of Ursa Major and were first formed into a separate group of twenty-three stars by Hevelius in his *Uranographia* published in 1690 after his death. It lies between Ursa Major and Bootes, low in the sky for most southern observers, and the area of the modern constellation is 465 sq. deg. The centre culminates at midnight about April 7th.

Canes Venatici lies in a region rich in extra-galactic nebulae, many of which make fine telescopic objects. It contains also the beautiful globular cluster M 3, but there are no galactic nebulae, either diffuse or planetary, and no open star clusters. Southern observers should not neglect clear dark nights with good definition low in the north when this constellation is above the horizon, for it well repays study.

445. 2 CVn. There has been no change in this orange and slate-blue pair since the measures of W. Struve in 1832, and common proper motion indicates a very long period binary. It is an easy object; the spectral colour of B is yellow.

446. NGC 4244. This edgewise spiral nebula appears as a faint streak of haze about 12′ × 1′ in pa. 45° with a somewhat brighter diffuse elliptical centre. It is barely visible to me with 20 cm and like all faint nebulae the dimensions are more evident by moving the telescope. Photographs give the size as 18′ × 3′ with an irregular axial dark lane.

449. NGC 4258. Photographs show an elongated spiral about 20′ × 6′ in pa. 165° with bright lengthened nucleus. Although very low in the sky, I see a large elongated fairly bright haze with diffuse elliptical nucleus, and it looks as if it would be an impressive object for northern observers. 10·5 cm shows it dimly. R is estimated as about 5 million pc.

486. MGC 4631. This edgewise spiral, which even 10·5 cm shows as a long faint hazy streak, is about 12′ × 1′ in pa. 85° with rather even light but it seems broader and brighter f., as if there may be absorption along the Np. edge. Photographs show a nebula 19′ × 4·5′ with the brightest region 1′ f. the centre, and an irregular dark axial lane.

488. NGC 4656–7. William Herschel in 1787 recorded this remarkable object as two nebulae but 'Both join and form the letter S'. Photographs show a single nebula 9′ × 1′ in pa. 33° with bright elliptical nucleus, the Nf. end corresponding to NGC 4657 being bright and sharply curved and the Sp. end wider and faint. This is an example of an irregular unsymmetrical eg. nebula, but not suited to small apertures. 30 cm has shown me a fairly bright centre 1′ × 0·5′ with a faint pointed ray Nf. curved at the brighter tip; the Sf. extension is difficult to see.

495. NGC 4736. This object, discovered by Méchain in 1781, is in large instruments a beautiful spiral nebula with bright closely packed whorls. 30 cm shows a very bright compressed haze about 1·5′ across with mottled centre, looking like an unresolved globular cluster; it is an easy object for small apertures. R is estimated as about 6 million pc.

501. α CVn. An excellent object for small apertures, this wide pale yellow pair has shown no real change since the measures of W. Struve in 1830. The proper motions are similar and denote a long period binary. R is about 40 pc.

513. NGC 5005. William Herschel discovered this elliptical spiral nebula in 1785. I see an extended haze about 3′ × 1′ in pa. 65° with bright elongated centre, but without the dark lanes Sf. shown by photographs. 15 cm shows this object reasonably well in good conditions.

515. OΣ 261. This moderately bright pair is clearly resolved with 7·5 cm; the separation is slowly increasing with diminishing angle since O. Struve's measures in 1843. Common proper motion denotes a long period binary.

518. NGC 5055. Méchain discovered this object in 1779 and recorded that it became invisible with even feeble illumination of his cross wires. Photographs show a beautiful spiral with narrow compact whorls, but all I see with 30 cm is an elliptical haze about 3′ × 2′ in pa. 100°, rising broadly to the centre which has a tiny nucleus difficult to see. In good conditions the nebula is easy with 10·5 cm. R is estimated as 4 million pc.

526. NGC 5194–5. This is the first extra-galactic nebula to be recognized as a spiral; Lord Rosse saw it as such in 1845 with his 6 ft mirror. It was discovered by Messier in 1773 when following a comet and he noted the companion as a small star. Photographs show a wonderful system of stars and dark matter in two immense spiral arms, one of which passes over the smaller irregular companion. The brighter stars of the spiral are bluish and those of the other are reddish. Unfortunately for most southern observers this object culminates at very low altitude; all I have seen with 30 cm are two bright round hazy spots 5′ apart in pa. 20°, respectively about 2′ and 1′ across. Smaller apertures show correspondingly less. R is about 2 million pc.

533. 25 CVn. This pale yellow binary has been under observation since W. Struve in 1831 found 1·1″ and 76°. It appeared single in 1859 and the stars are still slowly widening. The motion is retrograde and the period is about 240 years. At present 10·5 cm will resolve the pair in good conditions.

538. NGC 5272. This beautiful object can be plainly resolved with 10·5 cm, and even 7·5 cm will show a few faint outliers. It is very bright, round and symmetrical, and sparkles with innumerable starry points right to the broad centre 3' across while the outliers extend to 7' and probably are thinly scattered much farther. It was discovered by Messier in 1764 but he saw no stars in it. R is 12,000 pc.

Canis Major (CMa)

Canis Major, the large dog, is a conspicuous constellation lying mainly just S of the Milky Way between Orion and the long train of bright stars formerly composing Argo Navis. It is one of the Ptolemaic groups to which were assigned eighteen stars. The modern area is 380 sq. deg. which is dominated by the brilliant white Sirius culminating at midnight about January 1st.

This constellation is rich in fine objects for the telescope. Several double stars are particulary beautiful, and amongst the fifteen open clusters is the lovely group NGC 2362 surrounding 30 CMa. NGC 2359 is a diffuse gaseous nebula and IC 2165 is one of the four planetary nebulae which is available for small apertures. There are no globular clusters but several extra-galactic nebulae occur and two are given as examples.

211. NGC 2207. This conspicuous hazy elliptical nebula about 3' × 2' in pa. 85° lies in a field with many scattered stars; it has a well-condensed nucleus which looks elongated p. A broad band in the prism demonstrates its non-gaseous nature. 15 cm shows the elliptical shape well.

212. Σ 3116. 7·5 cm shows clearly the faint ashy companion close Nf. this bright pale yellow star, with an orange red star 5' Sp. The angle has increased slightly since W. Struve's measures in 1831 but the proper motion is very small and not much is known of this pair.

213. IC 2165. The brightest object in a field of scattered stars is this small round pale blue planetary nebula about 7" across, which shows a single prism image just perceptible with 7·5 cm. The light looks even with no central star. R is estimated as about 3,000 pc.

217. β 753. Burnham discovered this close pair in 1892 and little change has since taken place except very slow retrograde motion. The proper motion is small and little is known about this pair yet. 20 cm will resolve it in good conditions.

223. ν CMa. The colours of this wide pair, orange yellow and bluish, are clear with 7·5 cm; it lies in a field sown with stars, including some pairs and linear triplets. No real change has occurred since J. South measured the stars in 1821 and similar proper motions indicate a long period binary.

227. S 534. This is another of South's pairs, measured in 1825 and with no perceptible change since; similar proper motions point to a very long period binary. The field is beautiful, sown profusely with stars dominated by the pair.

228. α CMa. Sirius is exceeded only by some of the planets in apparent brightness and the history of the theoretical prediction and practical discovery of the small massive companion is well known. The period is 50·0 years; closest approach 3·7″ and 189° was in 1946 and widest separation 11·4″ and 61° is in 1974. The visibility of the small star depends greatly on good definition even when well separated from the primary; when close it is difficult in the largest instruments. Burnham has seen it well with 15 cm but I find 20 cm more certain, and a dark neutral filter is a great help in reducing the excessive glare. The spectrum is fine, crossed by four broad dark bars of hydrogen in red, blue and violet. R is 2·7 pc.

230. NGC 2287. This fine open cluster, recorded by Messier in 1765, was however known to Flamsteed much earlier, being in fact visible to the unaided eye. It is about 30′ across and contains some delicate pairs and triplets with a fine yellow star near the centre. R is about 400 pc.

231. AC 4. Dembowski measured this close pair in 1877 and the only change has been a steady increase in angle. The stars appear to form a binary system although the proper motion is small. 15 cm shows both stars, but not easily.

233. β 324. This pale yellow star is a close pair just separable with 10·5 cm which has shown little change since 1877. It is in a fine starry field with a wide white companion p. and a wide less unequal pair 4·5′ S. The proper motion is so small that little is known of the pair yet.

236. μ CMa. W. Struve in 1831 found 3·2″ and 343° for this pair; subsequent measures are rather erratic but there has clearly been little change and the stars probably form a long period binary. It is a beautiful orange pair in effective contrast with a fine field, and 7·5 cm shows it well.

237. B 122. Discovered by van den Bos in 1926, this close pair has shown little change since, but the stars are evidently connected by common proper motion. It is a bright deep yellow star in a starry field and 15 cm will resolve it.

238. ϵ CMa. This brilliant white star has a deep yellow companion well clear Sf. which 7·5 cm will show with attention; the field is fine, with many

87

scattered stars. Maclear measured this pair in 1850 and there has been no real change since; the proper motion is very small and little is known about it.

242. β 328. This bright white star has a wide companion N which looks fainter than m. 9 to me. The close pair was measured by Dembowski in 1875 as 0·3″ and 128°; the motion is steadily retrograde and although the separation has increased it does not seem to be changing much at present. This is no doubt a true binary, with doubt about whether the third star is connected. 20 cm will just resolve the close pair.

249. h. 3945. A really fine field is dominated by this well-separated pair, orange and pale bluish (by contrast), which small apertures show very well. Both angle and separation have slowly diminished since John Herschel measured the stars in 1837 but it is not clear yet if they are connected. However the spectroscopic parallax for each star indicates a distance of about 77 pc.

250. NGC 2359. Discovered by W. Herschel in 1785, this curious gaseous nebula was compared 51 years later by J. Herschel to 'the profile of a bust (head, neck and shoulders)'. It is a large rather faint even nebulosity in a fine field sown with stars, many of which shine through it. The rounded portion well defined N is about 6′ across, with a long edge straight in pa. 45° about 9′ long. 10·5 cm shows the object faintly but more aperture is needed to see the form well. R is not known.

252. NGC 2360. A beautiful open cluster of fairly bright stars nearly 20′ across, well concentrated towards the centre, and merging into the rich field with long irregular rays. It is a most attractive object, rich and delicate with 10·5 cm. R is about 800 pc.

253. NGC 2362. This most beautiful cluster contains about forty stars grouped round the very bright white 30 CMa which is set like a jewel in their midst. This star is a spectroscopic binary of period 154·8 days and near it are two companions (10·0 8″ 90°; 11·2 14″ 78°) forming an elegant triplet, both of which 7·5 cm will show with close attention. The cluster is irregularly round and makes a charming telescopic object. R is about 1300 pc.

256. See 78. This curious object is an orange red star immersed in a small orange nebula; the haze is more marked p. and in it is a small condensation or star (11·7 2·4″ 293°). The star itself was found by van den Bos in 1926 to be a close pair (7·7 9·2 0·52″ 171°) which I have not been able to resolve. Other faint stars near have been thought variable. The nebula does not seem to be gaseous; perhaps it is a dust nebula shining by reflected star light.

257. NGC 2380. In a fine field sown thickly with stars, mostly not bright and many in little groups, is a small round haze hardly 30″ across with a fairly bright nucleus. The prism extends it into a band, so that it is not gaseous but probably extra-galactic. 20 cm is needed to show it clearly.

259. NGC 2384. In this glorious region, spangled thickly with stars in bright knots on a profuse background, this is the Sf. of two clusters about 7′ apart, each about 4′ across. A fine orange star (8·0 9·5 6″ 211°) is Nf. and even small apertures will show something of these features. R is about 2,400 pc and for the Np. cluster (NGC 2383) is about 1,500 pc.

261. β 332. In this beautiful field sown with stars in many small pairs and groups, a bright deep yellow star has two well-separated white companions Np. and Sf. Higher magnification with 20 cm shows it to be a close pair, the fainter star white. There has been little change in the pair since Dembowski's measures in 1875 and the other stars have not altered much since 1832. Little is known about this group since the proper motion of the primary is very small.

Canis Minor (CMi)

The constellation of Canis Minor, the small dog, contains only 183 sq. deg.; it was known to the ancients as the companion of the larger animal and two stars were assigned to it, by which it is easily recognized. The brighter of these is Procyon ($7^h 36 \cdot 7^m$; $+5° 21'$. 0·5 dF3), a brilliant yellow star about five times more luminous than the sun and lying 3·4 pc distant. The small companion m. 13·5 and mean separation 5″ is quite beyond the capacity of amateur telescopes owing to the overpowering light of the primary. The period from proper motion studies is about 40 years, and from spectroscopic evidence 40·23 years. Procyon culminates at midnight about January 14th.

No objects of telescopic interest are found in this constellation except a few binary stars, of which two are given.

260. η CMi. This bright yellow star in a well-sprinkled field has a faint companion close Nf. which 10·5 cm will show with close attention. There has been no real change since Dembowski's measures in 1875 but shared proper motion indicates a binary system. Some scattered stars Nf. were recorded by William Herschel in 1785 as a cluster, subsequently NGC 2394, but it is not included amongst open clusters now.

273. Σ 1126. Following Procyon about 12′, this pale yellow pair has shown slow direct motion and slow closing since W. Struve's measures in 1829. Common proper motion indicates a binary of long period; at present 15 cm resolves the stars clearly and 10·5 cm makes the dual nature apparent.

Capricornus (*Cap*)

Capricornus, the goat, is the tenth constellation of the zodiac and it is curious that in ancient times the animal was usually represented with the tail of a fish. Ptolemy assigned twenty-eight stars to this group which is not conspicuous but easily recognized by the two stars α and β, following Sagittarius, the former being a pair to the unaided eye. The modern area is 414 sq. deg. and the centre of the constellation culminates at midnight about August 5th.

There are some interesting double stars in Capricornus and the beautiful globular cluster M 30, but no diffuse or planetary nebulae occur and no open clusters. The extra-galactic nebulae are almost without exception faint and difficult objects.

905. α Cap. In a field sprinkled with scattered stars are two bright golden stars which however are not connected, the proper motions being different. The less bright has a reddish companion wide Sp., easily shown by 7·5 cm; the following brighter star has a faint close companion Sf. which 15 cm will show with care and 20 cm exhibits as a very close pair (11·2 11·5 1″ 237°). There has been very little change in any of these pairs since discovery.

909. β Cap. This is a brilliant yellow star with a very wide white companion Sp.; the stars move together and have not changed appreciably since the measures of W. Struve in 1835. The brilliant star is a spectroscopic ternary with period 1374·1 days for A–BC and 8·68 days for B–C; the three stars are a remarkable mixture of spectral types, for A is a G0 giant, B is a normal B8 star and C a main sequence G5 dwarf. Also Burnham in 1883 during a lunar occultation discovered the white star to have a close companion (6 10 0·85″ 106°) which has since shown slow retrograde motion with some increase in separation; it is difficult but 30 cm will show it very close Sf. on a good night. This system is thus composed of five connected stars. Between the two bright ones somewhat N is a faint point which John Herschel discovered to be a pair (13·0 13·4 6″ 322°) and in 1830 recommended Admiral Smyth to try with his 5·9-inch refractor, remarking that only a telescope which showed this pair would have any chance with the satellites of Uranus. This was too difficult for Smyth, but 30 cm shows it clearly in good conditions—a very delicate object because of the proximity of bright stars.

912. π Cap. This bright white star has a white close companion Sf. which 7·5 cm shows well, a fine pair in a field of widely scattered stars. This is probably a binary, for no real change has occurred since 1846 and the proper motion of A must be shared by the other star.

913. ρ Cap. This bright yellow star, with another 4·5′ Sf. and orange, dominates a field of a few scattered stars; it has a rather faint companion measured by South in 1823 as 4·0″ and 177°, since when both values have slowly decreased. However in 1959–61 I could find no trace whatever of the small star in good conditions, so that the separation was beyond the capacity of 30 cm. The proper motion of A cannot have brought this about, and this pair will be interesting to watch.

914. *o* Cap. A fine striking combination, this bright wide unequal pale yellow pair is well suited to small apertures. Common proper motion indicates a physical connection, for there has been no real change since South's measures in 1823.

948. β 271. This attractive pair, deep yellow and whitish (in spite of spectral type) is well shown by 7·5 cm; it lies in a field of scattered stars which it far outshines. It was measured in 1878 at Cincinnati Observatory as 2·2″ and 231°, so that both values are increasing. Common proper motion is large and denotes a binary.

952. ζ Cap. Dominating a field of scattered stars, this brilliant golden yellow star has a faint companion wide Nf. which may be only a field star but is given as a test which 20 cm will show in the glare of A. See measured this pair in 1897 as 21″ and 14° and, if there is no connection, the proper motion of A should very slowly diminish the separation and increase the angle.

958. NGC 7099. Messier discovered this beautiful cluster in 1764 but was unable to see any stars in it; it lies in a fine contrasting field. The well-resolved centre is compressed and two short straight rays of stars emerge Np. while from the N edge irregular streams of stars come out almost spirally f. With outliers the cluster is nearly 4′ across. Resolution is just apparent with 7·5 cm and clear with 10·5 cm. R is about 11,500 pc.

Carina (Car)

Carina, the keel, is an extended constellation of area 494 sq. deg. formed by Gould in 1879 from the southern portion of the very large ancient group of Argo Navis, to which Ptolemy had assigned forty-five stars in all. The Milky Way passes through the Nf. region; it contains many bright stars and the leader Canopus (6^h 22·8^m; − 52° 40′) is second only to Sirius in apparent brightness but far superior in luminosity since its distance from the sun is much greater. This star was well known to the ancients, for it rises clear above the horizon at Alexandria and its declination has changed little in the past 2,000 years. The centre of the constellation culminates at midnight about January 30th.

Carina is very rich in objects for small telescopes, some of which are shown against magnificent star fields. There is a fine series of double stars and at least thirty-one open star clusters are known, including NGC 3532 which John Herschel described as 'the most brilliant object of its kind I have ever seen', while the single globular cluster NGC 2808 is a beautiful object. There are six planetary nebulae and several diffuse gaseous nebulae, including the wonderful region round η Car known as NGC 3372. As might be expected in an area involved in the Milky Way, extra-galactic nebulae are faint and inconspicuous; none of the ten examined, all in the p. portion of the constellation, was sufficiently bright to merit close attention.

240. Δ 39. 7·5 cm will resolve this bright pale yellow star. The components have shown very slow approach and increase in angle since John Herschel's measures in 1836, and common proper motion indicates that they are connected.

255. Rmk 6. The stars of this fine and easy binary are both dwarfs; separation has slightly diminished with slow steady increase in angle since 1835 and the period must be long. In the same field 8′ Nf. is another pair h. 3958 which is wide and easy.

284. NGC 2516. This beautiful open cluster, at least 50′ across, needs a large field and makes then a glorious sight with its scattered groups and irregular sprays of stars, effective for small apertures. A dainty pair h. 4031 (7·8 8·7 6″ 358°) is Sf. from the centre and another, h. 4027 (10·0 10·2 9″ 115°), is 10′ p. R is about 350 pc.

297. Rmk 8. Measures of this pair are somewhat erratic since those of Melbourne Observatory in 1877 but there has been little apparent change. It is a beautiful easy object, whitish and deep yellow, in a field of scattered stars. Similar proper motions probably denote a binary of long period.

311. h. 4128. John Herschel measured this pair in 1836 and both separation and angle have slowly diminished; if unshared by B, the proper motion of A would have caused considerable alteration so that this must be a binary system. The field is sown thickly with stars and 15 cm shows the pale yellow stars clearly apart.

313. h. 4130. The stars of this fine easy unequal pair, pale yellow and reddish, have common proper motion and are apparently connected; the angle is slowly increasing with little change in separation. The field is sown thickly with stars.

318. Rmk 9. It is likely that these two white stars form a binary of long period; they decorate a field sprinkled with stars on a faint profuse ground. Change has been small since the measures of John Herschel in 1836.

331. IC 2448. This conspicuous planetary nebula was missed by John Herschel and discovered by Fleming spectroscopically; it is 8″ across and the brightest object in a field of scattered stars. Even 7·5 cm shows the single prism image plainly. R is about 1,800 pc.

337. NGC 2808. In a fine field this beautiful object is a splendid example of the symmetrical strongly compressed type of globular cluster, composed of innumerable faint stars. It is about 5′ across and 15 cm will resolve it; to smaller apertures it is a bright nebulous haze with strong central condensation. R is about 7,500 pc.

343. NGC 2867. This bright pale blue planetary nebula lies in a field profusely spangled with stars; it is round, about 8″ across, of very even light with no visible central star. Even 7·5 cm will pick it out easily from the field and show the single prism image. R is about 800 pc.

349. R Car. This long period variable is a giant star of Mira type; it is orange red and near maximum dominates a delicate field sown with stars. The spectrum is very complex with many dark bands, and bright lines in green and blue. The period is about 309 days.

351. IC 2501. In a beautiful starry field this almost stellar planetary nebula shows a disk about 2″ across with sufficient magnification, and the single prism image is bright and clear. It was discovered spectroscopically by Fleming at Harvard Observatory, but even 7·5 cm will disclose the minute prism image plainly. R is about 1,650 pc.

356. υ Car. Since the measures of John Herschel in 1836 there has been no real change in this very fine pair, and the proper motions are sufficiently similar to indicate a long period binary. It is an admirable object for small apertures and a small pair h. 4252 (9·3 9·5 12″ 303°) about 5′ Sf. is also easy.

359. NGC 3114. Needing a large field and low magnification, this cluster is very beautiful even with small apertures; the stars are very numerous on the dark sky in elegant pairs, triplets and small groups but with little central condensation. R is about 500 pc.

360. Hrg 47. Proper motion is very small and little is known about this pair discovered by Hargrave in 1833; the only change has been some increase in separation. I find that 15 cm is needed to see the companion clearly, and the field on a dark night is really lovely.

364. IC 2553. This is another of the small planetary nebulae discovered spectroscopically by Fleming at Harvard; in a field sown thickly with stars it may be seen at once by its pale blue disk about 5″ across and the prism gives a single bright image which even 7·5 cm will show as a minute point of light. R is about 360 pc.

365. S Car. Near maximum this Mira-type variable of period about 150 days is a bright orange red star in a lovely field sown profusely with stars. The spectrum shows broad bands in red and orange, and others less marked in green and blue.

371. NGC 3199. John Herschel in 1834 discovered this remarkable gaseous nebula; it is a large diffuse fairly bright broad crescent about $7' \times 3'$, convex Sp. and well defined Nf. by a dark bay, with many stars involved. The field is beautiful, sown with small pairs and triplets in a striking manner. 15 cm shows the form of the nebula faintly but definitely. R is not known.

374. NGC 3211. In a beautiful starry field is a small even pale blue disk about 10″ across, fairly bright with no visible central star and a single prism image. It may be picked up easily with 10·5 cm, but both nebula and prism image need care with 7·5 cm. R is about 2,100 pc.

376. h. 4306. There has been slow retrograde motion but little change in separation of these stars since John Herschel measured them in 1836; they make an attractive object in a field sown with fainter stars.

382. IC 2581. The centre of this beautiful field is the bright yellow star CPD 3256 (4·9 F1) round which is a small spiral of stars ending in a delicate triplet. There is little separation of a cluster from the field in which are many fine groups needing at least 15 cm for effective display. R is about 1,000 pc.

387. NGC 3293. Marked concentric structure is shown by this beautiful open star group which is somewhat angularly round and about 5′ across; it is bright, with stars of different colours. R is about 900 pc (Plate 3).

390. NGC 3324. This is an extensive nebulous haze without much concentration, fairly bright but very irregular and only well defined on the edge Np.; it lies in a very rich star field and is more marked round the small pair h. 4338 (8·4 9·5 6″ 90°) of spectral type Oe5 which seems to provide the exciting radiation for the gas cloud. 15 cm will show the brighter regions of the nebula. R is about 3,000 pc.

391. Δ 94. This field is magnificent, spangled with stars in small groups and arcs, and dominated by an orange star with less bright white companion; even with small apertures it is a fine sight. The pair has shown no change since John Herschel measured it in 1836 and common proper motion indicates a binary system.

392. Gls 152. A fine wide unequal pair, orange and white, in a beautiful field sown profusely with stars. Since Russell's measures in 1871 both separation and angle have slowly increased but the proper motion of A may account for this and the stars may be unconnected.

396. NGC 3372. η Car with its associated star clusters and the great diffuse gaseous nebula enveloping it form one of the finest telescopic objects; on a clear dark night the region is beautiful beyond description, even for small apertures. The nebula is diversified by prominent dark lanes which indicate absorbing matter and it extends in irregular luminous clouds far beyond a large field. The bright orange η Car is surrounded by an orange red nebula about 3″ wide, just visible with 10·5 cm, and the spectrum of the star shows numerous bands with the red H α shining like a tiny lamp at one end; this too can just be seen with 10·5 cm. Photographs show nebulosity over about 4 sq. deg. R is about 1,100 pc (Plate 11).

402. h. 4383. The separation and angle of this pale yellow pair are increasing very slowly but the proper motion is shared by both stars. 10·5 cm will resolve them cleanly and the dual nature is apparent with 7·5 cm.

404. R 164. In an attractive field sown profusely with stars on a faint ground is this bright yellow star with faint white companion close Nf. which 10·5 cm will show with care. It is a true binary with angle and separation slowly lessening since Russell's measures in 1873.

405. IC 2621. This is a good example of a 'stellar' planetary nebula, only to be distinguished from the starry field by the single prism image, though with care a minute bluish disk can be made out. Even 7·5 cm will show the prism image with close attention. As a guide, the object forms the obtuse angle of a small flat triangle with two faint stars. R is not known.

406. NGC 3532. This magnificent cluster is about 60′ × 30′ and therefore needs a large field. The numerous bright scattered stars are obviously not distributed at random for, apart from many pairs, small straight and curved lines of stars are very evident. A number of bright orange stars will be noted. R is about 400 pc.

408. NGC 3582. Discovered by John Herschel in 1834, this is the brightest of a group of small gaseous nebulae in a rich starry field. The group is rather wedge like, about 7′ × 4′, with a faint star at the apex directed S. It may be regarded as one nebula with dark lanes, just visible in the prism with 15 cm. Two detached faint patches lie close S; this is an interesting field but needing a fair aperture. R is about 1,100 pc.

409. NGC 3603. This curious hazy object nearly 2′ across seems to be partly gaseous as judged by the prism; there is a central star with many fainter ones clustering round it in the haze, and 10·5 cm will show it. R seems to be still doubtful.

Cassiopeia (Cas)

This fine constellation with its six principal stars in the form of a flat distorted M lies in and north of a rich part of the Milky Way which is hidden from many southern observers. It is one of the oldest and best known of the northern star groups, to which Ptolemy assigned thirteen stars, and it represents the queen of Cepheus. The modern area is 598 sq. deg. and the centre culminates at midnight about October 9th.

There are some fine double stars in Cassiopeia but chief interest centres in the galactic clusters, of which forty-nine have been recorded; two of these were included by Messier in his catalogue. Few are really bright but many are exhibited against beautiful star fields which occur in profusion in this constellation. No globular clusters have been found and the known planetary nebulae are all very faint. Two of the extra-galactic nebulae are interesting in that they belong to the local system of these objects, and are about 400,000 pc from the sun; these are NGC 147 and NGC 185. A selection of interesting objects from Cassiopeia is given in the addendum.

Centaurus (Cen)

Centaurus, the centaur, is a very large southern constellation included in the *Almagest* of Ptolemy in A.D. 150, and he assigned thirty-seven stars to it. At present the two brightest of these, the well-known pointers to the cross, can hardly be seen above the horizon in latitude 30° N but 2,000 years ago they were about 10° farther from the S pole. Centaurus is in fact a very ancient group and to the Greeks appears to have typified the wise and benevolent Chiron in contrast to the wild predaceous centaurs represented by Sagittarius. The area is 1,060 sq. deg. and the centre culminates at midnight about April 6th.

The two bright stars α and β Cen do not point at present directly to Crux but somewhat north of it. However owing to the proper motion of α this direction is slowly swinging southwards and about A.D. 4000 will indicate the centre of the cross when the separation between the stars will be little more than half of the present 4·5°. Closest approach will occur about A.D. 6200, α Cen being then some 23′ N, and the pair will form a conspicuous and brilliant object in the southern sky. Such a conjunction between two first magnitude stars will not occur again for an immense interval of time.

Centaurus is a conspicuous constellation with an unusually large number of bright stars and offers a fine field for the telescope. There is a wide range of interesting double stars and some attractive open clusters are amongst the twenty known ones. Both globular clusters are splendid objects, NGC 5139 known also as ω Cen, being by far the richest in the sky, and the only other bearing comparison with it is NGC 104 in Tucana. There are three bright planetary nebulae and some interesting diffuse nebulae. Several extra-galactic objects occur and of these the strong radio emitter NGC 5128 is specially noteworthy.

410. h. 4423. Both separation and angle of this attractive yellow pair have slowly increased since John Herschel's measures in 1836; it is a dainty object in a black field with 7·5 cm. Common proper motion indicates that this must be a binary system.

421. NGC 3699. In a lovely field sown profusely with stars is a conspicuous round haze about 1·8′ across, brighter towards the centre with several faint stars involved. The single prism image shows its gaseous character; the edges are irregular and the light somewhat mottled while a dark rift runs almost across in pa. 60°, somewhat Sf. the centre. This rift is just visible with 20 cm, and 10·5 cm shows the nebula clearly in the starry field. R is not known (Plate 10).

422. VV 60. This is a fairly bright hazy grey somewhat elliptical object about 30″ across which shows a single prism image; the light is fairly even and it lies in a beautiful field. 10·5 cm shows the nebula quite clearly but 15 cm is needed to see the prism image.

426. I 78. Bailey measured this pair in 1894 as 1·4″ and 88° and the separation has since lessened with slow increase in angle; it is evidently a true binary of long period. The stars are equal and 15 cm will just separate them.

428. NGC 3766. This fine scattered cluster with broad central condensation is effective even for small apertures. It is at least 15′ across, merging into a rich field with a pattern of star loops giving a lobed appearance and containing orange, yellow, white and bluish stars. The age of this cluster has recently been estimated as 10^7 years and estimates of R vary from 900 to 1,900 pc (Plate 3).

430. NGC 3918. John Herschel discovered this remarkable planetary nebula in 1834 and observed it several times. It is so bright that even 5 cm will show the small disk and the single prism image; this is round, well defined, vivid pale blue about 10″ across and lies in a fine starry field. The prism image is elliptical from the overlapped images of doubly ionized oxygen, with a trace of a central star streak. R is about 1,000 pc.

442. Rmk 14. Separation and angle of this orange and white pair are slowly lessening; it is an easy object dominating a well-sprinkled star field and common proper motion indicates that the stars are connected.

482. γ Cen. This brilliant yellow binary has a period of about 85 years, the separation varying between 0·25″ in 1926 and 1·8″ in 1964. In 1961 10·5 cm showed the stars just apart; the motion is retrograde and changes in angle become very rapid shortly after minimum separation.

505. NGC 4945. A beautiful star field makes fine contrast with this long narrow luminous haze about $15' \times 1\cdot5'$ in pa. $40°$; it is slightly convex Np. and fairly uniform in brightness except towards the fading ends. Even $7\cdot5$ cm will show a faint streak about $10'$ long. This is an edgewise late-type spiral in low galactic latitude and therefore subject to considerable interstellar absorption. R is about $3\cdot8$ million pc (Plate 15).

506. R 213. Since the measures of Russell in 1878 there has been little change in this close deep yellow pair except perhaps some increase in separation. In 1961 the stars were just clear of one another with 20 cm; the proper motion seems to be shared, denoting a binary system and the colour looks too deep for the given spectral type.

509. NGC 4976. In a fine field sown with stars is this conspicuous somewhat elliptical nebula about $2'$ across with very hazy edges and rising to a small bright nucleus which shows a band in the prism. $10\cdot5$ cm shows the object plainly, a fairly bright yellow star $5'$ f. being a guide.

514. I 424. This bright pale yellow star has a white companion very close N which is just visible with $10\cdot5$ cm. Separation and angle have slowly increased since Innes measured the stars in 1902 and, as A is a very close pair which is so far quite beyond 30 cm, the system is probably ternary. $8'$ Nf. is the wide unequal orange and reddish pair Cor 152.

522. Dark nebula. This dark object stands out prominently on the luminous ground of the Milky Way which is here wonderfully rich and beautiful over a region of several square degrees. It is $10'-12' \times 4'$, irregularly elliptical and lobed, lying roughly N–S and sharply marked; it contains some scattered stars and a bridge of faint stars separates the smaller N part from the rest. $7\cdot5$ cm shows the object quite plainly and there are other but less-conspicuous dark patches in this rich region.

523. NCG 5128. Discovered by J. Dunlop in 1827, this remarkable object is a bright round luminous haze about $5'$ across, bisected by a clean dark bar about $1'$ wide in pa. $130°$ in which is a faint luminous streak coming in Np. Many stars are in the field, one being immersed in the S region of the nebula and one in the dark rift. Even $7\cdot5$ cm shows this object plainly; it is extragalactic and R is estimated at about 4 million pc. It is identified with Centaurus A as a powerful radio emitter. It is interesting to compare the simple drawing of John Herschel in 1834, corresponding with the above description, with the magnificent modern photographs of this object; nevertheless its precise nature still remains doubtful (Plate 12).

524. NGC 5139. Recorded by Ptolemy as a star, this wonderful cluster was really discovered by Edmund Halley in 1677. Photographs show outliers extending to $65'$ diameter but the main region is about $20'$ across and its myriad stars are broadly compressed towards the centre. It is powdered with faint stars with 7·5 cm, and with 10·5 cm looks like delicate tangled threads of beaded gossamer. Larger apertures show a pronounced lace-like pattern which seems to be made of small crossing curved lines of stars. Dark lanes and streaks are evident with moderate magnification and the star distribution is far from uniform. On a clear dark night it is a most impressive and beautiful sight. R is about 4,800 pc (Plate 6).

527. λ 180. This elegant pair was first measured by See in 1897 as 3·9″ and 230°, and little is known about it yet; 7·5 cm shows the companion plainly.

531. R 223. A fine orange star dominates the field sown profusely with stars; it has a faint white companion close Nf. which 7·5 cm will just show with attention. Little is yet known of this pair which is probably a binary system.

537. Δ 141. In a well-sprinkled star field this beautiful white pair is a fine object for small apertures. It was first measured by John Herschel in 1835 and there has been no change since. If a binary system, the period must be very long.

540. NGC 5281. Lacaille discovered this object as a 'small confused spot' in 1752 which 30 cm shows as a beautiful scattered cluster of fairly bright stars merging into a fine field and concentrated at the centre in a pattern of two crossing curved lines of brighter stars, yellow, bluish, white and orange. The central region is about 4′ across and 10·5 cm shows it well; on a clear dark night this is a most lovely field. R is about 1,600 pc.

541. NGC 5286. Discovered by J. Dunlop in 1827, this bright globular cluster shows faint star points with 10·5 cm. It is a fine object about 2·5′ across with many scattered outliers and broad concentration to the centre, but is far outshone by a bright deep yellow star 4′ Np.; this is the spectroscopic binary M Cen of period 437 days. Interstellar absorption is very considerable in this region, which makes distance estimates uncertain, but R seems to be about 10,000 pc.

543. Cor 157. Here is a beautiful field accented by an orange star with faint ashy companion well separated Np.; it needs close attention to see the small star with 7·5 cm, but 10·5 cm is easy. Change is slow and little is known yet about this pair.

544. Hwe 24. The colours of this well-separated unequal pair are deep yellow and reddish, clear with 10·5 cm. Glasenapp measured the stars in 1890 as 12·8″ and 354° and they may be closing slowly. Common proper motion is large, and this may be a binary system of long period.

546. NGC 5307. In a profuse star field is a small planetary nebula elliptical in pa. 160° and about 10″ across; it has a bright single image in the prism which may be seen with care with 7·5 cm where the object looks merely like a small star. The light is even with rather diffuse edges and no central star. R is about 2,400 pc.

547. Rmk 18. This bright unequal pale yellow pair in a well-sprinkled star field is a fine object for small apertures. There has been practically no change since John Herschel's measures in 1835 and common proper motion suggests a long period binary.

548. 3 Cen. A beautiful unequal white pair dominates this field of scattered stars; both angle and separation are very slowly diminishing since John Herschel's measures in 1836 and similar proper motion indicates physical connection.

549. β 343. Since Burnham's measures of 1·4″ and 130° in 1877, both angle and separation have steadily diminished; the stars are deep yellow and in 1961 15 cm showed them just in contact at about 60°. This should be an interesting pair to watch.

551. 4 Cen. This is another attractive pair for small apertures; the stars are pale yellow and ashy and have not changed appreciably since 1837. It is not clear yet whether they form a physical system, but A is a spectroscopic binary with a period of 6·93 days.

553. R 227. Since Russell's measures of 1·0″ and 348° in 1880, both values have steadily increased and in 1962 the stars were shown apart with 7·5 cm. This is no doubt a binary system with common proper motion. The field is fine.

554. NGC 5367. This curious object is a round rather faint haze about 2′ across surrounding a small pair (10·0 10·7 4″ 33°) and brightening it; it is difficult to decide with the prism if the haze is gaseous or not. Nothing seems to be known of this object; it does not look extra-galactic and may be a dust nebula.

556. β 1197. These two stars are slowly separating with increase of angle; they are yellow and white and ornament a field of scattered stars, 7·5 cm showing them clearly. This is a binary system with common proper motion, measured first by Burnham as 0·9″ and 179° in 1890.

557. β Cen. This brilliant bluish white star was long regarded as single until Voute about 1940 discovered a close companion. Owing to the proximity of A, good definition is essential to see it and I have found a deep neutral filter useful; 20 cm will then show it clearly. The only change so far is a slight diminution in angle which would be much greater if the proper motion of A were responsible.

559. Slr 19. In a field sown with scattered stars is a moderately bright deep yellow pair which in 1960 was just resolvable with 10·5 cm. Sellers first measured the stars in 1895 as 1·1″ and 230°; the motion is thus direct and this binary system will be interesting to watch.

560. Cor 167. Little can be said about this pair yet; the angle is slowly increasing with little change in separation. The field is attractively sown with stars, including several wide pairs and 7·5 cm resolves the close pair easily.

561. R Cen. With a period of 559 days, this variable of Mira type when near maximum is a fine red star dominating a field sown profusely with stars, while near minimum it looks crimson. The prism shows a spectrum of many dark absorption lines and bands, and also bright lines in blue and violet.

562. β 1110. There has been no real change in this pair since Burnham's measures in 1889; it is a fine object in a starry field and 10·5 cm shows the companion clearly. Not much is known about this pair yet.

564. Δ 159. Excellent for small apertures, this pair with stars deep yellow and white, was measured in 1836 by John Herschel as 9·6″ and 163°; there has been little change since but similar proper motions suggest a long period binary.

571. NGC 5617. A fine open star cluster about 15′ across with some central condensation, in a rich and beautiful region; it is well shown by 10·5 cm. R is about 1,000 pc.

575. α Cen. This well-known golden yellow binary of period 80·1 years is the nearest object to the solar system, the distance being 1·32 pc. A third star of m. 11, known as Proxima Centauri, traverses an enormous orbit round the bright pair and is at present nearer but is difficult for the amateur to find and recognize. α Cen is a very easy object for small apertures, even in bright sunshine, and separation will be greatest in 1981.

581. β 414. Burnham measured this close pair in 1889 and there has been no real change since, while common proper motion suggests a true binary system. There is no colour difference between the stars, which 15 cm will show apart.

595. κ Cen. This brilliant white star is a fine sight in a field well sprinkled with scattered stars. The faint companion, discovered by Innes in 1926, needs good definition, but then 15 cm will show it and 20 cm makes it comparatively easy. Little is known about these stars yet.

Cepheus (Cep)

Cepheus is an inconspicuous constellation of area 588 sq. deg. and represents the kingly father of Andromeda; it is an ancient star group to which Ptolemy assigned eleven stars, the brightest of which is only

m. 2·6. This is α Cep which will be the next bright pole star when the slow action of precession brings it there about A.D. 7500. About half of the constellation is immersed in the Milky Way which here approaches nearest to the north pole. The centre culminates at midnight about September 29th.

In addition to a number of interesting double stars, including the remarkable Krueger 60 near δ Cep, nineteen clusters are recognized in Cepheus, but few make good telescopic objects. The only globular cluster is the most northerly known; it was discovered at Palomar and is of open type, far beyond the reach of amateur instruments. There are no diffuse nebulae and of the planetary nebulae only NGC 40 is bright enough for selection, and has the added interest that the radiation is largely that of hydrogen instead of the usual ionized oxygen. The Milky Way acts as an efficient screen for extra-galactic objects and those that occur are faint. The addendum lists selected objects.

Cetus (Cet)

Cetus, the sea monster, is the fourth in order of size amongst the constellations with an area of 1,231 sq. deg. It is one of the ancient groups, to which Ptolemy assigned twenty-two stars, and lies mainly just south of the equator immediately following Aquarius in a rather barren part of the sky. The centre culminates at midnight about October 15th.

For such a large constellation Cetus is rather poor in good telescopic objects. There are many double stars, including the remarkable variable Mira with its fine spectrum, but neither open nor globular clusters occur. One planetary nebula is known and although extra-galactic nebulae are numerous, almost all are small and faint. Some seventy of these have been examined and only five are given. There is a sameness about these small spots of faint haze and the interest is concentrated mainly in finding them. For this exercise the NGC may be consulted. IC 1613 is a member of the local group.

9. β 395. With a period of 25·0 years this interesting binary is only 15 pc distant. The orange yellow stars were closest in 1946 and will be so again in 1971. In 1960, 30 cm showed them clearly apart in pa. 105° but only a dark line crossed the elongated image with 20 cm. The orbit has a high inclination.

14. NGC 246. Photographs show this planetary nebula to be $4' \times 3 \cdot 5'$ in pa. 120°; it is a rather faint luminous ring $2'$ across internally, pale bluish and fainter in the f. region. The prism shows it to be gaseous and there is a faint central star, and two others involved. A faint object with 10·5 cm. R is about 350 pc.

15. NGC 247. This large elliptical spiral nebula belongs to the Sculptor group which includes also NGC 55, 253, 300 and 7793, and is about 2·4 million pc distant. It lies in pa. 175° as a long not bright ellipse about 15′ × 3′, rising broadly to the long axis with ill-defined centre. A fairly bright star is projected on the central line Sf. The lengthened form of the nebula is faint but definite with 15 cm.

22. IC 1613. This very faint indefinite haze in a field with a few faint stars needs a very clear dark night to be seen with 30 cm. It is included as a type of dwarf extra-galactic system which may be quite common but is visible only because of relative proximity to the Milky Way. It was discovered photographically by Wolf and has a diameter of 12′ and integrated magnitude 9·6; as a guide, it lies 36′ in pa. 346° from the easy pair 26 Cet (6·1 9·0 17″ 254°). R is estimated as 600,000 pc.

36. h. 2036. The angle of this close unequal yellow pair has been steadily lessening with little change in separation since John Herschel's measures in 1835. It is a binary of fairly long period which 7·5 cm will resolve cleanly.

51. Σ 186. This yellow binary was measured by W. Struve in 1831 as 1·2″ and 65°; the separation lessened with direct motion until from 1892 to 1897 resolution was impossible. The stars are still widening now and small apertures show them well. The period has been estimated at about 158 years.

60. o Cet. Mira Ceti is the long-known red variable star recognized by Fabricius in 1596; the period lies between 320 and 370 days and at maximum brightness interferometer measures have given the diameter as 0·056″ which is the largest yet known. Although the distance is still uncertain, the diameter of the star is at least 300 times that of the sun. The spectrum is fine, with a succession of dark bands of various widths from red to violet and bright lines especially in red and yellow. The companion seems to be a white dwarf with little change in angle and separation so far; it can only be seen when A is near minimum.

63. NGC 908. In a field sprinkled with stars in effective contrast is this large fairly bright spindle about 4′ × 1′ in pa. 172°, rising broadly but greatly to the centre, which shows a broad band in the prism. A faint star is immersed on the f. edge S. This is an irregular edgewise spiral and 10·5 cm will show faintly the elongated form.

64. NGC 936. In photographs this object is a barred spiral nebula 6′ × 5·5′ but 30 cm shows a round bright symmetrical object like an unresolved globular cluster of concentrated type about 1·5′ across but evidently considerably larger as the edges fade away gradually. The central part is clear with 10·5 cm and also the continuous spectrum in the prism. About 13′ f. is another round but very faint spiral nebula; this is NGC 941.

66. ν Cet. These stars, golden yellow and ashy, have shown little real change since W. Struve measured them in 1831, and common proper motion suggests a long period binary system. 7·5 cm will show the companion clearly.

69. 84 Cet. A field of scattered stars is dominated by this fine yellow and reddish pair. Both separation and angle are diminishing very slowly; the motion is orbital and of long period.

71. NGC 1068. Discovered by Méchain in 1780, this fine somewhat elliptical nebula in pa. 20° rises to a very bright nucleus; it is about 2′ across in pleasing contrast with scattered field stars. There is definite evidence of concentric structure and the strong prism band shows a faintly beaded appearance suggesting bright lines in the nucleus. This is a spiral system distant about 12 million pc and a strong radio emitter; also the nucleus shows bright bands, in part of ionized oxygen similar to those in the spectra of planetary nebulae. It is thus an object of exceptional interest, the central part of which may be seen with 7·5 cm.

72. γ Cet. This beautiful pair dominates a field of a few scattered stars and is an excellent object for small apertures. A is brilliant white with a deep yellow companion close p. (N). Both angle and separation have increased slowly since W. Struve's measures in 1836 and shared proper motion suggests a long period binary system.

Chamaeleon (Cha)

This small constellation representing the reptile of the same name, occupying 132 sq. deg. between Carina and the south polar Octans, was proposed by Bayer in 1604. It consists of a few scattered stars of about magnitude 4 and some fainter ones, and the centre culminates at midnight about February 28th.

There is little telescopic interest in this constellation. Two pairs are given as well as the single planetary nebula. The few extra-galactic nebulae are small and faint.

366. NGC 3195. Little is known about this planetary nebula, discovered by John Herschel in 1835; it is round, about 30″ across, even in light and bluish with a single prism image. The field is scattered with stars on a very faint ground, four of them being near the nebula. It is clear when once seen with 10·5 cm but 15 cm is needed for the prism image (Plate 10).

399. δ Cha. This object consists of two bright stars (5·5 4·6) about 6′ apart, deep yellow and white. The former is the close pair which is clearly resolved with 20 cm. Innes measured the stars in 1901 as 0·6″ and 61° and the angle has slowly increased since. Common proper motion indicates a physical connection.

433. ε Cha. Since John Herschel found 1·6″ and 178° in 1836 for this pair, the separation has diminished with slight increase in angle and 15 cm shows the stars just in contact. This is probably a true binary because of common proper motion. The field is well sprinkled with stars, one of which, deep yellow and 2·5′ Nf., has a fainter well-separated companion.

Circinus (Cir)

Circinus, the pair of compasses, is a small southern constellation of area 93 sq. deg. constituted in 1752 by Lacaille. It lies in the Milky Way just S of and following the pointers to the cross, α Cir forming a right angle with them. There is little by which it may be recognized; it culminates at midnight about May 1st.

Both α Cir and γ Cir are double stars. There are three open clusters but none is a good telescopic object; the bright planetary nebula NGC 5315 will however repay observation. No extra-galactic nebulae can be expected owing to the screen of the Milky Way.

550. NGC 5315. In a beautiful field with a bright pale yellow star 4′ p. is this bright small nebula showing a strong elliptical prism image with a smaller fainter one close on the violet side, from oxygen and hydrogen respectively. The nebula is fairly well defined, about 5″ across and 10·5 cm shows it clearly as a bluish star while the prism image is easy with 7·5 cm. R is estimated as about 3,500 pc.

555. h. 4632. This fine unequal pair, orange yellow and white, lies in a beautiful field sown with scattered stars, with a curious coil of stars about 9′ Sp. Little is known about this pair yet; the angle seems to be diminishing slowly and 7·5 cm will show the companion with care.

578. α Cir. The motion of the fainter red companion of this very bright yellow star has been steadily retrograde since John Herschel in 1837 found 15·6″ and 244°. It is easy with 7·5 cm and the stars are probably connected in a long period orbit.

616. γ Cir. This bright yellow star is clearly resolved by 20 cm and in good conditions with 15 cm; the angle is steadily lessening since John Herschel's measure of 108° in 1836 but little change in separation has occurred. The stars probably form a long period binary system. A red star lies about 3′ N (f.).

Columba (Col)

Columba, the dove, appeared first as a constellation in Bayer's atlas of 1603. It is a small group of area 270 sq. deg. lying immediately S of Lepus and recognized by two stars of magnitude 3 and several less bright ones. It culminates at midnight about December 17th.

The telescopic objects of this constellation include a number of double stars and the fine bright globular cluster NGC 1851. There are several extra-galactic nebulae, of which two are given, NGC 1792 and 1808; these are somewhat similar in appearance and orientation and, as they are within 1° of each other, are no doubt neighbours in space. A few star groups appear in the NGC but none of these is classed as a true open cluster.

143. NGC 1792. Stars near the edges of this fine interesting field are fairly bright and contrast well with a bright elliptical nebula $3\cdot5' \times 1\cdot5'$ in pa. $135°$ which is fairly well defined. It rises in brightness broadly to the central axis, and $7\cdot5$ cm will show it. This is an extra-galactic spiral with continuous spectrum in the prism.

146. NGC 1808. This is another fine interesting field with a long bright elliptical nebula $4\cdot5' \times 1\cdot5'$ in pa. $145°$ contrasting well with scattered stars. It has a small bright lengthened nucleus about $20''$ across which $7\cdot5$ cm will show. In photographs this is a large barred spiral with dark lanes.

156. NGC 1851. This beautiful globular cluster rises sharply to a very bright centre; including outliers it is about $4'$ across and well resolved into gleaming points. It is round but somewhat unsymmetrical and resolution is doubtful with 15 cm but $7\cdot5$ cm is enough to show the strong central condensation and the prism band which denotes its starry nature. R is about 15,000 pc.

215. h. 3857. There are two bright orange yellow stars $70''$ apart in this field sprinkled with stars; the brighter is Sp. and nearly in the same line has an ashy companion easily visible with $7\cdot5$ cm. No change has occurred since John Herschel's measures in 1836 and similar proper motions suggest a binary system.

222. β 755. In a fine starry field this bright pale yellow star has a less bright ashy companion $21''$ in pa. $300°$; this pair (h. 3875) is practically fixed. 15 cm shows the bright star to be a close pair, which is evident without true resolution with $10\cdot5$ cm. Both angle and separation are increasing very slowly and all three stars belong probably to the same system.

Coma Berenices (Com)

The star group known as Coma Berenices, the hair of Berenice, was known to the ancients, but included either with Leo or with Virgo to the south. It was Tycho Brahe who in 1602 catalogued it separately as a constellation. The modern area is 386 sq. deg.; there are no conspicuous stars and as T. W. Webb has remarked, it is 'a gathering of stars which obviously requires distance only to become a nebula to the naked eye'. Indeed on a clear dark night one may pick out the constellation like a large faint detached portion of the Milky Way, itself nearly a whole quadrant south. R. J. Trumpler in 1940 published a careful survey of these stars, some forty of which form a physically related group 5° in diameter at a distance of about 80 pc. This group is now known as the Coma cluster, culminating at midnight about April 2nd.

Although so inconspicuous to the unaided eye, Coma is rich in telescopic objects for it lies in the wonderful region of bright extragalactic nebulae which stretches from Virgo through Canes Venatici to Ursa Major. Ten of these nebulae are given here but the number could easily be extended. There are also three globular clusters, including the very fine NGC 5024, and a number of interesting double stars.

436. 2 Com. This pale and deep yellow pair is a good object for 7·5 cm; the stars have common proper motion and no doubt are connected, but have shown no real change since W. Struve measured them in 1829. The period must be very long.

440. NGC 4147. W. Herschel discovered this globular cluster in 1784; it is fairly compact, moderately bright, about 1·5′ across and rises much in brightness to a broad centre. It is well resolved into faint stars which are clear with 20 cm, but 15 cm shows only granularity and it is a small hazy spot with 10·5 cm. R is about 25,000 pc.

441. NGC 4192. M 98 was discovered by Méchain in 1781 but it was too faint for him to see the elongation; however 10·5 cm will show a faint streak in the dark field. It is a spiral nebula which appears with 30 cm as a fairly bright pointed spindle about 7′ × 1′ in pa. 150° rising in brightness to the long axis with a round bright centre which readily shows a band in the prism. A very faint small haze 5′ Sp. is NGC 4186.

448. NGC 4254. Méchain found M 99 on the same night as M 98, and thought it rather brighter; it is a spiral nebula which appears as a round fairly bright luminous haze about 2·5′ across, rising steadily to a broad centre with no visible nucleus, and the prism shows a broad band. 7·5 cm will pick up this object.

452. Σ 1633. This fine equal yellow pair dominates a field sparingly sprinkled with stars. Common proper motion suggests a physical connection but there has been no real change since W. Struve's measures in 1831.

455. NGC 4321. M 100 is a large diffuse luminous haze about 4′ across, rising broadly and then suddenly to a small bright nucleus with no visible structure. Méchain discovered it at the same time as M 98 and M 99 and remarked that all three are difficult to find, and only on a clear night near culmination which for him would be at an elevation of 57°. From my observatory they culminate at an altitude of about 35° and I see them very easily with 10·5 cm—an interesting comparison of telescopic quality. This object is a very regular spiral nebula.

457. Σ 1639. The period of this binary is about 360 years; it was measured in 1836 by W. Struve as 1·2″ and 293° which by 1888 had diminished to 0·15″ and 211°; the stars then widened again while the angle continued to retrograde and the less bright star is now in the fourth quadrant. 20 cm will show them clearly apart.

460. NGC 4382. M 85 is a conspicuous hazy ellipse with faint envelope about 3′ × 2′ in pa. 25°, the central parts much brighter and showing a broad band in the prism. Large instruments show traces of spiral structure. About 7′ f. (N) is a fainter ellipse, somewhat smaller in pa. 145°, which photographs indicate as a barred spiral; this is NGC 4394. Méchain discovered M 85 in 1781 and recorded it as very faint, but it is easy with 7·5 cm, and 10·5 cm brings NGC 4394 into view.

470. NGC 4501. Messier discovered this object in 1781; it is a fine large ellipse about 4′ × 2′ in pa. 140°, rising much to a broad bright centre and giving a wide hazy band in the prism. Photographs show a beautiful spiral with close whorls. It is faint with 7·5 cm but the elongation may be seen.

472. 24 Com. This fine unequal pair, deep yellow and white, has shown no real change since W. Struve measured it in 1830; the stars have similar proper motions and no doubt form a long period system. B is in addition a spectroscopic binary of period 7·337 days.

474. NGC 4559. This large elongated spiral nebula, about 8′ × 2′, needs very clear weather, otherwise only the brighter central region about 2′ × 1′ is visible. It lies in pa. 140° and the outer parts are faint and diffuse. 15 cm shows the ellipticity.

475. NGC 4565. This remarkable edgewise spiral nebula was discovered by William Herschel in 1785. Photographs with large instruments disclose an extended spindle 20′ × 3·5′ in pa. 135° with enlarged central region and a broad dark bar running lengthways on the Nf. side. I can trace this object for 12′ × 1′ and the absorption lane is prominent, as well as the faint luminosity outside it near the bright centre. This is just visible with 20 cm while 10·5 cm will show the nebula itself as a faint extended haze. R has been estimated as 12 million pc.

493. NGC 4710. Photographs of this object show a narrow spindle with two dark absorption lanes on either side of the bright centre. I see it about 3′ × 0·5′ in pa. 30°, rising much in brightness to the central axis which seems mottled with a suggestion of a dark area Sp. the centre. It is faint with 10·5 cm but 15 cm gives the elongated form.

494. NGC 4725. This large spiral nebula appears as a diffuse elliptical haze about 4′ × 2′ in pa. 40°, the inner regions rising steadily and then suddenly to a bright small nucleus which shows a strong band in the general prism haze. The nebula is quite plain with 10·5 cm, while 15 cm shows the shape and the nucleus.

498. 35 Com. W. Struve measured these stars in 1829; the wide star has altered little but the close pair has diminished in separation with steady direct motion. All have similar proper motion and are probably connected. A is a fine orange yellow star with wide white companion; 20 cm will resolve the close pair.

502. NGC 4826. M 64 was discovered by Messier in 1780. I see it as a large bright ellipse about 4·5′ × 2·5′ in pa. 110°, rising much to a central nucleus, close N of which is a small dark absorption area distinctly concave inwards, visible even in the prism as a dark streak. This fine object is a compact spiral and it is shown by 7·5 cm as elongated with brighter centre. R is about 6 million pc.

511. α Com. This very interesting system has a period of 25·87 years; it appears in the field as a bright deep yellow star, and the orbit of the components is almost edgewise so that they appear to move nearly on a straight line in pa. 13° and 193°. They were widest apart about 1955 and will be so again in 1981; in 1960 they were clearly resolved with 30 cm at a separation of 0·5″. R is 17·5 pc.

516. NGC 5024. Messier discovered this beautiful globular cluster in 1777 and compared it later directly with the comet of 1779; he saw no stars in it although 10·5 cm indicates some of the scattered outliers distinctly. It is very rich and compact, irregularly round with rays of outliers about 4′ across, rising to a broad centre crowded with faint stars which 20 cm will show clearly—altogether a very fine object. R is about 20,000 pc.

519. NGC 5053. This globular cluster is very different from NGC 5024; it is a faint luminous haze, irregularly round about 4′ across and very liitle concentrated to the centre, where 30 cm shows very faint stars and some brighter outliers. It is not easy to find with 20 cm but as a guide it lies between two stars p. and f. about 14′ apart. R is estimated as about 15,500 pc; the cluster is thus considerably nearer than NGC 5024 and although the effect of interstellar absorption seems to be somewhat greater, its stars must be intrinsically much fainter. This cluster is therefore likely to be very old, with stars far advanced in evolution and nearly burnt out.

520. β 800. Considerable proper motion is shared by the stars, orange and red, of this unequal well-separated pair, distant only 15 pc from the sun. Burnham measured them in 1881 as 1·3″ and 121°, and the separation has much increased with only small retrograde motion, so that if in orbit this must be highly inclined. It is an easy object for 7·5 cm, and the colours are unusual.

Corona Australis (CrA)

Corona Australis, the southern crown, which follows immediately the curved tail of Scorpius, is nevertheless sufficiently far north to be included in the original forty-eight groups of Ptolemy who assigned thirteen stars to it. In the small area of 128 sq. deg. is an ellipse of fairly bright stars which serves to mark the constellation in the Milky Way. It culminates at midnight about June 30th.

Amongst the double stars is the interesting γ CrA of comparatively short period. No open star clusters occur but there are two globular clusters. Much diffuse dark nebulosity is present also, lit in places by immersed stars, as is the case with the curious variable nebula NGC 6729. There are two planetary nebulae, one of which needs the prism for its identification and is given as a test. As may be expected from the position of the constellation, no extra-galactic objects have been found in it.

758. NGC 6496. This globular cluster belongs to the most open type of these objects; 30 cm discloses a faint roundish haze about 2′ across without central condensation. Some faint stars may be seen in it but these may be field stars as the surrounding region is well sown. The cluster is shown by 10·5 cm as a dim hazy spot; interstellar absorption is rated here as m. 1·7 and R is esimated as 6,000 pc.

760. VV 133. In a field spangled profusely with stars, this planetary nebula is itself almost a stellar point as the diameter is not more than about 2″. The prism picks it out from the multitude of stars by the single image which can just be seen with 10·5 cm, the magnitude being about 11. As a guide, it forms the right angle of a triangle with two stars, about 50″ Sp. and 25″ Sf. R is given as 1,750 pc.

773. h. 5014. This fine bright equal pair is closing with retrograde motion, but in 1962 was still clearly divided by 10·5 cm; it is in a field sown profusely with stars. The period seems to be about 190 years and the spectroscopic parallax gives R as 55 pc.

776. NGC 6541. The combination of this globular cluster and its starry field is most beautiful; it is well condensed, round and resolved into gleaming stars, the outliers up to 6′ across. 15 cm shows stars in it but it is only mottled with 10·5 cm and is an easy luminous haze with 7·5 cm. Interstellar absorption is rated here at m. 1·6 and R is estimated as 4,200 pc.

813. κ CrA. Small apertures deal well with this bright wide pair in a fine starry field; there has been no real change since the measures of John Herschel in 1836 and if the stars are in orbit the period must be very long.

840. Brs 14. This is another fine pair for small apertures, the stars almost white. The only change since John Herschel's measures in 1837 is a slight decrease in angle, but common proper motion suggests physical connection between the stars in a long period orbit.

841. NGC 6729. This field lacks the faint starry background of neighbouring regions and appears to be obscured by diffuse nebulous material rendered luminous near immersed stars, as shown by this object which is a rather faint comet-like hazy ellipse about 1·5′ long with the small star R CrA near the Np. apex. This is a variable star (9·7–13·5) as also is the nebula and, as the spectrum of the latter is partly continuous, the nebula is probably made of dust and gas. Photographs show that the variability seems to be associated with obscuring material passing in front. Surrounded by similar luminous haze are the two fairly bright stars p. (NGC 6726 and 6727) and about 15′ Sp. is a fine equal pair (IC 4812) also immersed in haze. R for this extended nebula is about 150 pc (Plate 9).

846. γ CrA. The period of this binary is about 120 years and the separation does not change much, the motion being retrograde. It is a fine bright object, neatly resolved by 7·5 cm and a good pair to watch at intervals. R is about 17 pc.

855. IC 1297. In a fine starry field is this conspicuous pale blue planetary nebula about 10″ across, of even light with single prism image; the disk is fairly well defined with no visible central star, and 15 cm shows it plainly. R is not known.

Corona Borealis (CrB)

Corona Borealis, the northern crown, is an effective little circlet of stars between Bootes and Hercules which has an area of 179 sq. deg. It is one of the Ptolemaic northern groups to which eight stars were assigned and was known to the early Greeks as the wreath. Only later was the qualifying adjective northern added to distinguish it from its southern counterpart. It culminates at midnight about May 20th.

The only objects of telescopic interest in this constellation are a few double stars of which the relatively short period γ CrB and η CrB have been very well studied.

612. Σ 1932. The angle of this close yellow pair has increased steadily since the measures of W. Struve of 1·6″ and 274° in 1830, and the separation has diminished. It is clearly a binary of long period; in 1961 20 cm resolved it well.

617. η CrB. This bright deep yellow binary has been well investigated; the period is 41·6 years and for those with requisite means this is an interesting pair to watch. The stars are closest in pa. 290° and when widest in pa. 35° (as was the case in 1950). In 1961 with positions 0·6″ and 88°, I found clear resolution with 30 cm but only an elongated image with 20 cm. R is about 15 pc.

624. ζ CrB. For small apertures this is an attractive pale yellow pair. The only real change since W. Struve's measures of 6·0″ and 301° in 1829 has been very slow direct motion. Common proper motion suggests a physical connection between the stars and as A in addition is a spectroscopic binary of period 12·585 days, the system is probably ternary.

626. γ CrB. This bright pale yellow star dominates a field thinly sprinkled with stars; in reality it is a very close binary system with the orbit plane almost in the line of sight, so that when closest the stars are irresolvable even in large instruments. This happened between 1870 and 1877, and again now between 1960 and 1967, as the period is about 90 years. In 1961 30 cm showed only some elongation of the single image in a general N–S direction.

651. σ CrB. W. Struve in 1827 measured this bright deep yellow pair as 1·3″ and 89°, and both values have increased largely since then although general proper motion is common to both stars. This is a long period binary and makes a good object for small apertures. R is about 21 pc.

Corvus (Crv)

Corvus, the crow, is a small constellation of ancient origin to which Ptolemy assigned seven stars. It is distinguished by four prominent stars in a trapezium, and a fifth star α Crv which is so much less bright than the others that it may have decreased in light since Bayer lettered them in 1603. The group lies between Hydra and Virgo; the modern area is 184 sq. deg. and the centre culminates at midnight about March 28th.

I 30 cm Newtonian reflector

bservatory at Lavender Farm, Woodend

2 Nubecula Minor with NGC 104 and NGC 362 H. M. Johnson

Nubecula Major H. M. Johnson

3   387. NGC 3293. Open star cluster in Carina   A. R. Hogg

428. NGC 3766. Open star cluster in Centaurus   A. R. Hogg

4 497. NGC4755. Open cluster round κ Cru in Crux · · · · A. R. Hogg

640. NGC6025. Scattered cluster in Triangulum Australe · · · · A. R. Hogg

5 685. NGC6231. Open star cluster in Scorpius   G. Lynga

647. NGC6067. Open star cluster in Norma   A. R. Hogg

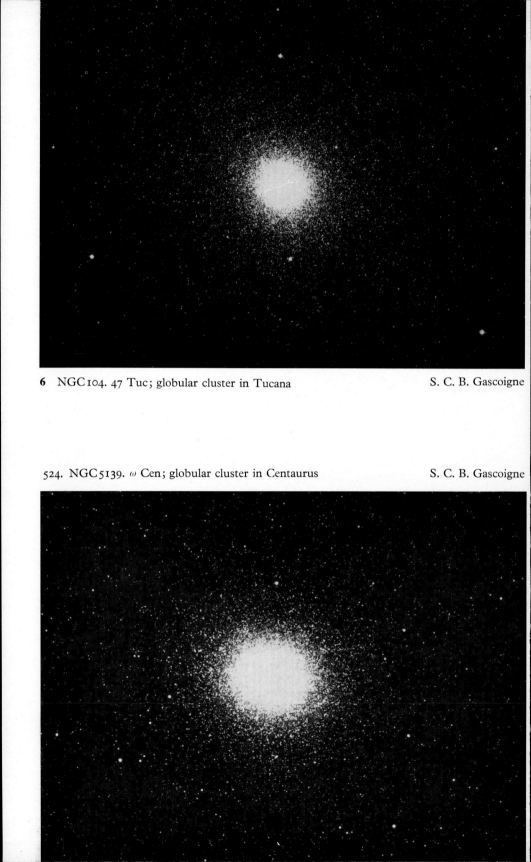

6   NGC 104. 47 Tuc; globular cluster in Tucana   S. C. B. Gascoigne

524. NGC 5139. ω Cen; globular cluster in Centaurus   S. C. B. Gascoigne

7   656. NGC6121. Globular cluster in Scorpius   V. L. Ford

691. NGC6266. Globular cluster in Ophiuchus showing asymmetry in the outer regions from
absorption   V. L. Ford

8 739. NGC6397. Globular cluster in Ara   S. C. B. Gascoigne

850. NGC6752. Globular cluster in Pavo   S. C. B. Gascoigne

9 373. NGC 3201. Open-type globular cluster in Vela J. Menzies

839, 841. Globular cluster NGC 6723 and extended variable gaseous nebula NGC 6729 in Corona Australis blotting out faint stars M. S. Bessell

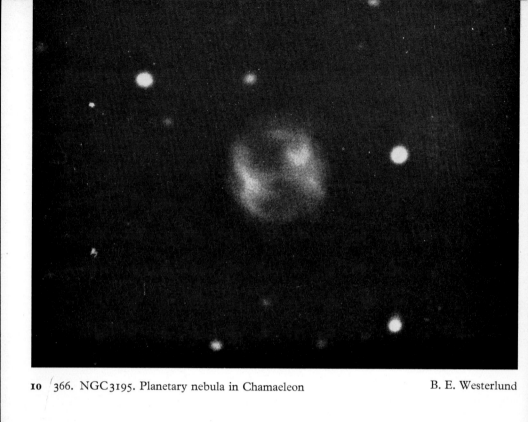

10 366. NGC3195. Planetary nebula in Chamaeleon   B. E. Westerlund

421. NGC3699. Gaseous nebula, probably planetary, in Centaurus   B. E. Westerlund

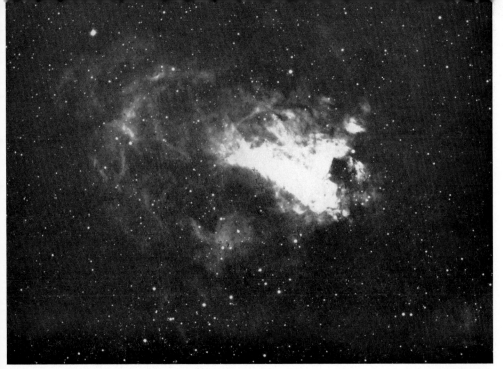

11 796. NGC6618. Gaseous nebula in Sagittarius   A. R. Hogg

396. NGC3372. Extended gaseous nebula round η Car in Carina   G. Lynga

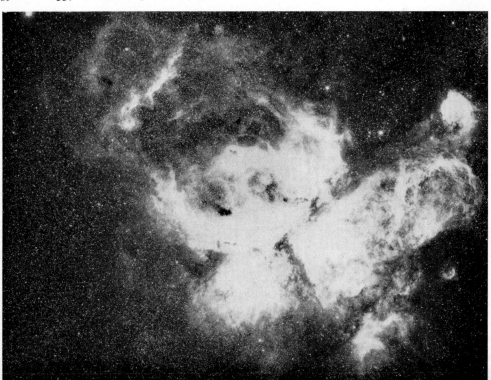

12   189. NGC 2070. Great gaseous nebula in Nubecula Major   A. R. Hogg

523. NGC 5128. Remarkable extra-galactic system in Centaurus   S. C. B. Gascoigne

13   3. NGC 55. Edgewise spiral system in Sculptor   A. R. Hogg

113. NGC 1549, 1553. Elliptical extra-galactic systems in Dorado   R. R. Shobbrook

14 91. NGC 1365. Bar-type spiral system in Fornax   B. M. Lewis

116. NGC 1566. Symmetrical spiral system in Dorado   R. R. Shobbrook

15   505. NGC4945. Edgewise spiral system in Centaurus   R. R. Shobbrook

530. NGC5236. Spiral system in Hydra   B. M. Lewis

16 434. NGC 4038, 4039. Interacting extra-galactic systems in Corvus   R. R. Shobbrook

1003. NGC 7582, 7590, 7599. Spiral systems in Grus   R. R. Shobbrook

The main telescopic interest of the constellation centres about some of the double stars, a planetary nebula NGC 4361 with a clear central star and two pairs of extra-galactic nebulae in contact, one of which NGC 4038–9 is a powerful radio emitter.

434. NGC 4038–9. These two elliptical extra-galactic nebulae, each about 2·5′ long, are inclined 40° and in contact f. Both are broadly but not brightly luminous with little central condensation and 15 cm is needed to show the forms well. This pair is very similar in appearance to NGC 4567–8 on the N edge of Virgo, but it is larger and better placed for southern observers. It is a strong radio emitter at a distance of about 20 million pc and has been thought to be either two systems in collision or one large system disrupting. Photographs show remarkable internal structure with faint extensions about 15′ across (Plate 16).

443. β 920. Burnham first measured this close yellow and white pair in 1879 as 0·8″ and 232°, since when both values have steadily increased so that 10·5 cm will now resolve the stars quite easily. This seems to be a true binary system.

450. β 605. This bright orange star was discovered to be a pair by Burnham in 1878 who found 1·3″ and 136°. Since then the separation has diminished and the angle increased. In 1961 in good conditions 30 cm showed the star as perfectly round, so that it should be interesting to watch for the reappearance of B.

458. NGC 4361. Discovered by William Herschel in 1785, this nebula was not recognized by him as a planetary, as it is more hazy and less well defined than the usual type. It is a prominent round object about 45″ across and white, with a clear central star which shows as a streak through the single prism image. Only this star can be seen with 7·5 cm, but 10·5 cm shows the hazy spot and the prism image. R is estimated at about 1,300 pc.

464. δ Crv. An attractive object for small apertures, this fine bright pair seems white to me although the spectral type of B indicates an orange star. There has been little change since J. South measured the stars in 1823 but the angle seems now to be increasing. The stars have common proper motion and no doubt form a binary system of very long period.

466. β 28. Dembowski measured this deep yellow and white pair in 1875 as 1·8″ and 354°, since when the separation has somewhat diminished and the angle steadily increased, being 36° in 1923. I was therefore surprised to find in 1962 that the fainter star stood in the fourth quadrant at about 310°, clearly and steadily shown by 20 cm and just visible with care with 10·5 cm. The period must be comparatively short and this binary should repay watching.

481. Σ 1669. This fine bright pair dominates a field of a few scattered stars and is an effective object for small apertures. Since W. Struve's measures in 1828, the angle has increased very slowly with little change in separation, and the common proper motion suggests a long period binary.

500. NGC 4782–3. In this field sprinkled thinly with faint stars is a double nebula, the components very similar, round, about 35″ across, considerably brighter to the centre and in contact in pa. 20°. Both give bands in the prism, indicating that they are extra-galactic objects, and are not bright but 10·5 cm will show them faintly. Photographs show nebular material connecting them.

Crater (Crt)

Crater, the cup, is a companion to Corvus on the back of Hydra, and precedes it with a rather larger area of 282 sq. deg. but the stars are less conspicuous. Ptolemy in the *Almagest* assigned seven stars to the group which culminates at midnight about March 12th.

Apart from a few double stars, the only other telescopic objects of any interest are extra-galactic nebulae but all of the twenty examined are relatively small and faint.

420. γ Crt. There has been no change in this pair since 1877 except perhaps a slight diminution of angle, and common proper motion suggests a long period binary. It is a fine object for small apertures, 7·5 cm showing both the stars clearly.

424. Jc 16. This pair was measured by Jacob in 1849 as 7·8″ and 77°, and the only certain change is a slight increase in angle but the stars seem to be connected through common proper motion. They make an easy pale yellow and ashy pair.

Crux (Cru)

The southern cross is the smallest of the constellations with an area of only 68 sq. deg., and yet more romantic interest has been associated with it than with any other. The early Portuguese navigators saw in it the symbol of their faith, and the mystery of the unknown lent it an additional charm in the minds of those from whom the southern skies were hidden. This is well expressed in the words of the distinguished traveller Alexander von Humboldt who in 1799 saw this star group from a small sailing vessel on the lonely waters of the tropical Atlantic Ocean.

'For several days the lower regions of the air had been filled with vapour, but on the night of the fourth to the fifth of July in 16° latitude we saw the southern cross clearly for the first time. It was steeply inclined and appeared from time to time between the clouds, the centre of which in the flickering sheet lightning shone with silvery radiance. If a traveller be permitted to mention his personal feelings, I may remark that on this night one of the dreams of my earliest youth was fulfilled.'

The two bright stars at the head and the foot of the cross have nearly the same R.A. and hence at culmination it is almost vertical, the siderial time being then about $12^h 30^m$. It is therefore possible to use this constellation as the hour hand of a celestial clock to give an approximate estimate of the local siderial time. It culminates at midnight about March 30th.

Crux lies almost wholly in the Milky Way which is very bright in this region and so renders conspicuous the large irregular dark nebula immediately Sf. known as the Coal Sack. This dust nebula is about $7° \times 4°$ and lies at a distance of 170 pc; its scattered solid particles are equivalent to about fourteen solar masses. Projected on it is a small star CPD 3376 m. 6·5 which on a clear dark night is distinctly visible to the unaided eye and may therefore be used as a test object. The constellation contains some beautiful stars, as well as ten open clusters including the vivid NGC 4755. No globular clusters nor luminous galactic nebulae, either diffuse or planetary, are present, and of course no extra-galactic nebulae, for which the Milky Way acts as an efficient screen.

438. NGC 4103. This open star gathering about 6′ across with little central condensation lies in a beautiful region sown with stars; it is well suited to a large field and effective with small apertures. There is a marked pattern of straight and curved lines of stars. R is about 1,000 pc.

456. NGC 4349. In a fine field this beautiful cluster of fairly bright stars is about 20′ across; it is open but rich, the stars in small groups, and makes a delicate object in a large field with 10·5 cm. R is about 950 pc.

462. α Cru. This brilliant bluish white pair is easily visible in bright sunshine with 7·5 cm, and 30 cm will show the wide companion as well. The stars form a physical system with long periods and there has been little change since J. Dunlop in 1826 measured them, although the separation of the bright pair seems to be diminishing slowly. This is a beautiful object which blots out the fainter stars of a rich field.

468. γ Cru. The spectrum of this brilliant orange star shows many prominent dark lines and is admirable for demonstration; the strongest are two in red and orange, two in yellow and green, a strong green band and lines in blue and violet. The star lies in a fine scattered field, the nearest star 2′ Nf. being white in comparison.

491. β Cru. A crimson red star EsB 365 m. 9·0 lies 2·4′ in pa. 260° in the same field as this brilliant white star in fine contrast, an excellent object for small apertures. The faint point about 45″ Np., which can just be seen with 25 cm, is a field star, of which there are many others scattered in this region.

497. NGC 4755. On a clear dark night this beautiful cluster has a jewel-like quality; it is rich and bright, about 10′ across with very marked geometrical pattern and the stars show delicate colours accented by the orange red κ Cru. It is a good object for small apertures, and magnificent with large ones. There is much discrepancy in estimates of the distance owing to the difficulty of measuring the interstellar absorption, for the cluster lies on the N edge of the Coal Sack; these estimates vary from 1,100 pc to a recent 2,360 pc (Plate 4).

499. μ Cru. This bright wide white pair lies in a starry field; the angle is slowly increasing, with no change in separation since J. Dunlop's measures in 1826. Common proper motion suggests a very long period binary system.

Cygnus (Cyg)

Cygnus, the swan, is one of the larger of the old constellations, to which seventeen stars were assigned by Ptolemy. It lies in the Milky Way following Lyra in a rich region of the sky and may be distinguished by the large cross made by its brightest stars, with γ Cyg in the centre. As portions of it extend to 60° N, it is low in the sky or even partly hidden for many southern observers. The modern area is 804 sq. deg. and the centre culminates at midnight about July 29th.

This constellation contains much of telescopic interest and many of the fields are sown profusely with stars. There are many fine pairs and although globular clusters are absent, at least twenty-eight open star clusters have been distinguished, few however standing out well as groups. Large tracts of diffuse and often very intricate nebulosity exist and one of these, NGC 7000 ($20^h 57^m$; $+44° 8′$) which is the so-called America nebula, is too large and faint to make a good telescopic object. Many planetary nebulae are known, mostly small and faint, but the bright NGC 7027 has been much studied and is a fine object. The Milky Way effectively screens off extra-galactic nebulae; few are known and none is bright.

866. β Cyg. This beautiful bright wide pair, deep yellow and pale bluish, dominates a field sprinkled with stars; the colours are very clear with small apertures for which it is an excellent object. No real change has taken place since the measures of W. Struve in 1832, and no doubt the stars are in orbit with very long period.

872. NGC 6819. This is a rich but distant galactic cluster and the stars are not bright, so that 20 cm is needed to resolve it well; the main part is about 5′ across and melts into a well-sown star field with two bright stars Nf. and Sf. Small apertures show it as a small hazy area. R is estimated at about 3,700 pc.

876. δ Cyg. This bright pale yellow star is difficult to resolve for many southern observers because of low altitude (only 7° maximum for my observatory), the star showing a short spectrum lying N–S from atmospheric dispersion. However this trouble may be diminished by using the edge of the field in the right way, found by trial, and in good conditions 15 cm has shown me the companion close Sp. Since W. Struve's measures of 1·8″ and 38° in 1830, the angle has steadily retrograded; measures of separation are rather erratic but this has not changed much. The period seems to be about 500 years but cannot be determined closely yet.

877. 17 Cyg. In a field sown profusely with stars, this bright yellow star has an easy orange companion wide Nf. The angle is slowly diminishing with no apparent change in separation, and common proper motion suggests a binary pair.

880. χ Cyg. The magnitude of this variable star is variously given from 2·3 to 5·1 at maximum, and it is credited with the largest amplitude of variation so far recorded. In its brighter phases it is a fine orange star in a rich field and shows the interesting absorption spectrum of Mira-type stars.

886. OΣ 390. This small triplet is in a beautiful field spangled with innumerable stars. A fairly bright pale yellow star has a companion Nf. which 7·5 cm will show, and a faint point wider S which needs 20 cm to see. There has been little change since O. Struve's measures in 1849 and proper motion is small, but this may be a ternary system.

893. NGC 6871. A large field is needed for this bright scattered cluster on a profuse starry ground; it includes the bright orange 27 Cyg and amongst others an unequal pair (7·0 9·5 11″ 300°), and is a good object for small apertures. R is about 1,100 pc.

904. NGC 6894. William Herschel discovered this planetary nebula in 1784 but did not notice the annular character, which indeed is not easy to see, although 30 cm will show it in good conditions. It is faint, round, about 45″ across in a field sown with stars and gives a single prism image. This object needs care in finding with a good aperture. R is estimated as about 7,000 pc.

906. Σ 2666. 7·5 cm shows quite clearly the companion of this bright white star, lying close Sp. The proper motion is very small and little is yet known of this pair, as the only change since W. Struve's measures in 1831 has been a slow increase in angle.

922. 49 Cyg. This bright golden yellow star has a whitish companion close Nf., easily seen with 7·5 cm in a field of scattered stars. Proper motion is small with the only real change since 1830 a very slow decrease in angle.

924. NGC 6960. In this field there is an irregular rather faint nebulous haze in which the fine yellow and orange pair 52 Cyg (4·3 9·2 6·0″ 70°) is involved. In making this observation it is necessary to see that other bright stars are free, for on some nights which seem to be clear, all bright stars will show haloes which are atmospheric in origin. This nebula is gaseous and forms part of a very large area of scattered wispy nebulosity including NGC 6992 and 6995, which photographs indicate to have a roughly circular outline. It is thought that these may be fragments of a supernova explosion at about 700 pc distance. The spectroscopic parallax of 52 Cyg indicates a distance of about 60 pc, so that there is no connection between star and nebula.

926. β 677. This bright orange star shines like a jewel in a fine starry field in beautiful contrast. A very faint point well clear Sf. needs care to see even with 30 cm. There has been little real change since Burnham measured the stars in 1878, but common proper motion suggests a physical connection.

933. NGC 6992–5. These two objects are portion of a great nebulous region including NGC 6960, and the prism indicates their gaseous nature. In rich surroundings there is a broad luminous band crossing the starry field from Np. to Sf., and extending far beyond; it is 5′–6′ wide at the broadest parts, not bright but quite plain and with irregular streaks in it. It is better defined along the N edges and involves many stars and star groups. The nebulous region is evidently complex and varied in brightness, and tails out to a very faint curved thin ribbon S and Sf.; the brightest parts may be seen with 20 cm.

940. 61 Cyg. Both separation and angle of this easy orange and red pair have steadily increased since W. Struve measured the stars in 1830 as 15·5″ and 91°; the path of B is slightly concave towards A and the stars form a binary of period about 650 years. A was the first star to have its parallax measured; this was done by Bessel in 1838 with the Königsberg heliometer. The accepted distance is 3·42 pc.

941. NGC 7027. In a field of small scattered stars this planetary nebula is conspicuous; it is somewhat elliptical, about 15″ across and gives a bright prism image extended towards the violet with a trace of continuous spectrum. Both it and the prism image are easy objects for 7·5 cm. A detailed study of the rich emission spectrum of this nebula has been made at Palomar and Mt Wilson; the brightest radiation comes from doubly ionized oxygen, then come singly ionized nitrogen and helium, and neutral hydrogen. Altogether the presence of seventeen chemical elements was confirmed. R is estimated as 1,100 pc.

942. Σ 2762. This bright pale yellow star is variable over a small range and seems to be a spectroscopic binary of period 1·13 days. It has a companion close Np. which 7·5 cm shows clearly and only the angle has changed by slow decrease since W. Struve's measures in 1829. The stars are no doubt connected.

944. τ Cyg. The companion of this bright golden yellow star was discovered by Alvan Clark in 1874, and has retrograde motion with a period of about 50 years. Definition has never been good enough at a maximum altitude of 14° for me to resolve this pair; separation is increasing and should be widest about 1972.

950. OΣ 437. 7·5 cm easily resolves this close orange yellow pair, the less bright star being Nf. The motion is slowly retrograde with increase of separation since O. Struve in 1845 found 1·4″ and 68° and this seems to be a true binary system.

955. NGC 7092. Messier discovered this bright scattered cluster in 1764 and dismisses it very briefly; it needs a large field and low magnification to hold it together and is well suited to small apertures. It is about 30′ across and R is 250 pc.

959. μ Cyg. William Herschel measured this bright yellow pair in 1780 as 6·6″ and 109°; the separation steadily diminished with direct motion to a minimum of 0·9″ in 1926. The stars are widening again and in 1961 they were clearly separated with 7·5 cm. The system is undoubtedly binary and the period may be about 450 years.

Delphinus (Del)

Delphinus, the dolphin, is a small constellation of 189 sq. deg. lying between Aquila and Pegasus, and is easily recognized by its compact group of stars. It has been known since ancient times and Ptolemy assigned ten stars to it. The centre culminates at midnight about July 31st.

In spite of its small size, Delphinus contains some interesting double stars, two planetary nebulae and two globular clusters, one of which NGC 7006 is so distant that it may be regarded as extra-galactic, only exceeded in this respect by NGC 2419 in Lynx.

903. NGC 6891. This is a bright bluish nebula, round and fairly well defined, about 12″ across and easily picked out in a rather barren field; it shows a single elliptical prism image with central star streak which is clear with 10·5 cm. R is estimated at about 1,750 pc.

910. NGC 6905. In a well-sprinkled star field is a rather faint bluish somewhat elliptical nebula about 45″ across, between two stars close N and S with other stars near; the edges are rather diffuse and the light is mottled with no visible central star. The single prism image is shown by 15 cm and the nebula itself dimly with 10·5 cm. R is estimated at about 2,200 pc.

915. i Del. Both angle and separation of this close pair are slowly increasing since Dembowski found 0·8″ and 343° in 1874. The proper motion of A would lessen the angle so that the stars seem to be in orbit. In 1961, 15 cm separated them.

916. β 987. There are two conspicuous yellowish stars in this fine field; the brighter is about 2′ Sf. and has a faint companion close Sf. which 15 cm shows clearly but 10·5 cm does not. The pair was measured by Burnham in 1880 as 2·3″ and 128°, and change has been small since then. Little is known about these stars yet.

918. NGC 6934. This broadly condensed globular cluster has a star nearly 2′ p. in pleasing contrast in a fine field; it is irregularly round, about 1·2′ across and partially resolved into very faint stars with faint suggestion of outliers. With 20 cm it appears merely granular, and as a round haze with smaller apertures. It readily gives a band in the prism. Interstellar absorption in this region is rated at m. 0·5 and R is estimated at about 17,000 pc.

920. β Del. Burnham discovered this close bright yellow binary in 1873 and the orbit is now accurately known; both spectroscopically and by measures the period is 26·79 years. The stars will be widest in 1977 when 20 cm should resolve them but in 1961 when nearly at minimum, 30 cm showed a single sharp image, slightly pear-shaped in pa. 150°. Motion is direct.

923. Σ 2723. W. Struve in 1831 found 1·5″ and 86° for this unequal pair, since when the separation has slowly diminished with steady direct motion. In 1961 the stars were clearly apart with 20 cm. This is a binary system of long period.

925. γ Del. This beautiful bright pair is an attractive object for small apertures; the colour of B has been given as greenish but I see it slightly paler yellow than the golden A, in conformity with spectral type. First measured by W. Struve in 1830, both angle and separation have slightly decreased but common proper motion suggests a physical system and the period must be long.

932. Σ 2735. This fine close pair is cleanly divided by 7·5 cm; the only appreciable change since W. Struve's measures in 1829 has been slow retrograde motion and the stars seem to be in physical connection.

935. NGC 7006. At about 45,000 pc this is one of the most remote globular clusters and it is only because of small interstellar absorption in this region and strong concentration of its stars that the cluster is fairly conspicuous. It is a moderately bright symmetrical haze about 1′ across, rising greatly to the centre and giving a band in the prism, but quite irresolvable with 30 cm. It may be seen with 10·5 cm, but needs care in finding.

Dorado (Dor)

The constellation of Dorado, the sword fish, was introduced by Bayer in 1604. It is irregular in form with an area of 179 sq. deg. and the most southern portion includes part of Nubecula Major, the remainder of which lies in Mensa. Because of this division and the special character of its very numerous telescopic objects, Nubecula Major is treated by itself under its own heading. Apart from the Magellan Cloud, Dorado is quite inconspicuous. The centre culminates at midnight about December 7th.

The list for this constellation is therefore limited to four extragalactic nebulae, a double star and the fine red variable R Dor.

113. NGC 1549–53. In this field are two bright extra-galactic nebulae about 13′ apart, both giving strong bands in the prism. One is round, about 1·5′ across with very bright nucleus; the other is elliptical, about 2′ × 0·8′ in pa. 150°, strongly concentrated and even brighter. 7·5 cm shows these nebulae plainly (Plate 13).

116. NGC 1566. Photographs show this object as a bright circular nucleus from which come two short dense symmetrical spiral arms surrounded by a larger faint envelope. I see it with 30 cm as a conspicuous ellipse about 3′ × 2′, rising greatly in brightness to a central nucleus; there is however no sign of the spiral arms. 10·5 cm shows the nebula clearly in the dark field (Plate 14).

126. R Dor. This orange crimson star ornaments a field sown with less bright stars, some quite close to it; it is an irregular variable of period averaging 338 days and has a fine spectrum crossed by many dark and bright lines and bands. 10·5 cm will show some of these near the maximum of the star.

128. h. 3683. The yellow stars of this long period and highly eccentric binary are now easily separable with 7·5 cm, though single to Innes in 1922. The Mt Stromlo measures of 1946 are given, but the separation was greater in 1963 and the angle about 80° and lessening. The stars are dwarfs at a distance of 16 pc from the sun.

131. NGC 1672. Photographs show a barred spiral nebula about 5′ × 5′, but only the brighter central region is visible with 30 cm as a fairly bright haze 3′ × 2′ in pa. 60°, with a well-defined small nucleus. 15 cm shows the general form but it is only a faint hazy spot with 10·5 cm.

Draco (*Dra*)

The large constellation of the dragon is marked by a number of widely scattered bright stars and, as it lies almost wholly north of 50° N declination, is largely hidden from many southern observers. It is of ancient origin and Ptolemy assigned thirty-one stars to it. No. 5 on his list, now Gamma Draconis, will always be remembered for it passes close to the zenith of Greenwich, and observations of it led James Bradley in 1725 to the discovery of the aberration of light. The modern area is 1,083 sq. deg. and the centre culminates at midnight about May 24th.

In such a large star group there are many interesting pairs. Neither galactic nor globular clusters occur and there are no diffuse nebulae. The single planetary nebula NGC 6543 is situated close to the northern pole of the ecliptic and is historically interesting because it is the first object in which nebular lines were demonstrated; this was in 1864 by William Huggins. Draco is rich in extra-galactic nebulae but most of these are small and faint. Six of the brighter ones are given in the addendum, as well as some other objects in the constellation.

Equuleus (*Equ*)

Equuleus, the foal, is said to have been made by Hipparchus about 150 B.C. from some small stars near Delphinus. Ptolemy in the *Almagest* three centuries later assigned only four stars to it, the brightest of which form a small narrow triangle which is not conspicuous. This smallest of the northern constellations with 72 sq. deg. is only slightly larger than the southern Crux. It culminates at midnight about August 9th and telescopic objects are limited to some interesting double stars.

934. 1 Equ. The orbit of this close yellow pair lies close to the line of sight and in 1917 and again in 1923 the separation was less than 0·1″; the stars are now widening and in 1961 15 cm resolved them cleanly. The period seems to be about 101 years. The wider white star has changed little since W. Struve measured it in 1832 but the angle is slowly decreasing. It is an easy object for 7·5 cm and the whole system is no doubt ternary.

936. 2 Equ. This dainty yellow pair in a well-sprinkled star field is cleanly divided by 7·5 cm; the motion is slowly retrograde with little change in separation since the measures of W. Struve in 1831 and the stars probably form a binary system.

943. γ Equ. This bright yellow star has a faint companion close p. which is not easy, but 20 cm will show it in good conditions; it was discovered by

Knott in 1867 and the motion is very slowly retrograde with little change in separation. Common proper motion suggests a physical connection between the stars.

946. β 163. The orbit of this binary is eccentric and highly inclined. In 1911–12 Aitken could not resolve the stars with the Lick 36-inch but separation is now increasing and in 1961 20 cm showed the stars almost in contact. The angle is hardly changing and the period is not yet known.

949. Σ 2786. 7·5 cm shows this small close white pair very clearly; the angle is slowly increasing with slight widening since W. Struve measured the stars in 1831. Little is known of this pair yet, but it seems to be a binary system.

Eridanus (Eri)

Eridanus, the river, is an ancient constellation and its origin has been linked with many streams. One of these is the Nile, the unknown source of which was symbolized with the disappearance of the winding train of stars below the southern horizon to its termination in Achernar, now α Eri. Ptolemy assigned thirty-eight stars to it and the modern area is 1,138 sq. deg. which places this amongst the largest of the star groups. Achernar culminates at midnight about October 14th and the centre of the constellation about November 10th.

Eridanus is rich in fine double stars but it contains neither open nor globular clusters. There are no diffuse nebulae but one of the planetary nebulae is an excellent telescopic object. As is likely in a large constellation well removed from the Milky Way, many extra-galactic nebulae occur but almost all of these are small and faint, with a general similarity which detracts from their telescopic interest. Some eighty of these objects have been examined and four have been selected.

46. p. Eri. These deep yellow stars make a fine sight in the well-sprinkled field; there is a slow decrease in angle and increase in separation, and a period of 219 years has been suggested. The distance is only 6·5 pc.

53. χ Eri. The brightness of this golden yellow star makes the faint companion difficult, and 25 cm is needed to show it to me. The angle is slowly increasing and the separation diminishing, but common proper motion suggests that the stars are connected.

75. θ Eri. This brilliant white pair is one of the gems of the southern sky, and completely dominates the field of a few scattered stars. Since the measures of John Herschel in 1835 the only change has been very slow direct motion, but the proper motions of the stars are similar and they no doubt form a long period system. The distance is about 37 pc.

78. β 11. This star is the following and brighter of two orange yellow stars (ρ Eri) 23′ apart; the companion is rather faint and just visible with 10·5 cm. There has been small change since Dembowski measured the pair in 1875, and physical connection seems likely.

82. Jc 8. The period of the close pair is about 45 years with retrograde motion; the whole system is ternary and 30 cm showed it in 1964 as a beautiful triplet. The third star is easy with 7·5 cm and the separation is increasing, also with retrograde motion. This is an interesting object for periodical observation.

84. NGC 1291. This extra-galactic system looks not unlike a distant unresolved globular cluster; the edges diffuse away gradually to about 2′ diameter with a small very bright central region which shows a strong prism band. It is easy for small apertures; photographs disclose an elliptical inner region 3·5′ × 3′ in a faint broad annulus about 10′ across.

85. Jc 1. There has been little change in this pair since Jacob measured it in 1858, and common proper motion makes physical connection likely. A is very bright orange and 10·5 cm will show the whitish companion.

88. NGC 1325. In a field of scattered stars, this remarkable object merits the description of John Herschel in 1835 who called it 'a complete telescopic comet'. It is a faint elongated luminous haze at least 3′ × 0·5′ in pa. 55° with a star m. 9·5 immersed just at the Nf. tip, and fading away Sp. I find it too diffuse for the prism; although classed as extra-galactic by Shapley and Ames, it certainly does not look like it. This object is not effective with small apertures.

101. Δ 16. This beautiful pale yellow pair dominates a field of scattered stars and is a fine sight with 7·5 cm. Since John Herschel's measures in 1836, there has been only very slow increase in angle, and shared proper motion suggests a long period binary system.

104. 32 Eri. A very fine pair, deep yellow and white, in a field sprinkled with scattered stars and with no real change since W. Struve's measures in 1833. The proper motions are similar and no doubt indicate a physical connection.

108. NGC 1531–2. This fine field with a few scattered stars contains two bright extra-galactic nebulae, one somewhat elliptical about 1′ long and almost at a right angle to the immediately following long narrow spindle with round bright centre, and about 5′ × 1′ in pa. 35°. Both objects are visible with 10·5 cm.

110. NGC 1535. In an effective field of scattered stars this bright pale blue planetary nebula stands out conspicuously; it is about 30″ across and well defined with fairly even light. No central star is visible but the prism image is elongated as if two images were overlapping and there is a definite central streak from the hidden star. The prism image is quite clear with 7·5 cm. R is estimated as 650 pc.

111. 39 Eri. This beautiful orange yellow star dominates a well-sprinkled star field and has a white companion Sf. in fine contrast. Slow retrograde motion is taking place with no certain change in separation, and considerable common proper motion indicates that the stars form a physical pair.

112. 40 Eri. This interesting ternary system is only 5 pc distant from the sun and all three stars have the high annual proper motion of 4·1″ in 215° with radial velocity of −45 k/s. The spectral types are dKo, wA and dM4. In the telescope a bright orange yellow star shows a pair of distant companions which by contrast appear indigo blue. These fainter stars, the brighter of which is a white dwarf, are both visible with 7·5 cm; the mutual period is about 250 years but their orbit round the bright primary must be very long in comparison.

117. β 744. Closest approach between this interesting pair of yellow stars took place in 1923 as 0·20″ and 87°; when Burnham discovered it in 1891 the values were 0·8″ in 307° and the period seems to be about 84 years. In 1963 the angle was about 280° and 20 cm was just able to divide the stars cleanly. A third star 8·3 45″ 41° shows common proper motion with the bright pair.

129. 55 Eri. This bright easy pair, deep and pale yellow, has shown practically no change since the measures of W. Struve in 1831. The estimated proper motions of the stars are not very different and this is probably a long period binary system.

Fornax (For)

Fornax, the furnace, is one of the southern constellations introduced by Lacaille in 1752. It immediately precedes Eridanus and lies in a bend of that river, but as α For is only of magnitude 4 there is little to distinguish it in the sky. The area is 398 sq. deg. and culmination at midnight takes place about November 4th.

The main interest of this constellation centres in its conspicuous extra-galactic nebulae which, with those of the neighbouring Sculptor, belong to a group about 2·4 million pc distant. In addition there is present the Fornax system or super-cluster, a large cloud of very faint scattered stars about 200,000 pc distant which is a member of the local group of sixteen systems including the Milky Way itself. This was discovered photographically as it is too large and faint to be a telescopic object in the usual sense, and in 1939 Hubble found two globular clusters in it, the number subsequently increased to five, of which the brightest is NGC 1049, well within the reach of amateur instruments. There are no galactic star clusters in Fornax, and the only gaseous nebula is the curious NGC 1360. α For is an interesting binary star.

65. ω For. This bright unequal pair is almost duplicated, except in brightness, by a faint unequal pair about 2′ p. There has been little real change since the measures of Jacob in 1858, but the stars have similar proper motion and no doubt form a long period binary system.

68. NGC 1049. This object looks like a hazy m. 11 star about 15″ across, rising much to the centre and showing a band in the prism. It is a globular cluster belonging to the Fornax system, an extra-galactic neighbour of the Milky Way, and itself too faint and scattered to be seen with the telescope. Another of its globular clusters (2^h $36 \cdot 5^m$; $-34°$ 59′) appears as a small round faint haze lying 35′ in 203° from NGC 1049 and a third (2^h $37 \cdot 9^m$; $-34°$ 46′) is 17′ in 169° from it, with a star m. 8 about 7′ p. (N). NGC 1049 may be seen with 15 cm but the others are more difficult.

73. NGC 1097. This large diffuse elliptical object about 5′ × 1·5′ in pa. 150° is brighter in the Np. region, where a faint star is involved at the extremity; the centre is bright and round, about 30″ across. Small apertures show the lengthened form quite well. This is a barred spiral system 9′ × 6′ in photographs and R has been estimated as 7 million pc.

81. α For. This bright yellow star has a less bright companion which has been changing rapidly over the past 20 years. In 1945 Mt Stromlo found 1·04″ and 124° but in 1960 the small star was already in the fourth quadrant, and 7·5 cm resolved the pair easily in 1963. Separation is steadily increasing and the period is not known with certainty. The companion seems to be definitely variable in magnitude.

87. NGC 1316–17. In a field with a few scattered stars are two conspicuous nebulae. One is an elliptical haze about 3′ × 2′ in pa. 60° with very bright nucleus easily extended into a long band by the prism; the other about 6·5′ N is round, less bright, about 40″ across and rising much to the centre which is also extended by the prism. Both are classed as spiral systems and 10·5 cm shows them plainly.

89. NGC 1350. In pleasing contrast with a scattered star field, this nebula although faint and diffuse in the outer parts is evidently well elongated, about 3′ × 1·5′, with a bright roundish centre about 30″ across giving a band in the prism. It is a spiral system which 10·5 cm shows as a small hazy spot.

90. NGC 1360. In a sparsely sprinkled star field is a large fairly bright but very diffuse irregularly elliptical nebula, at least 6′ × 4′ in pa. 20°. The centre is broadly brighter and there is a star m. 9 involved towards the f. edge.

This object is classed as a planetary nebula but little is known about it; it is too diffuse for certain testing with the prism, and the star does not seem to belong to it.

91. NGC 1365. This barred spiral nebula is the best object of its type for the southern observer. Photographs disclose very well-marked bar features in an elliptical system 6·8′ × 3·2′ which 30 cm shows as a bright round diffuse centre across which is a broad faint bar about 3′ long in pa. 70°. From the ends of this come streams of faint nebulosity, from the p. end in pa. 20° and from the f. end in pa. 200°, so that the general shape is that of a large open imperfect ellipse with dark areas on either side of the bar. Smaller apertures show correspondingly less but 15 cm indicates the bright central region clearly (Plate 14).

92. NGC 1379. An interesting field sprinkled with stars contains three nebulae, all fairly bright and giving bands in the prism. This is the most p., and is round with a bright centre, and about 1·5′ across. About 9′ Nf. is a narrow spindle, at least 2′ × 0·4′ in pa. 135° with a small concentrated centre (NGC 1381) and about 12′ Sf. is NGC 1387 similar to the first with small bright nucleus. 15 cm shows these nebulae easily and with a field of 30′ will show also NGC 1374 26′ Np. from the last, as well as its companion NGC 1375 which is 2·4′ S, while 30 cm will bring into view the faint NGC 1373 which is 4′ Np.

94. NGC 1380. Discovered by J. Dunlop in 1825 and described by John Herschel as 'a fine nebula', this object is not difficult for small apertures; it is an ellipse 3′ × 1·5′ in pa. 0°, rising much to the centre with a broad prism band. It is classed as a spiral system.

95. NGC 1399. This object, and the somewhat smaller NGC 1404 about 10′ Sf., lies in a beautiful field with several stars in fine contrast; it is about 1·5′ across. Both nebulae are round with much brighter centres, and show each a broad band in the prism. They are elliptical extra-galactic systems and can be made out with 10·5 cm easily. NGC 1404 lies in Eridanus.

Gemini (Gem)

Gemini, the twins, is the third constellation of the zodiac to which Ptolemy assigned eighteen stars; in ancient times these twins were known by various names but now universally as Castor and Pollux, the sons of Leda, represented by the two bright stars. It is a conspicuous group, stretching from these stars Sp. into the Milky Way. The modern area is 514 sq. deg. and the centre culminates at midnight about January 4th.

There are some fine double stars in Gemini, including the brilliant and interesting system of Castor. The best of the nine open clusters is M 35 which is effective for small telescopes. One globular cluster is recognized in NGC 2158 and there are three planetary nebulae, of which NGC 2392 is bright and shows the central star well. The extra-galactic nebulae are all small and faint.

206. NGC 2158. Once classed as a remote open cluster, this object is now recognized as globular in character, and 15 cm is needed to show some of its stars. It is irregularly triangular, about 2·5' across and well resolved into numerous faint stars with a stream emerging Sp. It is in effective contrast with a beautiful field of scattered stars on the Sp. edge of the galactic cluster M 35 and for small apertures looks somewhat nebulous. R is uncertain.

207. NGC 2168. Discovered by Messier in 1764, this beautiful cluster is an effective object for small apertures; it is more than 30' across and many of the stars are in curved lines and sprays which give it almost a cellular structure. R is about 700 pc.

210. η Gem. This brilliant orange star dominates a field sown with scattered stars in attractive contrast. The spectrum is fine, with broad dark bands in red, orange, green and blue. Burnham in 1882 discovered a companion at 0·96" in 301°; the separation has increased slowly with retrograde motion, giving 260° in 1961 when 10·5 cm showed the faint star pretty steadily although 30 cm needed the use of a dark neutral filter to make it visible—a good example of the value of small apertures on occasion. A is a spectroscopic binary of period 8·17 years so that the system is ternary.

229. OΣ 156. This close yellow pair lies in a field sown with stars over a profuse very faint ground. Since O. Struve's measures of 0·42" in 342° in 1844, the separation has slowly increased with retrograde motion and in 1961 the stars were clearly apart with 25 cm. Common proper motion suggests a long period binary.

235. 38 Gem. These two stars, yellow and pale orange, shine like gems in a field sown with scattered stars; it is a beautiful pair, even for small apertures. Since W. Struve's measures in 1829 the separation has slowly increased with retrograde motion and this is a true binary of long period. R is 26 pc.

243. Σ 1027. Here is an example of a distant pair of giant orange stars which has not changed appreciably since W. Struve's measures in 1830. It makes a dainty object in a field of scattered stars, clearly shown with 7·5 cm. The stars no doubt form a very long period binary and the spectroscopic parallax gives the distance as 420 pc.

245. Σ 1037. Very few known binaries have a more eccentric orbit than these two yellow stars; they were closest in 1921, and in 1965 about 1·3" in 326° when 15 cm showed them clearly apart, but in contact with 10·5 cm. The spectroscopic parallax indicates R as 45 pc, and the period is about 116 years.

251. λ Gem. This very bright yellow star dominates a field well sprinkled with scattered stars; it has a faint ashy companion Nf. which 10·5 cm will just show. Separation and angle are very slowly increasing since W. Struve measured the stars in 1829, and shared proper motion suggests a long period binary.

254. δ Gem. W. Struve measured this pair in 1829 and there has been slow direct motion since then, with little change in separation. A is very bright yellow and B a clear point which looks reddish; 7·5 cm shows it well. The stars appear to share the same proper motion and are probably connected physically.

258. NGC 2371–2. Discovered by William Herschel in 1785, this interesting object appears like two round nebulae in contact in pa. 65°, each rather less than 0·5′ across and only moderately bright. Each has a brighter nucleus and the prism shows them to be gaseous. Photographs with large instruments indicate that these objects are merely brighter regions of a single planetary nebula with very faint central star and elliptical envelope. R is estimated as 3,600 pc.

262. NGC 2392. A fine bright pale blue planetary nebula with very clear central star m. 9 in a good contrasting field; the single elliptical prism image with central star streak is very clear, even with 7·5 cm. It was discovered by William Herschel in 1787, who called it 'a very remarkable phenomenon'. It is about 30″ across and R is estimated at 700 pc.

266. α Gem. The system of Castor has been much studied since the bright pair was recorded by Cassini in 1678. The motion is steadily retrograde and the period about 420 years; also each star is a spectroscopic binary, the brighter of period 9·213 days and the other of period 2·928 days. In addition the red star YY Gem m. 8·6, wide Sf., has the same proper motion and is itself an eclipsing binary of two dwarf M stars with period 0·814 days. R for this sextuple system is 13 pc.

276. κ Gem. O. Struve measured this pair in 1853 and both separation and angle appear to be increasing very slowly. It is a fine pair, orange yellow and whitish, and 7·5 cm will show the fainter star. Common proper motion suggests a long period binary system.

Grus (Gru)

Grus, the crane, is a southern constellation introduced by Bayer in 1604; it lies south of the bright star Fomalhaut and is conspicuous because of an arc of stars concave towards the second magnitude α Gru. The area is 366 sq. deg. and the centre culminates at midnight about August 29th.

Being well removed from the Milky Way, there is no open cluster in Grus, and no globular cluster. One annular planetary nebula is known but it is rather faint. This is a region of clustering extra-galactic nebulae and many are included in this constellation. More than thirty of these have been examined but most are rather small and faint; three have been selected and in addition a striking field with three more in proximity. Some interesting double stars are included.

963. IC 5150. In a thinly sprinkled field this interesting object is a large faint greyish well-defined annular nebula about 2·5′ across with a single prism image. No central star is visible and a considerable area looks paler, but still luminous. 15 cm shows the nebula faintly; R is not known.

969. NGC 7213. This nebula is a bright round hazy object about 1·5′ across, rising much to the centre with the edges fading away; it looks like a remote globular cluster, which indeed it probably is on a gigantic extra-galactic scale, and gives a long band in the prism. 7·5 cm shows it dimly but quite definitely.

974. π Gru. The two components of this star, about 4′ apart, are not connected but make a fine sight in the star sprinkled field. The first is a bright orange red irregular variable (5·8–6·4 10·9 2·7″ 200° S) and has a companion close Sp. which 10·5 cm will show; it is not known if this is a true binary system. The spectrum of A is fine, with many dark bands, some in red and orange and very prominent ones in yellow, green and blue. The second star is brighter and yellow (5·8 12·0 4·7″ 209° Fo) and has a faint companion which 15 cm will show. This pair has common proper motion and may be a true binary with slow direct motion.

992. NGC 7410. In a rather barren field this is a large elongated nebula 5′ × 0·8′ in pa. 45°, with pointed ends and rising much to a large elliptical centre; it is a conspicuous object and visible as an extended band in the prism. It is an edgewise spiral and 10·5 cm shows its form.

997. β 773. This bright pale yellow star has a companion very close Sp., which 15 cm shows with care. It may be interesting to watch this pair, as little is known about it yet.

998. θ Gru. Jacob in 1851 found 2·7″ in 12° for this bright pair; the separation has diminished with steady direct motion, the angle in 1962 being about 75° when 10·5 cm was still able to resolve the stars clearly. Common proper motion indicates that this is a true binary but many years must pass before the period is known.

999. Δ 246. This is a beautiful and easy yellow pair in a thinly sprinkled star field. Discovered by Dunlop in 1825, the stars were first measured by John Herschel in 1835 as 8·1″ in 261° and change has been slow since then. The proper motions are similar and this suggests physical connection between the stars.

1001. I 1467. Innes discovered this interesting pair in 1926 and found 1·37″ in 42°, and in 1936 the position was 0·41″ in 11°. However in 1960 I found that the less bright star was very close Sp. in the 3rd quadrant and this was confirmed in 1961 when 15 cm showed it clearly in pa. guessed as 230°. The proper motion of A cannot account for this and the pair will repay observation. The star colours are orange yellow and whitish.

1002. NGC 7552. Photographs show this object as a barred spiral system about 3′ × 3′ with the bar very bright compared with the rest. This bar is what the telescope shows; it is fairly bright and lenticular, about 2·2′ × 0·8′ in pa. about 90°, with a small concentrated nucleus and two stars near S and p. 10·5 cm shows only the nucleus and some faint haze but 15 cm elongates it. This nebula is similar to, but less tilted than, NGC 7582 to which group it evidently belongs.

1003. NGC 7582–90–99. This striking field contains in an area about 16′ across three fairly bright extra-galactic spindles differently orientated, all visible with 10·5 cm. In R.A. sequence their apparent sizes and angles are: 4′ × 1′ in 150°; 2′ × 0·7′ in 45° and 4′ × 2′ in 50°. The second is the brightest, and the third the faintest and most diffuse. These nebulae form part of the Grus cluster which also includes NGC 7552 (Plate 16).

Hercules (Her)

Hercules, the Roman name of the Greek hero, is the fifth constellation in order of size, and occupies 1,225 sq. deg. between Ophiuchus on the south and Draco on the north. A number of scattered stars from the third magnitude downwards forms no particular pattern by which it may be recognized. The centre culminates at midnight about June 13th.

In such a large constellation there are many interesting pairs, and the spectrum of α Her is specially fine. Neither open clusters nor diffuse nebulae are known but four planetary nebulae have been found, of which only two are suitable for small telescopes. Of the three globular clusters, two are very beautiful and the third, NGC 6229, is the most northerly placed of these objects, with the single exception of one in Cepheus discovered photographically at Palomar and much beyond the reach of amateur instruments. The extra-galactic nebulae in Hercules are all small and faint.

648. IC 4593. This is a small bluish disk about 10″ across with prominent central star; a fairly bright star lies 5′ Np. The prism image is single with strong central star streak, and is clear with 10·5 cm. The nebula appears as a star with 7·5 cm. R is estimated at 1,000 pc.

674. ζ Her. Since William Herschel first measured this binary in 1782, more than five complete revolutions have taken place, the spectroscopic period being 34·42 years and the motion retrograde. The stars will be closest in 1967 and widest again in 1991. In 1961 the positions were 1·4″ in 50° and 10·5 cm showed the companion plainly, greenish by contrast with the almost orange primary. This is a good pair to keep under observation.

675. NGC 6205. This is the finest globular cluster available to northern observers and even at the comparatively low altitude of culmination in southern skies, it is wonderfully effective. The dense broad centre is very bright and sparkling and the outliers in extended rays cover a diameter of at least 6′; even 7·5 cm will show some of these and the cluster is well resolved with 10·5 cm. It was found by chance by Edmund Halley in 1714 and included in his catalogue of six nebulae in 1716. Messier rediscovered it in 1764 and could see no stars in it, which is a comment on the quality of his telescope. The latest estimate of R is 8,560 pc.

677. NGC 6210. This beautiful bluish nebula is in attractive contrast with a number of field stars; it is round, very bright with well-defined edges, about 20″ across and shows a fine prism image with another of hydrogen near on the violet side. An excellent object for small apertures. R is estimated as 1,200 pc.

679. NGC 6229. The low elevation of this northerly globular cluster at culmination, for most southern observers, demands a good clear horizon. 30 cm shows me a bright round symmetrical haze about 1′ across, rising much to the centre and with an occasional sparkle indicating resolution; the prism gives a broad strong band. This object is plain with 10·5 cm, forming a triangle with two bright stars. R is estimated at 25,000 pc.

683. Σ 2107. W. Struve measured this deep yellow close pair in 1829 as 1·1″ in 149°; separation diminished with direct motion until in 1901 it was 0·3″ in 330°. The stars are now widening and 20 cm resolved them cleanly in 1961; the period seems to lie between 150 and 200 years.

706. α Her. This beautiful bright pair, orange and white, is an excellent object for small apertures, the motion being slowly retrograde with little change in separation. The system is an interesting ternary one, since A is an irregular variable with a spectrum showing many dark bands and lines, some visible with 7·5 cm, and B is a spectroscopic binary of period 51·59 days.

707. δ Her. After the measures of W. Struve in 1830 of 26″ in 174°, it gradually became clear that the relative movement of these two stars was because of the difference of their proper motions. They were closest in 1960 at 9·5″

in 242° and separation is now steadily increasing with the angle in the distant future tending to the limit of 332°. This is a bright pair, pale and deep yellow, and should be interesting to watch; spectroscopic parallaxes show A at 28 pc and B at 40 pc distance.

715. NGC 6341. Messier discovered this beautiful globular cluster in 1781, but saw no stars in it. In clear weather it is well resolved, the centre broad and very bright with irregularly scattered outliers about 5' across, which even 10·5 cm will show quite plainly. The latest estimate of R is 8,400 pc.

727 ρ Her. The angle and separation of this beautiful pale yellow pair are very slowly increasing since the measures of W. Struve in 1830, and it is a true binary of long period. It is a fine object for small apertures.

744. μ Her. This bright golden star has a reddish companion wide Sp. which 10·5 cm will show; W. Struve in 1831 measured the stars as 30″ in 241° so that change has been very slow. In 1856 B was discovered to be a close pair (10·0 10·5 0·4″–1·8″) and the period was found to be about 43 years in an orbit of small eccentricity but high inclination. The stars were closest in 1957 and will be widest about 1989 in pa. 62°. The three stars form a physical system about 9 pc distance from the sun.

753. 90 Her. Since Dembowski's measures of this bright orange star in 1875, there has been little change. It seems to be a long period binary system and 10·5 cm should resolve it in good conditions.

756. Σ 2245. Both of these stars are deep yellow, which does not fit the recorded spectral type A2; they form a charming pair which 7·5 cm shows well. There has been no real change since 1829 but common proper motion suggests physical connection.

763. 95 Her. No significant change has taken place in these stars since W. Struve's measures in 1829; pale and deep yellow, they dominate the scattered star field with fine effect. Common proper motion suggests a long period binary system.

777. 100 Her. This is another fine bright pair which has shown no real change since W. Struve measured the stars in 1831; it is an excellent object for small apertures and the stars are probably linked in a very long period orbit.

784. Σ 2289. Slow retrograde motion is the only change in this pair since 1829; the stars are deep and pale yellow, clearly resolved with 20 cm, and 15 cm should do it also. This is probably a physical system.

816. OΣ 358. This yellow pair with no perceptible colour difference was found by O. Struve in 1845 to measure 1·2″ in 227°; the motion is thus retrograde with increase in separation and 7·5 cm resolves the stars well. This is a binary system with period estimated at about 300 years.

830. Σ 2411. This bright orange star in a fine field has an ashy companion wide f., which 7·5 cm will show with care. There has been no real change since 1829 when W. Struve measured the stars but common proper motion suggests a long period binary system.

Horologium (Hor)

Horologium, the clock, is one of the southern constellations added by Lacaille in 1752. It is an inconspicuous group of area 249 sq. deg. extended along the Sf. edge of part of Eridanus and the only bright star is the orange yellow α Hor, m. 3·8, at the Nf. end which culminates at midnight about November 24th.

Horologium lies well removed from the Milky Way and contains no galactic clusters nor gaseous nebulae. There are no double stars of note, but an interesting globular cluster and a number of extra-galactic nebulae.

83. NGC 1261. This well-condensed globular cluster lies in a fine field; 30 cm resolves it into crowded stars right to the centre. It is about 2·5′ across and the scattered outliers do not extend far; the stars are however very faint and hard to detect with 20 cm although the cluster looks granular. It is a fine bright object, conspicuous with 10·5 cm and R is estimated at 26,000 pc.

97. NGC 1433. Classed as a barred spiral system, this nebula is a large faint haze 3′–4′ × 2′ in pa. 100° fading away imperceptibly at the indefinite edges, with a small bright nucleus hardly 20″ across which easily gives a band in the prism. 10·5 cm shows only this nucleus, hazy and faint.

98. NGC 1448. In a field of scattered stars this long narrow nebula is not bright; it appears about 5′ × 0·5′ in pa. 40° and rises in brightness considerably to the central axis but needs close attention to see its length. It is an edgewise spiral system and 15 cm will give the shape faintly.

Hydra (Hya)

Hydra, the water snake, with an area of 1,303 sq. deg. is the largest of the constellations. It winds its way irregularly from the head near Procyon in Canis Minor to the tail at Libra, passing roughly from 7° N to 30° S through 7 hours in R.A. It is one of the old groups to which Ptolemy assigned twenty-five stars in all, but the only conspicuous part is the head with a curl of stars leading to Alphard, the m. 2 orange leader. This star culminates at midnight about February 9th.

Such a large area includes naturally many interesting double stars.

It does not encroach on the Milky Way and there is only one open cluster and no diffuse nebulae. Of the two planetary nebulae, NGC 3242 is admirable for small instruments while NGC 2610 is an attractive object for larger ones. The two globular clusters make a fine contrasting pair, and extra-galactic nebulae are very numerous. Most of these however are small and faint and indeed Hydra contains one of the most distant clusters of these objects yet studied. About eighty have been examined and nine are listed here, four of these being in one field.

295. NGC 2548. A large field is needed for this bright open cluster, at least 30' across; the stars are numerous with many pairs, triplets and small groups which make a fine effect. Near the centre is a delicate close pair. R is 500 pc.

306. NGC 2610. This attractive object is a round pale grey rather faint planetary nebula about 40" across in a beautiful starry field. A faint star m. 13 lies on the Nf. edge and a bright orange star 3' Nf. is in fine contrast; the single prism image is just visible with 20 cm and the nebula itself is faint with 15 cm. R is estimated at about 5,000 pc.

319. ϵ Hya. The companion of this brilliant yellow star was measured by W. Struve in 1830 as 3·2" in 196°, so that there has been steady direct motion with little change in separation; it is a spectroscopic binary of period 9·905 days and as the primary is itself a close pair of period 15·3 years, resolvable only in large instruments, the whole system is quaternary.

323. 15 Hya. The two wide companions of this bright yellow star belong to the field. The close companion is quite clear with 15 cm and seems to be in orbit; since Burnham's measures of 0·45" and 160° in 1878, separation has steadily increased with retrograde motion.

330. Σ 1316. In a field of many scattered stars this is a dainty deep yellow triplet, of which the faintest star is visible with care with 7·5 cm. W. Struve in 1832 found 6·8" in 146°; 13·0" in 153° and the separation of C has much diminished with direct motion since then. The proper motion of A does not explain this and it is likely that these stars form a ternary system.

334. NGC 2784. The bright elliptical centre of this edgewise spiral system is about 2' × 1', the faint extensions lying in pa. 65° reaching to about 4'. 15 cm shows only this centre which the prism spreads into a band. This is a good telescopic object in a field of a few scattered stars.

370. Hld 101. Since Comstock measured this yellow pair in 1888 as 1·5" in 114°, the separation has diminished, although 15 cm still showed the stars apart in 1962. Considerable proper motion is common to both stars which no doubt form a true binary and may be interesting to watch in the future.

378. β 219. There has been negligible change since this pair was first measured in 1876, and common proper motion suggests a long period binary. The stars are pale yellow and white, well resolved with 7·5 cm.

380. NGC 3242. This planetary nebula is so bright that both it and the single prism image are clearly shown by only 5 cm aperture. Photographs indicate a central star m. 11·3 in a broad spindle 26″ × 16″ in pa. 145° which lies in a fainter ellipse 40″ × 35″. I have made out these features with 30 cm, the spindle being brightest at the ends, and the elliptical prism image shows a long narrow central streak from the star. R is estimated at 600 pc.

388. NGC 3309–11. In this field are four nebulae, all giving prism bands as extra-galactic systems; all are more or less round, fairly bright and less than 1′ across. The two given are close together, another is 6′ Np. and the fourth is 7′ Sf., while two bright stars in the field are in fine contrast. 15 cm shows all of them.

389. U Hya. Of unknown period, this irregular variable is a bright red star of late spectral type, showing many well-defined dark lines, bands and flutings along the length of its spectrum. The more prominent of these are clear with 10·5 cm.

412. NGC 3621. Lying in a trapezium of four stars in good contrast with a scattered star field is this conspicuous hazy ellipse about 5′ × 3′ in pa. 160°, rising to the centre broadly with a wide prism band. It is a spiral system and quite easy, though faint, with 7·5 cm.

425. H III 96. This bright almost equal yellow pair is a fine object for small apertures; an orange red star is 8′ Nf. Jacob measured the stars in 1851 and there has been slight increase in separation with retrograde motion. This is a true binary of long period with considerable proper motion.

429. h. 4455. Discovered by John Herschel in 1836, this beautiful pair is a fine object for 7·5 cm with clear colours in the black field. There has been little change since discovery and common proper motion suggests a long period binary.

432. β Hya. The angle of this bright pale yellow pair is increasing and the separation has lessened since John Herschel measured the stars in 1837. 15 cm just separated them in 1961. The spectroscopic parallax of this long period system indicates a distance of 80 pc.

439. NGC 4105–6. In a star sprinkled field are two fine round nebulae with their concentrated centres about 1·5′ apart; both are extra-galactic as shown by conspicuous prism bands. They are clear though faint with 10·5 cm and form a triangle with a star about 2′ S.

479. NGC 4590. Messier saw no stars in this fine cluster when he discovered it in 1780, but faint outliers may be detected with 10·5 cm. It is very rich, broadly condensed to a central region about 2′ across and the outlying stars show evidence of a spiral pattern 5′–6′ across. 15 cm resolves this cluster clearly though faintly. R is estimated at about 12,000 pc.

521. NGC 5061. In a field sprinkled with stars is a bright symmetrical nebula about 1·5′ across with a nuclear centre; it shows a prism band and is extra-galactic. 10·5 cm shows this object plainly and also the nucleus; the small star 2·5′ f. is a close pair.

525. R Hya. This crimson red variable star has a period of about 387 days which is somewhat irregular. The spectrum is crossed by many dark bands, especially in green, blue and violet and near its maximum 10·5 cm will show many of these. The faint wide companion 21″ Np. may be merely a field star; 20 cm will show it.

529. HN 69. Small apertures deal well with this bright pale yellow pair, in which there has been no real change since the measures of J. South in 1825. Common proper motion suggests a long period binary system.

530. NGC 5236. This fine extra-galactic nebula was recorded by Lacaille in 1752; it is a large ellipse about 7′ × 5′ in pa. 60°, rising steadily to a very bright nucleus hardly 20″ across. This is a spiral system and I see evidence of concentric structure, apparent also with 20 cm; the spectrum contains some bright lines but the prism shows only a broad band. It is an easy object for small apertures. R is estimated at 4 million pc (Plate 15).

576. NGC 5694. This is one of the remote globular clusters which can be resolved only by large instruments; it is a conspicuous round symmetrical haze, well condensed towards the centre and about 1·0′ across. The prism readily spreads it into a band, showing its stellar nature, and it is a clear hazy spot with 10·5 cm. Estimates of R vary greatly with a mean of about 35,000 pc, the extent of interstellar absorption being uncertain in this region.

584. 54 Hya. Both angle and separation have slowly diminished since J. South measured these stars in 1823; they make a good object for small apertures, the colours yellow and reddish. The proper motion is common to both stars and suggests a binary system.

594. 59 Hya. Burnham measured this pair in 1874 as 0·8″ in 304°, and the angle has since steadily increased with little change in separation. These stars form a true binary system and the deep yellow disks are just apart with 20 cm.

Hydrus (Hyi)

Hydrus, the sea serpent, is one of the southern constellations introduced by Bayer about 1603. It stretches from Eridanus towards the south pole and its leader, the 3rd magnitude α Hyi, is the well-known very wide companion to Achernar. The area is 243 sq. deg. and the centre culminates at midnight about October 26th.

There is not much of telescopic interest in Hydrus. Two double stars are given and the brightest of a few extra-galactic nebulae, as well as the curious gaseous nebula NGC 602. It is interesting to note that a line drawn from α Hyi to β Cen is bisected by the south pole.

38. NGC 602. This curious nebula seems to be an outlier of Nubecula Minor; it looks elliptical, about 1·5′ × 0·7′ in pa. 135°, fairly bright with a dark rift dividing it into two parts irregularly. Some faint stars are involved and the prism image shows it to be gaseous. It is an easy object for 15 cm, but 20 cm is needed to see the prism image clearly.

52. h. 3475. John Herschel in 1837 discovered this dainty almost equal yellow pair; the angle was then 35° and has since slowly increased with no real change in separation. This easy object appears to be a true binary system.

80. h. 3568. This fine unequal pair, yellow and bluish white, is in a field with a few scattered stars; there has been little change since John Herschel measured it in 1835. Common proper motion suggests that the stars form a physical system of long period.

106. NGC 1511. This small nebula is nevertheless conspicuous in a field sprinkled with stars; it is fairly bright and quite narrow, about 2′ × 0·5′ in pa. 120°, rising in brightness to the central axis. It easily gives a band in the prism and is classed as an edgewise spiral system.

Indus (Ind)

Indus, the Indian, is another of the inconspicuous southern constellations which we owe to Bayer about 1603. It immediately precedes Tucana and Grus, and stretches to the polar Octans. The leader α Ind is an orange star of 3rd magnitude which I have seen clearly in bright sunshine with 5 cm aperture. The area is 294 sq. deg. and the centre of the constellation culminates at midnight about August 13th.

There is not much of telescopic interest in Indus. θ Ind is a fine pair and in addition two extra-galactic nebulae have been selected as examples of different types from more than thirty examined. In this region these objects are somewhat clustered but nearly all of them are small and faint.

945. NGC 7049. This is a small but conspicuous round haze about 40″ across with considerably brighter centre which shows a band in the prism;

the field is scattered with small stars. It is an elliptical system which 10·5 cm shows as a faint hazy spot.

947. θ Ind. This striking pair dominates a field with a few scattered stars, including a small wide pair 4′ S. A is very bright pale yellow and B is distinctly reddish, making an excellent object for small apertures. The separation has increased with retrograde motion since John Herschel in 1834 found 3·7″ in 305°, and as the considerable proper motion is shared by both stars, physical connection is likely.

957. NGC 7090. In a field with a few scattered stars on a very faint ground is a moderately bright lengthened haze at least 5′ × 0·5′ in pa. 130°, rising somewhat to the axis but without a bright nucleus. This is an edgewise spiral; 20 cm deals fairly well with it and 15 cm shows a faint streak.

Lacerta (Lac)

Lacerta, the lizard, is a small northern constellation half immersed in the Milky Way between Cygnus and Andromeda and, as it extends to about 56° N, it is low in the sky or partly hidden to many southern observers. Hevelius published it first in 1687 as including ten stars. Earlier Royer in 1679 had made a figure here which he called the sceptre and hand of justice in honour of Louis XIV, but this has been forgotten while Lacerta has remained. This illustrates the haphazard way in which some of the present constellations have originated. The area is 201 sq. deg. and the centre culminates at midnight about August 28th.

There are seven open star clusters in Lacerta but only two of them make good telescopic objects. Three planetary nebulae have been found, of which two are known only by photography. The few extra-galactic nebulae are small and faint.

967. NGC 7209. In a dense region of the Milky Way, this is a very irregular scattered cluster about 20′ across with stars m. 8–9 downwards, and the brighter ones avoiding the centre which has little concentration although the cluster is fairly rich. R is estimated at 600 pc.

972. NGC 7243. In a fine field this irregularly scattered cluster of moderately bright stars without much concentration and about 20′ across is fairly effective with small apertures. R is estimated at 1,100 pc.

973. Σ 2894. This unequal well-separated pair, bright yellow and reddish, is an easy object for 7·5 cm. There has been little change since W. Struve in 1831 measured the stars, and common proper motion suggests physical connection.

976. IC 5217. This planetary nebula is a tiny bright ellipse about $8'' \times 6''$ in pa. $0°$; it lies in a Milky Way field well sown with small stars, and though very low for many southern observers, 10·5 cm shows the single prism image in good conditions.

980. Σ 2906. Hardly any change has taken place in this pair since the measures of W. Struve in 1832, and the proper motion is small so that little is known about it. The bright star looks on occasion distinctly bluish, which makes the companion N appear reddish by contrast; 10·5 cm just brings this star into view.

989. Σ 2942. This fine orange star has a companion close p. which sometimes looks greenish by contrast. It can be used to show the value of small apertures when dealing with objects near the horizon, for I have seen B well with 7·5 cm when 30 cm would not show it because of poor definition. A faint third star (12·5 $10''$ $238°$) may be found too difficult by many southern observers. The pair was measured by W. Struve in 1831 as $2·7''$ in $282°$ and there has been slow retrograde motion since which the proper motion of A does not explain. The stars are therefore probably in orbit.

Leo (Leo)

Leo, the lion, is the fifth constellation of the zodiac, an ancient group to which Ptolemy assigned twenty-seven stars. It is large and conspicuous in two well-separated figures, the first an upright sickle with the leader Regulus capping the handle and the second an irregular trapezium of six stars following 1·5 hours later. The area is 947 sq. deg. and the centre culminates at midnight about March 1st.

There are some fine double stars in Leo, and the beautiful γ Leo is now accessible to quite small apertures. Main interest centres however in the large number of extra-galactic nebulae scattered through the constellation. About seventy of these have been examined and eleven have been selected, but the list could easily be extended. Two very faint objects, Leo I and Leo II which were discovered photographically, appear to be within about 500,000 pc of the sun and therefore to belong to the local group of which the Milky Way is a member. Neither suitable for telescopic observation.

345. ω Leo. The period of this bright yellow binary is about 117 years and the whole orbit has been observed. In 1962 when the positions were $0·44''$ in $321°$, 30 cm occasionally showed the stars apart but both values will steadily increase to $1·1''$ and $133°$ in 2040, so that for many years to come this pair may serve as a useful test for resolution. R is about 35 pc.

348. NGC 2903. Photographs indicate that this object is a fine extra-galactic spiral 14′ × 9′ in pa. 18° with large complex nucleus. 30 cm shows a very hazy indefinite ellipse about 5′ × 3′, concentrating much to a bright lengthened centre which gives a strong prism band. The nucleus seems closer to the f. edge. 10·5 cm shows a faint elongated haze in the black field.

355. R Leo. This fine red Mira-type variable star of period 313 days lies at the apex of an isosceles triangle with two white stars. It has a well-banded spectrum, the bands strong and broad in orange, yellow, green and blue, and also many lines. Some of these are visible with 10·5 cm when the star is near maximum.

363. α Leo. Regulus has a very wide orange red companion, easy with 7·5 cm, which has shown no relative change since W. Struve's measures in 1836. This companion is a close pair (13·5 2·7″ 87° in 1923) which is slowly closing, but I have never been able to see the faint star because of field glare. The distance of Regulus is 24 pc and it lies so close to the ecliptic as to be occasionally in effective conjunction with a major planet, or occulted by the moon.

369. OΣ 215. This nearly equal pair was measured by O. Struve as 0·5″ and 266° in 1844, since when the separation has slowly increased with retrograde motion. In 1962 the star images were clearly separated with 15 cm, but in contact with 10·5 cm. The spectroscopic parallax indicates a distance of 70 pc for this binary.

372. NGC 3190–3. These two nebulae contrast pleasantly with a field of scattered stars; the first is an edgewise spiral about 2′ long and quite narrow, in pa. 120° and the other, 6′ Nf., is round and about 1′ across. Both are much brighter towards the centre and give bands in the prism; they are plainly seen with 15 cm.

375. γ Leo. This beautiful pair has been widening with direct motion since W. Struve found 2·5″ and 103° in 1831, and now even 4 cm will resolve it. This is a true binary and the period seems to be near 600 years. Both stars are giants.

386. 49 Leo. Except for slight retrograde motion there has been no change in these stars since the measures of W. Struve in 1830; small apertures show them well, the colours pale yellow and white, and they seem to be connected. A itself is an eclipsing variable of period 2·4 days and may also be a variable of period 263 days.

395. NGC 3351. Photographs disclose here a beautiful spiral nebula, but Méchain in 1781 saw only a very feeble object, 10·5 cm showing in fact a rather faint small hazy spot. With 30 cm it is a bright symmetrical round haze nearly 3′ across in a field of a few scattered stars; the outer parts are very faint and there is a small bright nucleus showing a band in the prism.

397. NGC 3368. Méchain discovered this object in 1781, and 10·5 cm shows it quite plainly. Large instruments disclose a fine elliptical spiral 11′ × 8′ in pa. 150°, of which I see with 30 cm the brighter inner region 3′ × 2′. It is a conspicuous nebula rising greatly in brightness to the centre and showing a broad prism band.

400. NGC 3384. This object forms a right angle with two other nebulae about 7′ away, and stars in the field make a fine contrast. Two of the nebulae are bright and almost round, 1·5′–2·0′ across, with prominent prism bands; the third is a faint ellipse 2′ × 1′ in pa. 120°. 10·5 cm shows two of these without difficulty.

403. 54 Leo. A striking unequal pair, pale yellow and white, in a thinly sprinkled star field, and excellent for small apertures. Slow direct motion has occurred since the measures of W. Struve in 1830 and common proper motion suggests a long period binary. The radial velocity of B is variable and it may be itself a spectroscopic pair.

407. 65 Leo. This bright deep yellow star has a faint companion close f. (S) which 10·5 cm will show in good conditions. Burnham in 1878 found 1·8″ and 82°, so that both values are slowly increasing, and the stars appear to be in orbit.

414. NGC 3623. Messier discovered this nebula as a very faint object in 1780; it is an edgewise spiral system which I see as a conspicuous haze at least 4′ × 1′ in pa. 170° with bright central region readily giving a band in the prism. The central axis appears to lie closer to the f. edge because of a long dark absorption lane disclosed by photographs near this edge, which however I have not seen as such. Even 7·5 cm will show the elongated character of this nebula.

415. Σ 1527. W. Struve found 3·9″ and 10° for this pair in 1829, and direct motion has since slowly reduced the separation. This seems to be a long period binary; both stars are yellow, the less bright being deeper, and 7·5 cm shows them clearly in the black field.

416. NGC 3627. Messier discovered this object in 1780; it is 21′ following M 65 and yet a comet which he was observing passed between them on Nov. 1–2, 1773 without his discovering either because of the comet's brightness. It is a spiral system which 30 cm shows as a long spindle 5′ × 1·5′ in pa. 150° with very faint ends, rising to a broad elliptical centre containing a small nucleus. Small apertures show the central region only.

417. NGC 3628. This remarkable object is very long and narrow, about 12′ × 1·5′ in good conditions; it is an edgewise spiral in pa. 100° and photographs show a wide dark lane down the centre length with the southern portion of the nebula narrower and fainter. I have evidently seen only the northern part which with 15 cm looks long and narrow, but faint.

419. ι Leo. This interesting binary was discovered by W. Struve in 1832 as 2·2″ and 92° and motion proved subsequently to be retrograde with diminishing separation, the values in 1937 being 0·7″ and 15°. However in 1961 I saw the small star close Sp. in the third quadrant and it should soon be possible to determine the orbit. The stars are deep yellow and whitish, and 20 cm will resolve them.

427. 90 Leo. In a field of scattered stars this fine unequal pale yellow pair is an easy object for small apertures. There has been no real change since W. Struve's measures in 1829, but the proper motion of A is very small, and little is known of this pair yet.

Leo Minor (LMi)

Leo Minor, the small lion, is an inconspicuous northern constellation formed by Hevelius about 1660 from eighteen stars between Leo and Ursa Major. The area is 232 sq. deg. and culmination at midnight takes place about February 24th.

There is little of telescopic interest in this constellation. β LMi ($10^h 25 \cdot 0^m$; $+36° 58'$. 4·4 7·0) is a very close changing binary which I have never been able to resolve but the period may be short and the star would be worth observing occasionally in good conditions. The many scattered extra-galactic nebulae are almost all small and faint; of twenty-five observed, the best is probably NGC 3245.

352. Σ 1374. This small pair, deep yellow and white, may be used by southern observers as a test for steadiness and clarity of conditions near the horizon; if these are fair, 7·5 cm will show the stars clearly. W. Struve measured them in 1838 as 3·3″ and 275° and the separation is slowly diminishing with increase of angle. Common proper motion suggests a binary system.

381. NGC 3245. In a field sprinkled with stars is a small fairly bright elliptical nebula about 1′ long in pa. 0° with much brighter nucleus. 30 cm shows a faint extended envelope and photographs indicate traces of spiral structure. Care is needed to find this object with 10·5 cm.

Lepus (Lep)

Lepus, the hare, is one of the ancient constellations to which Ptolemy assigned twelve stars immediately south of Orion. The four chief stars form a trapezium which permits easy recognition. The area is 290 sq. deg. and the centre culminates at midnight about December 13th.

There are some good pairs in Lepus and an attractive little star group NGC 2017 which can hardly be called a cluster. Two outstanding objects are the well-resolved globular cluster NGC 1904 and the remarkable planetary nebula IC 418, but the extra-galactic nebulae are mostly small and inconspicuous, and only one is listed. The crimson variable star R Lep shows a fine spectrum near maximum.

141. R Lep. Near maximum this beautiful star gleams like a crimson jewel in a field well sprinkled with stars; the period is about 440 days. The spectrum is heavily banded with dark and some bright lines. This is 'Hind's crimson star' and small apertures show the colour well near maximum.

151. ι Lep. Since the measures of W. Struve in 1832, this beautiful white pair has shown no certain change, but common proper motion suggests a physical system. 7·5 cm shows the companion plainly.

153. κ Lep. This very bright star has a white companion close N which 7·5 cm shows clearly. Very slow change involving lessening of separation with direct motion indicates that the period must be very long.

159. 38 Lep. John Herschel records this pair as 'most beautiful' and it is probably a long period binary; there has been no appreciable change in separation and angle since the first reliable measures in 1879. The colours are pale yellow and white, easily seen with 7·5 cm.

160. 41 Lep. This beautiful deep yellow pair dominates a field sprinkled with stars; it was discovered by John Herschel in 1837 and the very slow retrograde motion has made little change in separation. It is a long period binary and the star about 1′ f. (S) has no connection with it.

163. NGC 1904. Méchain discovered this globular cluster in 1780 but was unable to resolve it, although 10·5 cm will show the outlying stars faintly. It is bright, of moderately condensed type and about 2·5′ across with outliers extending considerably wider. Large apertures show gleaming points right to the centre. It lies in a fine field and R is estimated at about 17,000 pc.

165. IC 418. This fine object has a bright bluish disk about 12″ across with a bluish central star, round which is a larger faint envelope. The prism shows two images close together from ionized oxygen and hydrogen and the central star streak looks beaded from a succession of bright and dark lines. Even 7·5 cm will show this beaded prism image with care. R is estimated as 1,200 pc.

167. β Lep. The faint companion of this brilliant deep yellow star is difficult unless definition is good, when 15 cm should show it. The separation seems to be lessening very slowly with direct motion and no doubt this is a physical system.

174. NGC 1964. In a star sprinkled field is a fairly conspicuous luminous haze about 2′ long and elliptical in pa. 45° with a bright stellar nucleus as well as three very faint stars involved Sp. It is an extra-galactic spiral and gives a band in the prism; 10·5 cm shows little more than the nucleus.

185. NGC 2017. This attractive group of apparently six stars, the faintest just visible with 7·5 cm, shows different colours, yellow, orange, bluish and ashy. Close examination discloses that the bluish star is a small pair (9·0 9·7 1·5″ 357°) and that the brightest star is also a close pair (6·8 8·3 0·8″ 149°) which 20 cm will resolve. These stars seem to form a physical system and there has been little change since Dembowski measured them in 1877.

193. γ Lep. This brilliant wide pair, yellow and orange in fine contrast, makes a beautiful low power object in a field sprinkled with many stars. Only 8 pc from the sun, the stars have similar proper motion and radial velocity.

197. β 94. 7·5 cm shows well this deep yellow and ashy pair in a field sprinkled with stars. Since Dembowski's measures in 1876 slow retrograde motion has made no certain change in separation. The proper motion of A would have an opposite effect, so that the stars must form a physical system.

Libra (Lib)

Libra, the balance, is the seventh zodiacal constellation and received its name in Roman times, for it was originally the claws of the following Scorpius which was regarded as a double group. Ptolemy in fact assigned eight stars to these claws, Libra not appearing in the *Almagest* of A.D. 150. The four principal stars form a trapezium preceding the head of Scorpius, none being brighter than the third magnitude. The modern area is 538 sq. deg. and the centre culminates at midnight about May 9th.

Most of the objects of telescopic interest in Libra are double stars. The constellation lies just outside of the Milky Way and no open clusters nor diffuse nebulae are known in it. There is a conspicuous globular cluster NGC 5897 and one small planetary nebula. The twenty-one extra-galactic nebulae examined all proved to be faint and mostly small.

568. Σ 1837. W. Struve measured this pair in 1829 as 1·4″ and 326°, and slow retrograde motion has made no real change in separation since. The proper motion is shared by both stars and resolution is clear with 10·5 cm.

569. Sh. 179. These two widely separated pale yellow stars have not changed since the measures of J. South in 1822, and have common proper motion. Dembowski in 1875 found the less bright star to be a pair (7·6 8·8 1·4″ 93°) with slow retrograde motion and 10·5 cm in good conditions will resolve it.

585. 5 Lib. 10·5 cm shows clearly the white companion of this orange star; it is widening with retrograde motion since Burnham in 1881 found 2·7″ and 250°. The proper motion of A does not explain this and the stars are probably connected.

588. μ Lib. There is no colour difference between these pale yellow stars which are quite clearly separated by 7·5 cm. Both angle and separation are increasing since Dembowski in 1875 found 1·4″ and 335° and common proper motion suggests a long period binary system.

593. HN 28. Orange and red is the unusual colour combination of this wide pair, an easy object for small apertures. Both angle and separation continue to increase since the early measures of J. South in 1823, but the proper motions are large and similar so that the stars must be in physical connection.

596. δ Lib. This pale yellow star is an eclipsing variable, the eclipse of the larger star by the smaller being annular. From the period of 2·327 days it is easy to pick observing times on different nights so that the changes in magnitude may be seen. The spectral type of the smaller star is G0 and the ratio of surface brightness of the two stars is 11·0, which explains the change in combined magnitude when the smaller star passes over the larger one.

599. σ Lib. The broad dark bands at the red end of the spectrum of this bright pale orange star are easily visible with small apertures, and there are narrower dark lines in green, blue and violet. This is a giant star.

605. ι Lib. The wide companion of this bright pale yellow star has accompanied it without relative change in position since William Herschel's measures in 1782, and the stars must be connected. In 1878 Burnham discovered the fainter star to be a close equal pair (10·5 10·5 1·9″ 12°) with slow retrograde motion. Good conditions are needed for 10·5 cm to show this, but 15 cm makes it easy.

608. NGC 5897. This large irregularly round globular cluster is conspicuous; the brighter stars are scattered through and round a faint hazy ground about 4′ across and rays of stars project thinly from this haze to a width of 7′. The stars are clear with 15 cm, but 10·5 cm shows merely granularity. This is a poorly condensed type of cluster and R is estimated at about 14,000 pc.

615. VV 72. This small planetary nebula about 5″ across is easily picked up in a well-sprinkled star field as a bluish disk about 1′ f. an orange yellow star m. 10. It is quite bright and on occasion the prism image has seemed double. 7·5 cm shows the nebula as a star and with care the prism image may be made out, faint but clear. R is not known.

625. β 122. A well-sprinkled star field is ornamented by this small yellow pair; it is a dainty object with 10·5 cm and just clearly resolved with 7·5 cm. There is slow direct motion since measures in 1868 but little change in separation.

Lupus (Lup)

Lupus, the wolf, is designated in the *Almagest* of Ptolemy as the wild beast, to which nineteen stars are assigned. It lies mainly between Centaurus and Scorpius, partly immersed in the Milky Way and near the region in which globular clusters are scattered so profusely. The modern area is 334 sq. deg. and includes many stars of moderate brightness without definite pattern. The centre of the constellation culminates at midnight about May 9th.

Lupus lies in a rich region of the sky and has many attractive telescopic objects. As well as some fine double stars there are five planetary nebulae, but one of these IC 4544 discovered photographically by Fleming of Harvard I have been unable to find. Three globular clusters are known, and four open clusters, although only one of the latter makes a good object. The few extra-galactic nebulae in this heavily veiled region are faint and small.

563. h. 4672. This bright close unequal pair shows good colour contrast; the angle was measured by John Herschel in 1837 as 302°, since when there has been very little change. 7·5 cm shows the stars clearly in the dark field.

565. IC 4406. In a well-sprinkled star field is a greyish blue fairly bright somewhat diffused disk about 20″ across, of fairly even light with single prism image and no visible central star. It is clear with 10·5 cm, and even 7·5 cm shows with care a faint prism image. R is estimated as about 1,200 pc.

566. R 244. Russell measured this unequal pair, pale yellow and white, in 1881 as 4·0″ and 125°, and little is known about it yet, as the proper motion of A may account for small subsequent changes. 7·5 cm shows the companion clearly.

573. Hd 232. This object is included as an example of a number of very unequal Harvard pairs where the magnitude of the companion, evidently estimated photographically, is much overstated visually. In this case the faint star should be seen easily with 15 cm, but requires care to pick up with 30 cm and can only be glimpsed occasionally with 20 cm. It is probably a field star, of which there are very many in the attractive field.

574. h. 4690. This fine wide pair, orange and white (or bluish by contrast), lies in a scattered star field and the colours are quite clear with 7·5 cm. There seems to have been little change for more than a century.

579. α Lup. This is another of the Harvard pairs (Hd 238) which will tax the powers of a 30 cm instrument; I have only seen the faint companion by shielding the brilliant white primary with a field bar. The stars are not likely to be connected.

586. h. 4698. This pair should be compared with Hd 232 above. The fine deep yellow star in a scattered star field has a white companion which may be seen steadily with 15 cm, and glimpsed occasionally with 10·5 cm; it is thus much brighter than the given m. 13·4. There has been only slight change for more than a century and common proper motion suggests a binary system.

592. h. 4715. A good object for small apertures, this close unequal pair in a field sown with stars has hardly changed since John Herschel's measures in 1836 and similar proper motions indicate a physical connection. A has variable radial velocity and may be itself a spectroscopic binary.

598. NGC 5824. Of strongly condensed type, this globular cluster is a very bright white symmetrical round haze giving a strong band in the prism; it is about 1′ wide and 30 cm shows a faint sparkle in it. It is an easy object for 7·5 cm and R is difficult to estimate because of uncertain interstellar absorption; the mean is about 37,000 pc.

601. NGC 5822. A large field is needed for this extensive group of stars nearly 40′ across. There is no central condensation and the numerous stars show very obvious patterns in the form of lines and ellipses; this feature is quite plain with small apertures. R is estimated at 600 pc.

602. π Lup. 10·5 cm clearly resolves this beautiful pale yellow pair which dominates a well-sprinkled star field. Since John Herschel's measures of 0·7″ and 111° in 1836, the separation has increased with steady retrograde motion and it is only a matter of time before the orbit will be known. This is a fine object for demonstration.

604. κ Lup. A most striking field, dominated by a bright pale yellow pair which makes a fine object for small apertures. There has been no real change for more than a century and as the proper motions are similar, it is likely that this is a physical pair in a vast orbit.

606. NGC 5873. This tiny bluish nebula, only 3″ across, is easily located at one of the acute angles of a small rhombus with three stars which focus sharply while it does not. The prism image is bright enough to be seen plainly with 7·5 cm, thus affording ready recognition; a faint star is very close Sp. R is about 4,000 pc.

607. NGC 5882. A pale blue disk about 7″ across is the most prominent object in a field sown with stars; it has a single prism image with evidence of a central star streak and the light is fairly even with well-defined edges. Even 7·5 cm will pick the object out of the field and the prism image is easy. R is given as 1,140 pc.

609. μ Lup. The close pair of this triplet may be just resolved with 10·5 cm; the bright stars are pale yellow, the wider companion looks reddish and the field is sown with stars especially N, the whole effect most attractive. The three stars form a physical system, the angle and separation of the close pair steadily lessening since John Herschel's measures of 2·1″ and 174° in 1836, but there has been little change for the wide star so far.

614. Hwe 76. In a field well-sprinkled with stars this pale yellow and white pair is an easy object for small apertures and is probably a binary system. Since the first measures in 1885 the only change has been slight direct motion.

619. NGC 5927. In a fine starry field this broadly compressed cluster is very rich in stars which are just apparent with 15 cm. The main part is about 3′ across; it is round with irregular edges and the outliers are scattered to 6′ wide. 7·5 cm shows a conspicuous nebulous haze. Interstellar absorption is strong in this region, assessed at m. 4·1, and the cluster is relatively close at 3,200 pc.

620. γ Lup. This close white binary has a period of about 100 years and the orbit is almost edgewise to the sun, thus causing the stars to fuse together at intervals which they did in 1926. I found them just separable with 30 cm in 1961, and a deep neutral filter was helpful in lessening the glare of the bright stars. This should be an interesting pair to watch at intervals.

623. h. 4788. In a field sown profusely with stars, this bright attractive pair, pale and deep yellow, is excellent for small apertures. Since the measures of John Herschel in 1836 of 3·1″ and 349°, steady direct motion has taken place with not much real change in separation. Little is known of this pair yet.

628. Hwe 79. Both angle and separation of this unequal pair, pale and deep yellow, are slowly lessening and common proper motion suggests physical connection. It lies in a starry field and is easy for small apertures.

630. NGC 5986. This globular cluster, about 2′ across, rises very broadly to the centre; it has irregular edges and the outliers are close and not much scattered. It is well resolved into faint stars which may be seen with 15 cm, while smaller apertures show a conspicuous hazy spot. Interstellar absorption is here assessed at m. 0·8 and R is estimated to be about 14,000 pc.

637. ξ Lup. This beautiful pale yellow pair dominates a field of scattered stars, with a faint pair of similar angle and separation 5′ p. There has been no change since John Herschel measured the stars in 1835 and common proper motion makes physical connection likely.

638. η Lup. No appreciable change has yet been detected in this very attractive white and ashy pair, which is in fine contrast with a starry field and makes an excellent object for small apertures. It is likely that this is a binary system of very long period.

639. NGC 6026. Once classed as extra-galactic, this object was reported in 1955 as a planetary nebula by G. de Vaucouleurs; it is a rather faint well-defined haze about 40″ across containing a stellar nucleus, and I found it independently to be gaseous in 1958 by means of the prism which shows a central star streak across the single nebular image. At least 20 cm is needed for this object, and there is a fairly bright orange star 6·5′ Sf.

Lynx (*Lyn*)

Lynx, representing the animal of the same name, is a fairly large constellation made by Hevelius about 1660 from nineteen stars, and R. H. Allen tells us that Hevelius chose the title because one needed to be lynx-eyed to examine it. It lies indeed in a very barren area of the sky between Auriga and Ursa Major with no prominent stars to mark it and, as it extends to 60° N, it is low in the sky and partly hidden to many southern observers. The area is 545 sq. deg. and the centre culminates at midnight about January 20th.

T. W. Webb remarks on the beauty of the pairs in Lynx, but none is bright and the absence of prominent stars makes a good equatorial mount necessary. There is one globular cluster NGC 2419 which is the most distant yet measured and may indeed be extra-galactic. Most of the numerous extra-galactic nebulae are small and faint, the brightest being NGC 2683.

269. NGC 2419. This is an example of an isolated globular cluster, far distant from any other and at about 60,000 pc the most remote from the sun. I see it as a diffuse round haze about 1·5′ across, rising broadly to the centre and rather faint as the integrated magnitude is only 11·5. A faint band in the prism shows its starry nature. There is a white star 4′ p. and a wide pair 9′ f. which may serve for identification. It is a really faint object with 15 cm.

320. Σ 1282. In a field with a few scattered stars is an elegant deep yellow pair, clear but not bright in the black field with 7·5 cm. No real change has taken place since the measures of W. Struve in 1830 but common proper motion makes physical connection between the stars likely.

324. NGC 2683. Photographs with large instruments show this object as an edgewise spiral system about 12′ × 4′ with dark absorption N of the nucleus. I see it as a fairly bright spindle 4′ × 0·7′ in pa. 40° with rather irregular elliptical centre and in good conditions traces of dark absorption N. It is a dim object with 10·5 cm.

340. Σ 1333. This close pair, in which both angle and separation are slowly increasing, may be clearly resolved with 10·5 cm and occasionally with 7·5 cm. Common proper motion makes physical connection probable.

341. 38 Lyn. Since W. Struve's measures in 1829, slow retrograde motion has made a slight increase in separation. This is a fine bright pair, pale and deep yellow, well shown by 7·5 cm and it is probably a long period binary system.

342. Σ 1338. This fairly bright yellow pair is not easy to resolve from my observatory, and 20 cm is needed to do it. W. Struve in 1829 found 1·8″ in 121° and the stars are still closing with direct motion. This is no doubt a binary system.

Lyra (Lyr)

Lyra, the lyre, is a very ancient constellation which received its present name from the Homeric myth of its invention from the shell of a tortoise by Hermes for Apollo. Ptolemy assigned ten stars to it and it may be recognized by the compact group of stars between Hercules and Cygnus led by the brilliant Vega, the 4th in order of brightness in the sky with a luminosity some fifty times that of the sun. The area is 286 sq. deg. and culmination takes place at midnight about July 2nd.

There are some fine double stars in Lyra, but no open clusters occur even though the Milky Way encroaches slightly. Two planetary nebulae are known but only the well-known ring nebula NGC 6720 is available for amateur telescopes and this is by far the brightest of its class. There is one globular cluster, and none but very faint extra-galactic nebulae.

817. α Lyr. This very brilliant pale yellow star has a strongly marked hydrogen spectrum, the three dark lines in red, blue green and violet being prominent in the prism. The companion wide S is just visible with 15 cm but it has no connection with Vega, the proper motion of which accounts for the steadily increasing angle and separation. R is 8·3 pc.

821. ε Lyr. Each member of this bright wide yellow pair is itself a pair, resolved well by 7·5 cm. The first is 5·1 6·0 2·9″ 0°. A2 A4 and the second is 5·1 5·4 2·3″ 100°. A3 A5. The separations have changed little since 1831 when they were measured by W. Struve but the motions are slowly retrograde. The whole system is quaternary but the periods are long.

826. β Lyr. This very bright pale yellow star is the well-known eclipsing binary with two unequal minima of 3·8 and 4·3 separated by maxima of 3·4. The stars are very close, elliptical from mutual tidal action, unequally bright and the light variability is caused by their mutual eclipse; the period is 12·925 days. The position of the nearby star has hardly changed since W. Struve's measures in 1835 and it seems to belong to the system also, with very long period.

832. NGC 6720. A comet passed very close to this object in 1779 and led to its discovery in that year by Messier. It is a bright pale blue elliptical ring 80″ × 60″ in pa. 80° with single prism image which even 7·5 cm will show clearly. The central star is plain in photographs but difficult visually, and I have never been able to see it. This is a most attractive object in a well-sprinkled star field. R is about 600 pc.

838. β 648. Because of magnitude difference, the stars of this close changing binary are difficult to measure, especially near minimum separation which took place about 1910. The period is about 62 years. Comparatively low elevation from my observatory has prevented me from resolving the stars, but 15 cm should do it in good conditions near maximum separation.

851. Σ 2470–4. These two well-separated pairs are in the same field about 11′ apart and they are remarkably similar in all respects except colour, the N pair being white and the S pair yellow. Since the measures of W. Struve in 1821, there has been very little change in Σ 2470 but the separation in Σ 2474 is decreasing with direct motion, which is bringing resemblance to the other still closer. In 1961 I found approximately 6·6 8·5 14″ 268° for Σ 2470, and 6·5 8·5 16″ 262° for Σ 2474. Both pairs are easy objects for 7·5 cm and are sure to interest the observer.

854. η Lyr. In the field containing this bright pair are three other smaller ones, all within 7′ distance. The stars look yellow and ashy, in spite of the spectral types, and this must be from low altitude here. 7·5 cm shows the fainter star which has not changed appreciably since W. Struve's measures in 1830. The proper motion is very small.

857. NGC 6779. Messier discovered this object in 1779 on the same night as the comet of that year. It is a conspicuous globular cluster of the less-condensed type and resolvable into faint stars with 20 cm; it is irregularly round, rising only broadly to the centre and about 2′ across. The field is sprinkled with stars and 10·5 cm shows the object plainly. R is about 13,500 pc.

Mensa (Men)

Mensa, named after Table Mountain in South Africa, was introduced by Lacaille about 1752. It lies far south, between Dorado and the polar Octans, and its stars are inconspicuous. The area is 153 sq. deg. and the centre culminates at midnight about December 13th.

The southern portion of Nubecula Major is located in this constellation and contains several objects of interest which are described under NMa. Apart from these, there is little but the globular cluster NGC 1841 and a few small pairs. Extra-galactic nebulae are all very faint and small.

137. NGC 1841. John Herschel discovered this object in 1836 and recorded it as a large rather faint irregularly round nebula showing signs of resolution. Recently it has been found to be a globular cluster of diameter 2·4′ and integrated magnitude 12·2, and 30 cm shows it as a fairly evenly luminous haze with irregular edges, about 2′ across, not bright but with a number of faintly gleaming stars in it. It is easy with 20 cm but without resolution, and even 10·5 cm shows a small dim spot in a field of scattered stars. R is not known.

183. I 277. This orange star, shining brightly in a fine field sown with stars and containing a number of nebulous star clusters, has a faint ashy companion close S (p.) which 10·5 cm will just reveal. Little is known about this pair which is probably a binary system projected on a background of part of Nubecula Major to which the distant star clusters belong.

Microscopium (Mic)

Microscopium, the microscope, is another of the southern groups introduced by Lacaille in 1852. It is a small constellation of area 210 sq. deg. immediately south of Capricornus, with no conspicuous feature for recognition. The centre culminates at midnight about August 4th.

There are no objects of telescopic interest beyond a few double stars and the extra-galactic nebula NGC 6925 which is much the brightest of a number examined.

917. NGC 6925. In an almost barren field is a fairly bright hazy ellipse about 2·5′×0·7′ in pa. 0°, rising much to a somewhat irregular nucleus which is easily visible in the prism as a band. This is an edgewise spiral and 15 cm will show the elongation clearly.

927. α Mic. This field of a few scattered stars is dominated by a bright yellow star which has an ashy companion wide Sf., shown clearly with 7·5 cm. There has been little change since John Herschel's measures in 1835 and the proper motion seems to be common to both stars, otherwise the separation would have been lessened appreciably.

951. β 766. Good conditions are needed to resolve this close yellow pair; in 1962 the stars were just separate with 20 cm. Burnham measured them in 1879 as 0·8″ and 314° since when there has been steady retrograde motion, and the stars appear to be in orbit.

953. Mlb 6. This close unequal deep yellow and white pair is clearly resolved with 7·5 cm. Measures are rather erratic since Burnham in 1879 found 4·0″ and 146° but subsequent changes are not explained by the proper motion of A and physical connection between the stars is likely.

Monoceros (Mon)

Monoceros, the unicorn, has been attributed to Bartschius in 1624 but it seems to have been formed much earlier, Scaliger having found it on a Persian sphere in the previous century. It is an inconspicuous constellation occupying 482 sq. deg. between Orion and Canis Minor. The Milky Way, here broad and diffuse, passes through its centre which culminates at midnight about January 5th.

This region is very rich in open clusters, at least forty being known in this group. These include the remarkable NGC 2244 which is associated with a large nebulous ring. There are two curious gaseous fan nebulae NGC 2245 and 2261. Amongst the stars the brilliant white triplet β Mon. is notable. No globular clusters nor planetary nebulae have been found and the few extra-galactic nebulae are small and faint.

204. 3 Mon. This close pair was first measured by Knott in 1872 and there seems to be slow direct motion but the proper motion of A is very small and little is known of the pair yet. 7·5 cm will show the companion with care.

214. ϵ Mon. This beautiful pair, pale and deep yellow, dominates a field of many stars, several in wide pairs and triplets; a red star lies 5′ in pa. 300°. There has been little change since the measures of W. Struve in 1831, and the binary character is still uncertain.

216. β Mon. The three stars of this beautiful white triplet form a narrow triangle, measured by W. Struve in 1831, and both separations and angles seem to be increasing very slowly. There is no doubt that this is a true ternary system. William Herschel discovered it in 1781 and thought it 'one of the most beautiful sights in the heavens'. It is a fine object for small apertures.

219. NGC 2244. This bright scattered cluster, with the strong yellow 12 Mon in the f. region, lies mostly in a dark space about 20′ across, round which is a large luminous band of nebulosity, most pronounced p. and N. This band is 20′ to 30′ broad and partly obliterates faint background stars, though many stars are scattered in it. The whole nebular ring is at least 90′ across and far too large for the usual ocular; it is gaseous and R has been estimated as 1,100 pc. 15 cm shows it plainly and the cluster is effective for smaller apertures.

220. NGC 2245. In a field sprinkled with stars this curious object looks like a wide wedge or fan of nebular haze with a small stellar nucleus at the apex, from which the luminosity appears to stream Sp. It is about 2′ long and nearly as wide where it fades away, and shows a gaseous image in the prism. It is easy with 15 cm, and faint with 10·5 cm; R is estimated as about 3,000 pc.

Photographs indicate that the nebulosity is about $5' \times 3'$ with little apparent structure.

224. NGC 2261. This is another fan nebula, smaller and brighter than NGC 2245, with a star m. 11 at the apex; the fan is about $1'$ long, enclosing an angle of $50°$, and fades away N. It is gaseous with single prism image which is just visible with 10·5 cm and R is estimated as 2,000 pc. Photographs show a nebulosity of about $2' \times 1'$ and considerable structural detail in which changes of form have been reported. The enclosed star is R Mon, reported slightly variable.

226. NGC 2264. A fine bright group of about 30 stars, extending $40' \times 20'$ in a prominent pattern, and at the N end the bright yellow star 15 Mon; this star has a companion wide N and there is a good deal of scattered nebulous haze. The nebulosity is gaseous and photographs indicate complex dark absorbing matter as well. R is estimated as 900 pc. With a large field this cluster is effective for small apertures.

234. NGC 2301. In a beautiful field is a bright open star group with an orange star in the roughly round central region about $6'$ across; there are extensions N, S and especially f., and even 7·5 cm shows the general structure. The central star makes a pair with a white star N, which has a faint companion p. R is estimated as about 900 pc.

239. NGC 2323. Found by Messier in 1772 when observing a comet, this splendid open cluster is about $20'$ across with broad central condensation. It contains scores of stars, many in pairs, triplets and small groups, with a bright orange star $7'$ S of the centre. Small apertures show this fine object well. R is estimated as 750 pc.

248. NGC 2353. This is a fine open group of stars with a definite concentric or roughly spiral pattern, about $20'$ across and well separated from the surroundings with a bright star S. It contains many pairs and small star groups, and is a good object for small apertures. R is estimated as 800 pc.

Musca (Mus)

Musca, the fly, was originally Apis, the bee, made by Bayer about 1603 but in Lacaille's chart of 1763 it is designated by the modern name. It is a small constellation of area 138 sq. deg. lying immediately south of Crux, partly in the Milky Way and recognizable by a group of fairly prominent stars. It culminates at midnight about March 31st.

Some fine telescopic objects occur in Musca. As well as several double stars there are two globular clusters, two interesting planetary nebulae and the remarkable diffuse nebula NGC 5189. However none of the six known open clusters is effective in the telescope, and extra-galactic nebulae appear to be absent in this heavily veiled region.

418. h. 4432. This pale yellow pair makes a good object for small apertures; the angle is slowly increasing but separation has not changed since John Herschel's measures in 1836. Physical connection between the stars seems likely.

431. Cor 130. An attractive field sown with stars is dominated by this bright pale yellow star; it has a companion very close Sf. which is just visible with 7·5 cm. Since the measures of Bailey in 1894 the stars have slowly approached with retrograde motion, and they appear to form a binary system.

437. h. 4498. In a field sown profusely with stars this elegant pair, deep yellow and white, makes a fine object for small telescopes. There has been no real change since John Herschel's measures in 1835 but common proper motion suggests that the stars are in orbit.

461. NGC 4372. This globular cluster is partially obscured by a lane of dark absorbing matter well shown in Milky Way photographs of this region; it is large and only slightly condensed, with thinly scattered outliers about 10′ across. A bright yellow star (CPD 1326 m. 6·8) about 5′ Np. interferes, but when it is hidden the cluster shows very numerous faint stars, a few of which can just be made out with 7·5 cm in the faint roundish cloud. It is difficult to estimate the amount of the considerable interstellar absorption here; the cluster appears to be comparatively near and R may be about 5,000 pc.

490. β Mus. Russell measured this very bright white pair in 1880 as 0·54″ and 317° and both values have steadily increased, so that 10·5 cm will now separate the stars. This is a long period binary, and a fine object in the starry field.

503. NGC 4833. This object was recorded by Lacaille in 1752 as resembling a small faint comet; it is a beautiful well-resolved and fairly compact globular cluster with small outliers scattered over and beyond it in small curved lines to a diameter of about 4′. A star m. 9 is projected on these outliers N in effective contrast. 7·5 cm shows a few faint stars in it, and resolution is clear with 10·5 cm. There is a strong absorption in this region, estimated as m. 2·4, and R is about 4,500 pc.

507. θ Mus. This elegant pale yellow and white pair ornaments a field sown profusely with stars. John Herschel in 1836 made the first reliable measures and there has been no real change since. This is an attractive object for small instruments and is probably a long period binary.

508. IC 4191. Not more than 5″ across, this small object may be picked out by its bright bluish disk from a profuse star field; as a guide a bright orange star (CPD 2192 m. 6·4) is 9′ S (p.). It has a bright elliptical prism image which 7·5 cm shows as a tiny point, and is an easy stellar object with 10·5 cm at the Np. apex of a narrow triangle with two fainter stars.

528. NGC 5189. A remarkable gaseous nebula discovered by John Herschel in 1835 and described by him as 'a very strange object'. It lies in a beautiful star field and is bright, about 1·5′ × 1′ in pa. 260° with irregular internal structure and three stars immersed. There is a knot of bluish light f., from which a bright curved bar passes axially p. The single prism image is very clear and may be seen with 7·5 cm which also shows the irregular structure. R is estimated as about 1,000 pc.

535. VV 66. This object is included to show the value of the direct-vision prism in distinguishing gaseous nebulae; it is a stellar point of m. 11·5 in a field sown with stars and impossible to pick out without the prism. As a guide for this, a faint well-separated pair is about 1·5′ p. (N). 15 cm will show the prism image clearly but faintly.

Norma (Nor)

Norma, the square, was introduced by Lacaille in 1752. It is a small constellation of 165 sq. deg. lying south of Scorpius between Ara and Lupus, and completely immersed in the Milky Way, which prevents any extra-galactic objects from appearing in it. α and β Nor are missing, and the brightest star γ Nor is of magnitude 4. This inconspicuous group culminates at midnight about May 21st.

There are few double stars, and although fourteen open clusters are known, many are not effective in the telescope. There is one moderately bright globular cluster and four small planetary nebulae, of which the easiest is given.

621. NGC 5946. This small moderately bright globular cluster lies in a beautiful star field with a number of fairly bright wide pairs, especially S, making a curious effect. It is about 1·2′ across, irregularly round, rises only broadly to the centre and is resolved into faint stars which can just be seen with 20 cm; a field star lies on the Sp. edge. 10·5 cm shows a faint hazy spot. There is strong absorption here, estimated as m. 5·1, and the cluster is relatively near at 3,300 pc.

629. Hld 124. Since the 1890 measures of Sellers as 2·3″ and 214°, there has been slow retrograde motion; the companion is a small point close Sp. which 7·5 cm shows clearly. Little is known of this pair yet; the stars are pale yellow in a well-sown field.

633. NGC 5999. With straggling outliers and no bright stars, this scattered cluster of numerous fairly bright stars about 10′ across stands out from the field. Many of the stars are in marked lines and closed curves, and the central region is an annulus about 2′ across. R is estimated as about 1,600 pc.

636. h. 4813. This bright yellow star has a small white point well clear f. which 7·5 cm shows easily. It dominates a field sown with stars, many in linear sequences on a profuse very faint starry ground—a fine effect. John Herschel in 1836 measured the angle as 97°, so that any increase has been very slight. This is probably a binary system with common proper motion.

641. ι Nor. This is a triple system, both motions retrograde. The close yellow pair has a period of about 27 years and the image was single with 30 cm in 1963 when the stars were closest. The wider star has a long period with slow retrograde motion; it looks reddish in contrast with AB and is an easy object.

647. NGC 6067. This is an attractive cluster, effective also with small apertures. The field is bright and sparkling with very numerous stars gathering towards the centre; the cluster is scattered with outliers over about 20′ with strong evidence of spiral and looped structure, and contains many delicate pairs, the brightest one near the centre. R is estimated as about 800 pc (Plate 5).

650. VV 78. This is the easiest of four small planetary nebulae recorded in Norma; it is about 25″ across, grey and round with no visible central star, and lies in a beautiful field profusely sown with stars. The prism shows the single image amongst the star streaks and 15 cm will show the nebula well. R is unknown.

653. NGC 6087. A very scattered open cluster with central group and two long arms of stars coming in from Sp., the whole field very fine and bright with golden yellow central star. It is still effective with small apertures. R is about 700 pc.

661. ε Nor. In a field sprinkled with stars is a fine wide unequal pair, pale yellow and bluish (by contrast) which has not altered since the measures of John Herschel in 1835. The proper motions are similar and indicate physical connection between the stars. A may be a spectroscopic binary.

662. NGC 6134. With extended rays merging with the starry field, this is an effective open cluster of stars about 15′ across, containing many small pairs and a ring of stars Np. 10·5 cm shows it quite well, though not brightly. R is estimated as 1,100 pc.

670. NGC 6167. This field is fine; there is a deep yellow star p. and the cluster falls away from it N, S and f. in curved wreaths of stars with knots along them and a little group of stars at the centre. The cluster is nearly 20′ across and 10·5 cm shows it fairly well. R is estimated as 700 pc.

Nubecula Major (NMa)

Nubecula Major, the large Magellan Cloud, is given separately for convenience as it lies in two constellations, Dorado and Mensa. It is easily picked out on any clear dark night as a large hazy region in the southern sky, and does not set outside the southern tropics. It has its upper culmination at midnight about December 13th.

This object is now known to be an extra-galactic system of irregularly spiral character belonging to the local group which includes the Milky Way itself. Being only 52,000 pc distant, in comparison with the Andromeda nebula M31 at 570,000 pc, a far better analysis of the content and structure of this system and its neighbour Nubecula Minor may be made than of any other external to the Milky Way. The telescope discloses vast regions of star clouds, open and globular clusters, gaseous nebulae both compact and diffuse, and innumerable scattered stars exposed for observation in a setting which is unique in the whole sky. Star clusters are extraordinarily numerous and many open clusters with very hot early-type stars rival in richness of population the older globular clusters. Large aperture is of great advantage here, but much may be seen with small instruments. I have examined nearly 200 objects listed in the NGC, largely the work of John Herschel from 1832 to 1836, and I hope that the selection here given will indicate some of the interest and beauty of this system (Plate 2).

134. NGC 1711. In a field sown with faint stars is a small bright symmetrical hazy spot with strong central condensation; some very faint stars in and near it show its stellar character and the prism gives a continuous spectrum. It is quite plainly visible with 10·5 cm.

135. NGC 1714. In an interesting field this is a bright, rather bluish irregularly round nebula, brightest near the Nf. edge, about 15″ across and showing a single prism image with some continuous spectrum. It is thus mainly gaseous, and may be seen with 7·5 cm. About 1·5′ Nf. is the very faint small round nebula NGC 1715, while 9′ S is the faint round nebula NGC 1735, and 7′ f. is a cluster of stars about 5′ across; this is NGC 1731.

136. NGC 1712–22–27. This fine field sown with stars contains three star clouds in a chain running from Sp. to Nf.; the central one is the smallest and includes a very small round gaseous nebula about 5″ across which shows plainly a single prism image. The clouds are faint with 15 cm but the prism image of the nebula may be made out.

138. NGC 1743–8. This beautiful field follows immediately the former somewhat N and contains several small gaseous nebulae showing single prism images; the two most prominent are denoted, the former larger, bright and irregular in form about 1·5′ across, and the latter small and round, hardly 20″ across; an orange star forms a right angle with them.

140. NGC 1763–9. Three bright well-defined gaseous nebulae are in this lovely field, all showing strong single prism images; they are enhanced by dark areas round them with relatively few background stars while Sp. is a rich scattered star cloud NGC 1761. The largest nebula is very bright and bean-shaped, about 4′ × 2′ in pa. 65° with fairly even light and many immersed stars. 20 cm shows this field well and smaller apertures indicate its interest.

144. NGC 1818. This fine compact cluster has a bright central starry region about 40″ across surrounded with a halo which 30 cm resolves into faint outlying stars extending to 1·5′ diameter. It is easily visible as a hazy spot with 10·5 cm, extended into a band by the prism. The spectra of the stars show them to be strongly blue and therefore young, so that this cluster is quite different in composition from the old globular clusters of the Milky Way system. About 6′ in pa. 300° is another, less concentrated and much fainter but showing stars; this object is just visible with 15 cm.

147. NGC 1837–45. For larger apertures, these objects form a beautiful large cloud of faint stars with many knots and wreaths, crossing the field from Sp. to NNf., and profusely dotted with m. 11–12 stars and a few brighter ones. This shows well the effect of distance on rich star assemblages.

150. NGC 1850–4–5. This beautiful field contains three star clusters within 12′ of one another. The first is a fine bright well-resolved globular cluster about 2′ across; 7′ Sf. is a small round knot of stars and 4′ S is a very rich star cloud 3′ × 2′ with brighter stars scattered through it. 10·5 cm shows all of these clearly and indicates their starry nature.

158. NGC 1903–10–16. Two bright round nebulae and a rich extended star cloud are in this lovely field sown with stars. The nebulae, each about 1′ across, have continuous spectra and are stellar, being unresolved globular clusters. The star cloud, about 6′ × 4′, is irregularly mottled with innumerable faint stars and many brighter knots. 10·5 cm shows all three objects clearly.

162. NGC 1935–6. In this attractive field sown with stars, five of the brightest are in beautiful contrast with a rich wedge-shaped star cloud directed S, near the apex of which are two round gaseous nebulae showing single prism images. The brighter of these is 40″ across and its prism image is plain with 10·5 cm. The whole region shows scattered nebulosity, partly gaseous and partly from irresolvable star groups.

169. NGC 1983–4. This is a beautiful region of scattered irregular star clouds, too complex for description. Parts of the field look almost nebulous but the prism does not disclose any gaseous nebulae. 15 cm shows the field fairly well.

173. NGC 2004. In a beautiful field sown with stars on a rich faint ground is a bright rather irregular globular cluster, giving a bright prism band. With outliers it is about 1′ across but the very bright condensed centre is much smaller. It is a conspicuous object with short radiating star arms N and Nf., and 15 cm shows it fairly well.

181. NGC 2029–32–35. Three irregular gaseous nebulae, all easy and bright, contrast effectively with a fine starry field; the second is the brightest, about 2·5′ across with a dark rift from S to N. The prism images are clear with 10·5 cm.

182. NGC 2027–41. This is an irregular tortuous star cloud extended across the field Sp. to Nf., well resolved and followed 6′ by a bright round symmetrical haze 1′ across with fine effect. A bright prism band indicates that the haze is an unresolved globular cluster. 15 cm deals quite well with this field.

186. NGC 2057–58–65. This complex field 20′ in diameter has at least eight small nebulae in it, three of which form a conspicuous triangle in the centre. None appears gaseous as each shows a prism band, so that they must be star clusters. Most of them are irregularly round, the largest about 2·5′ across.

187. NGC 2055–74. The region round the great looped nebula NGC 2070 is very complex; this field lies immediately Sp. and shows a lovely star cloud, very rich with many small groups and star knots in it, passing across from p. (S) to f. (N). It terminates f. with a very conspicuous S-shaped gaseous nebula with many immersed stars—a really fine object. 15 cm is needed to show the cloud well; the single prism image of the nebula is very clear.

189. NGC 2070. This wonderful field centred round the very hot bluish hazy star 30 Dor shows extensive clouds of luminous bluish haze contrasted with dark areas, and concentrated round the star in a series of well-defined loops. These are clearly outlined by the prism, demonstrating their gaseous nature which is evident even with 7·5 cm. The central star has many faint companions and the whole field is scattered with stars. 15 cm deals fairly well with the general structure of this nebula (Plate 12).

192. NGC 2080–86. Just S of the fine nebula NGC 2074 is this rich starry field containing several gaseous nebulae, the most prominent being double like a dumb-bell, followed by a small bright round nebula. About 7′ S of the former is a compact group of several nebulae. All are gaseous and show single prism images, of which the brightest may be seen with 10·5 cm.

194. NGC 2100. This is a small bright isolated knot of stars very clearly resolved; it lies in a fine field sown with stars and even 10·5 cm shows plainly the tiny star points in it. Two small faint irresolvable star clusters are in the same field, one 4·5′ p. which is NGC 2092 and the other 10′ f. which is NGC 2108, both giving faint bands in the prism.

200. NGC 2134. In a field with some scattered stars mainly N is a bright symmetrical nebulous haze about 1·5′ across with a concentrated centre. No resolution is apparent but a bright prism band reveals its stellar nature. About 5′ in pa. 200° is a small much fainter nebulous spot which also seems stellar.

203. NGC 2156–59–64. These three objects form a large triangle in a fine field sprinkled with scattered stars, and 10′ Sf. the brightest (NGC 2164) is another which is rather faint (NGC 2172). All are resolvable, the two fainter with difficulty, and the brightest is a fine compact globular cluster 2′ across with some scattered outliers. 15 cm shows all four fairly well.

Nubecula Minor (NMi)

Nubecula Minor, the small Magellan Cloud, lies in Tucana in the circumpolar region of the southern sky and is easily seen on any clear dark night as a hazy area, smaller and less bright than its neighbour. It too does not set outside the southern tropics, and reaches upper culmination at midnight about October 3rd.

This cloud is an irregular extra-galactic system distant 54,000 pc from the sun and belonging to the local group of sixteen members which includes the Milky Way system. The same variety of structure as in the large cloud is found here, but on a reduced scale. Nevertheless there are some attractive telescopic objects in it for larger apertures and seven of these are given from about twenty examined (Plate 2).

20. NGC 330. A very bright knot of stars, irregularly round about 1′ across in a field sown with faint stars; it is well resolved with sufficient magnification and 7·5 cm shows it plainly with some star sparkle. The stars must be very luminous to be evident in such a remote object.

21. NGC 346. This is an interesting region; in a field sown with stars is a large bright irregular haze about 4′ across with condensed elongated centre in pa. 130°. The prism indicates that it is gaseous, the image being easy even with 7·5 cm. 10′ Sp. is a small bright round nebula, and 12′ S (f.) are two small nebular spots about 30″ across which show prism bands and must therefore be clusters; these are IC 1611 and 1612.

24. NGC 371. In this interesting field sprinkled with stars is an almost nebulous star cloud about 5′ across, irregular and not bright. 11′ Nf. are two smaller star groups close together, the more northerly about 2′ across (NGC 395) and the other about 1′ (IC 1624). These are clearly visible with 10·5 cm and show the effect of distance on scattered clusters.

25. NGC 376. In a field scattered with medium and faint stars is a small bright irregular knot of faint stars less than 30″ across, clearly resolved with

20 cm and giving a strong band in the prism. It is easy with 7·5 cm, and 10·5 cm shows some indication of its starry character.

29. NGC 419. This remote star cluster is a bright round hazy object about 1·5′ across, symmetrical and rising to a broad centre; it is conspicuous in a field sown with faint stars and the prism extends it into a band. A small pair (7·2 10·0 3·6″ 350°) lies 8′ Sf., and 7·5 cm shows both pair and object clearly.

31. IC 1644. In a field with a few scattered stars on a very faint ground this fairly bright bluish nebula may be picked out at once by its small disk about 10″ across; it has a single prism image, plainly visible with 10·5 cm. This object has been described as planetary but if it is really in Nubecula Minor at 54,000 pc distance, the absolute magnitude would be $-9\cdot2$, the diameter at least 5 pc and the mass probably several hundred solar masses. These quantities are much greater than those of any galactic planetary nebula. It must therefore either be relatively near, and merely projected against the small cloud, or be a diffuse nebula without planetary character as recognized in galactic objects.

34. NGC 456. This object is one of a chain of small star clusters, looking partly nebulous but not gaseous in the prism. The chain is nearly 20′ long, running irregularly from Np. to Sf. and is sprinkled over with brighter stars; 10·5 cm will show this character. In appearance it looks very remote.

Octans (Oct)

Octans was established by Lacaille in 1752 to commemorate the invention of the octant by John Hadley in 1730. It occupies the rather barren region round the south celestial pole and there is little to distinguish the comparatively small area of 291 sq. deg. The stars are not designated in magnitude sequence, for the brightest is the orange yellow ν Oct m. 3·1 while α Oct is only m. 5·2. The nearest star to the pole visible to the unaided eye is σ Oct m. 5·5 which is about 50′ distant.

There are few objects of telescopic interest and no conspicuous extragalactic nebulae. NGC 2573 ($3^h 54^m$; $-89° 52′$) was discovered by John Herschel in 1837 who described it as round, small and faint and called it 'Neb. Polarissima Australis'. Photographs show it as an extra-galactic spiral 2·0′ × 0·65′ with bright nucleus, but I have never been able to find it. However others may wish to try; the R.A. is diminishing very rapidly because of precession.

921. Δ 232. Change has been slight since John Herschel measured this well-separated pair in 1836 but there seems to be slow direct motion and the stars may be physically connected. It is an easy object, and the more northerly of the two stars constituting μ Oct.

961. λ Oct. This bright elegant close pair, deep yellow and white, is very easy with 7·5 cm. It seems to be a long period binary, the only change being slow retrograde motion since John Herschel's measures in 1836.

Ophiuchus (Oph)

Ophiuchus, the serpent bearer, is an ancient constellation to which Ptolemy assigned twenty-four stars. It is a large group of area 948 sq. deg. stretching from Hercules to Scorpius on both sides of the equator and Serpens appears on each side of it. The brighter stars are widely scattered without pattern and this may be the reason why the compelling figure of Scorpius with a very short inclusion of the ecliptic is in the zodiacal sequence while Ophiuchus with an ecliptic passage nearly three times as long is not. The centre culminates at midnight about June 11th.

The southern part of Ophiuchus is in the Milky Way, the centre of which lies in this direction near the junction with Scorpius and Sagittarius. The region is heavily obscured with diffuse nebulous matter, both luminous and dark. There are six open star clusters but none makes an effective telescopic object. The globular clusters are however remarkable, as twenty-two of these bodies have been identified and they show great variety in brightness, size and resolvability, and in the extent to which they are obscured by interstellar material. Many planetary nebulae are known but most are beyond amateur instruments; however NGC 6572 is remarkably bright and NGC 6369 is annular. There are some attractive double stars, but none of the few extra-galactic nebulae is bright enough for selection.

659. ρ Oph. This is a beautiful field filled with bluish luminous haze which blots out the Milky Way stars. Three bright stars form a triangle, in which this is the brightest at the wide apex f.; it is a close unequal yellow pair, clearly resolved with 7·5 cm. Both angle and separation of this long period binary are slowly diminishing and the proper motion is common to the other two bright stars. The p. star of these is β 1115, also a close long period binary (6·8 8·2 0·8″ 350°) in retrograde motion with so far little change in separation, and 20 cm should resolve it. The luminous haze extends roughly between $16^{\rm h}\ 16^{\rm m}$ to $16^{\rm h}\ 35^{\rm m}$ and $-22°\ 40'$ to $-25°\ 35'$, and is evidently a vast diffuse nebula on which some scattered stars appear but the Milky Way background is obliterated, and faint stars only begin to appear beyond the general limits given. The nebula is relatively close at 160 pc; altogether a wonderful region of the sky.

665. Σ 2048. This easy and attractive pair, deep yellow and orange, is changing only very slowly since W. Struve found 4·7″ and 303° in 1831, but common proper motion suggests that the stars are in orbit.

668. λ Oph. This binary has a period of about 133 years; the stars were closest in 1945 and are now widening with direct motion. They are both pale yellow and in 1961 were just in contact with 15 cm, the values being 0·8″ and 342°.

669. NGC 6171. Of extended and only broadly condensed type, this globular cluster is about 3′ across, resolved into faint stars and irregularly scattered outliers which are just apparent with 15 cm, while 10·5 cm shows only a patch of haze. Interstellar absorption has been variously estimated here; R seems to be 12,000 pc.

678. NGC 6218. Messier discovered this object in 1764 and saw no stars in it, although 7·5 cm will show some. It is a beautiful large well-resolved globular cluster with a broad hazy centre of faint stars and curved rays of outliers up to 8′ across; the field also is fine. Allowing an absorption of m. 1·2, R is about 6,000 pc.

682. 21 Oph. In 1844 O. Struve found 0·87″ and 173° for this pair, and slow retrograde motion with little change in separation followed for many years. However in 1961 the companion was difficult to see and this pair should repay watching. It is a pale yellow star in a field sown with small stars, and 5′ S is the small wide unequal pair Σ 2105, the brighter star red.

684. NGC 6235. This is one of the less-concentrated type of globular cluster, a hazy luminous body about 1·5′ across full of tiny gleaming points with no conspicuous outliers. 20 cm shows some of these stars but 15 cm failed, and 10·5 cm gives only a small hazy spot in the field. With an estimated absorption of m. 1·1 in this region, R is about 16,000 pc.

688. 24 Oph. Both angle and separation of this bright pale yellow pair are slowly increasing since Burnham in 1889 found 0·7″ and 264°, and in 1960 15 cm clearly resolved the stars. Proper motion is small but there is little doubt that this is a true binary system.

689. NGC 6254. Messier discovered this cluster in 1764 and failed to see any stars in it, though these are plainly evident with 7·5 cm. It is a large broadly compressed gathering of innumerable stars, the central region about 3·5′ and the scattered outliers to 8′ across while two straight rays of four to five stars emerge N (p.). Being rather barren the field looks as though obscured; estimating this absorption as m. 1·7, R is about 6,000 pc.

691. NGC 6266. Discovered by Messier in 1771, who thought it resembled a small comet, this charming object in a beautiful field is conspicuous for small apertures but needs 15 cm to begin the resolution. It is a mass of innumerable faint stars about 3′ across, bright and symmetrical with strongly compressed centre. Absorption is however considerable, rated as m. 2·4, and R is about 7,000 pc (Plate 7).

692. IC 4634. This nebula shows a bright pale blue disk about 10″ across in a field of scattered stars; the single prism image is clear, with evidence of a second close on the violet side and a trace of very narrow continuous spectrum from a central star. 15 cm is needed to show the disk but even 7·5 cm indicates the prism image clearly. R is estimated as about 2,600 pc.

693. NGC 6273. Discovered by Messier in 1764, this fine object is somewhat elliptical, about 3′ across, rising very broadly to the centre and resolved into innumerable faint stars with almost no widely scattered outliers. Two brighter stars immersed Np. and Nf. are probably field stars, as the field is well sown. 10·5 cm shows a conspicuous granular haze with a few very faint stars in it, the beginnings of resolution. Allowing for absorption, R is estimated as 7,000 pc.

695. NGC 6284. In a field sown profusely with small and faint stars is a round haze about 1′ across, easy to see with 10·5 cm but needing 20 cm to resolve it irregularly into gleaming points. It is a distant moderately concentrated globular cluster and, allowing m. 1·1 for interstellar absorption, R is about 17,000 pc.

697. NGC 6287. The Milky Way field in which this globular cluster lies is partly veiled by absorbing matter, estimated at m. 2·9, which blots out most of the background stars. The cluster is about 1·5′ across, irregularly round, not bright and just resolved into very faint stars with 30 cm. All that 10·5 cm shows is a faint round spot in an almost empty field. R is about 8,000 pc.

698. NGC 6293. In a fine starry field is a bright compressed well-resolved globular cluster about 2′ across with irregular edges but no conspicuous outlying stars. 20 cm is able to resolve it partially but 15 cm shows only granularity. With absorption of m. 1·3 in this region, R is estimated as 14,000 pc.

699. η Oph. This brilliant white star was resolved by Burnham in 1889 as 0·35″ and 275°; separation increased with retrograde motion to a maximum of 0·65″ and 233° in 1925 and the stars then closed in, so that in 1961 I could not resolve the elliptical image with 30 cm. This is clearly a binary system which will be interesting to watch. The distance is about 24 pc.

703. NGC 6309. This small elliptical nebula 15″ × 8″ in pa. 145° is fairly bright and somewhat mottled; it lies in a sparingly sprinkled field and shows a single prism image which may just be seen with 10·5 cm. A star is close Np. R is estimated as 1,900 pc.

704. NGC 6304. This is one of the nearer globular clusters but heavy absorption, assumed as m. 3·9, makes resolution difficult, 30 cm showing in good seeing conditions some extremely faint stars in it. It is moderately bright and broadly compressed, about 1·8′ across and symmetrical; 10·5 cm shows it plainly as a round haze. R is estimated as about 5,000 pc.

705. 36 Oph. These two orange yellow dwarf stars make an impressive and easy pair in a field sprinkled with a few stars and the distance is only 5·6 pc. They were measured by South and J. Herschel in 1823 as 5·3″ and 225°, and both values have since decreased. This is a very long period binary system.

708. NGC 6316. Like most of those in Ophiuchus, this globular cluster is immersed in the Milky Way and yet the field stars are not prominent because of strong absorption which is here assessed as m. 3·3. It is a hazy luminous spot about 1′ across with very indefinite edges, not resolvable with 30 cm but evidently of compact type, not bright but showing a good prism band. It is an easy but faint object with 10·5 cm. R is estimated as about 9,000 pc.

709. U Oph. This bright pale yellow star has a faint companion wide Np. which is a good test for 20 cm; there has been no certain change since 1820, but the proper motion is small and it is impossible to know if the stars are connected. A is an eclipsing variable of period 1·677 days.

710. 41 Oph. Only in 1915 was this fine orange pair discovered by Aitken as 0·5″ and 298°. Both angle and separation appear to be increasing steadily and in 1963 the stars could be plainly seen with 20 cm, and doubtfully with 15 cm. This is no doubt a true binary system.

711. NGC 6325. This globular cluster has the same strong absorption as NGC 6316 but is more distant at about 16,000 pc. It is of fairly compact type, a round haze about 1′ across with no sign of resolution, faint but not difficult with 20 cm. The field shows only a few scattered stars.

712. o Oph. These two bright stars, orange and yellow, are connected by common proper motion but relative change is very slow, there being slight retrograde motion since William Herschel measured them in 1782.

716. NGC 6333. Messier discovered this globular cluster in 1764; it is large, rising broadly to the centre with irregular edges and well resolved, the scattered outliers about 3′ across, some of which are visible with 20 cm. It is an easy object for 7·5 cm. Considerable obscuration, estimated as m. 2·4, dims the lustre of this cluster which is relatively near at about 6,000 pc.

718. β 126. This dainty white triplet needs 15 cm to show the third star, but the close pair is clear with 7·5 cm. Motion between the three stars is very slow but this is probably a ternary system; the field is fine.

719. NGC 6342. A combination of heavy absorption, estimated as m. 3·7, and distance makes this globular cluster rather faint and irresolvable; it is fairly compressed, irregularly round, about 40″ across and shows a good prism band. A field star is near Sp. 15 cm shows the object quite plainly and R is estimated as about 12,000 pc.

721. NGC 6356. This is a well-condensed type of globular cluster, a bright luminous haze with fading edges, about 3′ across with no sign of resolution; the stars must be very faint and numerous. The bright centre 1·5′ across is an easy object for 7·5 cm. There is considerable absorption in this region, assessed at m. 2·8, and R seems to be about 10,000 pc.

722. Dark S nebula. This dark nebula is familiar to astronomers from photographs of the Milky Way, in which it is outlined against the background luminosity from innumerable faint stars. This background is unfortunately less bright here than in many other regions, and makes a very clear dark sky necessary for successful observation. The nebula is about 20′ across in a general Np.–Sf. direction and is widest around the Sf. loop, where it is clearly defined by stars inside it. Dark nebulae in general may be seen fairly well with small apertures because of less field brightness.

724. NGC 6355. A few very faint stars may be made out with 30 cm scattered through this irregularly round haze about 1′ across, and signs of resolution are also apparent with 20 cm. 10·5 cm shows a faint but quite clear hazy spot with a group of scattered stars N and f. R is not known for this distant cluster.

729. NGC 6366. Strong obscuration assessed as m. 4·7 interferes with the study of this relatively near open-type globular cluster; it is a large round gathering of very faint stars about 4′ across with little central condensation which 25 cm should show, but only a dim haze is visible with 15 cm. R is about 2,000 pc.

730. NGC 6369. This pale annular planetary nebula about 25″ across lies in the Milky Way but the field is rather barren because of strong absorption. The darker centre can just be made out with 20 cm but the single prism image is plain with 15 cm, quite well defined. R is estimated as 7,000 pc, but this seems excessive in view of the obscuration.

732. Σ 2173. With a period of 46 years, this deep yellow binary has been well observed. The stars were closest in 1957 and separation will continue until 1990. In 1961 the values were 0·6″ and 160° and the stars appeared just in contact with 20 cm. This is a good pair to watch; the distance is about 18 pc.

737. NGC 6402. Messier discovered this object in 1764; it is a large fairly bright hazy cluster, only broadly condensed and resolved into innumerable faint stars, a few of which 20 cm will show. With scattered outliers it is about 3′ across and somewhat elliptical, and with 10·5 cm conspicuous though faint. Considerable obscuration in this region is assessed at m. 2·9 and R is about 6,000 pc.

738. NGC 6401. 30 cm will hardly resolve this fairly bright elliptical hazy globular cluster about 1′ across; it is in a star sprinkled field and rises only broadly to the centre. The star in the Sf. part is no doubt a projected field star; 10·5 cm shows this and the faint spot of haze quite plainly. R is unknown.

742. 61 Oph. Small apertures show this bright wide pair well; W. Struve measured it in 1827 as 20·5″ and 94° and there has been no real change since. Proper motions are small but similar and the stars are probably connected.

743. NGC 6426. This globular cluster owes its faintness mainly to distance, although absorption in this region is assessed as m. 1·7. All one sees in a field sprinkled with stars is a faint round haze about 1′ across, somewhat brighter to the centre where some faint stars may be glimpsed with 30 cm. Care will be needed to find it with 20 cm. R is estimated as 25,000 pc.

761. NGC 6517. This is the faintest of the telescopically discovered globular clusters with an integrated magnitude of 12·7, but it is easier to see than some others because it is only 45″ across and rises considerably to a central nucleus. It is round and fairly symmetrical with no signs of resolution, and 15 cm should show it. The faintness is mainly because of heavy absorption, assessed at m. 5·4, which blots out the background stars. R is estimated as about 9,000 pc.

765. τ Oph. These close deep yellow stars shine like jewels in a field of scattered stars, and are cleanly separated with 7·5 cm. This is a binary system with a period estimated at 277 years and the motion is direct. W. Struve in 1836 found 0·43″ and 200°; the separation increased to a maximum of 2·2″ about 1898 and after remaining steady for many years, the stars are now closing again.

772. 70 Oph. This fine bright yellow and orange binary is very easy for small apertures; on spectroscopic evidence the period is 87·71 years and A is also a spectroscopic pair with period of 18·10 years. The stars are now closing, which will continue until 1991; in 1961 they were 4·5″ in 90°. The distance is 5·1 pc.

774. Σ 2276. Another easy object for small telescopes, this elegant pair on a faint starry ground is slowly widening without perceptible change in angle since the measures of W. Struve in 1830. Proper motion is small but there is little doubt that the stars are connected.

781. 73 Oph. It will be interesting to watch this pair in the future; the stars are in a very eccentric orbit of high inclination and long period which may be about 400 years. W. Struve in 1831 found 1·5″ and 260°; the stars then closed and in 1905 were only 0·1″ apart. Widening began again but in 1961 I found much difficulty in separating the stars cleanly with 30 cm, the pa. being about 35°. The motion is retrograde.

786. NGC 6572. This remarkably bright bluish planetary nebula shows a small disk 10″ across and in the prism the strong image is followed by another less bright on the violet side, with evidence of a third still farther along; these come from ionized oxygen and hydrogen. There is also a long thin spectrum streak, stronger towards the red, which is that of the otherwise invisible central star. In the field the nebula is at the apex of a train of following stars; it and the prism image are easy with 7·5 cm. R is estimated at about 900 pc.

Orion (Ori)

Orion, the hunter, has been admired throughout historical times as one of the most brilliant and symmetrical constellations; being bisected by the equator, it is equally well seen from both hemispheres. Ptolemy assigned thirty-eight stars to it, including the nebulous one which had been remarked in very early times. The area is 594 sq. deg. and the centre culminates at midnight about December 13th.

Many of the bright Orion stars are very hot, young and of early spectral type; this applies particularly to those like the multiple θ Ori which are immersed in the great nebula and which stimulate its luminescence. Such stars are using up their stores of hydrogen so rapidly that their lives cannot be long astronomically unless they have means of continual replenishment of the element from the vast regions of nebular material surrounding them. It appears that in the Orion nebula stars are still in the process of active formation.

Orion is specially rich in beautiful double and multiple stars, and nebulous haze both bright and dark is found in many regions. There is no globular cluster, but ten open clusters are known, some of which are brilliant scattered groups; in addition two large star associations have been studied. One is in the region of Orion's belt, and the other is round λ Ori; these are too large for telescopic objects. One of the two planetary nebulae is listed, but all of the extra-galactic nebulae are faint.

145. 14 Ori. Since its discovery by O. Struve in 1844, the separation of this fine close pair has hardly altered but the motion has been steadily retrograde. The period has been estimated at about 500 years. 20 cm separates the stars cleanly deep and pale yellow. About 6′ S the pair Σ 643 (8·5 8·5 3″ 301°) has the same proper motion.

149. Σ 652. This deep yellow star has a close companion which 7·5 cm will show in good conditions. There has been little real change since the measures of W. Struve in 1830 and, though the proper motion is small, the stars seem to share it and no doubt form a long period binary system.

152. ρ Ori. This beautiful easy pair, orange yellow and white, is in a field well sprinkled with stars. Common proper motion suggests physical connection but no change has been observed since W. Struve's measures in 1832.

154. β Ori. Even 5 cm will show the companion of this brilliant bluish white star; there has been very little change between them since W. Struve's measures in 1831 and the period must be long. B is itself a very close equal pair of spectroscopic period 9·86 days.

157. τ Ori. Two faint wide companions can be made out by 15 cm near this brilliant pale yellow star, one in pa. 250° and the other in pa. 60°; 30 cm will show the former as a pair (11·5 12·3 3·5″ 51°) and it is a good test of definition, being only 35″ removed from A. The stars seem fixed but, as the proper motion of the primary is very small, physical connection is doubtful.

161. η Ori. The components of this beautiful white pair are just separated with 10·5 cm. Dawes measured them in 1849 and the separation has somewhat increased with slow retrograde motion, evidently of long period. A is a spectroscopic binary of period 7·99 days and there is evidence of a third star with period 9·2 years.

171. 33 Ori. This fine white pair in a field well sprinkled with stars is clearly divided by 7·5 cm. No real change has occurred since the measures of W. Struve in 1831.

172. δ Ori. This is an attractive combination of wide bluish white pair and star field, suitable for all apertures. A is a spectroscopic binary of period 5·732 days and in its spectrum interstellar lines which do not share the Doppler motion of the star were first detected by Hartmann in 1904. Being so close to the equator this is a useful star for determining the field diameter of oculars; the time in seconds taken by the star to drift centrally through the field, divided by 4, gives its diameter in minutes of arc.

176. λ Ori. This brilliant and easy white pair was measured by W. Struve in 1830 and there has been no real change since; the proper motions are very small. Photographs show that both stars are immersed in faint extended nebulosity and R is estimated as 500 pc.

177. NGC 1976. One of the most attractive objects in the sky, this great nebula is too well known to need description; faint extensions from it appear to cover most of the constellation of Orion. The prism shows the gaseous nature very plainly. Immediately N is the extension known as M 43, which is a star immersed in bright luminous haze with a curved tail and dark areas near. The average radial velocity is $+17\cdot5$ k/s and R is estimated as 460 pc.

The star group known as the trapezium (θ Ori) lies in a darker bay near the heart of the nebula. Six stars are visible in it with 15 cm, and five with $10\cdot5$ cm, although I have seen the fifth star steadily with $7\cdot5$ cm. Because of the ease with which the two fainter stars may now be seen, it is remarkable that they were missed by William Herschel with his great instruments. In fact, E was discovered by W. Struve in 1826 and F by John Herschel in 1830, who wrote in 1849 that the four trapezium stars are 'accompanied by two excessively minute and very close companions, to perceive both which is one of the severest tests which can be applied to a telescope'. This is certainly not the case now, and it has been thought that both stars have increased in brightness since discovery, though they do not seem to be variable now. It is of course easier to see an object known to be there than to discover it, but the Herschels, father and son, were most experienced observers always alert for new discoveries. It should be remembered also that steady atmospheric conditions are most important in making visible faint stars in bright luminous haze, and large instruments are much more sensitive in this respect than small ones. At the Slough observatory of William Herschel the trapezium stars culminated only $33°$ above the southern horizon.

178. 42 Ori. The field shows a large straggling star group involved in luminous clouds which are extensions from the great nebula. This very bright star needs good definition to see the close companion with $10\cdot5$ cm; the pair seems to be a true binary, and both separation and angle are slowly diminishing.

179. ι Ori. This star is in the group immediately S of the great nebula; the field is beautiful and the brilliant white star, itself a spectroscopic binary of period $29\cdot136$ days, has a well-separated white companion which has remained fixed since the measures of W. Struve in 1831. A bright wide white pair ($4\cdot7$ $5\cdot6$ $36''$ $226°$) points towards it. Most of these bright early type stars show interstellar lines in their spectra.

184. σ Ori. Three companions combine with this bright white star to form an irregular cross bar to a narrow triangle of stars with a delicate equal pair at one base angle—a charming pattern. The bright star is itself a very close pair which I have never succeeded even in elongating. There has been no real change since the measures of W. Struve in 1831.

188. ζ Ori. This brilliant white pair needs good definition because of glare; it may be cleanly resolved with $7\cdot5$ cm. This must be the reason why William Herschel overlooked the companion; it illustrates the great advantage of previous knowledge of what may be seen and makes his own discovery of the planet Uranus such a wonderful feat. The angle of the pair is slowly increasing with no real change in separation.

190. NGC 2022. A small but conspicuous grey object of even light lies in a field sown with stars; it is slightly elliptical in pa. 30° and about 20″ across. The prism image is single and no central star is visible; this image may be seen with 10·5 cm. R is estimated as about 3,000 pc.

191. NGC 2024. This region shows extensive irregular mottled luminosity, with here a dark roughly rectangular area about 10′ × 4′ lying Np.–Sf., with a few stars on the edges. The dark patch may be made out with 10·5 cm, but too large a field will include some of the glare from ζ Ori which is 17′ Sp. The 'horse's head' nebula so well known from photographs with large instruments lies about 30′ S of this star but I have never been able to see it, although a long thin ribbon of irregular haze is faintly shown by 30 cm. This is the brighter f. edge of a large nebulous patch into which the dark nebula projects.

195. NGC 2068. Méchain discovered this gaseous nebula in 1780 and described it as 'two fairly bright stars enveloped in nebulosity'. Close attention shows that the whole field is nebulous, of which this is a brighter part, rounded and defined on the N by a darker area there. It is about 4′ across and the wide pair of stars stare out of the luminosity like eyes. The prism discloses its gaseous character and it is not difficult to find with 7·5 cm.

196. 52 Ori. W. Struve measured this pair in 1831 as 1·7″ and 200°, so that the separation is slowly diminishing with direct motion. It is an attractive yellow pair in a field sprinkled with stars, the stars just in contact with 7·5 cm.

199. α Ori. Betelgeuse is an irregular variable of general period 5·8 years, and variable radial velocity indicating pulsation. The spectrum is very fine, crossed by a large number of sharp lines and bands, many of which may be seen with 7·5 cm. The sharpness of the lines indicates a giant star of very low density which was confirmed by interferometer measures of the apparent diameter, giving a value of 0·047″. At a distance of 100 pc, this gives the actual diameter as 4·7 A.U., sufficiently large to include the whole orbit of Mars.

208. NGC 2169. In a region sown with stars this bright open cluster stands out well, even with small apertures. It is about 5′ across and would be completely triangular if the Sp. apex were not missing. It includes a close pair (7·3 8·0 2·6″ 110°) and R is estimated as 700 pc.

Pavo (Pav)

Pavo, the peacock, is one of the constellations introduced by Bayer about 1603. It covers an area of 378 sq. deg. between Telescopium and the circumpolar Octans, and the only conspicuous star is the m. 2 white α Pav on the northern edge. The centre culminates at midnight about July 13th.

The chief ornament of this constellation is the beautiful globular cluster NGC 6752, one of the gems of the sky. There are no open clusters but two planetary nebulae are known; both are difficult and NGC 6630 is given as a test. Some thirty extra-galactic nebulae have been examined; the brightest are NGC 6684 and 6744, and the elongated spindle IC 5052 is also given.

797. ξ Pav. This very bright orange star shines like a jewel in a field of scattered stars; it has a white companion which 7·5 cm will show. For 30 years after the first measures in 1895 there was little change but the angle is now increasing. The proper motion of A is very small and not much is known about the pair. A was shown in 1928 to be a spectroscopic binary of period 2,214 days.

805. NGC 6630. This object is not easy for 30 cm; it requires a dark clear night with good equatorial setting and will be seen as a very faint round haze about 30″ across in a field sprinkled with faint stars. The single prism image can just be made out. As a guide are four stars m. 12·5–13 about 1·5′ away, p., Sp., Sf. and f. The integrated magnitude is given as 15·3 but visually it must be brighter than this. R is not known.

824. R 314. Russell measured this close pale yellow pair in 1880 as 1·0″ and 260°; both angle and separation have since increased and in 1960 7·5 cm showed both stars clearly. It is impossible to say much about this pair yet.

825. NGC 6684. The brightest of the numerous extra-galactic nebulae in Pavo is round and symmetrical, about 45″ across, rising sharply to an almost stellar nucleus with a definite prism band. The bright pale yellow θ Pav is 6′ Np. and interferes with observation but 15 cm shows the nebula clearly; it is classed as spiral.

849. NGC 6744. Photographs show this object as one of the largest of the barred spirals, about 21′ × 15′; I see it as a large irregularly elliptical faintly luminous haze more than 5′ across with some faint stars involved. The centre about 30″ wide is bright and looks granular, giving a strong band in the prism. In good conditions 10·5 cm shows this nebula plainly.

850. NGC 6752. On a clear dark night this is a most lovely object; it is a moderately condensed type of globular cluster, the central region about 3′ wide and the unusually bright outliers extending over 15′, involving an elegant pair (7·7 9·3 3·0″ 238°). Many of the brighter stars of the cluster are in curved and looped arms, and look distinctly reddish. Even 7·5 cm shows scattered stars in and around a nebulous haze. R is about 5,800 pc (Plate 8).

928. IC 5052. In a field well sprinkled with stars on a very faint ground is a rather faint edgewise spiral nebula in the form of a spindle about 4′ × 0·5′

in pa. 135° which rises somewhat to the long axis but with no real nucleus. It is an easy interesting object which 20 cm shows fairly well.

929. Rmk 26. This is an attractive pair for small apertures; both angle and separation are diminishing since John Herschel in 1835 found 3·2″ and 100°, and similar proper motion suggests a long period binary system.

939. Hd 305. For many of these Harvard pairs where the magnitudes have been determined photographically, I find the faint star considerably fainter than designated. This pair is a possible exception as the companion of the bright yellow star may be glimpsed with 25 cm on a clear dark night of good definition, a real test of instrument and conditions. The proper motion is considerable and shared by both stars which may be in orbit, but little is known about them yet.

Pegasus (Peg)

Pegasus, the winged horse of Greek mythology, is one of the ancient northern constellations, to which Ptolemy assigned twenty stars. It is a very large group of area 1,121 sq. deg. extending from near the equator to 35° N and is recognized by the great square of bright stars, of which however the Nf. one is α And. In addition there are some stars representing the fore feet, and a curved arc for the head and neck, in the upright position for southern observers. Culmination of the centre occurs at midnight about September 1st.

Some interesting double stars are found in Pegasus. There are two globular clusters, the beautiful NGC 7078 and a remote system, discovered photographically at Palomar, much beyond amateur instruments. A small planetary nebula has been recorded as projected on NGC 7078. Of twenty of the extra-galactic nebulae examined, three of the brighter have been included.

954. NGC 7078. This beautiful globular cluster in a field well sown with stars rises to a very bright central peak and is resolved into a mass of faint stars with scattered outliers in irregular rays up to 7′ across. This resolution is just apparent with 10·5 cm, and it is interesting to note that when Maraldi discovered this object in 1745, he described it as being composed of many stars, but Messier in 1764 could see none. A small planetary nebula is projected on this cluster but I have never been able to find it with the prism as the background illumination is too bright. The latest estimate of R is 9,960 pc.

960. κ Peg. This very bright yellow star is an interesting system in itself, for Burnham in 1880 discovered it to be a very close binary of period 11·5 years and one of the stars was found by Luyten in 1934 to be a spectroscopic binary of period 5·97 days. It is not known if the wide companion belongs to the system also; it was measured by W. Struve in 1831 as 11″ in 308° but the proper motion of A may account for the subsequent changes. It can be seen in the glare of the primary with 15 cm.

962. Σ 2848. This is an attractive pale yellow pair in a field of scattered stars, an easy object for 7·5 cm. No real change has followed the measures of W. Struve in 1829 and little is known of the stars yet.

971. Σ 2878. This pair is evidently a long period binary with slow retrograde motion which is the only change since W. Struve's values of 1·4″ and 131° in 1830. The less bright star close Sf. may be seen surely with 10·5 cm, whiter than the other.

979. 34 Peg. The faint companion of this bright yellow star is close Sp. and not easy, but 25 cm will show it in good conditions. Change has been very slow since Burnham's measures in 1878 but considerable common proper motion suggests that the stars must be connected.

983. 37 Peg. This interesting binary has an orbit almost in the line of sight and a period of about 143 years. When W. Struve measured it in 1831 the values were 1·2″ and 113°, but between 1887 and 1897 and again between 1914 and 1916 it could not be resolved. The stars are now widening and in 1964 20 cm showed them clearly apart in pa. 118°; this should continue until at least 1980. It will be interesting to watch this pair.

986. NGC 7331. Photographs disclose a fine edgewise spiral 9′ × 2′ in pa. 165° with a dark band along the central region p. I see with 30 cm a pointed ellipse 2·5′ × 0·5′ rising much to a bright elongated centre, with an indefinite longer and wider very faint envelope. The centre looks granular and readily gives a band in the prism, but no dark lane is visible. The nebula is faint and elongated with 15 cm.

987. NGC 7332. In this well-sprinkled star field is a small narrow elliptical nebula about 1·5′ × 0·5′ in pa. 155°, fairly bright and rising much to a small round centre. About 5′ f. (S) is a faint narrow nebulous streak 1·5′ long in pa. 90°; this is NGC 7339, of more even light than the other and just perceptible with 20 cm, while the first may be made out with 10·5 cm. Both are extra-galactic spirals.

990. ξ Peg. This very bright yellow star has a faint companion well-separated Sf. which 20 cm will show steadily in the glare. The stars share considerable proper motion and are no doubt connected; there has been slow retrograde motion since John Herschel found 123° in 1820.

995. 52 Peg. O. Struve in 1845 found 0·9″ and 181° for this yellow pair and with steady direct motion the separation increased to 1·2″ in 1900. The stars are now slowly closing and in 1961 20 cm showed them just in contact. The period is apparently several hundred years.

996. β Peg. Dominating a field with a few scattered stars this brilliant orange star has a fine absorption spectrum in the prism, with broad dark bands in red and orange, and a series of narrower bands in green, blue and violet. Some of these are plain with 10·5 cm.

1006. NGC 7619. In this field sprinkled with stars are two bright round nebulae about 7′ apart, the more f. being NGC 7626. Both are about 1′ across, rise much to the centre to a tiny star-like nucleus, and they show conspicuous bands in the prism. They make a large cross with two stars m. 8 lying N (p.) and S (f.). 15 cm shows them clearly and both are classed as elliptical extra-galactic systems.

1007. Σ 3007. This dainty unequal pair, deep yellow and ashy, is clearly shown by 7·5 cm in a black field. W. Struve in 1829 found 5·7″ and 79° and the only change has been steady direct motion. Common proper motion indicates that the stars are probably in orbit.

1013. 78 Peg. This fine bright deep yellow star forms a large triangle with two stars less bright S and Sp. I do not find it easy to resolve although 20 cm will show the companion very close Sp. in good conditions. Direct motion has occurred since Dembowski found 1·4″ and 192° in 1876 and the stars seem to be in orbit.

1017. 85 Peg. Measurement of this very unequal close binary is difficult, but the period is about 26·5 years. The stars were closest in 1961 at 0·4″ and 327° and will be widest about 1969 with 0·8″ and 145°. This is not an easy object and needs good definition, but it is interesting and worth following by those with adequate optical means.

Perseus (Per)

Perseus, the Greek hero, is one of the ancient northern constellations which is only partly visible to many southern observers. It lies in the Milky Way between Andromeda and Auriga from 31° N to 59° N, and may be recognized by a group of moderately bright stars low in the north preceding the brilliant Capella. The area is 615 sq. deg. and the centre culminates at midnight about November 7th.

There are no very striking double stars in Perseus but the well-known eclipsing variable is β Per. Of the twenty known open clusters, much the most attractive are the companions NGC 869 and 884 which indeed are mentioned as a nebulous star amongst the twenty-six assigned to Perseus by Ptolemy. No globular cluster occurs and only two planetary nebulae are available for amateur instruments. There are few extra-galactic nebulae, the brightest being NGC 1023.

47. NGC 650–1. Méchain discovered this object in 1780 which Messier thought later was composed of faint stars; it is however a planetary nebula with bright irregular centre, about $85'' \times 40''$ in pa. $40°$ which with small apertures seems divided into two parts, the brighter Sp. It gives a single prism image, easily visible with 15 cm. R is estimated as 2,500 pc.

59. NGC 869; **61.** NGC 884. These two brilliant clusters, about $30'$ apart, are listed for completeness; they do not rise above the horizon of my observatory. Each is given as $30'$ in diameter, integrated magnitude 4·4, containing more than 100 stars and R is estimated as 2,200 pc. T. W. Webb describes them as 'gorgeous' and Admiral Smyth as 'affording together one of the most brilliant telescopic objects in the heavens'. They have been known since the time of Hipparchus.

67. NGC 1023. Photographs show a large elongated ellipse which is probably spiral, the centre very bright. With 30 cm it is a fairly bright elliptical haze $3' \times 1'$ in pa. $80°$, rising much to the centre and showing a band in the prism. The elliptical form is plain with 15 cm.

70. NGC 1039. Messier discovered this cluster in 1764 and noted the easy visibility of its stars. It is a fine scattered group needing a large field as it is about $30'$ across, effective for small telescopes with numerous stars and good central condensation. R is estimated as 400 pc.

77. Σ 336. This easy unequal pair, orange and whitish, lies in a field of scattered stars; proper motion is common to both stars but there has been only slight change since W. Struve measured them in 1831.

79. β Per. The orbit of Algol has been well investigated spectroscopically; this is an eclipsing variable of period 2·867 days, the companion being cool enough to be called dark. In 1934 McLaughlin suggested a third, also dark, companion of period 1·873 years in relation to the close pair; this third star has been compared to a planet, but without any convincing evidence.

96. Σ 425. This dainty equal yellow pair is in a field of scattered stars and is clearly shown by 7·5 cm. The stars appear to form a true binary system with slowly diminishing angle and separation.

99. IC 351. In this field of faint stars the most conspicuous object is an unequal wide pair, and nearly $4'$ Np. is a hazy disk about $5''$ across which shows a single prism image. 20 cm shows this image also but with 15 cm the planetary nebula appears only as a faint star. R is estimated as about 2,800 pc.

103. ζ Per. The brilliant pale yellow star has an ashy companion well separated Sp. which 10·5 cm shows with care. There has been no real change since

W. Struve's measures in 1830, but the proper motion of A is small and little is known about these stars yet.

105. ε Per. 7·5 cm shows easily the slate coloured companion of this brilliant pale yellow star; change has been negligible since the measures of W. Struve in 1832 but common proper motion suggests physical connection between the stars.

120. 56 Per. This is a bright golden star with a yellow companion Nf. in a field well sprinkled with stars. Steady retrograde motion has taken place with little change in separation since the measures of O. Struve in 1847 and the stars seem to be in orbit. The distance is about 28 pc.

Phoenix (Phe)

Phoenix, the mythical bird which rose again from its own ashes after destruction by fire, is one of Bayer's additions to the constellations about 1603. It lies south of Sculptor between Grus and Eridanus, with little to distinguish its scattered stars except the orange yellow α Phe of m. 2·4. The area is 469 sq. deg. and the centre of the group culminates at midnight about October 5th.

The objects of interest in this constellation are restricted almost entirely to some double stars, for neither star clusters nor gaseous nebulae occur and of the thirteen extra-galactic nebulae examined, only NGC 625 is fairly large and bright.

1011. θ Phe. Small apertures find an attractive object in this elegant unequal white pair, which has shown little change in separation and slow direct motion since John Herschel's measures in 1835. The stars are probably in orbit.

26. β Phe. This very bright yellow pair is clearly divided with 15 cm; separation is slowly increasing with slow retrograde motion and the period must be long.

27. ζ Phe. This beautiful white pair ornaments a field sprinkled with a few stars. Change is very slow but the stars are probably connected and the brighter is an eclipsing spectroscopic binary of period 1·67 days, the combined masses nine times that of the sun.

42. NGC 625. In a field sprinkled with a few stars is a fairly bright lengthened haze about $3' \times 1'$ in pa. 80°, considerably brighter to the central axis and giving a band in the prism. This is an extra-galactic edgewise spiral, and 15 cm shows the form clearly.

Pictor (Pic)

Pictor was originally the painter's easel of Lacaille in 1752, and the name was simplified by Gould in 1877. It is a small constellation south of Columba of area 247 sq. deg. and contains only scattered stars, making recognition difficult. The centre culminates at midnight about December 15th.

Apart from some double stars, this constellation is devoid of interest for the amateur. The few extra-galactic nebulae examined were all small and faint.

133. ι Pic. This beautiful bright yellow pair dominates a field sprinkled with scattered stars, an excellent object for small apertures. There has been no real change since J. Dunlop measured the stars in 1826 but considerable common proper motion suggests that the stars are connected. A shows variable radial velocity and may be a spectroscopic binary.

164. θ Pic. John Herschel measured these bright pale yellow stars in 1835 and no sensible change has occurred since; they share the same proper motion. In 1901 Innes discovered that the brighter f. star was a close pair (6·9 7·3 0·45″ 197°) for which separation has slowly increased with retrograde motion. In 1960 30 cm separated the stars, the companion very close S (p.).

221. μ Pic. Since John Herschel measured this pair in 1836 there has been ittle real change; it is a bright white star with a companion close Sp. which 7·5 cm shows with close attention. Not much is known about this pair yet.

Pisces (Psc)

Pisces, the fishes, is the last of the zodiacal constellations and was assigned thirty-four stars by Ptolemy. It is a large group of 889 sq. deg. area in a rather barren region of the sky. The main distinction by which it may be recognized is two irregular chains of small stars, one roughly from north and the other from west, meeting in the pale yellow α Psc of magnitude 4·3, south of the triangle of Aries. The centre of the constellation culminates at midnight about September 27th.

The only objects of interest for the amateur observer are a number of double stars and a few extra-galactic nebulae. None of these latter is really bright and from seventeen of them examined, only two have been selected.

1008. Σ 3009. This beautiful pair, orange and whitish (by contrast), ornaments a field with a few stars, and small apertures deal well with it. W. Struve measured the stars in 1829 as 6·8″ and 229° and there has been no real change since. However shared proper motion suggests that the stars are connected.

2. 35 Psc. The brighter star of this long period pair was discovered to be a spectroscopic binary in 1934 with a period of 0·842 days; the system is thus ternary as the stars have common proper motion. It is an easy object for 7·5 cm.

4. 38 Psc. This is an elegant yellow pair in a field sprinkled with faint stars, neat and dainty with 7·5 cm. Both stars are dwarf, with no real change in angle and separation since 1836. R. G. Aitken found in 1908 that the brighter star is itself an extremely close pair.

10. 55 Psc. With similar proper motion but no real change since 1830, the period of this binary must be very long; the stars are in fine contrast, orange yellow and ashy, in a field sprinkled with scattered stars.

17. 65 Psc. This fine pair of giant yellow stars has remained unchanged since 1832 and similar proper motion suggests that they are in an orbit of long period. It dominates a field of scattered stars, excellent for small apertures.

30. β 303. The separation and angle of this close yellow pair in a thin field seem to be increasing very slowly and no doubt the stars form a true binary. 20 cm resolved them but 15 cm was not successful.

32. ϕ Psc. This pair has shown little change since measured by W. Struve in 1832; the colours are orange yellow and white, and 7·5 cm will show the companion. Similar proper motion suggests physical connection between the stars.

33. ζ Psc. The colours of this pair, yellow and whitish, are contradicted by the spectral types, which shows how easily the eye may be deceived by difference in brightness. It is an easy object and makes a lovely sight in a moonlit field. The less bright star is itself a spectroscopic binary of period 9·075 days. Change has been inappreciable but common proper motion and similar radial velocity indicate a very long period system.

37. NGC 524. In this round very symmetrical nebula, discovered by William Herschel in 1786, photographs show faint traces of spiral structure; it is about 1·5′ across with an almost stellar nucleus and gives a strong prism band. It is an easy object for 10·5 cm.

39. η Psc. Since Burnham discovered this close unequal pair in 1878, slow direct motion has occurred but little is known about the stars yet. Like all such pairs with very bright primary, good steady definition is needed to show the faint star and 30 cm should be able to do it.

43. Σ 138. 10·5 cm resolves this elegant yellow pair well. Common proper motion suggests that the stars are connected but the only change since W. Struve's measures in 1830 has been very slow direct motion.

45. NGC 628. Photographs show this object as a beautiful symmetrical spiral system about 8′ in diameter, the two arms regularly coiled and with many scattered condensations in them. I see a rather faint round haze 4′ across with a broad brighter centre and suggestion of concentric zoning. Méchain discovered it in 1780 but found it very difficult to observe, and indeed 10·5 cm shows only a dim round haze.

56. α Psc. This fine pair dominates a field of a few scattered stars, and even 5 cm will resolve it clearly. It is a binary system of long period, with slow diminution in both angle and separation.

Piscis Austrinus (PsA)

Piscis Austrinus, the southern fish, is an ancient group to which Ptolemy assigned twelve stars. It is easily recognized by the bright star Fomalhaut with a few stars near. This star is the mouth of the fish into which old star charts show the stream of water from Aquarius ending; it has a brilliant spectrum crossed by prominent dark absorption lines of hydrogen. The area of the constellation is 245 sq. deg. and the centre culminates at midnight about August 25th.

Stars are the only galactic objects which occur in Piscis Austrinus, and among them are several attractive pairs. There are many extra-galactic nebulae but few are prominent; from more than twenty examined, the brightest has been selected and also a field containing three of these objects.

964. η PsA. This bright pale yellow star lies in a field with five small wide pairs; in good conditions it is clearly divided by 7·5 cm and makes an attractive object. Since 1876 the angle has diminished very slowly with little change in separation and it seems to be a binary system of long period.

965. NGC 7172. In this interesting field well sprinkled with stars are three small extra-galactic nebulae. In R.A. sequence, the first is round, diffuse, about 1′ across rising only broadly to the centre and not bright. The second (NGC 7173) is small, round with a nucleus, fairly bright about 30″ across. The third (NGC 7176) is the brightest; it is elliptical in pa. 250°, about 1′ across and seems to be composed of two irregular parts in contact with a tiny nucleus only in the Nf. one, so that John Herschel called it a double nebula. All three show their nature by prism bands. They are visible faintly with 15 cm, but 20 cm is much better.

984. β PsA. This is an excellent object for small apertures; the stars are pale yellow and white, the less bright star appearing sometimes reddish; the field is comparatively barren, a fainter star being 2·5′ in 200°. John Herschel measured this pair in 1836 and there has been no real change since, but common proper motion makes it likely that this is a binary system.

985. NGC 7314. In a sparsely sprinkled star field this is a large diffuse fairly bright elliptical haze about 3′ × 1′ in pa. 160°, rising only broadly to the long axis and giving a band in the prism. It is an extra-galactic spiral system which 15 cm shows rather faintly, but 20 cm indicates the general shape.

988. h. 5356. In this field is a fine combination of a bright yellow star (CD 17873 m. 6·3 Go) with 1·5′ Sf. a close unequal less bright and less yellow pair; these show well with 7·5 cm in a black field. In 1837 John Herschel found 4·4″ in 58° for the pair, since when the separation has diminished with slow direct motion. The bright star has the same proper motion as the pair and all three seem to be connected.

991. γ PsA. This beautiful pair with a few scattered stars in the field is an excellent object for small apertures, the stars pale and deep yellow showing their colours well. Since John Herschel's measures in 1835 of 3·6″ and 276°, change has been slow with retrograde motion but the stars are connected by common proper motion.

994. δ PsA. In a sparingly sprinkled field this bright deep yellow star has a faint companion close Sp. which 7·5 cm will show with care. Since Burnham measured the stars in 1879 there has been no appreciable change, but common proper motion indicates that they may be in orbit.

Puppis (Pup)

Puppis, the poop, is one of the constellations formed by Gould in 1877 from the ancient and very large Argo Navis. It has an area of 673 sq. deg. and is the most northern of Gould's divisions, extending along the Milky Way from Monoceros to Carina. The Milky Way is rich in this region and sown with bright scattered stars, so that Puppis offers a fine selection of objects for the observer. The centre culminates at midnight about January 9th.

This constellation includes at least forty open star clusters; some of these are attractive telescopic objects but many are less so because they do not stand out well enough from the usually very rich star fields. I have therefore been sparing in selecting these, but have included several double stars which combine well with most impressive backgrounds and should give the observer a good conception of the great beauty of this region. There is one globular cluster NGC 2298 and six planetary nebulae, of which however three are beyond amateur instruments. NGC 2467 is a remarkable gaseous nebula not classed as planetary. Extra-galactic objects are almost entirely screened off by the Milky Way.

205. h. 3834. This elegant unequal pair, yellow and orange, is in a fine field sown with fainter stars and three other bright ones; the nearest of these is 3·3′ Np. and shares the considerable proper motion of the pair with similar parallax, so that this is no doubt a ternary system at 29 pc distance. The separation of the pair is increasing with slow retrograde motion, and 7·5 cm shows it cleanly.

218. Δ 30. This beautiful pair, yellow and reddish, has shown slow diminution in both separation and angle since measured by John Herschel in 1835. Each star is also a close pair, forming a quaternary system. A and B (6·0 6·1 0·85″ 266° in 1947) are now separating with retrograde motion. C and D (9·1 9·2 0·7″ 110° in 1947) were single from 1914 to 1916 and are now separating with rapid direct motion. The respective angles in 1962 were about 250° and 150°, and 20 cm was able to resolve the pairs. This system will be interesting to watch.

225. Δ 31. A well-sprinkled star field is dominated by this orange yellow and white easy pair; the proper motion is very small and there has been little change since 1835, so that not much can be said about these stars yet.

232. NGC 2298. A small rather irregular globular cluster lies in a field sown with stars; it is well resolved and fairly compact, about 1·5′ across with some scattered outliers. The object is easy with 10·5 cm but 15 cm is needed to show evidence of resolution. R is estimated as about 25,000 pc.

241. h. 3928. This elegant pair lies in a field sown with scattered stars, an easy object for 7·5 cm. Both angle and separation have slowly diminished since John Herschel's measures in 1836 and this is probably a true binary.

246. β 757. 7·5 cm shows this bright pale yellow pair very well in the black field dotted with faint stars. Pritchett in 1881 measured the stars and there has not been much change since but the proper motion seems to be shared.

247. L² Pup. Unusually bright for a long period variable, this orange red star dominates a field sown with stars. The spectrum is crossed along its length by a series of dark bands and lines, some of which are visible with 10·5 cm. The period is 141 days.

263. Δ 49. This bright white pair accentuates a beautiful field sown profusely with stars, many of which form marked curvilinear patterns. The angle is so far fixed but the separation seems to be diminishing slowly, and if these stars are in orbit the period must be very long.

264. Σ 1104. Clearly divided by 7·5 cm, this beautiful golden yellow pair lies in a profuse starry field; the angle is steadily increasing with no clear change in separation since W. Struve measured the stars in 1831, and they appear to be in orbit with shared proper motion.

265. σ Pup. A brilliant orange star with white (by contrast) companion makes a fine sight in the star sprinkled field, and 7·5 cm shows it well. The stars have similar proper motion and there has been no real change since the measures of John Herschel in 1836. A is also a spectroscopic binary of period 257·8 days, both stars being giants while the companion is a dwarf.

267. HN 19. This is an attractive almost equal deep yellow pair which dominates the field of scattered stars. J. South found the angle 105° in 1825 and it has slowly increased without change in separation. The proper motions are similar and suggest that this is a binary system.

268. NGC 2422. This is a wonderful field of bright white scattered stars in an open cluster about 30' across, preceded by a fine orange star. The two pairs are Σ 1120 (5·6 9·5 19" 36°) and Σ 1121 (7·9 7·9 7·5" 303°) in both of which there has been no change since the measures of W. Struve in 1830. R is about 500 pc.

272. H III 27. An excellent object for small telescopes, this beautiful almost equal pale yellow pair dominates a fine starry field; there has been little change since Jacob's measures in 1853. A faint star (14 7" 222°) found by Burnham in 1899 I have not been able to see. Similar proper motions suggest a binary of long period, and the spectroscopic parallax indicates R to be 80 pc.

274. NGC 2437–8. A beautiful open cluster of medium bright stars about 25' across, rich and broadly concentrated towards the centre. In the Nf. region is a pale bluish planetary nebula 50" across which on close examination will be seen to be annular with paler centre and single prism image. Several stars are projected upon it for the nebula at 1,600 pc lies far behind the cluster at 700 pc. Messier discovered the cluster in 1771 but did not see the nebula, which however is plainly visible with 10·5 cm amongst the stars.

275. NGC 2440. Photographs with large instruments give this object an irregular outline and make it look like the result of an explosion. It is a bright bluish hazy nebula about 20" across in a fine starry field; the prism shows only one image and no central star is apparent. It is easy to find with 7·5 cm, and also the prism image. R is estimated as about 2,000 pc.

278. NGC 2447. Messier discovered this object in 1781; it is a beautiful open cluster about 25" across, merging into a rich field and contains many small pairs, triplets and elegant groups, including two orange stars Sp. It is an attractive object with 10·5 cm; R is estimated as about 750 pc.

279. NGC 2452. This planetary nebula is round, about 20" across, fairly well defined with no visible central star and a single prism image. It lies in a fine field sown with stars which 9' Nf. gather into a small fan cluster (NGC 2453). 15 cm shows the nebula and a very faint prism image. R is about 3,000 pc.

280. 5 Pup. This pair was measured by W. Struve in 1831 as 3·3″ and 17°, and both values have slowly diminished since then. It is a fine object in a starry field and 7·5 cm shows it well. The stars are connected by similar proper motion.

281. NGC 2467. William Herschel discovered this remarkable object in 1784; it is a bright round fairly even luminous haze nearly 4′ across containing many faint stars, and lies in a rich and beautiful field. It is gaseous as the single prism image indicates; 10·5 cm will show this, and 7·5 cm shows the nebula itself. R is estimated as 1,000 pc.

282. NGC 2477. This is a rich open cluster of stars about 25′ across, broadly concentrated to a denser centre of 12′; the stars are very numerous and many are grouped in curved lines and sprays with dark sky between, making a beautiful effect. 15 cm shows this cluster fairly well. R is about 700 pc.

283. I 26. Discovered by Tebbutt in 1895 as 0·8″ in 27°, this difficult pair seems to be gradually closing with slow direct motion. Good conditions in 1962 allowed 25 cm to separate the stars; they are probably in orbit and should repay watching by those with adequate optical means.

285. β 202. This elegant white pair lies in a lovely and impressive star field. In 1876 Burnham found 8·2″ and 165° and subsequent measures are somewhat discrepant although change is clearly very slow. Not much is known about this pair but I think the magnitude of B is overestimated as 9·2, for it was difficult to see with 7·5 cm.

286. h. 4038. John Herschel discovered this pair in 1837 and noted as very remarkable the unusual colour combination of very pale yellow and red; this is visible with 7·5 cm and a fine field makes this an attractive object. Both separation and angle have shown only doubtful change and little is known of this pair yet.

288. h. 4046. In this beautiful and varied field is a bright orange star with white companion wide f., near which N is a deep red star, while immediately preceding A is a faint close pair which 20 cm will show. With sufficient aperture these stars make an attractive colour group, and other faint stars are near. There has been little change in this group since 1837 and the proper motion of A is small.

291. Δ 63. This elegant white unequal pair is in a very fine starry field with a pronounced curved line of stars coming in S and ending in a small wide pair 3′ f.; 10·5 cm shows this well. John Herschel measured the pair in 1836 and there has been no real change since but the stars are connected by common proper motion and may be in orbit.

293. h. 4051. This yellow star is the brightest in a beautiful field spangled with stars, including a remarkable elongated irregular group near the Sf. edge.

The two faint companions are probably field stars, which are numerous in this rich region. 20 cm shows them plainly, and 15 cm at least the p. star. The field is most attractive even with 10·5 cm.

296. β 454. This fine orange star with a close white companion shines like a jewel in a lovely field, scattered profusely with stars with an arc of brighter stars N. 7·5 cm resolves the pair well; slow retrograde motion has taken place since Burnham's measures in 1892 and this is probably a binary system with common proper motion.

300. h. 4093. John Herschel in 1835 measured this bright yellow pair and there has been no apparent change since; in an attractive field it is an excellent object for small apertures. The stars are connected by common proper motion.

Pyxis (Pyx)

Pyxis, the compass, was introduced by Lacaille in 1752 from part of the very large ancient constellation of Argo Navis. Later it fell into disuse but was resurrected by Gould in 1879. It is a small group of area 221 sq. deg. which follows Puppis north of Vela, and the Milky Way passes through the Sp. corner. Three stars of the fourth magnitude in line serve to distinguish it and the centre culminates at midnight about February 3rd.

None of the six open star clusters is specially impressive, but NGC 2818 has been selected as being superposed on the single known planetary nebula. The best of a few extra-galactic nebulae is NGC 2613, and four double stars are given, two being difficult.

303. I 489. This object appears as a bright pale yellow star in an attractive field. It was discovered by Innes in 1911 to be a binary (0·5″ and 108°) and slow retrograde motion has since taken place. I have not been able to resolve it with 30 cm, the star appearing elongated in about 60° in 1961, and observers may wish to see what they can do with it.

305. β 205. This is another difficult close pair; the angle is steadily diminishing with doubtful change in separation, measures being erratic. In 1962 I saw the star elongated and almost divided, the angle about 40°, and it will be interesting to watch this binary. 25 cm showed the elongation clearly.

307. NGC 2613. In a beautiful starry field is an elongated spindle about 4′ × 1′ in pa. 110°, and only the extended elliptical axis is bright, the pointed ends being very faint. The prism gives a broad band from the bright centre. This is a fine object but needs 20 cm to deal well with it, although 10·5 cm shows it faintly.

309. β 208. Both angle and separation of this binary star are slowly increasing and it should soon be possible to determine the orbit, closest approach in 1901 having been 0·20″ in 117°. 7·5 cm is at present capable of resolving it, the star colours orange yellow and whitish. The distance is only about 16 pc.

329. h. 4166. Little is known about this pair; the angle has not changed since John Herschel's measures in 1836. Both stars are pale yellow and ornament a field sown profusely with stars. It is a fine object for small telescopes.

339. NGC 2818. The same NGC number refers to both planetary nebula and galactic cluster although they are unconnected, R for the nebula being given as 3,600 pc and for the cluster as 1,500 pc. The nebula is pale grey, not bright, about 40″ across of somewhat uneven light with a single prism image; it lies in the p. region of a cluster of scattered stars about 7′ across. Together these objects make an interesting field but 15 cm is needed to show them clearly.

Reticulum (Ret)

Reticulum, the net, originated in 1752 when Lacaille renamed an earlier group. It is a small constellation of area 114 sq. deg. immediately Np. the large Magellan Cloud and is characterized by a small group of stars surrounding the orange yellow α Ret of magnitude 3·4. The centre culminates at midnight about November 19th.

There are several conspicuous nebulae in Reticulum, and three of these are given. The best of the double stars is θ Ret; no clusters nor galactic nebulae occur.

86. NGC 1313. Although photographs show this object as a barred spiral 9′ × 6·5′ it is not easy to make out this feature visually. 30 cm shows a fairly bright irregular hazy ellipse about 3′ × 2′ in pa. 25° with suggestions of faint arms at either end in the directions Np. and Sf., the bar being an ill-defined brightening of the central axis. A supernova appeared in this extra-galactic system in December 1962 of m. 10 and 2·5′ S of the centre, and it formed a small pair with a less bright star near Np. Though rather faint, the spectra of both stars were compared and that of the supernova appeared to be beaded along its length, as if containing bright lines. It gradually faded and a year later could not be found. At its brightest the supernova was plainly visible with 7·5 cm, the nebula itself being very faint.

114. NGC 1559. This bright pointed elliptical nebula lies in pa. 55° in a field scattered with stars; it is about 3′ × 1·5′ and rises broadly in brightness to a central axis without visible nucleus. It is a conspicuous object classed as a barred spiral and photographs show much internal structure. 15 cm shows it clearly though not brightly.

115. θ Ret. In an attractive field sprinkled with stars this pale and deep yellow pair makes a good object for small telescopes. The motion is slowly retrograde and the separation, after a minimum of 3·6″ in 1907, seems to be increasing again. The period of this binary must be very long.

119. NGC 1574. Several stars in the field make an effective contrast with this bright round nebula, which rises to a small central nucleus giving a strong band in the prism. It is about 1·5′ across and even 7·5 cm will show it faintly as a round haze.

Sagitta (Sge)

Sagitta, the arrow, is a small narrow northern constellation entirely immersed in the Milky Way between Aquila and Vulpecula. It is of ancient origin and Ptolemy assigned five stars to it; these make an elongated group 10° north of Altair in Aquila. The area is only 80 sq. deg. and the centre culminates at midnight about July 17th.

There is one open cluster and two of globular type; one of these is the beautiful M 71 but the other, discovered photographically at Palomar, is much beyond amateur instruments. Of five small planetary nebulae, three are given as the others are beyond reach, and a few double stars complete the list. The Milky Way is of course an effective screen for extra-galactic objects.

853. β 139. Dembowski measured this close pale yellow pair in 1875 and there has been little change since. The stars are probably connected in an orbit of long period and 20 cm will show them both just clear of one another.

879. ζ Sge. This bright yellow star with a reddish companion Np. is itself a very close binary of period 23 years (5·3 6·3 0·17″–0·32″) and well beyond the reach of most amateur observers. There has been no real change in the easy wider pair since W. Struve measured the stars in 1831, and the system seems to be ternary.

883. NGC 6838. Méchain discovered this beautiful object in 1780 but could see no stars in it; it was formerly classed as an open galactic cluster but is now considered to be globular in type at a distance of about 4,000 pc. It is very rich and well resolved, with several long starry arms extending over the field from the centre about 3′ across; small apertures make it look nebulous although 10·5 cm will show some of its stars.

888. 13 Sge. The field containing this bright orange star is really fine, sown with innumerable stars; in the prism the spectrum shows very broad dark bands especially in red and yellow. I have never been able to see the wide companion and think that it must be fainter than m. 12. Burnham measured it in 1878 and there has been little change for 50 years; as the proper motion of A is small, it may be merely a field star, of which there are very many.

896. θ Sge. This pair makes a good object for small apertures and is in a fine star field; the colours seem to me considerably less yellow than correspond to the spectral types. Since W. Struve's measures in 1832 there has been only slight increase in angle but the stars are connected by common proper motion. Close Np. is the beautiful scattered star group NGC 6873 which has a bright effect and needs a large field.

898. NGC 6879. For those with good instruments this tiny planetary nebula is given as an exercise in finding. It is a disk about 2″ across and m. 12 in a field with faint profuse ground and shows a minute single prism image which with care may be seen with 20 cm. As a guide, the nebula forms a right angle with two stars of m. 8, one 6′ f. and the other 10′ N, while the elegant pair Σ 2634 (8·0 9·5 5″ 13°) is 14′ Sp. in pa. 240°. The nebula is shown as a faint star by 15 cm.

901. NGC 6886. In a field well sprinkled with stars this small planetary nebula forms the right angle of a small triangle with two brighter stars 1·5′ and 0·5′ distant; it has a slightly hazy disk 5″ wide, fairly well defined with single elliptical prism image. 15 cm will show this image clearly. R is given as 2,500 pc.

908. IC 4997. This small bluish nebula forms a conspicuous wide pair with a yellow star about 1′ Sp. in a field sown profusely with stars. It is about 5″ across with single prism image and another suspected towards the violet, as well as a central star streak. This image is visible with care with 7·5 cm. R is given as about 1,750 pc.

Sagittarius (Sgr)

Sagittarius, the archer, is the ninth constellation of the zodiac, to which Ptolemy assigned thirty-one stars. It has a large area of 867 sq. deg. containing a number of scattered bright stars; much of it lies in the Milky Way adjoining Scorpius and Ophiuchus, and the remainder stretches eastwards to Capricornus. The Milky Way in this region hides the centre of the galactic system and has a profuse concentration of star clouds and clusters, planetary nebulae and diffuse nebulae both luminous and dark. It is not surprising therefore that Sagittarius is the richest constellation in the total number of these objects, and it is in addition very well placed for southern observers. The centre culminates at midnight about July 5th.

Some difficulty in selection from so many objects has been experienced. Twenty-seven open clusters are known and six of the most effective have been chosen. Because of their intrinsic interest, all but two of the twenty-two globular clusters are given; those excluded were found at Palomar photographically and are beyond the reach of amateur instruments. The planetary nebulae are very numerous but most of them have been found photographically and are very small difficult objects; seven have been included as well as the more prominent diffuse nebulae. A single extra-galactic system NGC 6822 belonging to the local group is given and a number of interesting binary stars completes the list.

745. NGC 6440. Although relatively near to the sun at 3,500 pc distance, this globular cluster lies in a region of such heavy absorption, assessed at m. 7·0, that it appears small and obscure in a field from which the background stars of the Milky Way are blotted out. It is about 1′ across, round and rising a good deal to the centre with no sign of structure or resolution. It is plain though faint with 10·5 cm.

746. NGC 6445. This pale grey planetary nebula is 22′ Nf. the globular cluster NGC 6440 and looks somewhat smaller and less bright, with uneven light and hardly rising to the centre. It is distinguished at once by the single prism image while the cluster shows a band; this image may be seen with 15 cm. R is estimated as about 4,000 pc, which seems excessive.

751. NGC 6476. Needing a wide field, this region is very beautiful with a glittering array of innumerable stars on an irresolvable luminous background. Even when so profuse as to be nebulous, these star fields look quite different from the smooth nebulosity with few stars which characterizes true nebulae, such as that round ρ Oph. There are many dark nebulae which will be found by sweeping in this magnificent region and they show quite well with small apertures because sky light is less obvious.

754. Dark nebula. This is one of the dark nebulae outlined against the profuse star fields here; it is irregularly rectangular, 30′ × 10′, lying N–S and followed about 20′ by a round dark area 6′ across. A few of the brighter stars are scattered on these areas but the luminous ground is extinguished. They exhibit well with 15 cm and are fairly effective with 7·5 cm.

755. NGC 6494. Messier discovered this star cluster in 1764; it is a fine open star group about 30′ across and needs a large field. There is little central condensation but, as in many of these galactic clusters, the stars form a pattern of lines and loops with some straight radial rays; this is easily seen with 10·5 cm. R is estimated as 500 pc.

759. h. 5003. This beautiful pair, orange and yellow, in a starry field is well shown by small telescopes. There has been hardly any change since John

Herschel's measures in 1836 but the stars are probably connected. A minute point wide Sp. (13·0 26″ 239°) is likely to be a field star, and 25 cm will show it.

762. NGC 6514. Messier saw this fine nebula in 1764 but could make little of it; photographs show an irregular mass of bright nebulosity 25′ wide on which are superposed three tortuous dark lanes meeting near the centre, one of which divides again. These lanes about 45″ wide may be seen with 10·5 cm, and near their junction at the apex of the f. broadly deltoid nebulosity lies a small quadruplet of two brighter stars 11″ apart, each with a closer faint companion. I find 20 cm necessary to show all four, but 10·5 cm will show three. The whole field is very fine with irregular diffuse nebulosity and many stars in and around this. Very little apparent change in the quadruplet has yet been detected. R is about 1,600 pc.

764. NGC 6520. This cluster about 4′ across has an orange star in the centre, round which are arcs of stars looking almost like a close spiral; it is in a grand field, the background of which is luminous with the combined radiance of innumerable faint stars. On this is projected a remarkably dark nebula lying close Np. and very irregular, about 6′ × 4′, with parts of it standing out strongly and sharply against the luminous ground; there is an orange star on the Np. edge. Barnard found the dark nebula by photography in 1883 and it is one of the best for telescopic observation, small apertures dealing with it well. R for the cluster is estimated as 1,700 pc.

766. NGC 6522. William Herschel discovered this small globular cluster in 1784 on the same night as NGC 6528 which is 15′ f.; it is a fairly bright nebulous spot nearly 1′ across in which faint stars may be seen with 25 cm, but it is merely granular with 15 cm, of moderately condensed type with a star on the f. edge. The field sown profusely with stars is really a 'window' in the Milky Way close to the direction of the galactic centre but somewhat obscured by absorbing matter. Allowing for this, R is estimated as 8,700 pc.

767. NGC 6523. Messier discovered this fine nebula in 1764; it needs a large field and shows very extensive luminosity of varying brightness, involving two bright stars, with dark irregular lanes and followed by a bright open star cluster (NGC 6530). The whole field is wonderfully fine and varied, and small apertures show it well. The nebula is gaseous, extending over 90′ × 40′ in photographs, and R is estimated as 1,500 pc.

769. NGC 6528. This globular cluster in the same 15′ field as NGC 6522 is smaller and less bright but is actually nearer at an estimated 7,200 pc, there being considerably greater absorption assessed at m. 4·2. It is of fairly condensed type and 30 cm will not resolve it. Even 7·5 cm shows plainly the difference between these clusters.

770. NGC 6531. Messier discovered this cluster in 1764 and thought it was nebulous although 10·5 cm shows it as an obvious star group. It is a fine open cluster more than 20′ across and gathers somewhat towards the centre where is a bright yellow star; being in a very rich region of the sky, it is difficult to delimit. R is estimated as 900 pc.

775. NGC 6544. In a beautiful field sown profusely with stars this irregularly round and well-condensed globular cluster about 1·5′ across is resolved with stars right through it, although only granular with 10·5 cm. It has only recently been classed as of globular type and R is not known.

778. NGC 6553. This object has been assessed by Lohmann as the nearest of the globular clusters but the absorption of m. 6·3 is so heavy that it appears as a rather faint haze just resolvable on occasion with 30 cm. There is little central condensation and it is markedly elliptical, about 2′ × 1·5′, in a field sprinkled with stars. It is easy to see with 10·5 cm. R is 1,300 pc.

779. IC 1274–5. There is a good deal of scattered diffuse nebulosity in this region, concentrated round stars which probably render it luminous. These objects are close together, the former a hazy triplet and the latter a hazy pair, from 2′ to 3′ across. These seem to be dust nebulae shining by scattered light, for the prism shows the spectra to be continuous.

780. β 245. This fine easy pair has not changed appreciably since the first Harvard measures in 1868 and it is probably a long period binary system. The field is sown with scattered stars on a faint profuse ground.

782. NGC 6558. John Herschel discovered this remote globular cluster in 1834 and resolved it into faint stars which are just visible in good conditions with 30 cm; it is round, fairly bright, well condensed and about 1′ across, but little is known about it yet. It lies in a beautiful star field and 10·5 cm shows it with care.

785. NGC 6563. In a field sown thickly with stars is a pale blue well-defined even disk 45″ across, giving a single prism image which may be seen by 15 cm with care. This delicate nebula is faintly visible with 7·5 cm and R is given as about 5,000 pc.

787. NGC 6569. Absorption of m. 3·3 in this region makes this globular cluster difficult to resolve, the distance being estimated as about 7,000 pc. It is bright, rising broadly to the centre, about 1·5′ across, round and symmetrical, and looks granular but there is no certain resolution with 30 cm, although the prism shows a broad band. It lies in a fine starry field, and is easy as a hazy spot with 7·5 cm.

789. NGC 6567. The region of this small nebula is charming beyond description, and 20′ f. the field glitters with innumerable stars—a wonderful scene. The nebula itself is 8″ across, slightly hazy and quite bright, with a faint star close f. and a single prism image which is clear when found with 7·5 cm. R is given as about 2,000 pc.

790. η Sgr. This brilliant orange star dominates a field sown with scattered stars on a profuse faint ground, and the white companion close Sf. is steadily visible with 7·5 cm. Recorded measures of this pair are rather erratic but both angle and separation seem to be slowly increasing since Burnham in 1879 found 2·8″ and 100°, and it is probably a long period binary system. The spectrum of A is fine, with several dark broad and narrow bands, easily visible with 7·5 cm.

793. NGC 6603. Messier found this cluster in 1764 and described it as a large nebulosity containing many stars. About 4·5′ across, it is a roughly round well-condensed group of stars which resembles an open globular cluster. The field is beautiful and indeed the immediate region is like a vast cluster and quite indescribable in richness and variety. The cluster is not bright with 10·5 cm but may be picked out easily from the field. R is estimated as 2,200 pc.

796. NGC 6618. This most beautiful object, projected on a very fine star field, is in the form of the figure 2 with long extended base in pa. 120°; it is very bright and because of the gradation of light from the central axis, it has a rounded plastic appearance which lends an added charm. It is roughly 15′ × 3′ in the brightest portions but much broader with extended haze; the area inside the curl is very dark and shows well in the prism, indicating the gaseous nature. 10·5 cm gives the shape quite well. The full dimensions of this nebula as revealed by photography are 46′ × 37′ and R is estimated as 1,800 pc. It was discovered by Messier in 1764, who remarked on its extended form (Plate 11).

798. NGC 6624. 30 cm resolves this bright well-condensed irregularly round globular cluster into faint stars scattering away in diffuse edges, but 20 cm shows only a mottled appearance. It is about 1′ across and easily picked up as a hazy spot with 7·5 cm. Interstellar absorption here is assessed as m. 2·1 and R is estimated at 12,000 pc.

799. NGC 6626. Messier discovered this object in 1764 as a round nebulosity without stars in it, and it is easy to find with 7·5 cm. It is one of the nearer globular clusters at 4,000 pc, but absorption of m. 2·6 diminishes its brightness. However it is a fine object with 30 cm, bright round and symmetrical and well resolved into stars, the outliers extending to 3·5′. 15 cm shows this resolution by mottling the haze with faint stars; it lies in a well-scattered star field.

801. 21 Sgr. This pair, orange and greenish (by contrast), lies in a field well sprinkled with stars. Many measures have been made since Jacob found 1·8″ and 297° in 1846 and have shown very slow retrograde motion. This is probably a true binary and it may be resolved surely with 7·5 cm.

802. NGC 6629. William Herschel discovered this object in 1784 without recognizing it as a planetary nebula. It is a pale grey rather hazy disk about 15″ across in a field scattered with stars and shows a single prism image. This image when once found is clear with 10·5 cm. R is estimated as 2,200 pc.

803. β 133. This moderately bright pale yellow star may be cleanly divided with 10·5 cm. Schiaparelli measured it in 1875 as 1·8″ and 265° and both values are slowly diminishing. The stars seem to form a binary system.

806. NGC 6638. Because of its distance of 14,000 pc combined with inter-stellar absorption amounting to m. 2·0, this globular cluster is not easy to resolve; however faint stars may be glimpsed in it with 30 cm. It is a conspicuous object about 70″ across with a broad centre and 10·5 cm shows it clearly but faintly.

807. NGC 6637. Lacaille found this object in 1752 and compared it with the nucleus of a comet. It is a beautiful well-resolved cluster about 2·5′ across in a fine field with a bright star 4′ Np., and is somewhat elliptical and moderately compressed with the outliers not widely scattered. Resolution is apparent with 15 cm and it is an easy round haze with 7·5 cm. Absorption here is rated as m. 2·9 and R is estimated as about 6,500 pc.

809. IC 4725. Discovered by Messier in 1764, this is an effective star group for small telescopes but it needs a large field nearly 40′ wide; it is a fine bright cluster somewhat gathered to a broad centre with three deep yellow stars in line, from which runs a remarkable widening curve of equal stars. R is estimated as about 600 pc.

810. NGC 6642. Little appears to be known about this globular cluster yet; it is a compact irregularly round mass of faint stars about 1′ across, concentrated centrally with scattered outliers. 20 cm is just able to show a few of these stars and the object is a plain hazy spot in a star-strewn field with 10·5 cm.

811. NGC 6644. This object furnishes a good example of the value of the prism in distinguishing a gaseous nebula, for its diameter is only 2·5″. It is a bright bluish point amongst innumerable scattered stars and the single prism image may be seen distinctly like a tiny star with 7·5 cm when the actual star streaks are too faint to be visible. R is estimated as about 2,500 pc.

812. NGC 6645. William Herschel discovered this object in 1786 and described it as 'a beautiful cluster of very small stars of various sizes, 15′ in diameter and very rich'. This description is apt; the brightest stars are about m. 10 and there are many small pairs, triplets and small groups in it. It has a lobed and radial structure and the open centre about 2′ across is ringed with stars. This is a delicate object for 10·5 cm, and plain as a group with 7·5 cm. R is about 900 pc.

814. NGC 6652. This distant globular cluster is rather irregular, about $50'' \times 30''$ in pa. 100° and definitely resolved into clear gleaming points with faint scattered outliers. It is fairly compact and lies in a field profusely scattered with small stars. A few of its stars are shown by 20 cm, but hardly by 15 cm, although it is an easy hazy spot with 7·5 cm. With absorption assessed here as m. 1·8, R is estimated as 16,000 pc.

815. NGC 6656. Only 3,100 pc distant, this is one of the nearest globular clusters and well-resolved into unusually bright stars for these objects. The broad centre is about 7' across and the scattered outliers extend to 15'; it is a most beautiful object in a fine starry field, even though the absorption here amounts to m. 1·8. It was discovered by Ihle in 1747, and when Messier observed it in 1774 he saw no stars in it, although 7·5 cm shows the brighter ones quite plainly.

818. NGC 6681. Messier discovered this object in 1780 and saw no stars in it, which in fact needs 15 cm to demonstrate; it is a bright round compact well-resolved globular cluster with outliers about 1·5' across and lies in a fine starry field. 7·5 cm shows an easy hazy spot. R is estimated as about 20,000 pc.

820. IC 4776. This planetary nebula has a small bright bluish disk about 6'' wide in a rather empty field; the single prism image has a short narrow streak which denotes a central star. This prism image may be seen with 7·5 cm but is not easy to find. R is estimated as nearly 3,000 pc.

833. NGC 6715. Messier discovered this object in 1778 and remarked on its bright centre; it is a strongly compressed globular cluster about 2' across with irregular diffuse edges. 30 cm shows granularity but no real resolution, and it is an easy hazy spot for small apertures, showing a broad prism band. Absorption is here assessed as m. 1·4 and R is estimated at about 15,000 pc.

835. NGC 6717. One of the bright yellow components of ν Sgr lies 2·5' N and interferes much with the observation of this globular cluster; it appears as a round compact object about 30'' wide, clearly shown by 10·5 cm and some of its stars visible with 15 cm. These stars are not numerous and are immersed in an unresolved haze. The cluster has only recently been recognized as globular in type and little is known about it yet; it is evidently fairly remote.

839. NGC 6723. J. Dunlop discovered this fine object in 1826 and resolved it easily into stars. It is a broadly compressed type of globular cluster, irregularly round and looking like an almost hemispherical heap of star dust, the outliers extending to 4' across, and being in irregular rays. 10·5 cm will show some faint stars in the conspicuous haze. Absorption in this region is very small and R is estimated as 10,500 pc (Plate 9).

842. ζ Sgr. This brilliant close pair was discovered by Winlock in 1867 and has performed several complete revolutions since, the period being 20·8 years.

The stars will be widest in 1971, and could not be resolved with 30 cm in 1960. This is an interesting pair to watch at intervals; a red star is 1·2′ Np.

843. h. 5082. These three stars have shown little change since John Herschel's measures in 1836 but the proper motion of A is so small that one cannot say much about them yet. 10·5 cm shows all three, but only two are visible with 7·5 cm. This is a very pretty object in a field sprinkled with stars, a bright yellow one being 10′ N.

844. HN 126. This small yellow binary is the leader of a field sown profusely with stars. It was resolved as very close by William Herschel in 1801 and Burnham found 0·6″ in 353° in 1890. Separation reached a minimum of 0·4″ about 1900 and is now slowly increasing with retrograde motion. In 1960 the stars were shown clearly apart by 20 cm.

862. β Sgr. There has been no real change in this pair since John Herschel measured the stars in 1834, but they probably form a physical system of long period. Bright pale yellow and ashy white, this is a fine object for small telescopes.

864. HN 119. The first good measures of this pair were made in 1877 as 8·2″ and 140°, and change has been slow since. Common proper motion suggests a long period binary; in contrasting colours it is a fine pair for small apertures.

869. AQ Sgr. This star is a good example of one of the brighter irregular variables with a fine spectrum crossed along its whole length by many dark lines and bands; these may be seen fairly well with 15 cm. The star itself is moderately bright and deep red, in contrast with a white star near Np.

871. NGC 6809. Lacaille recorded this object in 1752 and compared it with the nucleus of a large comet; Messier could not find it in 1764 but succeeded in 1778. It is an open type of globular cluster nearly 10′ across, irregularly round, rising only broadly towards the centre and beautifully resolved into stars scattered in a haze of fainter ones. Even 7·5 cm will show this to be a cloud of faint stars. It is an excellent example of its type, particularly well seen as interstellar absorption is negligible in this region. R is estimated as 6,800 pc.

874. NGC 6818. Even 7·5 cm will show plainly this planetary nebula and its single prism image. It is large and conspicuous for these objects, pale grey blue with even light and no visible central star, nearly 25″ across and somewhat elliptical. R is estimated as 870 pc.

875. NGC 6822. This large faint object needs a clear dark night for observation. It is an elliptical haze about 8′ × 4′ in pa. 20°, rising only very broadly towards the centre and including some faint stars which no doubt belong to the field. It may be seen plainly but faintly with 20 cm. Photographs show dimensions of 15′ × 11′ and an integrated magnitude of 8·7. This is a member of the local group of extra-galactic nebulae to which the Milky Way system belongs and R is estimated as 400,000 pc.

892. NGC 6864. Discovered by Méchain in 1780, this is an easy object for small telescopes and a good example of the strongly compressed type of globular cluster. It is symmetrical, about 1·5′ across with a strong central peak but too distant to be resolved with 30 cm. Interstellar absorption is small in this region and R is estimated as about 30,000 pc which places it amongst the most remote of these clusters.

897. h. 5173. This pair is difficult to measure but change is very slow although the common proper motion is high, which suggests physical connection between the stars. A is a bright deep yellow star and the faint companion Sf. may be made out with 15 cm; the distance is only 5·7 pc so that it must be either a red or a white dwarf. A brighter wide companion is about 1′ f.

907. h. 5188. In this field is a bright almost white star with a companion close Nf. which looks reddish. Another white less bright star is about 0·5′ Np. while 5′ Np. is a reddish star. The close pair points to a small almost equal pair about 2·5′ Nf. (10·5 10·8 4·7″ 188°) and all this may be seen with 7·5 cm. The angle of the close bright pair is steadily diminishing and it may be a physical system.

911. β 763. Burnham first measured this close pair in 1879 as 1·2″ and 204° and the angle has since steadily increased. Separation measures are erratic but the value seemed to me in 1960 less than 1·0″, for 15 cm showed the stars in contact with dark line between, and 20 cm was needed to separate them. Common proper motion suggests a long period binary system.

Scorpius (Sco)

Scorpius, the scorpion, is the eighth zodiacal constellation but the ecliptic passes only through the extreme Np. corner. It is a striking group lying almost entirely in the Milky Way and one of the few which has some resemblance to the object it is supposed to represent. It is rich in varied interest for the telescope and very well placed for southern observers. The area is 497 sq. deg. and the centre culminates at midnight about June 3rd.

There are some attractive double stars in Scorpius, including the leader Antares. About twenty small stars in an area 10° × 7° round this brilliant orange red star show similar proper motion to it and evidently form an association, known as the Antares cluster, which is also involved in a dust nebula. Thirty-five open clusters are known, of which the most effective eight have been selected, as well as all eight globular clusters. Many planetary nebulae have been found, mostly very small and faint, and five of the easier ones are given. Mention should also be made of the remarkable gaseous nebula NGC 6302. There are no extra-galactic objects in Scorpius.

634. 2 Sco. This bright yellow star has a companion close p. which looks whiter, an attractive object for small apertures. The first measures in 1881 gave 2·7″ and 277°; separation reached a maximum of 3·1″ in 1902 and is now slowly lessening with only slight change in angle. It looks as if this may be a binary with orbit almost edgewise to the line of sight.

642. ξ Sco. This interesting system consists of a bright yellow pair of period 44·7 years, closest at 123° in 1949 and widest at 7° in 1970; in 1963 the stars were just in contact with 10·5 cm. The third star was measured by W. Struve in 1825 as 6·7″ and 79° since when the separation has increased with retrograde motion, and it is clearly connected in a large orbit with the pair. In the same field 5′ Sf. is the smaller deep yellow pair Σ 1999 (7·4 8·1 12″ 99°) which has similar proper motion and radial velocity to ξ Sco, but it will be long before orbital motion can be established.

643. β Sco. Dominating a field of scattered stars, this splendid pale yellow pair has shown only slight retrograde motion since the measures of J. South in 1823 and similar proper motion indicates that the stars are connected. In 1880 Burnham found a star very close to A (8·5 0·9″ 88°) which reached maximum separation of 1·1″ in 1900 and is now closing with slow direct motion. I could not be sure that I saw it in 1960 and it may be beyond 30 cm now. The whole system is quaternary since A was found in 1940 to be a spectroscopic binary of period 6·828 days.

644. Brs 11. Since the measures of John Herschel in 1837, this pair has not altered except for slight decrease in angle; the proper motions are similar and imply a connection between the stars. This easy yellow pair makes a fine sight in a field of scattered stars on a very faint starry ground.

645. ν Sco. Like ε Lyr, this is a system of two connected close pairs, more compact and less bright but much better placed for southern observers. Angle and separation between the pairs have hardly changed for 150 years, showing a very long period. A consists of two bright stars (4·5 6·0 1·3″ 4°) and B is a less bright pair (6·9 7·7 2·2″ 54°) and in each case both separation and angle are slowly increasing. 15 cm will resolve A, and B is easy for 7·5 cm. This quaternary system makes an attractive telescopic object.

646. 12 Sco. A fine object for small apertures, this elegant pair was measured by John Herschel in 1834 as 4·6″ and 83°, and change has been slow since then. The stars are connected by common proper motion.

649. NGC 6072. In a well-sprinkled star field this nebula may be picked up without difficulty with 20 cm; it is about 40″ across, fairly bright, round and somewhat brighter towards the centre but the single prism image shows no central star streak. R is estimated as about 6,000 pc.

652. NGC 6093. Méchain discovered this object in 1781 and compared it with the nucleus of a comet; it is round and well condensed, bright and resolved into innumerable stars which may just be seen with 15 cm, while 7·5 cm shows a conspicuous hazy spot. With scattered outliers it is about 3′ across and lies in a beautiful field with contrasting stars. Absorption in this region is assessed at m. 0·9 and R is about 10,500 pc.

654. σ Sco. This brilliant pale yellow star has a wide white companion p., a fine sight in a field sprinkled with a few stars, and well shown with 7·5 cm. There has been no change since J. South measured the stars in 1822 but they are linked by common proper motion.

656. NGC 6121. Lacaille discovered this beautiful cluster in 1752; it is crowded with stars running to a broad haze at the centre, across which is a bar of brighter stars. The outliers are in curved arms, forming a marked concentric pattern reaching to 12′ across and visible with care even with 7·5 cm. Interstellar absorption here is estimated as m. 1·9 and R is about 2,300 pc (Plate 7).

657. h. 4850. This is a really fine pair in a field of scattered stars, excellent for small telescopes. John Herschel in 1835 found 7·5″ and 349° and the separation has slowly diminished since. Common proper motion suggests a binary system of long period.

658. NGC 6124. A large field is needed for this scattered galactic cluster about 25′ across; it contains several orange stars as well as numerous pairs, triplets and small groups, quite well shown by 10·5 cm. R is estimated as 600 pc.

663. NGC 6144. This irregular globular cluster with little central condensation lies behind a diffuse nebula surrounding Antares, which makes the field somewhat bright. It is about 2′ across and hazily resolved with faint outliers scattered in and around it, and a star on the p. edge. 15 cm shows this star and a faint patch of haze and 20 cm gives the beginnings of resolution. Absorption is rated here as m. 1·3 and R is estimated as about 9,000 pc.

664. NGC 6139. Compared with NGC 6144 this globular cluster is much more compressed and at nearly the same distance, estimated as 9,500 pc, is considerably brighter, but strong absorption of about m. 3·3 makes resolution into stars difficult. With 30 cm it appears granular with glimpses of very faint outliers. It is about 1·5′ across, a fairly symmetrical round haze, quite plain with 10·5 cm.

666. α Sco. Antares is a brilliant orange red star with a fine spectrum of well-distributed dark lines and bands. The companion close p. has not changed in position since the earliest observations and may be seen in good conditions with 7·5 cm. Its colour is pale green which I have seen well with 30 cm in bright sunshine against the blue sky, but this is an effect of contrast for the spectral type shows that the star is pale yellow. It is true that Dawes in 1856 saw it emerge from behind the dark limb of the moon before Antares itself and noted the colour as green, but in the most favourable case only very few seconds are available for judgment. Further, in 1936 a luminous red nebula about 75′ in diameter was discovered surrounding Antares and this would condition the eye of the observer long before the companion emerged. Antares is a red supergiant and one of the largest measured stars, the interferometric diameter being 0·040″. If R be taken as 100 pc, the actual diameter is nearly 300 times that of the sun.

667. NGC 6153. This small nebula about 20″ across is pale blue and lies at the S corner of a small rhombus made of an orange star, a white star and a small close pair—an attractive combination. The light is even and well defined with single prism image which 10·5 cm shows plainly, while the nebula is easy with 7·5 cm. R is estimated as 1,800 pc.

676. β 1116. 10·5 cm will just show close N the companion of this star; both angle and separation appear to be increasing slowly but the proper motion of A may be responsible. Many of the field stars are in linear order, especially f.

681. h. 4889. This easy pair was measured by John Herschel in 1835 as 7·2″ and 5°, and there has been little change since; it lies in a field of many scattered stars on a faint starry ground, and the stars are probably connected.

685. NGC 6231. Lacaille noted this glorious cluster in 1755 as seven or eight small close stars but it is really a striking group for small telescopes. The central more condensed region is about 20′ across but scattered outliers extend much farther. There are many bright white and yellow stars, and many pairs and triplets, which sparkle in patterns of lines and small groups. R is estimated as 600 pc (Plate 5).

686. I 576. This bright white star is in beautiful contrast with a rich star field. The faint companion p. was measured by Innes in 1913 as 5·0″ and 269°, and 20 cm will show it. Little is known of these stars yet.

687. NGC 6242. This cluster is included as one of the few recorded in his first catalogue by Lacaille in 1752 with his indifferent optical means; he calls it a feeble oval lengthened spot. It is a scattered star group about 10′ across, somewhat extended N–S with a bright orange red leader 2·5′ Sf., and merges into a fine field. The group is fairly effective with 10·5 cm. R is estimated as 800 pc.

694. NGC 6281. In a large field this region is very beautiful, with a pyramidal group of stars about 8′ across standing out prominently in the centre; it contains several pairs and two bright orange stars, and the linear pattern is most striking. It is quite well shown by 10·5 cm. R is estimated as about 800 pc.

696. IC 4637. In a field sprinkled with stars is a small round bluish nebula about 10″ across which shines in the prism like a bead on a narrow line of spectrum from the central star. It lies at the Nf. end of an irregular trapezium with three stars. 10·5 cm shows only a faint hazy star and 15 cm is needed for the prism image. R is given as nearly 5,000 pc.

700. Hwe 86. Some of the stars in this fine field are in curved lines almost encircling an elegant close pair, bright yellow and reddish, which is quite clear with 7·5 cm. Change has been slow since Russell in 1880 found 2·3″ and 139° and not much is known of these stars yet.

701. NGC 6302. This remarkable object was discovered by Dunlop in 1826, missed by John Herschel and rediscovered by Barnard about 1883. It is an elliptical or spindle-shaped bluish nebula 1·5′ × 0·5′ in pa. 80° with exceptionally high surface brightness, rising to a very bright small nucleus. It gives a strong single prism image which is quite clear with 7·5 cm, and is a most interesting object in the star sprinkled field. It is apparently not a true planetary nebula and R has been estimated as about 3,000 pc.

702. h. 4926. This orange red star shines like a gem in a field profusely scattered with stars; the two whitish companions have hardly changed since John Herschel's measures in 1835 but the proper motion of A is small and little is known about them yet. Both may be seen with 10·5 cm but only the nearer one Np. with 7·5 cm.

714. Mlb 4. A period of about 42 years has been found for this close orange pair; a third star (10·0 32″ 135°) has similar proper motion and the system may be ternary. In 1962 all three stars were visible with 7·5 cm. The orange pair was closest in 1933 and will be again in 1975. The distance is 6·8 pc.

720. NGC 6337. This charming object was discovered by John Herschel in 1834 and described by him as 'a beautiful delicate ring of a faint ghost-like appearance'; it looks as if suspended in a field sown profusely with stars, some of which are seen through it, and needs at least 20 cm on a clear dark night. It is about 40″ × 30″ and shows a single prism image. R is not known.

734. NGC 6383. A bright yellow star with two faint companions (h. 4962) lies in a small star cluster about 3′ across, the whole bearing a striking resemblance to 30 CMa in NGC 2362, but neither so vivid nor so rich. The field is fine and both of the companions are visible with 10·5 cm. R is about 700 pc.

735. NGC 6380. It is hard to recognize this hazy irresolvable object as a globular cluster, observation being impeded by a star m. 8·5 which is projected on the S edge. It is more than 1′ across, and faint; 20 cm will show it but 15 cm only doubtfully. Little is known about it yet.

736. NGC 6388. In an attractive field of scattered stars on a faint profuse ground is a bright symmetrically round well-compressed globular cluster, mottled but not truly resolved with a faint haze of outliers 3·5′ across—a beautiful object, easy and conspicuous with 7·5 cm. Interstellar absorption here has been variously assessed; allowing m. 2·0 for this, R is estimated at 10,000 pc.

740. NGC 6405. This cluster was first recorded by Lacaille in 1752, and Messier saw it as a group of faint stars in 1764. It needs a large field, being about 25′ across with open centre and well-marked loops and arcs of stars radiating from it—a good object for small telescopes. R is estimated as about 400 pc.

741. IC 4663. It is not difficult to pick up this pale bluish grey disk about 20″ across and fairly well defined in a beautiful scattered star field on a profuse faint ground. The single prism image is clear with 15 cm but 10·5 cm shows only the nebula itself as a dim round haze. R is not known.

748. NGC 6441. This interesting field sown with stars shows a bright round symmetrical broadly condensed haze about 2′ across, white in contrast with the brilliant orange star G Sco 4·5′ p. A star is nearer Sp. and fainter ones nearer still. The haze looks granular but not resolved, even when the star is covered. This is a fine object for small apertures, even though considerable absorption interferes with resolution; assessing this at m. 3·0, R is about 7,500 pc.

749. NGC 6451. Merging into a fine starry field is a group of stars about 6′ wide, of marked rectilinear pattern with a narrow dark rift roughly N–S. It is a curious gathering, not bright, and needs 15 cm to show it clearly. R is 1,200 pc.

750. NGC 6453. This very distant globular cluster immediately precedes the brilliant open cluster M 7; it is a small irregular haze in a starry field, about 1′ across, only broadly compressed and too faint to be resolved. Some faint stars are near but they do not look like outliers. 10·5 cm shows it as a dim spot, clear with 15 cm. Allowing an absorption of m. 2·6, R is about 22,000 pc.

752. NGC 6475. Lacaille recorded this group, visible to the unaided eye, in 1755 and noted its pattern; it is the most southerly object in Messier's catalogue and a remarkable sight in a large field with its structure of quadrant and straight lines. With outliers it is more than 40′ wide, and very effective for small telescopes. The fine orange star included Sp. is the very close pair λ 342 (6·4 6·5 0·4″ 260°) which I have seen elongated p.–f. but not resolved with 30 cm. R for the cluster is about 220 pc.

757. I 1013. There are two fairly bright stars in this attractive field; this is the pale yellow one 4·5′ Sf. It was measured by Innes in 1913 as 0·74″ and 178° and there has been retrograde motion since with little change in separation. 25 cm will resolve the stars cleanly. The proper motion is evidently shared by both stars, which suggests a binary system.

Sculptor (Scl)

Sculptor, the sculptor, was formed by Lacaille in 1752 from a group of inconspicuous stars between Cetus and Phoenix, and it has no distinguishing characters since the brightest stars are only of magnitude 4·5. The area is 475 sq. deg. and the centre culminates at midnight about September 27th.

This constellation lies in a region rich in extra-galactic nebulae, some of which are large and bright and so make fine telescopic objects. Prominent amongst these is NGC 253, a beautiful example of an edge-wise spiral. There is also the Sculptor system or super-cluster (0^h $57\cdot7^m$; $-33°$ 59′) which is a widely dispersed and sparse aggregation of very faint stars and at 110,000 pc distance is closer to the Milky Way system than any other members of the local group except the two Magellan Clouds. It is about 30′ in diameter and was discovered photographically but is not a telescopic object in the usually accepted sense. Apart from stars, the only galactic object in Sculptor is the globular cluster NGC 288.

1010. Hwe 93. This elegant unequal pair is not difficult for small apertures; it was measured by Burnham in 1881 and there has been no appreciable change since. The stars are connected by common proper motion.

1015. NGC 7793. Bond in 1850 discovered this conspicuous object with the Washington 26-inch refractor and likened it to a comet, but it culminated for him at only 18° elevation; however there is some resemblance. It is a large elliptical luminous haze rising greatly but very broadly towards the centre, about 6′ × 3·5′ in pa. 70°, in a rather barren field. It gives a very broad band in the prism and is an easy but rather shapeless object with 15 cm. This is a very open extra-galactic spiral system and R is about 3 million pc.

1. κ Scl. This bright yellow pair in a rather thin field is cleanly resolved with 10·5 cm; the separation is increasing with very slow retrograde motion and no doubt the stars form a long period binary as they share a common proper motion.

3. NGC 55. A fine example of a spiral system seen edgewise, estimated to be at a distance of 1·9 million pc. 30 cm shows a bright remarkably elongated spindle 25′ × 2·5′ in pa. 70°, asymmetric with very bright p. region knotted or curdled and a long f. region mottled and less bright. 10·5 cm shows the brighter lengthened central part and the spindle shape is clear (Plate 13).

7. NGC 134. Between two stars, this conspicuous object, about 6′ × 1′ in pa. 47° is spindle-shaped, the outlying regions faint and the extended centre bright and suggesting some structure. Another faint spindle (NGC 131) is about 7′ p. and just visible with 20 cm, which shows NGC 134 fairly well. These are both edgewise spiral systems.

16. NGC 253. The best example of an edgewise spiral, which even 7·5 cm will show about 20′ long; it is very bright with 30 cm, particularly the elongated centre, and at least 30′ × 3·5′ in pa. 52° with evidence of a dark rift especially p., and three stars involved. The field is fine also. R is estimated as 2·2 million pc.

18. NGC 288. In a star sprinkled field this open-type globular cluster appears as an irregular cloud of stars about 6′ across with only small central condensation. Even 10·5 cm will show very faint stars in a dim haze. R is about 12,000 pc.

19. NGC 300. This extra-galactic object is included because of its interest in being a probable member of the local group at an estimated distance of 1 million pc. Photographs indicate a very large elliptical spiral system with many luminous condensations in it, although 30 cm shows only a diffuse haze rising broadly to the centre, irregular and extended generally p.–f., about 3′ × 2′. It is a faint indefinite haze with 15 cm.

41. NGC 613. Photographs show this object as a fine barred spiral. I see with 30 cm a bright elongated nebula about 4′ × 1·5′ in pa. 120°, rising very much to a rather lengthened nucleus which the prism spreads into a band. 10·5 cm will show it, but very faintly.

44. τ Scl. The separation of this close yellow pair is lessening with direct motion and in 1960 15 cm was needed to resolve it. Both stars are dwarfs at a distance of about 40 pc and seem to be in orbit.

48. ε Scl. This easy bright yellow pair was measured by John Herschel in 1836 as 5·5″ and 70° since when both angle and separation have diminished. The stars have common proper motion and are probably in orbit.

Scutum (Sct)

Scutum represents the shield of the Polish hero John Sobieski; it was introduced by Hevelius about 1660 and occupies a small area of 109 sq.

deg. in the Milky Way between Aquila and Sagittarius which is difficult to locate visually. It culminates at midnight about July 1st.

In this small constellation nine open clusters have been recorded, as well as the globular cluster NGC 6712. There are many planetary nebulae, mostly small and faint, and the curious diffuse nebula IC 1287. Extra-galactic objects can hardly be expected because of the screen of the Milky Way.

808. IC 1287. Photographs show here a large diffuse nebula $44' \times 34'$ which is rendered luminous by the pair Σ 2325 (6·0 9·3 12″ 257°) immersed in it. These stars are yellow and ashy white, clearly seen with 7·5 cm, and have not changed since W. Struve's measures in 1829 so that the period must be very long. The nebula itself is gaseous, vaguely diffused and faint, and a clear dark night is needed for its observation. R is estimated as 240 pc.

819. NGC 6694. Messier discovered this cluster of fairly bright stars in 1764; it is a gathering about 6′ across containing some forty stars and stands out fairly well from a field scattered over with stars but is rather inconspicuous with small apertures. R is estimated as about 1,200 pc.

823. Σ 2373. This dainty pair, pale and deep yellow, lies in a beautiful field sown profusely with stars, and 7·5 cm shows it well. There has been little change since W. Struve's measures in 1832 and not much is known of the stars yet.

828. NGC 6705. This attractive galactic cluster is well suited to small apertures; it was first seen by Kirch in 1681, and Messier in 1764 noted that it contained a large number of small stars with a brighter leader. It lies in a starry field but is well concentrated and separated from it, about 10′ across. The outer regions show marked concentric structure while the inner stars are in groups with dark lanes between them, giving a lobed appearance. R is estimated as 1,700 pc.

831. NGC 6712. Rising only broadly to the centre, this globular cluster is moderately bright, irregularly round about 2·5′ across and is resolved into a mass of faint stars, which may be made out partly with 20 cm. There seems to be a dark lane running into the f. region of the cluster in the direction Sp. and almost cutting off a portion. 10·5 cm shows a conspicuous luminous haze and the field sown with stars is in fine contrast. Interstellar absorption here is assessed at m. 2·7 and R is estimated as about 6,000 pc.

834. IC 1295. This planetary nebula follows at 24′ in pa. 120° the globular cluster NGC 6712 and lies in a beautiful field; it is faint but not difficult as it is about 90″ wide. There is no visible central star but the centre is somewhat brighter and in good conditions the single prism image may be seen. The nebula is shown by 20 cm, but hardly by 15 cm. R is doubtful, perhaps about 9,000 pc.

Serpens (Ser)

Serpens is the serpent which Ophiuchus carries, and appears on either side of him. The constellation is therefore in two parts of total area 637 sq. deg. It is one of the star groups in the *Almagest* of A.D. 150 and Ptolemy assigned eighteen stars to it. The first portion is a scattered star group north of Libra and culminates at midnight about May 17th; the second is mainly in the Milky Way between Ophiuchus and Sagittarius where it is subject to heavy obscuration, and culminates at midnight about June 21st.

There are five open clusters in Serpens but only one is an effective object; this is the remarkable NGC 6611 which is associated with the gaseous nebula IC 4703. Of the five globular clusters, two are beyond the reach of amateur instruments but the others are interesting objects and it is instructive to compare NGC 6535 with NGC 6539. All of the known planetary nebulae are small and difficult and none of the extragalactic nebulae is bright. Some interesting double stars are included.

610. NGC 5904. Messier discovered this globular cluster in 1763 and saw no stars in it although the outliers may be seen with 7·5 cm, and 10·5 cm resolves it plainly. It is large, the rich compressed part being about 2' across while curved unsymmetrical arms bending away S and f. extend much farther. The field is sprinkled with stars. Interstellar absorption is low in this region and R is estimated as 9,200 pc.

613. 5 Ser. This is the bright yellow star 22' Sf. NGC 5904; the reddish companion may be seen with 10·5 cm. In 1831 W. Struve found 10·1" and 41° and subsequent change has been slow. The large common proper motion suggests however a long period binary system.

622. δ Ser. There is no colour difference in this attractive pale yellow pair which is excellent for small telescopes. W. Struve in 1833 found 2·7" and 197° so that the separation is increasing with retrograde motion. Proper motions are similar which suggests that the stars are connected.

627. β 619. It will require steady air to resolve this deep yellow star with 30 cm. Little change has occurred since Burnham discovered the pair in 1878 and not much is known about it yet but the stars are connected by common proper motion.

768. NGC 6535. This distant globular cluster is a small faint object, resolved into a few stars on a hazy irregularly round area about 1' wide; 15 cm shows only a dim roundish haze with a very faint star or two in it. Although the absorption in this region is assessed at m. 1·1, the field is well sprinkled with stars on a faint ground and R is estimated as 14,500 pc. This field should be compared with that containing the comparatively near NGC 6539 where the stars are blotted out by heavy absorption.

771. NGC 6539. Interstellar absorption is so heavy here, assessed at m. 7·0, that this globular cluster is quite faint, even though R is estimated as only 1,600 pc which makes NGC 6553 in Sagittarius the only globular cluster nearer to the sun. The heavy veiling is shown by the blotting out of the Milky Way stars in the field and the cluster itself is a faint round haze nearly 3′ wide, rising a little and broadly to the centre with no resolution apparent with 30 cm, although a few faint stars near may possibly be outliers. The cluster is just perceptible to 15 cm.

788. β 131. This beautiful little triplet was linear in 1880 but the angle of the faintest star has increased since then while that of the close pair has hardly altered and the separations have remained fixed. Little is known of these stars yet; 7·5 cm shows the pair only and 15 cm is needed for the third star.

794. NGC 6611. Messier discovered this remarkable object in 1764 and noted both stars and haze. It extends to at least 20′ across, a scattered open cluster of fairly bright stars immersed in bright nebulous haze which is most marked in the irregularly elliptical centre about 10′ × 6′; the prism shows that the haze is gaseous and it is easily perceptible with 7·5 cm lying in the star group. Photographs indicate that the nebula is actually 35′ × 28′ with an emission spectrum and R is estimated as about 1,200 pc. This is a good example of the association of gaseous nebulosity with cluster stars; the nebula is listed as IC 4703.

795. Σ 2303. This fairly bright yellow star has a companion close Sp. which 7·5 cm shows with care. Since W. Struve's measures in 1831 of 3·2″ and 216°, changes have been slow but the stars are probably connected. The field is almost blank, though lying in the Milky Way, because of the heavy absorption in this region.

800. AC 11. Dawes discovered this close yellow pair in 1854 and measured it as 0·4″ and 178°. In 1905 separation was less than 0·1″ in 22° and is now increasing, the motion being retrograde. The period is still uncertain; in 1961 the stars could just be divided with 20 cm, and they will be interesting to watch.

804. 59 Ser. This fine unequal pair, deep yellow and white, is in an almost blank field, the Milky Way being blotted out by dark absorption clouds in this region; 7·5 cm shows it well. There has been a very slow increase in angle since 1828 and the stars are probably connected. This would make the whole system quaternary since Miss Tilley in 1943 found spectroscopically that A is a ternary star with an A2 + A0 pair of period 1·850 days, coupled with a G0 star in a period of 386 days.

822. Σ 2375. Small apertures deal well with this fine bright pair. The angle is increasing slowly with little change in separation since W. Struve's measures in 1829 of 2·2″ and 108°, and no doubt this is a true binary system. The field has some scattered stars on a very faint ground, but there is considerable absorption in this region.

836. θ Ser. Since W. Struve measured it in 1830, this attractive pale yellow pair has remained practically unchanged. Common proper motion suggests that the stars are connected but the period must be very long. It is excellent for small telescopes; an orange star is 7′ Nf.

Sextans (Sex)

Sextans, the sextant, was formed by Hevelius about 1680 in honour of the observatory instrument which he had used since 1658; the nautical sextant was invented by Hadley in 1730. It is a small constellation of area 314 sq. deg. on the equator between Leo and Hydra, and has no visual distinguishing feature. The centre culminates at midnight about February 21st.

Beyond a few double stars, the only objects of telescopic interest in Sextans are extra-galactic nebulae. NGC 3115 is the brightest of these, and two others are given which are sufficiently close to one another to occupy the same field.

357. γ Sex. Alvan Clark discovered this difficult binary in 1854 with only 12 cm aperture; the period is about 79 years and I have never seen the bright yellow star even elongated. The components were closest for several years round 1962 but in a few years should separate sufficiently for resolution with 30 cm. They will be widest for several years round 1999.

361. NGC 3115. This elliptical extra-galactic nebula looks like a bright pointed spindle about 4′×1′ in pa. 45° with very faint halo, the small lengthened centre very bright. 10·5 cm shows this centre and 15 cm deals fairly well with the nebula. R is estimated as about 4 million pc.

367. NGC 3166–9. These two nebulae, discovered by William Herschel in 1783, are about 8′ apart and similar in appearance, both being round, about 1·5′ across rising well to the centre in brightness and conspicuous in the star sprinkled field. NGC 3169 has however evidence of a larger faint envelope, and both are in reality irregular elliptical spirals of which only the bright central regions are easily seen. 15 cm shows both sufficiently to give good prism bands.

394. 35 Sex. Since W. Struve's measures in 1832 there has been no real change in this pair. Both stars are orange but B looks more yellow and they make a good object for small instruments. Similar proper motions suggest that the stars form a long period binary system.

401. 40 Sex. Slow increase in both separation and angle characterize this fairly bright pair, which shows no colour difference between the stars. It is an easy object for 7·5 cm and the components are probably in orbit.

Taurus (Tau)

Taurus, the bull, is the second constellation of the zodiac, to which Ptolemy assigned thirty-three stars. It is a large conspicuous group introduced by the Pleiades rising in the east, followed by the triangular Hyades containing the brilliant orange Aldebaran. The Milky Way not far from its anticentre in Auriga passes through the extreme following region of Taurus and is comparatively faint here. The area is 797 sq. deg. and the centre culminates at midnight about November 30th.

There are nine open clusters, two of which are the well-known moving star groups of the Pleiades at 126 pc distance, and the Hyades at 41 pc. Both of these are too large for telescopic objects. Many of the stars in the Pleiades are involved in irregular nebulosity from the reflection of their light by minute solid particles. This has been seen by quite small instruments but I have never been sure of my observations because all bright stars tend to be surrounded by luminous haze, even in telescopes of first-class quality, and on some otherwise clear nights this is most marked. None of the other clusters is particularly impressive, the best being NGC 1647. Only one of the planetary nebulae repays observation, and this is the very interesting M 1. There is no globular cluster and no extra-galactic nebula of note, but many attractive double stars are available.

93. Σ 422. The colours of this attractive pair appear orange yellow and whitish, in spite of the spectral type of the companion, an example of the easy deception of the eye. The angle is slowly increasing with little change in separation and the motion is orbital. The bright yellow star 11′ S is 10 Tau m. 4·4 G5.

100. 30 Tau. This beautiful and easy pair, pale yellow and reddish grey, lies in a field well sprinkled with stars. No real change has occurred since the measures of W. Struve in 1830 but common proper motion suggests that the stars are connected.

102. OΣ 65. The plane of the orbit of this close pale yellow binary is nearly in the line of sight; the stars will be widest in 1969 and in 1962 they were resolved by 25 cm in pa. about 205°. The period is about 57 years.

107. Σ 495. Slow direct motion with so far little change in separation is taking place with this easy yellow pair and, as proper motion and radial velocity are similar, the stars no doubt form a long period binary.

109. 47 Tau. Burnham discovered this deep yellow pair in 1877 and there seems to have been little change in separation since. 20 cm shows the small star lying close N (p.). The motion is slowly retrograde and the proper motion of A is small.

118. β 87. Since Dembowski's measures in 1875 there has been no appreciable change in this pair; the proper motion is very small and not much is known about it yet. A is a giant orange star with a white companion close S (f.) and 7·5 cm will show it.

121. ADS 3201. This small pair, about which little is known, lies almost midway between the two very bright pale yellow components of κ Tau; these stars are 5·5′ apart and dominate the field. 10·5 cm just shows the pair, which makes a good test in the glare of the two stars.

123. Σ 559. In a field sprinkled with faint stars this elegant equal pale yellow pair is a good object for 7·5 cm. The stars have common proper motion and no doubt form a binary system, although there has been little change since W. Struve's measures in 1830.

124. α Tau. Aldebaran has a fine absorption spectrum crossed by many prominent dark bands and lines, some of which are shown by 7·5 cm. It is a giant star of diameter forty-three times that of the sun, and R is 20 pc. A faint star (13·5 31″ 112°) has the same large proper motion and may be in physical connection; I have never been able to see it.

125. Σ 572. A very slow increase in separation with retrograde motion has occurred since W. Struve measured this pair in 1830 and the stars appear to be in orbit. They are both yellow and the field is sprinkled with many faint stars.

130. NGC 1647. This open galactic cluster without central condensation needs a large field as it is about 35′ across; the stars are fairly bright and numerous with several well-separated pairs, and outside the S edge is the bright orange star BD 719 m. 6·1 Ko. R is estimated as about 500 pc.

168. Σ 716. A field of scattered stars is dominated by this pale yellow pair, a good object for small apertures. In 1829 W. Struve found 4·9″ and 197°, and only slow direct motion has taken place since; the stars are connected by similar proper motions.

175. NGC 1952. This nebula was discovered by Bévis in 1731 and again by Messier in 1758 when observing a comet, and this led to the formation of his catalogue of 103 nebulous objects as an aid to his comet seeking. It is familiar from photographs with large instruments which show extreme turbulence in the still-expanding gas as the result of a supernova explosion recorded in 1054. It is a bright elliptical haze about $4' \times 2 \cdot 5'$ in pa. 125° in beautiful contrast with a starry field and shows a single prism image with however some continuous spectrum. This image is clear with 7·5 cm and the object itself quite easy. I see no sign of structure beyond irregular edges and a faint curved extension Sf. R is about 1,200 pc. Some 26' f. is the elegant pair Σ 742 (7·2 7·8 3·5" 269°).

Telescopium (Tel)

Telescopium, the telescope, was formed by Lacaille in 1752 between Pavo and Sagittarius. Its three principal stars form with θ Ara a small quadrilateral immediately south of Corona Australis, and this is the extreme Np. corner of the constellation, the rest containing only insignificant stars. The area is 252 sq. deg. and the centre culminates at midnight about July 6th.

There are a few double stars in Telescopium, a single globular cluster NGC 6584 and one planetary nebula IC 4699. The only other objects of interest are extra-galactic nebulae; from twenty of these, NGC 6868 is selected as the brightest.

783. ϵ Tel. This bright deep yellow star has a faint companion wide Sp. which I glimpse with 25 cm, but not with 20 cm. It is probably a field star, of which there are many, and if so the proper motion of A will diminish the separation to a minimum of about 9" in 295° in 400 years.

791. NGC 6584. 20 cm will show resolution in this conspicuous but not bright globular cluster; it is of the broadly condensed type and irregularly scattered outliers are about 2·5' across. The stars are evidently very faint but are visible right through the broad centre and the very diffuse edges. 10·5 cm shows this object easily as a faint haze. Absorption is rated here at m. 1·1 and R is estimated as about 13,000 pc.

792. IC 4699. With care the tiny grey disk of the planetary nebula may be picked out from a starry field by 30 cm; as a guide there is a star m. 11 rather more than 1' N and a small pair about 1' Sp. Otherwise the single prism image makes matters easy, even for small apertures. The diameter is about 3" and R is estimated as 2,160 pc.

837. I 113. Discovered by Innes in 1900, little can yet be said about this pair; it makes a fine sight in a field well sprinkled with stars and both separation and angle may be diminishing slowly. 7·5 cm shows the small star with care.

881. Δ 227. This beautiful pair is an excellent object for small telescopes; both stars are bright and are in fine contrast, orange yellow and white, dominating the field. There has only been slight retrograde motion since John Herschel's measures in 1835. The proper motions are very small though similar, and this suggests a long period binary.

895. NGC 6868. This nebula is the brightest of the many extra-galactic objects in Telescopium and may be made out with 10·5 cm. It is round, rising steadily to the centre, about 1·5' wide and shows a strong prism band. It is classed as of elliptical type and was discovered by John Herschel in 1834.

Triangulum (Tri)

The small group of Triangulum, the triangle, is an ancient one to which Ptolemy assigned four stars. It is seen as a narrow triangle of third and fourth magnitude stars north of the triangle of Aries and has an area of 132 sq. deg. It culminates at midnight about October 23rd.

The chief interest in this constellation centres on NGC 598 or M 33, a very large irregular spiral nebula well known from many beautiful published photographs. It is a member of the local group of sixteen systems including that of the Milky Way, and in it may be seen the component stars, clusters and diffuse nebulae characteristic of these objects; one of the last is separately listed as NGC 604. Several other extra-galactic nebulae occur in Triangulum, but more distant and of smaller interest.

40. NGC 598. Messier discovered this nebula in 1764. Photographs show a very large spiral system extending about 80' × 50', well resolved into stars with numerous condensations as in M 31 in Andromeda but not tilted so much to the line of sight; the distance is about 600,000 pc. 30 cm shows a large round haze rising very broadly to the centre which is about 4' wide, but close attention reveals that the whole field of 20' is filled with faint hazy patches. There is a vague broad arm emerging N and curving f. where it includes NGC 604 about 11' in pa. 50° from the centre. A broader diffuse arm emerges S and turns p. Some minute stars are immersed near the centre and in the spiral arms. NGC 604 appears as a small fairly bright nebulous spot about 50" wide, of irregular form with a faint single image in the prism showing its partly gaseous nature. M 33 is a most remarkable object and worthy of close observation.

58. 6 Tri. This bright golden yellow pair dominates a field with a sprinkling of faint stars, easy for small apertures. Separation is slowly increasing with retrograde motion and it is a binary system of long period. In addition each star is a spectroscopic binary of respective periods 14·73 days and 2·24 days.

Triangulum Australe (TrA)

Triangulum Australe is the southern counterpart of the northern constellation, published by Bayer in 1603 although apparently suggested by Pieter Theodor about a century earlier. It lies between Ara and Circinus and may be recognized by its three prominent stars following α and β Cen southwards. The area is 110 sq. deg. and the centre culminates at midnight about May 22nd.

As well as some double stars there is one open cluster and one planetary nebula, both good telescopic objects. Extra-galactic nebulae are all very faint.

611. I 332. In a field sown profusely with stars is a bright pale yellow star with a companion very close Sf. which is clearly separated with 20 cm. About 1′ away Nf. is a fairly bright white star. Innes discovered this pair in 1901 as 1·1″ and 108° and little is known about it yet.

631. Rmk 20. This pale yellow equal pair dominates a field sown profusely with stars, and 7·5 cm shows it well. Areas in the field, particularly N and S of the pair, seem devoid of stars, indicating dark nebulae. Since John Herschel's measures of 2·4″ and 156° in 1835, separation and angle have slowly diminished and the stars are connected by common proper motion.

632. NGC 5979. This nebula shows a pale greyish blue disk about 15″ wide in a crowded field of stars; the light is even with no visible central star and the single prism image is slightly elliptical. 10·5 cm shows the nebula plainly as a small round haze and even 7·5 cm will distinguish it from a star and show the prism image faintly. R is not known.

635. Slr 11. The companion of this bright yellow star may just be made out with 10·5 cm; angle and separation have slowly increased since the 1893 measures of Sellers as 0·9″ and 94° but the proper motion of A is very small and little can be said about this pair yet. The same applies to the two wide companions Nf. and Sp.; these have hardly changed since John Herschel's measures in 1836 and may be only field stars, of which there are very many on a profuse ground.

640. NGC 6025. This is a fine open group of pretty bright white and yellow stars about 15′ wide in a rich star field; it shows a definite pattern of curved and straight lines but has no central gathering. It is an effective object with 10·5 cm. R is estimated as about 700 pc (Plate 4).

660. ι TrA. This object is given as an example of an optical pair; the stars are deep yellow and white and lie in a fine field sown with stars. In 1836 John Herschel found 25″ and 25° and in 1961 the values were 13″ and 12° which may be explained by the proper motion of A. The small star is easy with 7·5 cm and A itself is a spectroscopic binary of period 39·89 days.

Tucana (Tuc)

Tucana, the toucan, was introduced by Bayer in 1603; it lies south of Grus and Phoenix and is easily located by some bright scattered stars and the small Magellan Cloud in the Sf. corner. The total area is 295 sq. deg. and the centre culminates at midnight about September 17th.

Even excluding Nubecula Minor which is treated under its own name, Tucana has some fine telescopic objects. These include double stars and the beautiful globular clusters NGC 104 and 362, the former being in size and richness second only to NGC 5139 in Centaurus. Many extra-galactic nebulae occur also, the brightest being NGC 7205. There are two planetary nebulae, only one of which I have been able to find; this is NGC 7408.

968. NGC 7205. This extra-galactic nebula is a conspicuous object about $3.5' \times 2'$ in pa. $65°$, rising broadly to the centre with no apparent nucleus. It is fairly bright but diffuse and gives a broad band in the prism. 15 cm shows it faintly but 20 cm is needed to reveal the shape.

977. δ Tuc. A bright white star with a companion well clear p., looking definitely reddish and forming a beautiful pair which 7·5 cm shows well. There has been no real change since the measures of John Herschel in 1836, and similar proper motion suggests a binary system of long period.

993. NGC 7408. John Herschel discovered this nebula in 1834 without recognizing its planetary character; it needs a good aperture and 30 cm shows a slightly elliptical faint haze about $70''$ wide, rising a little and broadly to the centre. The prism gives a single image, indicating the gaseous nature. A few scattered stars are in the field. R is estimated as about 3,300 pc.

6. NGC 104. This wonderful object, also known as 47 Tuc, is crowded with innumerable stars steadily increasing to the dense very bright centre, the scattered outliers reaching to $23'$ diameter. Even 7·5 cm shows granularity in the large bright haze and 10·5 cm resolves it well, while larger apertures present a most impressive and beautiful sight. The most recent estimate of the distance is 4,780 pc, and the close brighter unequal pair $2'$ Sp. the centre is much nearer (Plate 6).

8. β Tuc. A beautiful field containing the very bright wide pale yellow pair and a third bright star (CPD 52 m. 5·2 A2) about $10'$ Sf. These stars have similar proper motion and probably form a physical system which seems to be sextuple, for the third star and one of the pair are very close binaries, and the other has a very faint close companion. I have not been able to resolve these stars with 30 cm.

23. NGC 362. This beautiful globular cluster is well resolved to a very bright compressed centre, the main part 2′ wide and the scattered outliers reaching to 4′. It is symmetrical and approximately round. 15 cm resolves it well, 10·5 cm shows undoubtedly some very faint stars in it, and it looks granular with 7·5 cm. R is estimated as about 12,000 pc.

35. κ Tuc. This pair is particularly beautiful in a moonlit field, the stars yellow and orange; both angle and separation are slowly diminishing. The distance is 21 pc and the common proper motion is similar to that of I 27, which is 5·3′ Np. This star itself is a close pair (7·9 8·5 0·9″–1·1″) of period 81 years, and B is now in the second quadrant. This is an excellent pair to observe periodically for changing angle, and 15 cm should always resolve it.

Ursa Major (UMa)

Ursa Major, the great bear, is the third in size of the constellations with an area of 1,280 sq. deg. It is an ancient and well-known star group to which Ptolemy assigned twenty-seven stars, and the figure made by the seven brightest is familiar to every northern astronomer. It lies between 29° N and 73° N and is in consequence largely hidden from many southern observers. The centre culminates at midnight about March 11th.

Such a large constellation naturally contains many attractive double stars. There are no open clusters and the two globular clusters recently discovered by photography are both too faint for amateur instruments; indeed at 125,000 pc they are extra-galactic. Only one planetary nebula is known, the large faint NGC 3587. Extra-galactic nebulae however exist in profusion, many of them in groups of which the nearest is the M 81 group at about 2·1 million pc. Their variability in size, shape and brightness offers much interest to the observer. This list of objects in Ursa Major is restricted to the few which are visible from my observatory; others are given in the addendum.

411. ξ UMa. This interesting system only 7·7 pc from the sun consists of two bright yellow stars with a period of 59·86 years, each of which is itself a spectroscopic binary, A with period of 669·2 days and B of 3·98 days. It is a fine object in a field sprinkled with stars, and clearly resolvable by 7·5 cm for a good deal of its orbit. The stars were closest about 1933 and will be widest about 1974.

413. ν UMa. This brilliant orange star in a thin field has a well-separated white companion Sf. which is clearly visible with 10·5 cm. Since W. Struve's measures in 1830 there has been very little change but common proper motion suggests a physical connection between the stars.

423. 57 UMa. W. Struve in 1831 found 5·4″ and 11° for this unequal pale and deep yellow pair, and the only subsequent change has been slow retrograde motion. The companion is now in the fourth quadrant and 7·5 cm will show it in good conditions. The stars are connected by common proper motion.

435. NGC 4062. In a field of a few stars is this faint elongated spindle about 4′ × 1′ in pa. 100°, brightening only broadly to the axis with no visible nucleus. It is a regular edgewise spiral and 20 cm will bring out its form.

Ursa Minor (UMi)

This small constellation of area 256 sq. deg. is an ancient star group to which Ptolemy assigned seven stars, but the origin of the name is uncertain. It is now distinguished by the proximity to the north pole of its leader Polaris which makes this the most useful navigational star in the sky. This use, and the name, are however comparatively modern for in the time of Hipparchus about 150 B.C. the star was more than 12° distant from the pole. Closest approach will be 26′ 30″ in A.D. 2095. Although circumpolar, most of the constellation lies between R.A. 13^h to 18^h and the centre culminates at midnight about May 13th.

Polaris itself is a wide unequal pair with rapidly changing R.A., as well as being a Cepheid variable of period 3·97 days and a spectroscopic binary of period 29·6 years. Apart from this star and a few small pairs, there is little of telescopic interest in the constellation. The brightest of a few inconspicuous extra-galactic nebulae is NGC 6217 which will be found in the addendum.

Vela (Vel)

Vela, the sails, is one of the three large groups into which Gould in 1877 divided the ancient Argo Navis; it lies north of Carina between Puppis and Centaurus, almost completely immersed in the Milky Way which in this region is divided across by an irregular lobed band of dark absorbing material. The Nf. corner alone is free, and here a few extra-galactic objects may be found. The area of the constellation is 500 sq. deg. and the centre culminates at midnight about February 11th.

The leader of many bright scattered stars in Vela is γ Vel with a wonderful helium spectrum. There are many attractive double stars and twenty-two open galactic clusters are known. Many of these are not effective telescopic objects, and five of the best are given. There is one globular cluster NGC 3201, and two planetary nebulae. Two diffuse gaseous nebulae are given, one being the remarkable faint streak in a rich field found by John Herschel in 1834. The brightest of several small extra-galactic nebulae is NGC 3256.

290. γ Vel. This brilliant white star is by far the brightest Wolf-Rayet star known, and its beautiful spectrum of bright broad helium lines is evident with 7·5 cm. The wide white companion, which 30 cm will show in bright sunlight, and a small white pair about 1′ Sf. combine to make a most striking field. No real change between the two stars has occurred for more than a century and although the proper motions are very small, the stars may be connected.

292. NGC 2547. A large field is needed to show this striking and attractive group which is about 17′ across and stands out against a background powdered with faint stars. Many stars are in chains and loops, and there are many pairs and small groups, including a somewhat skew miniature of Crux. R is about 500 pc.

298. I 67. Since Innes discovered this close pale yellow pair in 1901, there has been a slow decrease in both separation and angle. In 1960 20 cm showed the stars clearly apart. Proper motion does not account for the changes and the stars no doubt are in orbit.

301. h. 4104. A less bright star at 18″ in 38° makes a fine triplet with this bright pale yellow pair, in which there has been little real change since the measures of John Herschel in 1836. Not much is yet known of these stars. The field is striking since most of the brighter stars are in wide pairs and triplets, and there is a tendency to a spiral pattern. Small apertures deal well with this object.

302. Δ 70. Since Jacob's measures in 1851, there has been no certain change in this pale and deep yellow pair, a dainty object with 7·5 cm. This is probably a physical system and there is evidence that A is a spectroscopic binary.

304. Slr 8. Sellers measured this pair in 1892 as 0·4″ and 302°; the separation increased to 1·0″ in 1925 and is now closing with retrograde motion. This is clearly a binary system; the stars make a fine pair, orange yellow and whitish, which 20 cm just separates.

312. IC 2391. This bright scattered cluster including the brilliant *o* Vel makes a fine wide field object for small apertures. A. R. Hogg finds a distance of only 150 pc for a group of twenty-one stars and recommends proper motion studies because of its nearness.

314. NGC 2660. This is an example of a very distant galactic cluster which looks almost like a globular cluster about 1·5′ across. It is a well-compressed knot of faint stars lying in a rich field with an orange star 2′ S, and 10·5 cm shows the beginnings of resolution. R is estimated as about 5,000 pc.

315. IC 2395. Small telescopes show this striking open star group well; it is excellent with 10·5 cm. About 20′ across, the stars are not numerous but there is some central condensation. R is estimated as about 600 pc.

316. δ Vel. This pale yellow pair is evidently difficult to measure since recorded values are somewhat erratic; there is however slow retrograde motion. 10·5 cm shows the less bright star close Sf. in the blaze of A. R is about 21 pc and this seems to be a true binary system.

322. Hd. 205. 7·5 cm shows the companion of this bright pale yellow star quite clearly. The pair was first measured by Bailey in 1894 as 3·7″ and 81°, since when the separation seems to have diminished but angular measures are erratic and perhaps there has been little change, so that not much is yet known about these stars.

326. R 87. In a field sown with stars this bright pair, pale and deep yellow, is an attractive object, easy for 7·5 cm. Both angle and separation are slowly lessening but the proper motion is very small and it is not yet clear whether the stars are connected. A is a spectroscopic binary of period 0·915 day.

327. NGC 2736. This remarkable object, discovered and figured by John Herschel in 1834, is a faint long narrow nebular streak lying in pa. about 20° in a rich star field. It is evidently gaseous and may be traced for more than 20′, hardly 0·5′ wide, varying somewhat in brightness and rather better defined on the f. edge. 20 cm shows it very faintly and discontinuously, a test for a clear dark night.

328. h. 4165. Since John Herschel in 1837 found 1·4″ and 88° for this pale yellow pair, the separation has slowly diminished with steady direct motion; this seems to be a true binary system and 15 cm resolved it plainly in 1961.

335. NGC 2792. In a field of scattered stars this planetary nebula is round, greyish and about 10″ across; the light is fairly uniform and the edges well defined. 10·5 cm will just show it and the single prism image with care, but 15 cm makes it easy. R is estimated as about 4,500 pc.

336. h. 4188. This bright white pair in an attractive field suits small apertures well. John Herschel discovered it in 1835, since when there has been very slow diminution in separation and angle. The stars seem to be connected.

338. I 11. In a fine starry field this bright pale yellow star needs 15 cm to resolve it, the stars just in contact with no perceptible colour difference. It was measured by Sellers in 1896; the motion is slowly direct and it is without doubt binary.

344. NGC 2899. This field is lovely, sown with fairly bright stars on a profuse faint ground. In it is an irregularly round luminous haze about 1·5′ across, rising broadly to the centre and showing its gaseous nature by a single prism image. 15 cm will show the nebula but its location needs care. This object is not listed either as a planetary or a diffuse nebula, and little seems to be known about it. John Herschel discovered it in 1835, and the position and gaseous character show that it must be a galactic object.

347. ψ Vel. The period of this bright yellow binary is about 34 years; closest approach should be about 1971 and widest separation about 1981. In 1961 30 cm resolved the pair as 0·5″ in 210° and for those with good instruments this is an interesting system to watch. R is only 15 pc.

350. h. 4220. Dominating a field well sprinkled with stars, this fine pale yellow pair is clearly divided by 7·5 cm. John Herschel in 1836 found 3·0″ and 202° so that the separation has lessened with slow direct motion. The stars seem to be in orbit, and the less bright looks deeper yellow than the primary.

354. h. 4245. Little is known of this elegant pair, orange yellow and bluish, which shines in a lovely field profusely sown with stars. John Herschel discovered it in 1835 and there has been no real change since then.

358. Δ 81. This bright unequal pair, pale yellow and bluish, ornaments a lovely field, a real treat to see. Changes since John Herschel's measures in 1836 are small and uncertain, but the proper motion is shared by both stars and they probably form a long period binary system.

362. NGC 3132. The central star is prominent in this bright white annular planetary nebula about 30″ across in a field of scattered stars. The single prism image is slightly elliptical with central star streak, easily seen with 7·5 cm. The light appears even without any of the bluish tint usual with planetary nebulae. Photographs show intricate, somewhat concentric structure, as if several outbursts of gaseous material had emerged from the star. R is estimated as 600 pc.

368. λ 118. A most beautiful field with this orange star central, and another less bright about 7′ in 200°. There is a faint companion well separated Sf. which 20 cm brings to view but not 15 cm. Motion seems to be retrograde but little is known about this pair yet and the companion may be a field star.

373. NGC 3201. This globular cluster is one of the less-condensed types, irregularly round, about 5′ across and well resolved into faint stars, some of which are in short curved rays like jets of water from a fountain; 10·5 cm will show these. The field is sown with stars but the cluster lies near the large irregular cloud of obscuring matter which cuts across the Milky Way in this region, and absorption is assessed at m. 2·2; allowing for this, R is about 3,800 pc (Plate 9).

377. Rmk 13. This bright white pair shines like twin gems in a rich field; a third star is wider S (p.). These stars have shown little change since measured by John Herschel in 1836 and they may all be connected. Even with 10·5 cm this is a beautiful object.

379. NGC 3228. For a wide field this is an effective star group with small apertures; it is about 20′ wide in a field spangled with innumerable stars. The brightest stars are of spectral types B8–Ao and from their absolute magnitudes R is estimated as 500 pc and the age of the group as 250 million years.

383. NGC 3256. An example of an extra-galactic system in low galactic latitude which is visible only because of a thinning out of the absorbing matter in this region. This is shown by the rich scattered star field in which is a fairly bright elliptical nebula about 1·5′ × 1′ in pa. 60°, rising well to the centre and giving a bright prism band. 10·5 cm shows it faintly but clearly. It is a member of a group of extra-galactic nebulae lying mainly in Hydra and R is estimated as 18 million pc.

398. μ Vel. Russell in 1880 first measured this bright close yellow pair as 2·8″ and 55°; since then the separation has steadily diminished with direct motion, so that it is now difficult to see the less bright star. The proper motion is shared by both stars and they form no doubt a true binary which will be interesting to watch in the future.

Virgo (Vir)

Virgo, the virgin and sixth of the zodiacal constellations, is the second largest group with an area of 1,294 sq. deg. It lies on either side of the equator and the leader is the brilliant Spica, preceded to the north by some scattered less bright stars. The centre culminates at midnight about April 12th.

Being well removed from the Milky Way, there are no open clusters in Virgo and no gaseous nebulae, either diffuse or planetary, while the only globular cluster is NGC 5634. The constellation lies however in an area remarkably rich in extra-galactic nebulae; more than 200 of these objects have been examined and about thirty selected. The list could easily be extended but there is a certain sameness in many of these spots of luminous haze, and those given will be sufficient to indicate their general telescopic appearance. Attention is drawn to NGC 4594 as one of the very few of these systems with dark absorption lane visible with amateur instruments. Several double stars are scattered through the list.

444. NGC 4216. This extended rather faint edgewise spiral nebula about 5′ × 0·8′ in pa. 20° has a bright elliptical centre. The field shows only a few faint stars but 10′ Sp. is another fainter spindle in pa. 0° (NGC 4206) while 13′ Nf. is a third smaller one in pa. 60° (NGC 4222). 15 cm shows only the first of these, and then little beyond the central region.

447. Σ 1627. A good object for small apertures, with no real change since the measures of W. Struve in 1830; the field is sprinkled thinly with stars. Similar proper motions suggest a long period binary.

451. NGC 4281. An example of the way in which nebulae are crowded in the region of Virgo, the field of 12′ contains five small objects, of which this is the brightest; it is the most f. and about 1·5′ × 0·5′ in pa. 85° with a clear nucleus. The faintest is NGC 4277 about 5′ Sp. and needs care to see with 30 cm. The others are easy, the largest NGC 4273 being inside a triangle of three others, and all give prism bands.

453. NGC 4303. M 61 was discovered by Messier in 1779 who mistook it at first for a comet; it is a fine large nebula, nearly round, bright and rising broadly to the centre, about 3′ across and classed as a spiral system. It is easy but not bright with 7·5 cm.

454. 17 Vir. There has been no real change in this wide unequal pair since W. Struve measured the stars in 1829; A is deep yellow and B looks white, though the spectral type indicates orange. 7·5 cm shows the stars well and common proper motion suggests that they are connected. A small nebula (NGC 4324) is 9′ f. (S) which 10·5 cm shows plainly as a faint ellipse.

459. NGC 4374. M 84 was discovered by Messier in 1781; it is a round bright and conspicuous haze about 1′ across, rising much to a small diffuse nucleus and giving a strong band in the prism. There is a much larger very faint hazy envelope. The bright central region is an easy object for 7·5 cm.

463. NGC 4406. Messier discovered M 86 in 1781; it follows M 84 about 18′ and is somewhat larger, elliptical in pa. 125° and rises more broadly to the centre. It too gives a strong prism band and photographs show no discernible structure. These two nebulae, which are easy objects for 7·5 cm, form an equilateral triangle with NGC 4388 to the S; this is a narrow spindle, about 2′ × 0·5′ in pa. 90°, while 10′ N of this, almost between M 84 and M 86, is the faint small NGC 4387.

465. NGC 4472. Discovered by Messier in 1771, M 49 is another easy object; it is a round nebula in a thinly sprinkled star field, rising broadly to a bright centre about 1′ wide, but the gradually fading envelope is much larger, shown in photographs as 11′ across. The centre gives a strong band in the prism, and a faint star is immersed about 1′ f.

467. NGC 4486. This is a fine large round nebula about 3' across and rising much to the centre in brightness; it looks symmetrical and gives a strong prism band. It was found by Messier in 1781 and is an easy object for small apertures. Photographs show no discernible spiral structure but a curious straight jet proceeds from the nucleus in pa. 20° and is thought to be connected with the intense radio emission from this object. R is estimated as about 11 million pc.

469. NGC 4517. This edgewise spiral nebula, about 8' × 1' in pa. 84°, rises only broadly in brightness to the central axis. Photographs show a dark absorption lane passing just N of the centre; I have not seen this but the N border near the centre looks irregular, as if dark matter were invading it. A star is on this N edge. 15 cm shows this object faintly.

471. NGC 4526. Two bright stars 15' apart make a fine contrast with this bright elliptical nebula 3' × 1' in pa. 112° which lies between them, with a fainter star near S. The centre is very bright and gives a strong band in the prism. Small apertures deal quite well with this object.

473. NGC 4552. Messier discovered this object in 1781 as a very faint and difficult hazy spot, while missing many others considerably brighter. It is round, about 1·5' across and has a bright nucleus giving a strong prism band. 7·5 cm shows it as a faint hazy star. It is an elliptical-type system.

476. NGC 4567–8. Rendered familiar by photographs with large instruments, this pair of extra-galactic nebulae resembles NGC 4038–9 in Corvus, but is fainter. Each nebula is about 1·5' × 1'; they are inclined at 60° to each other and touch at the f. ends, and it is not known whether they are coming together or receding. 20 cm is needed to show them clearly; about 12' N is the small spindle NGC 4564.

477. NGC 4569. Photographs show this object as a large diffuse spiral about 12' × 6'. I see it as a diffuse elliptical haze 4' × 1·5' in pa. 25° with a small bright nucleus which may be seen with 7·5 cm. Messier found it in 1781 and compared it with the neighbouring M 89 in faintness.

478. NGC 4579. Messier discovered this spiral nebula in 1779 and remarked that the least illumination of his cross wires caused it to vanish. It is fairly bright, broadly elliptical, about 2·5' × 1·5' in pa. 65°, and quite easy with 7·5 cm where the nucleus looks like a faint star.

480. NGC 4594. This is the best example of a dark lane in an edgewise spiral nebula. The object itself is about 5' × 1·5' in pa. 92° with very bright elliptical centre and pointed ends. The lane about 15" wide extends along the whole length just S of the nucleus and 15 cm will show it, but 20 cm is needed to demonstrate the faint illumination outside it S. R is estimated at 4·4 million pc.

483. γ Vir. Since the first measures by Cassini in 1720, this bright yellow binary has been much investigated. The orbit is very eccentric with period of 171 years; closest approach was in 1836 at 0·25" in 151°, and widest separation in 1922 at 6·0″ in 322°. The stars are now closing again with steady retrograde motion, but are still very easy for 7·5 cm. Both stars are dwarfs and R is 10·5 pc.

484. 31 Vir. This bright star has a faint companion well clear Nf. which 10·5 cm will show with care. Since Burnham's measures of 3·7″ and 29° in 1880, the angle is slowly increasing with little change in separation. Similar proper motions suggest a true binary system.

485. NGC 4621. Discovered by Messier in 1779, this elliptical nebula has a bright centre 30″ wide, surrounded by a fainter envelope about 1·5′ × 1·0′ in pa. 165°. It is smaller and less bright than M 60 which is 25′ f., and is an easy though faint object for 7·5 cm.

487. NGC 4649. This symmetrical round haze rises much to a bright centre and is about 2′ across; some 2·5′ Np. is the much less bright diffuse NGC 4647. Both are extra-galactic, and the brighter may be seen with 7·5 cm, the other doubtfully with 10·5 cm. Messier discovered M 60 in 1779, but understandably missed its companion.

489. NGC 4666. An edgewise spiral nebula fairly bright in the central region; it is 4′ × 0·8′ in pa. 40° and the central axis looks in part mottled from the numerous condensations shown in photographs. The extended form is plain though faint with 10·5 cm.

492. NGC 4697. William Herschel discovered this fine nebula in 1784, an easy object even for 7·5 cm. The small elliptical very bright centre is surrounded by a hazy envelope 2·5′ × 1′ in pa. 70°, and some scattered stars S and f. are in effective contrast.

496. NGC 4754–62. This interesting field contains two nebulae of differing type and 11′ apart. The first is round and about 1′ across, rising much to the centre; the other is a bright spindle 3′ long and very narrow, lying in pa. 30° and both give strong prism bands. 15 cm is needed to show the forms, but they are easy objects for 10·5 cm.

504. 48 Vir. Burnham first measured this almost equal pale yellow pair as 0·48″ and 229° in 1879, since when the separation has increased with slow retrograde motion. 20 cm shows the stars clearly apart; they form a binary system of long period.

510. θ Vir. This fine easy pale yellow pair was measured in 1830 by W. Struve and the only change has been very slow retrograde motion. Common proper motion suggests that the stars are connected.

512. β 931. The faint companion of this orange star may be used as a test for small apertures, as the stars appear to be relatively fixed. 10·5 cm will show it in good conditions and it is easy with 15 cm.

517. 54 Vir. This dainty well-separated pair is a good object for small telescopes. It was first measured by J. South in 1823, and both angle and separation seem to be lessening very slowly. The stars evidently form a physical system, and each member may also be a spectroscopic binary.

534. NGC 5247. Photographs show this object as a fine open two-branched spiral. I see it as a round diffuse rather faint haze about 4′ across, with a small bright nucleus giving a band in the prism, and there is distinct evidence of concentric structure denoted by uneven light. The object is just perceptible with 10·5 cm; it was discovered by William Herschel in 1785.

539. 84 Vir. This beautiful orange and pale yellow pair dominates a field of scattered stars and is well resolved by 7·5 cm. Both separation and angle have slightly diminished since W. Struve's measures in 1828, and the stars are connected by common proper motion.

542. 86 Vir. A bright yellow orange star has a faint companion wide Sf. which 20 cm shows to be a close pair (11·6 12·8 2″ 272°) and the close star is also clear with this aperture. Relative movement between these four stars has been small since Burnham measured them in 1879, but the proper motion of A is small, and little is really known about them yet.

552. Σ 1788. In 1831 W. Struve found 2·4″ and 54° for this fine yellow pair, and slow increase in both values has since occurred. This is a good object for small apertures and the stars are connected by common proper motion.

570. φ Vir. The stars of this unequal yellow and orange pair are relatively fixed, and 7·5 cm shows the small one clearly. The proper motion is shared, which suggests a physical system and there is evidence that B is a spectroscopic binary.

572. NGC 5634. This distant but fairly bright globular cluster 2′ wide is clearly resolved into faint stars, just perceptible with 20 cm; it is broadly condensed and lies in a triangle of three stars. 7·5 cm shows it faintly and 10·5 cm gives the prism band clearly. Absorption is small in this region and R is estimated as about 23,000 pc.

582. NGC 5746. Photographs show this object as an edgewise spiral with a dark lane on the f. side of the nucleus, but I have not been able to see this. It is 5′×0·7′ with a bright elliptical centre lying in pa. 170° and there are contrasting stars in the field. It is quite plain though faint with 10·5 cm.

597. β 348. This difficult pair has shown no certain change since Dembowski's measures in 1875; it is a bright orange star with the companion very close Sf. which 30 cm shows only in good conditions. The system is no doubt binary as the proper motion is shared, and it is included as a test.

Volans (Vol)

Volans, the flying fish, is one of Bayer's southern additions in 1603. It follows the large Magellan Cloud between it and Carina as an irregular group of moderately bright stars. The area is 141 sq. deg. and the centre culminates at midnight about January 18th.

Apart from a few double stars, the only objects of telescopic interest in Volans are extra-galactic nebulae, all faint and mostly small, but one large example is included.

244. γ Vol. This bright golden and pale yellow pair in a field of scattered stars is an attractive object for small apertures. There has been no apparent change since John Herschel measured the stars in 1835, which are connected by common proper motion.

270. h. 3997. 7·5 cm will separate this pair into two almost equal pale yellow stars; these have slowly increased in angle and separation since John Herschel measured them in 1836, and they appear to form a binary system.

271. NGC 2442. John Herschel discovered this object in 1834 and thought it was a double nebula with 'some sort of hooked appendage'. This was in fact the brighter of two arms from opposite ends of a barred spiral nebula. 30 cm shows a diffuse rather faint elliptical haze $3' \times 1·5'$ in pa. about $45°$ with an excentric nucleus, and from each end very faint extensions may be seen, that from Nf. towards Np. being somewhat brighter. 10·5 cm shows a faint ellipse in a starry field.

277. ζ Vol. A star sprinkled field is dominated by this brilliant orange star with a white companion well separated Sf., an attractive object for small apertures. The stars have not altered appreciably since John Herschel's measures in 1835, and they are connected by common proper motion.

289. ε Vol. This star is like a bright white gem in a field sprinkled with stars; it has a yellowish companion well clear Nf., easily seen by 7·5 cm. A is a spectroscopic binary of period 14·17 days. This is another of the pairs measured by John Herschel in 1835 and subsequent change is doubtful. If the stars are in orbit, the period must be very long.

Vulpecula (Vul)

Vulpecula, the little fox, was introduced by Hevelius about 1660 across the Milky Way between Aquila and Cygnus. Its stars are scattered and not bright, and there are no distinguishing marks. The area is 268 sq. deg. and the centre culminates at midnight about July 26th.

The screening effect of the Milky Way practically excludes extra-galactic objects from this constellation. There are nine open star clusters, of which three are given, and three planetary nebulae. Of these, one is beyond amateur reach, one is the beautiful NGC 6853 and the third NGC 6842 is a good test for a clear dark night. Three of several double stars have been selected.

858. 2 Vul. I have not found this close pair easy, even with 20 cm. Dembowski in 1876 measured the stars as 1·9″ and 125° and though subsequent values are rather conflicting, there is not much evidence of real change. The proper motion is very small and little is yet known about this pair.

865. NGC 6802. This is an interesting elongated cluster of faint stars 5′ × 1·5′ in pa. 10° with two wide brighter pairs near, and others in the field. The stars are clear with 30 cm, and some may be seen hazily with 15 cm while 10·5 cm shows a small faint hazy bar. R is estimated as 1,700 pc.

885. NGC 6842. In a field well sprinkled with stars is this dim round haze about 40″ wide, rising only little and broadly to the centre, with a difficult single prism image for 30 cm. No star is very near, but as a guide 6′ f. is a large semicircle of a few m. 9–10 stars convex to the nebula. The integrated photographic magnitude is 13·6, making a severe test for clear conditions. R is about 4,800 pc.

887. NGC 6853. This wonderful object, reported by Messier in 1779, is large and bright pale blue. 30 cm shows the whole elliptical periphery faintly, about 6′ × 4·5′ in pa. 120° while the broad very bright central hour-glass region has a general axis in pa. 20°. The prism maintains the general shape, but more diffusely, as if more than one visible frequency is present. The field is spangled with stars and most attractive in contrast, while several of the stars are projected on the nebulosity. The shape is roughly rectangular with 7·5 cm, and the prism image easy. At 220 pc this is one of the nearer planetary nebulae.

889. 16 Vul. O. Struve measured this pair in 1844 as 0·6″ and 79°, since when both separation and angle have increased; similar proper motion makes it likely that this is a binary system. In 1961 15 cm showed the deep yellow stars just in contact.

899. NGC 6882–5. These two open star clusters are really one, connected by curved lines of stars, and need a large field where they make a striking pattern. The former at 8′ diameter is smaller than the latter which is about 20′ wide; both are clear with 10·5 cm but larger aperture is a great improvement. R is estimated as about 1,000 pc.

902. Σ 2653. This dainty unequal yellow pair lies in an attractive starry field and is quite clear with 7·5 cm. W. Struve in 1831 found 2·5″ and 255° and there has been slow direct motion since. The stars are connected by common proper motion.

919. NGC 6940. Needing a large field, this delicately beautiful star cluster condenses somewhat to an open central network about 20′ × 15′ with a brighter orange star there. The cluster is very rich but needs at least 15 cm to show it well. R is estimated as about 1,000 pc.

ADDENDUM FOR
NORTHERN OBSERVATORIES

This addendum gives a list of selected objects between 50° N and the north pole for northern observers. The arrangement and mode of selection are similar to those of the main list, but with fuller descriptions in the table itself, taken from various sources. The northern constellations from which these objects have been selected are described in the alphabetical constellation sequence earlier in the book.

Name	R.A.	Var.	Dec.	Var.	Description	Con.
	h m	m	° ′	′		
Σ 3053	0 0·0	+0·51	+65 49	+3·3	6·0 7·5 15″ 70° gG5. A1. Fine easy pair, yellow and bluish; no real change since 1832	Cas
NGC 40	0 10·2	0·53	+72 15	3·3	Small fairly bright planetary nebula with faint prism image and central star streak. R is 1,000 pc	Cep
NGC 147	0 30·4	0·54	+48 13	3·3	Faint large elliptical eg. nebula 4·5′ × 2·5′ in pa. 30°, brighter in centre. R is 400,000 pc	Cas
NGC 185	0 36·1	0·55	+48 4	3·3	Irregularly round eg. nebula 2·5′ across, not bright without apparent nucleus. R is 400,000 pc	Cas
η Cas	0 46·1	0·58	+57 33	3·3	3·6 7·4 11″ 295° dF9. dMo. Beautiful long period (500 years) dwarf binary yellow and orange; direct motion	Cas
γ Cas	0 53·7	0·60	+60 27	3·2	1·6–2·3 11 2·2″ 254° Boe. Irregular variable and unequal pair, as test; little change since 1888	Cas
NGC 457	1 15·9	0·62	+58 4	3·2	Fine large scattered cluster 12′ across near φ Cas; stars numerous with central condensation. R is 1,400 pc	Cas
NGC 581	1 29·9	0·66	+60 27	3·1	M 103. Beautiful field with triangular cluster and some red stars. R is 1,200 pc	Cas
NGC 663	1 42·6	0·68	+61 0	3·0	Fine large open cluster 14′ across passing into the field. R is 1,200 pc	Cas
α UMi	1 48·8	5·2	+89 2	3·0	2·1–2·3 8·9 18″ 218° F7. Easy yellow pair with little change since 1834. A is a Cepheid variable of period 3·97 days and a spectroscopic binary of period 29·6 years	UMi

Name	R.A.	Var.	Dec.	Var.	Description	Con.
	h m	m	° ′	′		
48 Cas	1 57·8	+0·83	+70 40	+2·9	4·6 7·5 0·4″–1·1″ A4. Close pale yellow binary of period 63 years; it was widest in 1935	Cas
ι Cas	2 24·9	0·82	+67 11	2·7	4·8 7·0 2·3″ 240° A4; 8·2 7·2″ 114° dG4. Long period pale and deep yellow triplet, the close pair in retrograde motion with a probable dark companion	Cas
Σ 331	2 57·3	0·71	+52 9	2·4	5·4 6·8 12″ 85° B8 A1. Bright easy white pair with no real change since 1828. Common proper motion shows physical connection	Per
Σ 320	2 59·4	1·34	+79 13	2·4	5·7 9·5 5·0″ 233° gM1. Fine orange and bluish pair with very slow increase in separation and angle since 1831	Cep
Σ 362	3 12·3	0·79	+59 51	2·2	8·5 8·8 7·1″ 142° Ao. Elegant white pair in fine field; no real change since 1831	Cam
Σ 385	3 25·0	0·81	+59 46	2·1	4·4 9·0 2·4″ 161° B9. Fine unequal white pair with little change since 1829	Cam
Σ 460	4 1·6	1·68	+80 34	1·6	5·6 6·6 0·9″ 65° (1924) dF1. A2. Close yellow and white pair with steady direct motion	Cep
NGC 1501	4 2·7	0·86	+60 47	1·6	Fairly bright planetary nebula 50″ across with single prism image, in a fine field. R is 4,000 pc	Cam
NGC 1502	4 3·4	0·88	+62 12	1·6	Scattered galactic cluster about 8′ across containing the bright white pair Σ 485. R is 900 pc	Cam
NGC 1528	4 11·4	0·75	+51 7	1·5	Large bright star cluster about 22′ across, well shown by 7·5 cm. Central condensation and some spiral structure. R. is 500 pc	Per
1 Cam	4 28·1	0·79	+53 48	+1·3	5·8 6·8 10·4″ 308° B2. B1. Easy white pair with no real change since 1832	Cam
NGC 2146	6 10·7	1·60	+78 23	−0·0	Fairly bright eg. spindle 4·5′ × 1′ in pa. 147°. Photographs show an irregular dark lane S of centre	Cam
12 Lyn	6 41·8	0·88	+59 30	0·6	5·5 6·1 1·7″ 89°; 7·5 8·7″ 309° A2. Fine bright triplet of long period, the close pair with slow retrograde motion	Lyn
Σ 958	6 44·0	0·83	+55 46	0·6	6·3 6·3 4·8″ 257° dF4. dF6. Attractive equal pair of dwarf yellow stars with little change since 1830, connected by common proper motion	Lyn

ADDENDUM

Name	R.A.	Var.	Dec.	Var.	Description	Con.
	h m	m	° ′	′		
NGC 2403	7 32·0	+0·96	+65 43	−1·3	Large bright eg. spiral 16′ × 10′ in pa. 140° between two medium stars; photographs show many condensations. R is 2 million pc	Cam
Σ 1122	7 41·2	0·95	+65 17	1·4	7·0 7·0 15″ 5° F2. Elegant easy yellow pair in a fine region. No real change since 1830	Cam
Σ 1127	7 42·4	0·93	+64 11	1·4	6·8 8·0 5·5″ 340°; 9·2 11″ 174° A2. Elegant white triplet with little change since 1830	Cam
NGC 2655	8 49·3	1·30	+78 25	2·2	Fairly large elliptical eg. nebula in pa. 90° but only the bright centre 1′ across is likely to be seen	Cam
Σ 1306	9 6·0	0·88	+67 20	2·4	4·9 8·5 2·2″ 18° dF4. Fine close yellow binary of long period, about 700 years, now widening with steady retrograde motion	UMa
NGC 2841	9 18·6	0·69	+51 11	2·5	Bright elliptical eg. nebula about 5′ × 1·5′ in pa. 152°, a regular spiral with bright nucleus	UMa
23 UMa	9 27·6	0·78	+63 17	2·6	3·8 9·0 23″ 271° A4. Fine wide unequal pair, pale yellow and ashy; no change since 1830	UMa
NGC 2985	9 46·0	0·93	+72 31	2·8	Almost round fairly bright eg. nebula 3′ across; a condensed spiral with small bright nucleus	UMa
NGC 3031	9 51·5	0·85	+69 18	2·8	M 81. Beautiful bright elliptical spiral 16′ × 10′ in pa. 155°, condensed towards the centre, discovered by Bode in 1744. R is 3 million pc	UMa
NGC 3034	9 51·9	0·86	+69 56	2·8	M 82. Long narrow bright irregular eg. spindle 7′ × 1·5′ in pa. 65°, with dark rifts shown in photographs. Discovered by Bode in 1744. R is 3 million pc	UMa
NGC 3147	10 12·6	0·89	+73 39	3·0	Nearly round symmetrical spiral nebula 3′ across with very bright nucleus	Dra
Σ 1415	10 13·9	0·81	+71 19	3·0	6·3 7·3 17″ 168° gA8. gF0. Wide easy pale yellow pair with no change since 1832; both stars are giants	UMa
NGC 3556	11 8·7	0·59	+55 57	3·3	Fairly bright irregular eg. spiral 8′ × 1·5′ in pa. 84° with several condensations shown in photographs	UMa

Name	R.A.	Var.	Dec.	Var.	Description	Con.
	h m	m	° ′	′		
NGC 3587	11 12·0	+0·59	+55 17	−3·3	M 97. Large round planetary nebula about 3′ across, fairly bright with two fainter areas near the centre and single prism image. Discovered by Méchain in 1781. R is 800 pc	UMa
NGC 3613	11 15·7	0·59	+58 17	3·3	Fairly bright narrow elliptical eg. nebula 1·8′ in pa. 95°; 16′ Sf. is the smaller and fainter NGC 3619	UMa
OΣ 235	11 29·5	0·57	+61 22	3·3	5·5 7·3 0·3″–1·0″ dF4. Close yellow binary with steady direct motion and period 72 years. Closest in 1977	UMa
65 UMa	11 52·5	0·52	+46 45	3·3	6·5 8·0 3·7″ 41° A2. Elegant easy white pair with very slow direct motion. Another star 6·8 A0 is wide Sf.	UMa
NGC 4096	12 3·5	0·51	+47 45	3·3	Long narrow eg. spindle, 6′ × 1′ in pa. 18°, fairly bright with large excentric nucleus	UMa
IC 3568	12 31·7	0·24	+82 50	3·3	Bright round planetary nebula 18″ across with even light and single prism image. R is 1,900 pc	Cam
Σ 1694	12 48·8	0·09	+83 41	3·3	5·3 5·8 21″ 325° A2. A0. Fine wide pale yellow pair of long period, in very slow retrograde motion	Cam
ζ UMa	13 21·9	0·40	+55 11	3·1	2·4 4·0 14″ 151° A2. A6. Beautiful pair with very slow direct motion. A is a spectroscopic binary of period 20·54 days	UMa
Σ 1770	13 35·7	0·40	+50 58	3·1	6·6 7·9 1·9″ 121° gM3. Elegant orange and red pair; no change since 1831	UMa
NGC 5457	14 1·4	0·35	+54 35	2·9	M 101. Large irregularly round fairly bright eg. nebula discovered by Méchain in 1781. Photographs show a beautiful spiral about 20′ across with many condensations in the arms, nine of which are NGC objects. The four brightest are Sp., p., Sf. and f., all within 6′ of the centre	UMa
Σ 1831	14 14·4	0·32	+56 55	2·8	6·6 9 5·9″ 140° dG2. Deep yellow pair with little change; a fainter pair is 1·5′ Sp.	Dra
NGC 5866	15 5·1	0·27	+55 57	2·3	Fairly bright lenticular eg. nebula 3′ × 1′ in pa. 125° with brighter centre	Dra
NGC 5907	15 14·6	0·26	+56 31	2·2	Very long eg. spindle 11′ × 0·6′ in pa. 156°, fairly bright with condensed nucleus and dark lane	Dra

Name	R.A.	Var.	Dec.	Var.	Description	Con.
	h m	m	° ′	′		
NGC 5985	15 38·6	+0·20	+59 29	−1·9	Elliptical spiral nebula 4′ × 2′ in pa. 5° with brighter nucleus. 8′ Np. is the brighter and smaller NGC 5982	Dra
Σ 1984	15 49·8	0·26	+53 3	1·8	6·5 8·8 6·4″ 277° A2. dF5. Easy pale and deep yellow pair with slow direct motion since 1830	Dra
Σ 2054	16 23·1	0·14	+61 49	1·4	6·0 7·0 1·1″ 351° gG7. Close yellow pair with slow retrograde motion	Dra
η Dra	16 23·3	+0·14	+61 38	1·4	2·9 8·1 5·5″ 142° gG6. K2. Fine deep yellow pair of uncertain change, first measured in 1843. Σ 2054 is 11′ Np.	Dra
NGC 6217	16 34·9	−0·50	+78 18	1·2	Rather faint elliptical eg. spiral 1·8′ × 1·2′ in pa. 155°, with slightly brighter centre	UMi
17 Dra	16 35·0	+0·24	+53 1	1·2	5·6 6·6 3·4″ 106° B9. A0. Fine white pair with slow diminution in angle and separation since 1831	Dra
μ Dra	17 4·3	+0·21	+54 32	0·8	5·8 5·9 2·2″ 74° dF6. dF6. Long period binary with steady retrograde motion	Dra
ψ Dra	17 42·8	−0·18	+72 10	0·3	4·9 6·1 30″ 15° dF5. dF6. Fine wide yellow pair; common proper motion	Dra
NGC 6503	17 49·9	−0·11	+70 10	0·2	Fairly bright eg. spindle 5′ × 1′ in pa. 125° with brighter elliptical centre	Dra
NGC 6543	17 58·6	−0·03	+66 38	−0·0	Bright bluish planetary nebula 22″ × 16″ with central star and single prism image. R is 520 pc	Dra
Σ 2278	18 2·0	+0·18	+56 25	+0·0	7·1 7·6 8·1 A5. A0; AB 37″ 26°; BC 6·1″ 146°. Elegant triplet with little change	Dra
39 Dra	18 23·2	+0·15	+58 46	0·3	4·9 7·7 3·7″ 354° A2. Fine pair with very slow retrograde motion	Dra
NGC 6826	19 43·4	+0·26	+50 24	1·4	Bright round planetary nebula 20″ across with central star and single prism image, visible with 7·5 cm. R is 540 pc. 29′ p. is the bright wide yellow pair 16 Cyg	Cyg
ε Dra	19 48·4	−0·03	+70 8	1·5	4·0 7·6 3·2″ 12° gG3. Yellow and bluish pair with slow direct motion	Dra
κ Cep	20 10·6	−0·34	+77 34	1·8	4·4 8·0 7·4″ 122° B9. Easy white pair with little change since 1832	Cep
NGC 6939	20 30·4	+0·20	+60 28	2·0	Galactic cluster of numerous faint stars 8′ across, fan-shaped p. R is about 2,000 pc	Cep

Name	R.A.	Var.	Dec.	Var.	Description	Con.
	h m	m	° ′	′		
Σ 2751	21 0·8	+0·28	+56 28	+2·4	6·2 6·8 1·7″ 353° B9. Close white pair with very slow direct motion	Cep
Σ 2790	21 17·9	0·28	+58 25	2·5	5·8 9·9 5·0″ 44° gM1. B3. Fine orange and bluish pair with little change since 1832	Cep
β Cep	21 28·0	0·13	+70 20	2·6	3·3 7·9 13″ 250° B1. A4. Fine white pair; no real change since 1832	Cep
μ Cep	21 42·0	0·31	+58 33	2·8	3·6–5·1 M2. Irregular variable with fine band spectrum	Cep
Σ 2840	21 50·3	0·34	+55 34	2·8	5·9 6·8 19″ 196° B6. A1. Fine wide white pair; little change since 1832	Cep
ξ Cep	22 2·3	0·28	+64 23	2·9	4·6 6·5 7·7″ 278° A3. dF7. Beautiful white and yellow pair; slow retrograde motion	Cep
Kr 60	22 26·3	0·37	+57 27	3·1	9·3 10·8 1·5″–3·3″ M3. Remarkable orange binary in rapid retrograde motion. Period 44·3 years	Cep
δ Cep	22 27·3	0·37	+58 10	3·1	3·8–4·6 7·5 41″ 191° F4–G6. Fine wide pair, deep yellow and bluish, with little change. A was the first of the Cepheid variables with the period of 5·37 days	Cep
Σ 2950	22 49·4	0·39	+61 26	3·2	6·1 7·3 1·7″ 295° gG3. Yellow and ashy; slow diminution in angle and separation	Cep
NGC 7510	23 9·4	0·42	+60 18	3·3	Small galactic cluster of medium stars 3′ across, irregularly fan-shaped, in a fine field. R is about 1,100 pc	Cep
o Cep	23 16·6	0·41	+67 50	3·3	4·9 7·8 2·9″ 213° gG7. Yellow long period binary with slow direct motion	Cep
NGC 7654	23 22·0	0·44	+61 19	3·3	M 52. Large scattered cluster of numerous stars 13′ across, found by Messier in 1774. R is 700 pc	Cas
6 Cas	23 46·4	0·48	+61 57	3·3	5·6 8·0 1·7″ 197° A2. Ao. Close pale yellow binary with common proper motion but little certain change	Cas
NGC 7789	23 54·5	0·50	+56 26	3·3	Beautiful large cloud of mostly faint stars 20′ across. R is 1,200 pc	Cas
σ Cas	23 56·5	0·50	+55 29	3·3	4·9 7·0 3·1″ 326° B3. B3. Fine white pair in a beautiful field. Little change since 1832	Cas

BIBLIOGRAPHY

The following works have been consulted:

Aitken, R. G. *Catalogue of Double Stars within 120° of N pole*. Carnegie Institution of Washington, 1932.

Allen, C. W. *Astrophysical Quantities*. 2nd ed. Athlone Press, London, 1963.

Allen, R. H. *Star Names and their Meanings*. Stechert, New York, 1899.

Aller, L. H. *Gaseous Nebulae*. Chapman & Hall, London, 1956.

Becker, W. *Sterne und Sternsysteme*. Steinkopff, Dresden, 1950.

Becvar, A. *Skalnate Pleso Atlas of the Heavens*. Sky Publishing Corporation, Cambridge, Mass., 1949.

Boss, B. *Albany Star Catalogue*, 1931. *San Luis Star Catalogue*, 1928. Carnegie Institution of Washington.

Brown, R. *Primitive Constellations*. Williams & Norgate, London, 1899.

Cederblad, S. Bright Diffuse Galactic Nebulae. *Med. Lund. II*, **119**, Sweden, 1946.

Collinder, P. *Galactic Clusters*. Lund. Ann. 2, Sweden, 1931.

Dreyer, J. L. E. *New General Catalogue of Nebulae and Star Clusters*. Mem. Roy. Ast. Soc. 1887.

Dreyer, J. L. E. *Index Catalogues of Additional Nebulae and Star Clusters*. Mem. Roy. Ast. Soc. 1894; 1907.

Gascoigne, S. C. B. and Westerlund, B. *Uppsala–Mt Stromlo Atlas of Magellanic Clouds. Epoch 1975*. Issued for Mt Stromlo Observatory by the Australian National University, Canberra, 1961.

Herschel, John F. W. *Results of Astronomical Observations at the Cape of Good Hope, 1834–1838*. Smith, Elder & Co., London, 1847.

Herschel, William. *Catalogues of New Nebulae and Star Clusters*. Phil. Trans. Roy. Soc. 1786; 1789; 1802.

Hogg, Helen S. Star Clusters. *Handb. der Phys.* **53**, 129, 1959.

Holmberg, E. Photometry of Extragalactic Nebulae. *Med. Lund. II*, **136**, 1958.

Innes, R. T. A. *Southern Double Star Catalogue*. Union Obs. Johannesburg, 1927.

Jeffers, H. M., van den Bos, W. H. and Greeby, F. M. *Index Catalogue of Visual Double Stars, 1961.0*. Lick Obs. Pub. XXI, 1963.

Kinman, T. D. Globular Clusters. *Observatory*, **78**, 122, 1958.

Lacaille, N. L. de. *Nébuleuses du Ciel Austral*. Conn. des Temps., 1784.

Lick Observatory. *Studies of the Nebulae*. Lick Obs. Pub. XIII, 1918.

Lohmann, W. Globular Clusters. *Zeit. f. Astrophys.* **30**, 234, 1952.

Messier, M. *Catalogue des Nébuleuses et des Amas d'Etoiles*. Conn. des Temps., 1784.

Moore, J. H. and Neubauer, F. J. *Spectroscopic Binary Stars*. 5th ed. Lick Obs. Bull. 521, 1948.

Norton, A. P. *Star Atlas and Reference Handbook*. 14th ed. Gall & Inglis, Edinburgh, 1959.

Payne-Gaposchkin, C. and Gaposchkin, S. *Variable Stars*. Harvard Observatory, 1938.

Reinmuth, K. Die Herschel-Nebel. *Abh. Heidelb. Akad. Wiss.* **13**, 1926.

Sagot, R. et Texereau, J. *Revue des Constellations*. Soc. Astron. de France, 1963.

Schlesinger, F. and Jenkins, L. F. *Catalogue of Bright Stars*. 2nd ed. Yale Univ. Observatory, 1940.

Shapley, H. *Star Clusters*. McGraw-Hill Book Co., New York, 1930.

Shapley, H. and Ames, A. *Survey of External Galaxies brighter than m. 13*. Harv. Ann. 88, No. 2, 1932.

Smyth, W. H. *Cycle of Celestial Objects*, 1846. Revised ed. (Chambers, G. F.). Oxford Univ. Press, 1881.

Trumpler, R. J. *Open Star Clusters*. Lick Obs. Bull. 420, 1930.

Vaucouleurs, G. de. *Bright Galaxies S of −35° Declination*. Mem. Com. Solar Obs. (Mt Stromlo Observatory), 1956.

Vaucouleurs, G. de and A. de. Radial Velocities of Bright Southern Galaxies. *Mem. Roy. Ast. Soc.* **68**, 1961.

Vorontzov-Veljaminov, B. A. *Gas Nebel und Neue Sterne*. Verlag Kultur und Fortschritt, Berlin, 1953.

Webb, T. W. *Celestial Objects for Common Telescopes, 1859*. Revised ed. Dover Publications Inc., 1962.

Wilson, R. E. *General Catalogue of Stellar Radial Velocities*. Carnegie Institution of Washington, 1953.

Woolley, R. v. d. R. *et al. Double Star Results*. Mem. Com. Obs. **9** (Mt Stromlo Observatory), 1948.

INDEX

Individual objects are not indexed separately, for the two general lists in
R.A. sequence fulfil this function, particularly for NGC objects